Purity Lost

THE JOHNS HOPKINS UNIVERSITY STUDIES
IN HISTORICAL AND POLITICAL SCIENCE
124th Series (2006)

1. Benjamin Ehlers, *Between Christians and Moriscos: Juan de Ribera and Religious Reform in Valencia, 1568–1614*
2. Eric R Dursteler, *Venetians in Constantinople: Nation, Identity, and Coexistence in the Early Modern Mediterranean*
3. Steven A. Epstein, *Purity Lost: Transgressing Boundaries in the Eastern Mediterranean, 1000–1400*

Purity Lost

Transgressing Boundaries in the Eastern Mediterranean,
1000–1400

STEVEN A. EPSTEIN

The Johns Hopkins University Press
Baltimore

Excerpt from *Invisible Cities* by Italo Calvino, copyright © 1972 by Giulio Einaudi editore s.p.a., English translation by William Weaver, copyright © 1974 by Harcourt, Inc., reprinted by permission of Harcourt, Inc.

© 2006 The Johns Hopkins University Press
All rights reserved. Published 2007
Printed in the United States of America on acid-free paper
2 4 6 8 9 7 5 3 2 1

The Johns Hopkins University Press
2715 North Charles Street
Baltimore, Maryland 21218-4363
www.press.jhu.edu

Library of Congress Cataloging-in-Publication Data
Epstein, Steven A., 1952–
Purity lost : trangressing boundaries in the Eastern Mediterranean, 1000–1400 /
Steven A. Epstein.
p. cm. — (Johns Hopkins University studies in historical and political science)
Includes bibliographical references and index.
ISBN 0-8018-8484-5 (hardcover : alk. paper)
1. Middle East—Relations. 2. Cultural relations. I. Title. II. Series.
DS63.18.E67 2006
956'.014—dc22   2006010565

A catalog record for this book is available from the British Library.

For Jean

And Polo said, "The inferno of the living is not something that will be; if there is one, it is what is already here, the inferno where we live every day, that we form by being together. There are two ways to escape suffering it. The first is easy for many: accept the inferno and become such a part of it that you can no longer see it. The second is risky and demands constant vigilance and apprehension: seek and learn to recognize who and what, in the midst of the inferno, are not inferno, then make them endure, give them space."

Italo Calvino, *Invisible Cities*

CONTENTS

Preface xi

Introduction 3

1 The Perception of Difference 9

2 Mixed Relationships in the Archipelago 52

3 Treaties and Diplomacy 96

4 Renegades and Opportunists 137

5 Human and Angelic Faces 173

Conclusion 204

Notes 209
Selected Bibliography 233
Index 243

PREFACE

In her novel *Last Letters from Hav,* Jan Morris imagined a city somewhere in the Mediterranean or the Black Sea. Hav was a place where Chinese, Muslim, Middle Eastern, and European civilizations mixed in a truly polyglot, multicultural environment. There Venetians, Turks, Greeks, Arabs, and many others flourished and, for a season, ruled. Real cities like Iskenderun, Smyrna, Salonika, Caffa, and Acre for a time resembled Hav, though no actual place ever contained quite its rich stew of ancient and modern legacies, eastern and western influences. But nowhere else in the world would such an imaginary, invisible city be remotely plausible. There has long been something about the eastern Mediterranean (like the East Indies) that makes it so possible a setting for all sorts of cultural exchanges that even the arrival of some intrepid Chinese was not inconceivable, as the Mongols proved in the thirteenth century. Other spots, for example in the Indian Ocean, come to mind as potential settings for a Hav, but they lack the Mediterranean's potential for sparking a world system of cultural and economic exchanges. After all, when we hear about how the Dutch, the English, and others from northwest Europe established worldwide empires and trade, we are looking at peoples (and even the Portuguese and Spanish fit here) first trying to emulate and then to surpass the traditional monopolists of the East's fabled riches. Without a Silk Road, or pepper, or Jerusalem, what was the point to exploring the Atlantic? Even Columbus's dream of a rear attack on the Ottoman state was simply another tribute to the allure of the eastern Mediterranean, and all the religious attention to the Holy Land and Mecca was going to remain fixed on these sacred places.

Less noticed have been the people who actually made the eastern Mediterranean and how their rich array of ethnicities and cultures required the successful, however defined, to learn the ways of others. For all the great lingua franca in the region, from Greek to Arabic, Farsi, and French, there remained over the centuries durable diasporic cultures like the Armenian and Jewish, and these peoples defined the benefits and challenges of adaptability. Learning another's tongue and methods was one thing, actually incorporating them into one's business or family required something more, a true mixing based if not on mutual respect then a shared self-interest, or in some cases forceful appropriation. The eastern Mediterranean partly overlaps the later territory ("field") of the orientalists and the contested ideas about orientalism and the imperialist project.[1] There were orientalists *avant la lettre*, particularly those scholars engaged in anti-Islamic polemic, crusade, and mission in the twelfth and thirteenth centuries.[2] Their observations add important details to the stories of people in mixed relationships.

This book investigates relationships between people who were usually separated in the Middle Ages by various constructed boundaries. Those boundaries, which postulated "pure" types on both sides of the line, included color, religion, language, and ethnicity. Part of this book is about the boundaries themselves, how they were raised and maintained, and how the categories they defined were conceived as pure but not necessarily equal; another part (most important to me) is about how people defied, overlooked, or transcended these boundaries in order to establish relationships with those different from themselves, even with spiritual beings like angels. Pure and impure, unmixed and mixed—for the historian these labels need specific contexts. Hence this book seeks out those people living outside the neat labels.

The main argument of this book is that mixed relationships are the prisms that refract the pervasive claims of ethnic, racial, religious, and cultural purity. A passage from the Book of Ecclesiasticus (13:9) states "that every beast loves its like, so every person the one nearest."[3] Some people nonetheless loved or engaged with the unlike, and the boundary that they crossed in doing so obliged them to reflect upon their own identities. Defining just what counted as a mixed relationship preoccupied the medieval people discussed here, and the skills developed in these relationships were one of the major engines of historical change in the eastern Mediterranean region. Relationships count as mixed when the parties do not share a common creed, language, skin color, or other marker of difference.[4] Although every human relationship is in some sense mixed, the argument here concerns relationships that crossed one of the big boundaries or broke the rules set by the boundary makers. For mixed relationships to exist, there had to be ideas about pure types, however fallacious—what Sally McKee has called "the myth of ethnic purity."[5] The mixed and the pure are equally constructed and often frustratingly vague identities. Since individuals defined themselves as groups or were assigned to them, we must examine and fathom the various divisions among humans by religion, ethnicity, or race. In turn, mixed relationships changed their members by blurring divisive distinctions and creating ties in place of obstacles.

Some mixed relationships turned out badly, and their histories do not show the unfolding of progressively more tolerant and diverse values in the eastern Mediterranean. As K. Anthony Appiah has observed, identities (and by extension concepts of purity) may arise out of relationships.[6] Instead of people bringing clear ideas about themselves to new ties, they may learn and define what they are by engaging with others. Either way, historians can use relationships to analyze how and what past peoples learned from crossing the big boundaries, where the potential lessons were more dramatic and perilous.

The aim of this study is to show that a world system first appeared in the region I call here the eastern Mediterranean, broadly construed (see map on page 2). This system depended on the degree to which individuals succeeded in thriving inside mixed relationships and making them accomplish individual and collective goals. The texture of daily life inside mixed relationships made all the rest possible: crusades, long-distance trade, slavery, new empires, and more. This emerging world system rewarded people who were multilingual and flexible enough to connect to others often quite different from themselves. But there were costs as well as benefits to those in mixed relationships and to the wider world. Numerous examples of these mixed effects appear throughout this book. Knowing more languages was a social good; color symbolism could sharply divide and rank people; the ties with good angels brought out the best in some people, but heeding one bad angel cost humanity Paradise itself.

It is a pleasure to thank those who have helped me find my way in the course of this project. Helen Evans and Father Justin made it possible for me to use two images I needed to make an argument about angels. Jonathan Boyarin, Jean Brown Epstein, Norman Golb, George Gorse, Sally McKee, Ed Muir, and Glenn Peers offered valuable comments and assistance. John Ackerman, Benjamin Z. Kedar, Barbara Rosenwein, and anonymous reviewers read the entire manuscript and certainly helped me to improve it. I am most grateful to Pam LeRow, who helped save parts of the manuscript from oblivion and prepare it for publication. I am greatly indebted to Henry Tom and his colleagues, especially Claire McCabe Tamberino, at the Johns Hopkins University Press for much astute advice and support in bringing this work into print. I am also grateful to Julia Ridley Smith for perceptive and expert copyediting. I cannot thank by name the many students of all levels in Colorado and Kansas who listened patiently to parts of these arguments, asked good questions, and above all kept me employed at many rewarding tasks during these years of writing. Their own hard work gave me the time to write this.

Purity Lost

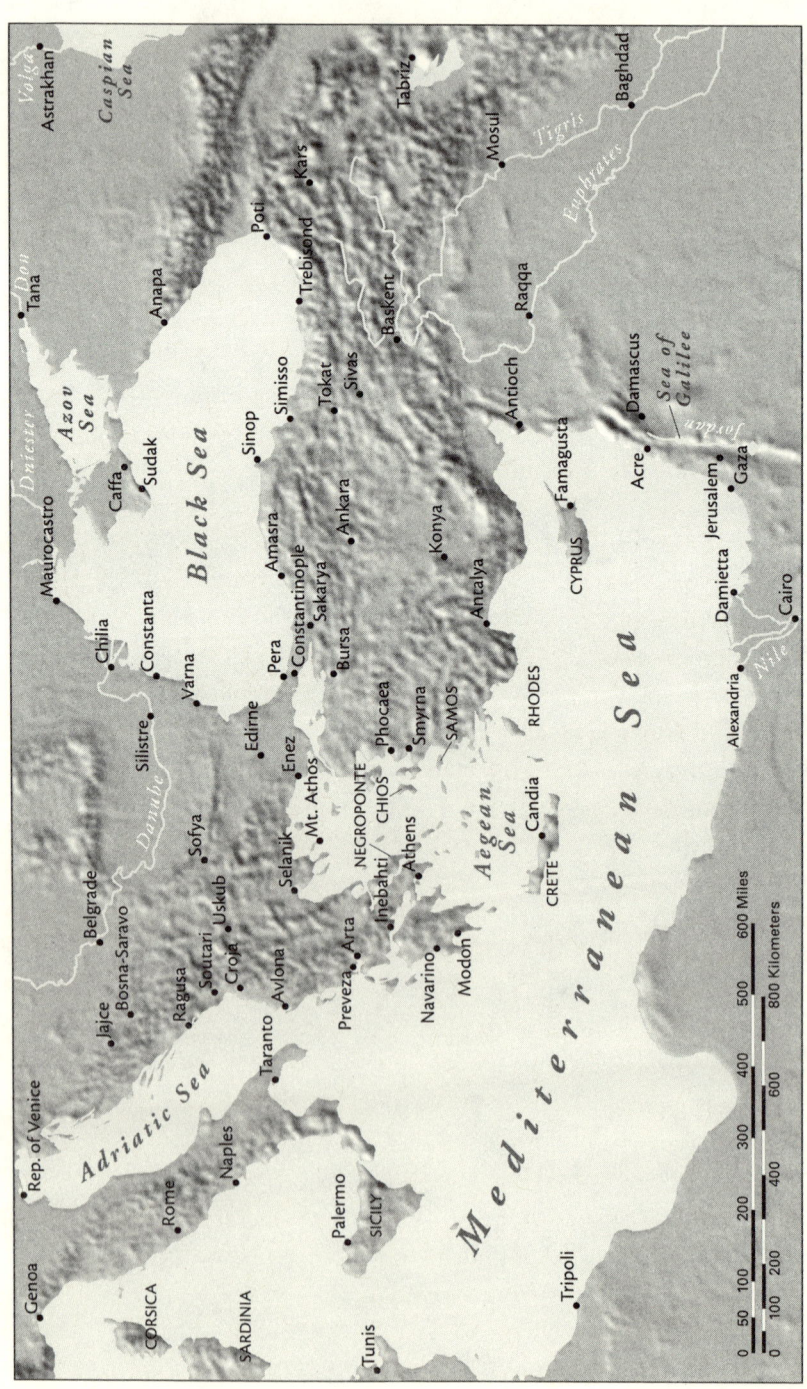

The Eastern Mediterranean. *Source:* The University of Kansas Cartographic Services, Darin Grauberger and Jonathan Thayn.

Introduction

Many standard histories discuss trade, marriage, slavery, diplomacy, or specific peoples or states in the premodern eastern Mediterranean. Rarely are such topics explored from the perspective of relationships, and mixed relationships receive hardly any notice. The marriage in which the families and even partners at first needed an interpreter is the point here, not the typical union. What was the status of children coming from these mixed marriages? Masters and slaves were often different colors and ethnicities. Does slavery somehow thrive on such mixing? Inside slavery, the master chose the relationship while the slave endured it, but the interests of both coincided in the hope to survive bondage. What is the role of choice in all mixed relationships? Business partners are often uneasy when they do not share a creed. What types of oaths or enforcement mechanisms would satisfy these parties? Treaties between different ethnic groups are more complex. What language or rules should prevail in these circumstances? All these bonds, motivated by temporary common interests, challenged the values of the pure, who preferred their own kind, however defined. The master narratives of commerce or marriage, to take two examples, become quite different when reconstructed from the foundations of mixed ties. Relationships of all types make up the fabric of daily life; the ones examined here also challenged pervasive claims of purity.

The people quietly crossing the boundaries of the eastern Mediterranean have received less scholarly notice than its geography, trade networks, and clashes of cultures.[1] Nonetheless, the prospects for developing any type of world system depended on mixed relationships and methods of communicating across language barriers. The focus of this book is on how daily interactions among ordinary as well as grand people shaped the master narratives of empires. Economic historians sometimes assume too readily that bargaining was transparent and trade uncomplicated by language barriers and different ethical systems. Historians of conflict often privilege the battlefield as the place where ethnic, national, or imperial groups work out their differences and shape any emerging world system. Insider or partisan analysts of individual groups often search for ethnic origins and stick mainly to essentialist, reaffirming narratives located thoroughly inside the group being studied. And finally, the great works of Mediterranean synthesis, from Henri Pirenne and Fernand Braudel to that of Peregrine Horden and Nicholas Purcell, must incorporate the undeniable splits of the sea into its eastern versus western, or northern versus southern shores.[2]

All these perspectives benefit from being reexamined through the prism of mixed relationships. This book is a sampling of relationships drawn from a variety of source materials. The category of relationships must be expansive and draw us outside conventional thinking to consider ties from the mundane to the angelic as possibly mixed. Modern scholars and past observers have yielded valuable works of high quality that will continue to influence people's understanding of this small part of the globe where so many different threads come together. How does one write the history of mixed relationships, in this or any other region of the world? A manageable unit of analysis is required, so this study focuses on the region stretching from the Black Sea down to Egypt. Examining the complex stories in this region demands special attention to the hallmarks of the historian's craft: accuracy and sincerity. Bernard Williams has recently clarified these necessary virtues for writing history; in his conception, they go beyond the usual professional canons to challenge historians to choose questions, sources, and approaches capable of providing fresh insights and stories that make honest sense of human experiences.[3] Because identities and relationships can limit or subordinate as well as liberate people, we must be careful not to force the history of mixed relationships into a theory of progress or modernity.[4]

A historical perspective on the problem of mixed relationships demands a sharp focus on the lives of actual people. Every type of source, from chronicles and theological works to contracts and wills, reveals medieval people pondering and sometimes entering mixed relationships and forming new identities, personal and collective. These identities were not fixed but instead were constructed over time to serve the needs of particular groups in a context. Rather than adding to the innumerable studies on specific peoples or groups, this book investigates the margins or boundaries between one thing and another. The skin is a good place to look for boundaries and their makers.[5] Inside the skin people are all (courtesy of genetics) half one thing and half another, part mother and part father—hence the orphan searching to fill some gap beyond heredity about the unknown, sometimes unknowable parent. This halfness is also external, since even parents who might be close cousins in an isolated ethnic group still contribute different cultural ways to their offspring. Half one thing and half another, with the skin acting as a membrane to separate what is inside a person (however it got there) from external influences affecting personal identity.

Isidore of Seville (ca. 560–636) in his great survey of human knowledge also saw people as mixed beings—inside spirit, outside flesh.[6] A history of human skin and attitudes toward it could make a difference here, but no such study apparently exists. So this one explores the skin's most distinctive quality—not its toughness, texture, pliability, or other traits but the one people have always fixed upon—its color.

Skin color in this region is not a clear marker and in every direction it seems to change—darkness in the south, whiter (lighter) to the north, yellow toward the east. And there in the middle of all this color, the brown or olive Mediterranean skin, with all its varieties and exceptions. Skin color is a deeply flawed, complex, but still venerable proxy that supposedly represents other traits as well, from temperament to physical strength. These cultures perhaps valued as well how the skin forms and covers facial features, which also signal information about the person. Hence, there is a science, a body of consistent knowledge, called physiognomy, where skin color plays only a small part in a wider collection of attributes as delicate as eye lashes or as robust as noses. Where skin color alone was too common or crude a benchmark, facial features served past peoples as alternative, reliable signs of personal character and ability. Assigning personal identity took the shortcut of examining the human face, partly covered by the skin. This method also allowed for other ways to enter deeper into the person, as the skin made way for people to see, taste, hear, and smell the world. Outsiders used these very senses to pigeonhole others.

Half one thing and half another defines all people, and so every relationship or identity is in some sense a mixed one. But a deeply mixed relationship that crossed one of the big boundaries of religion, ethnicity, language, or skin color forced people to think about their own identities, sometimes resulting in painful, undesirable responses. Mixed ties made everyone, not just the mixers, ponder the boundaries of what should be permitted and what could not. This story rests on the idea that mixed bonds and the people entering into them explain what actually happened in the eastern Mediterranean in the centuries before modernity. Nonetheless, purity never lacked apologists. Dominant modes of thinking about the constructed boundaries continued to view mixed relationships with suspicion. Considering this history from the perspective of these relationships can yield new interpretations in fields as diverse (and usually unconnected) as diplomacy and science. This book is, like many others, literally an essay, an attempt to pull together evidence on a new subject—the mixed tie. This study of a little corner of human experience cannot also become a history of purity in all its forms, but this is not a neglected topic. Indeed, the master discourse from the Middle Ages forward remains largely in the hands of the boundary makers.

The book takes the reader on a journey through ideas about color and mixing, quotidian commerce in the East, and then through the topics of treaties, renegades, and angels. I ask the reader only to be willing to see these disparate subjects from the perspective of mixed ties and then test the arguments made here about them. The first chapter begins on familiar territory, with ancient legacies of race and skin color, languages, and creeds, and follows these themes into the medieval period. Chapter 2 investigates some special places, islands or isolated spots, where mixing was most common or unavoidable, and reveals how people lived inside various mixed relationships, from marriages and business contracts to the bonds between slave and master. Here, as throughout this study, language differences are important, partly because contemporaries saw them as real obstacles but also because multilingual people bridged these gaps. Inside the interpreter's mind thoughts shifted from one tongue or discourse and its context to another. Such people, including notaries, facilitated the efforts of others to form a tie of some kind. Economic self-interest sometimes looms larger than the claims of racial or religious superiority.

Chapter 3 takes a common surviving source, treaties and other documents, and looks at them as contracts between contacts making and sustaining mixed relationships. The more different the parties were, the more they are valued here. Treaties set the boundaries of the permissible, and they regulated encounters already being lived on the ground. Chapter 4 looks at those who broke rules and relationships, the renegades and opportunists, for their stories of betrayal reveal how contemporaries saw the complex claims of personal honor and group loyalty. Betrayal, like treason, is sometimes a question of dates, so a proper context reveals a renegade in one culture to be a hero in another. Chapter 5 proposes a possible theoretical framework for the practical approaches toward mixing taken in the previous chapters. This chapter begins with physiognomy and concludes with angels, whose faces and behaviors engaged all the peoples of the region. Physiognomy, that complex legacy of ancient thought, is a neglected tool for understanding how people used the appearance and movements of the body as ways to label and value others. It was the science of human differences. Angels, another old feature of human thought about the spirit world, show how people put faces to beings who were better than mere mortals. Physiognomy and angels, both deeply implicated in ideas about purity, provoke fresh ways to explain enduring ideas about how people appear and act. The theme of mixed relationships helps to explain how human bonds with the angels mimicked ethnic hierarchies and helped to shape attitudes about equality.

The emphasis here in studying mixed relationships leans much more toward the individual than the collective. The social, economic, and even spiritual opportunities open to the people studied here were affected by their beliefs about their ethnic loyalties and what their physical appearances meant to themselves and others. Specific contexts shaped personal decisions to join or leave groups, and also determined the scope, if any, for such choices. People entered many relationships, some mixed and some not, and sorting out conflicting claims of loyalty is an important task here. Often the mixed relationship was or became the paramount one, challenging the "pure" ones. Hence, this study depends on many microstories of the microregions, within the context of relationship and language.

These stories, selected because they are clearly about mixed relationships, represent only a small fraction of the ties that bound. The premise here is that the mixed relationships and identities, in the context of all the others, make sense of the changes these societies were experiencing. The medieval world, defined in the West as Europe on the make, has traditionally been dominated by the chronologies and perspectives of those scholars working on northwestern Europe. Here the Middle Ages takes in the Venetian and Genoese sea empires, and the land-based states of Byzantium, Mamluk Egypt, and the Mongols. These diverse interests converge on the eastern Mediterranean. The new and old peoples of the medieval period all draw on a classical heritage, whether it be the polis, Roman law, or the Arabia of Muhammad. Mixed relationships were not simply a constant of life across the ancient, medieval, and modern worlds. Beneath the surface these ties complicated and illuminated the majority story, the way things usually were. Relationships changed over the centuries, however, and a classical perspective serves as the first step toward exploring a world after 1000, when this region became the center of a true world system. Yet there are many important stories before 1000, and they should not be neglected, nor should stories from the fifteenth century and beyond which show the legacies of earlier mixing. Above all, the dangerous illusion of a static portrait must not obscure the dynamics of the system that arose and virtually collapsed between 1000 and 1400. Remembering that change over time helps us stay connected to the intrepid few who crossed the barriers, broke the so-called rules, and made something new as they forged their own identities and changed the cultures around them.

For all these reasons, studying mixed relationships is the best way to analyze two contradictory tendencies: an acceptance, however grudging or feigned, of diversity, however defined in tension with the venerable claims of superiority that inevitably privileged the pure over the rest. What counts as acceptance here is simply the context that fosters or permits a mixed relationship to exist at all, no matter how temporary, impure, or fragile its life might be. Creeds stressed the purity of their own spiritual values, and believers found it very hard in the Middle Ages to tolerate those who believed something else. People might complicate matters by changing their beliefs or appearing to do so. Racism privileged skin color as a proxy for other traits and was no friend to anyone muddying the fake clarity of white and black. This book investigates how in one corner of the world purist values ran up against the realities of daily life. The results of this mixing complicated the stark appeals of all types of purity. Some people looked for their own peaceful space, not simply the inferno of the living that Italo Calvino imagined for those who did not claim that space.

CHAPTER ONE

The Perception of Difference

The three main examples of human differences discussed in this chapter are religion, language, and race/color. In the eastern Mediterranean, the lines separating Islam, Christianity, and Judaism were fairly stable, and relationships across these barriers were clearly transgressive, requiring a strong dose of self-interest to overcome preferences for coreligionists and the penalties for mixing. Languages too reflected sharp differences among speakers of Arabic, Persian, Greek, and the western Romance and Slavic tongues. Concerns about linguistic purity certainly existed; in the late fourteenth century, Ibn Khaldûn worried that a unifying, pure version of Arabic was being lost through the corrupting influence of Persian and Turkish speakers.[1] Still, no new languages or religions appeared that bridged these differences. The ancient legacies in this region were that the Greeks were monolingual and the Romans bilingual, especially their leaders.[2] The Arabs later seemed reluctant to learn new languages, especially Frankish and Turkish.[3] Conversely, minorities like Armenians and Jews needed to learn the languages of their conquerors. This book looks to those who solved part of the problem of linguistic difference by learning new languages and hiring interpreters.

Missionaries, crusaders, and ghazi warriors tried to resolve the issues of religious difference by conversion, peaceful or otherwise. Mixed relationships occurred across these barriers as people learned new languages or changed their faiths. Differences in physical appearance, manifested in the children from such unions, challenged claims of purity, for here real mixings occurred and produced something new—a different type of person. Race and color thus are more problematic than creed or language, and require a lengthy introduction to show how modern assumptions can distort past traditions.

Everyone agrees that early nineteenth-century thinkers constructed scientific raciology in a cultural context that treated this modern idea with awe. Believers in this ideology devised an increasingly complicated and bizarre rationale for dividing the human family into a hierarchy based on race. But pseudoscientific raciology has proved to be more durable than other past fantasies, like phrenology and mesmerism, that once enjoyed intellectual respectability. If Paul Gilroy is right that other modern ideas about race derive from fascism (itself partly a child of raciology), then a dangerous filter exists between postmodern generations and the origins of racial classification.[4] If racial categories are a superficial veneer on older and grander notions of a universal humanity, then maybe race can be refinished, scraped away along with fascism. Gilroy's pursuit of antiracism is admirable, but his faith in a premodern universal humanity seems too optimistic. William C. Jordan has reminded medievalists of the vast gap between modern concepts of race and the vocabularies past peoples used to describe ethnic and national differences.[5] Current preoccupations about race, projected back into the Middle Ages, can do much harm because they give modern racism a pedigree.

In another recent analysis of racism, George Fredrickson has looked more closely at the alleged era of the brotherhood of man. His main argument is that racism "originated in at least a prototypical form in the fourteenth and fifteenth centuries rather than the eighteenth or nineteenth (as is sometimes maintained) and was originally articulated in the idioms of religion more than those of natural science." The idiom of religion is a clue to his strong belief that Jews as well as Africans were the objects of western racist attitudes. Fredrickson does not find racism before the later Middle Ages because what ethnic discrimination then existed lacked "a world view that would persuasively justify such practices." The equality bestowed by baptism was a powerful sustaining ideology for believing in a basic equality among humans. For Fredrickson, it would take a strong countervailing ideology to undermine this core value of western Christian culture. A possible candidate, color prejudice, according to Fredrickson did not exist in the Middle Ages but originated in the early modern era.[6]

The western tradition of the brotherhood of humanity partly depended on religious teachings regarding the common parents of all people: Adam and Eve. These assumptions, coupled with intense studies of Greek and Roman attitudes toward color and ethnic prejudice, yielded a consensus that the ancient world was free of any values resembling modern racism.[7] Building on this work, David Goldenberg has recently approached the problem of racism from its other end by looking for cultural changes that gave birth to overtly racist assumptions about subgroups of humanity. Drawing on wide research in ancient sources and western religions, Goldenberg started with the venerable and nearly universal metaphor of color symbolism, especially in the stark form of white/black, positive/negative traits. Associating colors with good and bad things resulted in color prejudices revealing what people preferred and disliked. Color prejudice, expressing itself in somatic preferences within various groups of people, can lead to ethnic prejudices when the colors become attached to specific peoples. The big leap occurs when specific colors become tied to groups who were never precisely red, yellow, black, and white. It is exactly at this point that color prejudice (but not necessarily racism) emerges, and Goldenberg has a hard time fixing the moment. He concludes that the first seven centuries of the common era witnessed a slow transition as the color black became tied to slavery and evil.[8] This theme of the curse of Ham affected slave systems beyond the ancient and medieval worlds, but Goldenberg has demonstrated that sometime in the last centuries of antiquity, in the eastern Mediterranean, ideas about color, ethnicity, and slavery came together with terrible consequences for darker-skinned peoples.

The classicist Benjamin Isaac has recently located the invention of racism directly in classical antiquity. Isaac defines racism as "an attitude toward individuals and groups of peoples which posits a direct and linear connection between physical and mental qualities. It therefore attributes to those individuals and groups of people collective traits, physical, mental, and moral, which are constant and unalterable by human will, because they are caused by hereditary factors or external influences, such as climate or geography." The core of racism is "that it tries to establish a hierarchy of groups of human beings, basing itself on an imagined concept: race, that is, on illusory common characteristics which override individual differentiation."[9] Like most modern biologists, Isaac does not believe races are real, but historians are forced to explain them because people have for a long time acted as if they are. Isaac has also rightly focused on racism's crucial ingredient with the simple word *unalterable;* whatever race is, in theory people cannot change it. A racial hierarchy, presuming human inequality, inevitably privileged claims to an original purity. Isaac is sure that geographic and climatic determinism were so strong in classical antiquity that the elements of what he has, alas, in the end called *protoracism* were present thousands of years ago, long before the raciologists of the nineteenth century. Ancient ideas on superior and inferior peoples, not only defined by color, had a long sequel in the Middle Ages. Even Ibn Khaldûn (1332–1406) in his famous *Muqaddhima* recycled older views on blacks as inferior, closer to animals, and born to be slaves—all bad traits caused by the excessive heat of the south. But he believed that if they moved to a temperate climate, their descendants would become more white over time.[10]

Fredrickson, and Goldenberg and Isaac, by coming at the problem of racism from two chronologically opposed perspectives, have in effect challenged medievalists to fill in the middle of the story and resolve inconsistencies in the grand narrative of western racism. My argument is that color prejudice, as repellent as it is, can and did take the form of a sustaining ideology. Color, as well as ethnic origins and other physical characteristics, had been since antiquity a proxy for additional information about people. Fredrickson took two groups victimized by modern racism, blacks and

Jews, and searched for a common thread that would explain the origins of the sustained, ideological reasons the majority community used to enslave and persecute them. He did not cast his net far enough; these two groups are not the entire story of diversity in the Middle Ages. Still, his summary conclusion on racism, that it "exists when one ethnic group or historical collectivity dominates, excludes, or seeks to eliminate another on the basis of differences it believes to be hereditary and unalterable," is a powerful tool for analyzing our subject.[11] The ideologies of color prejudice and a belief in the universalizing effects of baptism were not necessarily in conflict. After all, baptism had not trumped sexism, and its universalizing effects may have retarded as much as advanced equality for women. The conclusions of Goldenberg and Isaac point to the eastern Mediterranean as the place to explore early Judaic, Christian, and Muslim ideas on color, prejudice, and slavery. Goldenberg repeatedly warns against the error of reading back into the past what Gilroy has called modern raciology.[12] Still, Goldenberg exonerated the ancient Jews from ethnic prejudice and the worst consequences of the curse of Ham, and he found some responsibility for these trends in early Christian writers and even more in early Islam. Isaac is convinced that ancient antisemitism was a type of racial prejudice if the Jewish characteristics were perceived as unalterable.[13] These conclusions merit a closer look, as this study pays attention to the context in which late ancient thinkers wrote and, more importantly, to the activities of their audiences—how people actually implemented these values in their relationships.

Fredrickson's work also raises an important question: Why does it matter where the precise origins of modern racism are? His excellent analysis of the modern issues can easily be detached from this earlier problem and still provide a satisfactory account of contemporary dilemma. If we can explore a hypothetical time when a belief in a common humanity was supposedly the norm, then the Middle Ages may supply the evidence for testing the hypothesis that an idea of "universal humanity" once commanded widespread belief and respect. If enough medieval people embraced this humane belief, then we should be able to find instances where others claimed better treatment based on this bond among Christians. It is not going to turn out that scientific raciology is older than we think, or even that the modern concept of race itself can be pushed back into the Middle Ages. People have been thinking about the human race and its constituent parts for millennia. Also, simple color prejudice, the classifying of people by skin color as a reliable proxy for other characteristics, is deeply ingrained in western culture and long antedates Europe's encounter with the New World.

The question of the human race and its constituent parts raises the issue of identity from two perspectives: how people self-identify, and how others identify them.¹⁴ A person over the course of a lifetime constructs many allegiances based on religion, ethnicity, skin color, place of habitation, gender roles, family, and other influences. This process of self-identification is even more complex for persons of mixed parentage because for them the choices or results of the mixing are more numerous. Far from being blank slates, people mature and make choices in a world where others are constantly pigeonholing them on the basis of perceived, imagined, or assigned differences. Students of identity formation are familiar with these issues, which in a medieval context are especially complex because the sources address identity in unfamiliar vocabularies and languages. One purpose of this study is to place the issue of identity in its proper context by looking closely at just who is claiming or being defined by specific labels. Also, mixed relationships problematize identity on a physical level as traits or colors become blurred, and on the personal level as individuals attempt, with varying degrees of success, to renegotiate their standing in the traditional hierarchies.

The grand themes of discovery, slavery, and the fate of the Indians in the early modern period have obscured previous experiences of travel, bondage, and ethnicity. One problem is that from a medieval perspective the Americas look like the fourth New World encounter, depending on how one counts them. The exploration of sub-Saharan Africa began earlier in time and affected the wider context in which the exploration of the Americas occurred.¹⁵ Yet, beginning with the Viking settlement on Greenland in about 1000 and their subsequent encounters with the Inuit (*skraelings*), the Norse sagas have something to say about the Arctic New World. After that "discovery," there was another New World found as Europeans like the Polos of Venice trekked across the vast expanses of Asia to find China in the thirteenth century. So, there are at least four New Worlds—the Arctic, Asian, African, and then the Americas. And *before them all*, back in the Middle Ages, color prejudice existed, at times even with few or no people of color to deprecate.

The great French historian of antisemitism, Léon Poliakov, concluded his study of the Aryan myth with these optimistic words: "The Judaeo-Christian tradition was both anti-racist and anti-nationalist, and the social structure and barriers of the Middle Ages, with its feudal, horizontal hierarchies, no doubt helped the Church to translate this ideal into reality. If all men were equal before God, vertical and geographical distinctions should make no difference to the value of human beings."¹⁶ Most scholars, it seems, have fallen in with this consensus. Many classical historians seem proud of the nonracist societies and systems of slavery (excepting Sparta) they study; modernists claim that the rise of racism and racialism are nineteenth-century phenomena and only explicable in that context. Early modernists make some tentative claims to the topic of race as it concerns events like Columbus's voyage and the rise of the slave trade. Scholars of the long period in between, the Middle Ages, have contributed little of value to this debate. And so sweeping generalizations like Poliakov's (and Fredrickson's) sustain an image of the medieval period as one in which religious assumptions prevail (the Age of Faith syndrome). The particular banality Poliakov has in mind concerns Adam and Eve as the parents of humanity, an idea that later anthropologists termed the monogenesis theory of human origins. The task here is to look more closely where Poliakov saw a reprieve from racism. If it can be established that racist assumptions permeate medieval thought in the monasteries and the haunts of merchants, then we can begin to ask new and exciting questions about the history of race in a medieval context. The fruits of this research can contextualize modern debates on race and human difference. More varieties of human inequality can help us to clarify this old habit of dividing people into groups based on distinctive positive and negative traits.

Let us for the moment define racism as the valuing or disvaluing of people on the basis of skin color or ethnicity—and consider ethnicity to be a question of blood, or in some cases, like the Tartars, simple self-identification. The valuing can have a practical cast, as the means to determine the price of a slave, or be a sweeping judgment on an entire "race" where noneconomic values come into play. This definition is a parallel to Fredrickson's, and it also stresses the innate value or quality attached to these characteristics. Racism has been so thoroughly discredited as an ideology that it has become a tainted weapon wielded against others. Inside a group, the same ideology functioned to make people feel better about themselves, to have a more fixed common identity. Seeing racism this way does not neutralize the term but rather encourages a close look at the reasons why other, equally specious reasons for self-value are just as racist as the ones used to justify demeaning others. In other words, the valuing is just as bogus as the disvaluing when the bases of the distinctions turn out to be groundless. Reaffirming personal or group identities on the basis of specious values cannot make people feel good about themselves for long.

Two ideas, sometimes considered to be the results of modern raciology, clearly originate deep in the Middle Ages if not before. First, color prejudice, often part of its venerable cousin ethnocentrism, is very old, though people have periodically refurbished its justifications. Just what determines the color of skin then becomes the interesting question, and whether these causative agents are inherent or environmental. The skin becomes the boundary between these two influences, as well as the contested territory where the results appear as color. This chapter focuses primarily on what is beneath the skin, though the dichotomy is not strict. Second, people have believed (justifiably or not) for a long time that there are human types that breed true, even in the context of an overarching belief in the unity of the human species. As in the farmyard, like usually produced like, but familiar things like mules and grafted fruit trees gave people pause when considering their own breeding. Cultural characteristics were also understood as passed down, but the focus here is more on the innate physical aspects that helped medieval observers *define* a type of people and perceive human differences. Why does it matter that the chronological and cultural contexts to this problem are longer and deeper than people think? The tension between innate differences and a common humanity may never have been satisfactorily resolved by past peoples, let alone by us. If that is true, then we are not witnessing the end of racism in any form, but its typical mutation into a more modern guise, perhaps this time, as Fredrickson fears, regarded as cultural differences that will be portrayed as innate.[17] What matters to students of medieval and modern ethnicity is discovering the proper context for seeing just what counts as innate and unalterable about people, and what structures of inequality define particular societies.

The eighteenth-century French naturalist Georges Buffon (1707–88) can serve as a benchmark or standard for determining the antiquity of ideas about innateness that have sometimes been seen as more recent. Buffon lived at the dawn of modern raciology, yet he remained an ardent believer in the unity of humanity as a scientific principle. He used language drawn from older traditions as well as Enlightenment discourse. As Buffon's biographer Jacques Roger noted, "since the translation of Aristotle's works into Latin, the Latin word 'generatio' and its French equivalent 'génération' (in English 'generation') have traditionally referred to the process by which living beings engender beings similar to themselves."[18] Medieval authorities were just as much at a loss as Buffon was to explain the mechanism of this inheritance of traits, but they had been observing it for centuries and understood it to be a fact of life. For example, the great Latin dictionary of the thirteenth century, the *Catholicon*, offered a sophisticated definition of *genus* which rooted this word in themes of blood, descent, and origin.[19]

In the volume of Buffon's *Natural History* devoted to humanity, he unequivocally observed that "the first and most remarkable of the varieties [of the human species] is that of color, the second is that of shape and size, and the third is that of the nature of different peoples." To Buffon, this observation was no novelty but a received truth superseding even gender. Color was first, before but not identical to his concept of *race*, a word he used to describe groups like the Lapps, Tartars, and many others. He was especially interested in the Jews, whose traditions about endogamy proved to his satisfaction that the truism—children resemble their parents—defined the group. Ideas about the Jews constituting a specific lineage helped to define them as a group with distinctive blood ties. Buffon also accepted ancient theories positing distance from the equator as determining human differences. Climate was undeniably a major factor in thinking about race in the eighteenth century, as it had been in the previous twenty-five. Buffon knew, however, that no matter where they were born (he was thinking of temperate France), black Africans remained black. Climate did not change this fact, and color was for Buffon the most important thing. Lastly, everything that Buffon learned about natural history strengthened his certainty that human beings constituted a single species. He was an ardent supporter of monogenesis, but he did not come to this conclusion by the same means as the medieval theologians who viewed Adam and Eve as humanity's parents. Buffon's monogenesis relied on observation, and he recognized varieties that were passed down the generations. Climate caused many of these differences, but so too did diet, disease, and other factors. In a medieval context, the task is to look for cracks in the belief in monogenesis, and signs that color and other factors like language, food, and burial customs helped to rank human beings.[20]

As it was passed on from the ancient to the medieval worlds, color symbolism became deeply entrenched in religious discourse, with bad consequences for darker peoples. First the eastern Mediterranean became the place where travelers, merchants, and holy warriors came together to forge new cultural attitudes about differences of creed, color, and ethnicity. From there subsequent generations traveled onward to encounter the Mongols to the east and the Africans to the south. Even when other paths led to Africa or the Far East, the habits of thinking developed in the eastern Mediterranean defined the ethnographic gazes of all the parties involved. This vast subject, covering so much space and time and so many peoples, requires that the analysis proceed through a series of carefully selected examples of how Christian-Jewish-Muslim interactions and cultural assumptions in the eastern Mediterranean shaped later expectations about the wider world. Sometimes these interactions hint that color prejudice and racism were occasionally countered by civilizing ties and humane values.

The Song of Songs

The Song of Songs, or the Canticle of Canticles, has long been where exegetes and modern scholars look for the classical inheritance and its beneficiaries with respect to the themes of color, ethnic prejudice, and racism. Perhaps the Bible's oddest book, this love story has few literal spiritual values and so has always demanded closer scrutiny. Around 240 the Egyptian theologian Origen composed a commentary that set the tone for all subsequent exegetes by stressing that the allegorical meaning of the book conveyed its spiritual message.[21] As Gregory of Nyssa observed in the fourth century, this text only became clear "once the literal meaning has been purified by correct understanding."²² This text cried out for an allegorical interpretation, and this level of exegesis might provide a look at what commentators believed about what was beneath and external to the skin. Being attributed to Solomon saved this love story from some ancient poetry anthology and instead made it the exegete's sternest test: where was the spiritual message in this tale?²³

The problem first occurred to the ancient Hebrews, who concluded that the story was an allegory for God's love of his people Israel.²⁴ Origen concluded that the story was an allegory of Christ's love for his church. He was the first major exegete to deal with the critical phrase "Fusca sum et formosa, filiae Hierusalem" (I am dark and comely, daughters of Jerusalem).²⁵ Origen interpreted this passage as meaning that the woman should not be criticized for her color, which was either natural or caused by outdoor exercise. But his mystical interpretation quickly moved to the fact that the woman was *nigra* (black) and not descended from a distinguished people that had accepted the light of the law of Moses. She was nonetheless beautiful, neatly here because she was made in the image of God. Still, Origen ties the woman of the Song to the Ethiopian Moses married (see below) and concludes that both came from an ignoble type or race.²⁶ Hence the tradition was established that the dark woman in the song was an Ethiopian like the Queen of Sheba. Origen also wrote that the Ethiopian woman was dark or black not by nature nor from the creator but because of the sun, and the blackness was thence handed down through the seed; thus he developed a theory of cause and inheritance.²⁷ He further complicated matters by concluding that as she rose to meet her beloved, the woman became *dealbata,* whitened, another proof that her blackness was caused by the sun. This analysis planted the seed of the idea that interior blackness of the soul had other causes and worse consequences.

Origen revisited these questions in two contemporary homilies on the Song.²⁸ Here he added the thought that the woman had become white through penitence, without which her soul would have remained black and ugly. With penitence, she was still black outside, but beautiful!²⁹ Many subsequent exegetes turned to these difficult questions, but their work for the Latin West was summarized in the standard, ordinary gloss.³⁰ The standard gloss naturally took no interest in the literal or historical sense of the Song, and nothing appeared here about Ethiopia or slavery. What was present was the idea that the woman was black as a result of affliction or penance. There was also a closer look at sunlight, which must owe something to Origen. The sun may burn but also illuminate. Far from the original context of the Song and its earliest commentators, this exegesis ended up promoting an unintended racism as sin, evil, and black became inextricable.

Pierre Abelard and Saint Bernard of Clairvaux, who had little else in common, applied their talents in the 1130s to explicating this text. Abelard did so in only a small way; Bernard wrote a long series of sermons exploring the Song word by word. What actually drew them to this text remains unknown, but a major challenge appeared early in the now standard fourth line, the famous "Nigra sum, sed formosa, filiae Hierusalem" (I am black but comely, daughters of Jerusalem). Here the Ethiopian woman opens her argument for her right to love. This is not the theme that engaged biblical scholars, at least not at first. The Ethiopian gave these men from northern France a chance to discuss blackness, an engaging theme even in the absence of black people. Perhaps one or two Africans passed through Paris during the early twelfth century, maybe Abelard saw one, and Bernard may have seen a Moor on his trip to Italy. Yet they were already prepared by their cultural contexts to explore these themes, and so we have some access to contemporary attitudes toward color, long before the conventional, modern "discovery" of these issues. Whether or not this is "racism before race" is another question to explore.

In the fourth letter of his correspondence with Héloise, Abelard finally responds to the personal issues and distress she has expressed in her previous letters. Coming to the unhappy memory of how Héloise entered religious life after their disastrous marriage, Abelard thinks of his ex-wife in the black robes of a Benedictine nun. His mind skips from this relationship and the nun's habit to Moses' marriage to an Ethiopian.[31] This was another relationship that fell under censure, at least from Moses' siblings Aaron and Miriam. A rich vein of exegesis exists on this early "mixed" marriage.[32] In this case the Lord suddenly appeared and in angry terms denounced the critics of his prophet. Perhaps Abelard was thinking of himself here and hoping for such vindication. This Aethiopissa led him straight to the more famous one of the Canticle, another criticized bride. Abelard first quotes her response to these daughters of Jerusalem, "Nolite me considerare quod fusca sim quia decoloravit me sol." This line, which we look at more closely with Bernard, means "Do not look upon me because I am black, because the sun discolored me." An ancient theory of human difference, the latitude explanation, explains what happened to the Ethiopian. For Abelard and other medieval writers, the classical consensus, based on mostly Mediterranean thinkers from Hippocrates to Isidore, held that a moderate, Mediterranean climate was best. Extremes in the north and south produced outer races naturally defective in their ways.[33] Yet what interested Abelard were the internal consequences of blackness.

Abelard next turns to the contemplative soul and Héloise's black robes, also suitable for her status as a mourner. He takes a closer look at the Ethiopian. She is black on the outside, in her flesh, and it is this exterior that strikes her critics as "more deformed" (*deformior*). Abelard looks beneath the skin, where the Ethiopian is more beautiful (*formosior*) and whiter (*candidior*)—in her bones and teeth! This is a curious image; the redeeming, interior whiteness beneath the black flesh. (J. T. Muckle helpfully notes that Aristotle had observed the white bones and teeth of Ethiopians. Perhaps this inspired Abelard—yet another cultural benefit to the revival of Aristotelian thought and logic.[34]) How does Abelard explain this exterior blackness, the sun's baleful effects? In this life the tribulations of repeated adversities bodily afflicted the Ethiopian—"quasi in carne negrescit"—so she grew or became black in the flesh—but there is no mechanism for this transformation. Leaving no doubt that trials cause blackness, Abelard notes that as whiteness (*candidus*) denotes prosperity, blackness denotes adversity. But these signs were on the outside, and the inner person continues to preoccupy Abelard. Inside, her white bones reveal her shining virtue. Outside, while she is exiled in the pilgrimage of this life, she holds herself base and abject so that she might be exalted in the next. There is a lot more on the theme that blackness is an adversity to be endured in this world, a true tribulation. When Abelard approached the subject this way he was bound to evoke the well-known negative attributes of blackness, and he does. Abelard mentions the "deformity of blackness" (*negredinis deformitas*). Even though the flesh of the black woman is softer (*suavior*) (how can he know this?), it is also deformed because it deviates from the standard of whiteness and purity.

Abelard brings this discussion of blackness back to clothing, and there we may leave it. Black as mourning, black as the robes of a Benedictine nun—here is a general conception of darkness. But when it comes to the question of the flesh, blackness conjures up other unattractive associations. The Bible says "black but comely"; what then can it mean except the reverse of the obvious, even if one must dig down to the white bones to find redeeming virtue? Abelard was no ethnographer generalizing about Ethiopians. He was a disgraced theologian trying to shake himself loose from Héloise's apt criticisms. Yet their common calamity, Abelard's misfortunes (he seldom reflected on hers), drew his mind to a fellow sufferer, the Ethiopian. He did not accept her theory of blackness and instead proposed that tribulations caused her color. If that had been the case, then the Ethiopian, like Abelard miscast by life's vicissitudes, might have become a sympathetic character to medieval audiences. Instead, the Ethiopian became synonymous with deformity, her only redeeming feature her sparkling white teeth. Here's an image with a sequel.

A vexing passage from Jeremiah eases the way into Bernard's extended commentary on the Song of Songs. Here is another Ethiopian, this one a man. According to Jeremiah "Can the Ethiopian change his skin or the leopard his spots? Then may you also do good that are used to doing evil . . ."[35] The prophet, no optimist about human nature, is plainly implying that the answer is *no*—to the Ethiopian, the leopard, and the sinner. This passage occurred to Bernard as he explored the meaning of the dark woman's claim at the start of the Song of Songs, a work to which he devoted a large collection of sermons intended for learned audiences. For Bernard, the Ethiopian woman had become a holy sinner (*sancta peccatrix*), for she had changed her skin (metaphorically) and restored it to a new brightness or whiteness (*candor*). So, she could claim to be black but comely.[36] How could she change her skin? She mourned, or cried, and from her innards she vomited out the bilious or melancholic humors (*felleos humores evomuit*). Apparently Bernard subscribed to the humoral theory of human difference. Can he really have believed that removing black bile, by whatever means, resulted in changing the Ethiopian's skin color? Perhaps not, but he had to find some mechanism for accomplishing this unlikely event.

Bernard's response to blackness is complicated because he cannot discuss the Ethiopian and Solomon (here also assumed to be black and a tradition worth exploring) without finding a way to bring some brightness or fairness out of all this darkness. He finds a way, and the path is tortuous but rewarding because of the rich mine of information about color. Here is a summary of what Bernard has in mind.[37] A black curtain covered the tabernacle of the ancient Hebrews, and this is how he sees black skin, as something cloaking a deeper nature that might be good or evil. Even darkness can have some positive connotations; Bernard writes that she grows dark (using that lovely verb *nigresco*) in the zeal for brightness, the prize of beauty. Blackness can become a stage on the road to purity, to improvement. The most common word here for Bernard is always some variant of *candor*—with all of its positive contexts.

Bernard combines these insights by developing the thought that the blackening (*denigratio*) of one makes many bright/white, and here he also has in mind the sacrifice of Jesus. It is John 11:50 that supplies the connection: It is better that one man die for the people, so that the entire gens (people) not perish. For Bernard, this passage declares that it is better that one man become black than that all of humanity be lost to the blackness of sin. Here it is not such a bad thing to be black. Bernard explains. It is better that the substance of God be covered up (*obnubiletur*, another verb that implies color, meaning to be obscured by clouds, not likely white ones) in the form of a slave if the lives of slaves are thereby redeemed. The word *servus* is of course complex in twelfth-century France, being equally applied to slaves and serfs, but Bernard makes the clear leap from black to slave. Yet he keeps pulling himself back to the idea that the blackness is in exterior things. Even Solomon was only black in his skin. Black outside but not inside. Even Adam and Eve were black skinned and also stained inside by sin, here the curious word employed is in their protoplasm—the original precious bodily fluid.

These references to secondary figures are preparatory to Bernard's return to Jesus, whom he wishes to compare to the Ethiopian woman. Jesus is in some manner black, at least to the senses, while faith naturally reveals him to be white (*candidus*) and comely (*formosus*).³⁸ Jesus' blackness concerns how he appears to others and how they are disposed to view him. According to Bernard, Jesus appeared black to Herod, beautiful and therefore not black to the thief and the centurion. The other thief saw Jesus as black and deformed. Bernard observes that the resurrected Jesus in heaven will return to being *candidus* and *rubicundus* (fair and ruddy), as in Canticle 5:10. Jesus will no longer appear in *pelle nigra,* black skin—but in *veste alba*—in a white covering.

Allegory proves a difficult subject for Bernard, but he does not employ skin color in a simplistic manner. To be sure, Bernard has a hard time rehabilitating bleakness, but he has distinguished between exterior black, which is complex, and interior black, which is always bad and sinful. At the end of this sermon, Bernard explains how the church sometimes emulates blackness; it is not ashamed to seem or to be called black, provided of course that the blackness is outside.³⁹ Images like the blackness of penance, or compassion, or persecution, if hard to understand, do lend positive meaning to the color.

The Canticle gives a good excuse for the Ethiopian's blackness; as she says, "Do not look upon me that I may be dark, because the sun has discolored me." (Latitude again.) Then Bernard puts in the Ethiopian's mouth a more extended plea for compassion. "Do not judge me as deformed because I appear less attractive under the weight of persecution, less adorned according to worldly glory."⁴⁰ Here Abelard and Bernard seem to agree that blackness is a type of misfortune. In one interpretation, Bernard suggests that the woman came too near the sun, and so she became dark, black, and ugly. But he prefers to believe that she is suffering from persecution and hence has become black.

Jewish attention to the Song of Songs did not end with the writing of the Talmud. Rashi (d. 1105), also active in northern France, wrote an influential commentary in Hebrew that associated sin and blackness.⁴¹ Yet for Rashi a person's blackness could be cleansed as easily as dark curtains could be washed. Sinning in Egypt and worshiping the golden calf were evil deeds and helped turn this woman dark, but repentance was capable of reversing the bad effects. Even if at times Rashi associated blackness with ugliness, he raised no ethnic issues as did his near contemporaries Abelard and Saint Bernard.⁴² In the mid-thirteenth century Ezra ben Solomon of Gerona wrote that the woman's swarthiness or darkness resulted from exile as well as sin. She was also "situated amongst my children who are enslaved, at hard labor, performing all of their work in the field."⁴³ This context evokes the sun's effects and notes slavery, not in the Bible but relevant to the Mediterranean in this period. Finally, Levi ben Gershom (Gersonides 1288–1344), working in Provence, thought the woman was black because she lacked philosophical principles, but comely because she was disposed to see them! Here blackness resulted from ignorance, the sun, and excessive involvement in worldly matters.[44] These nuggets from the rich veins of Jewish scriptural exegesis did not refer to Africa or Ethiopia. Still, as the neglected Latin translation of Rashi's commentary suggests, exegesis was not an endeavor where mixed analysis, drawing on Jewish and Christian traditions, would flourish.

For Abelard and Bernard, the Ethiopians posed issues about blackness on the surface and beneath. These problems were not going away. In almost every way the claims of white purity trumped blackness. For some Jewish thinkers, less inclined to write about ethnicity, sin, exile, ignorance, and other factors caused a blackness that was not indelible, or African. Jewish discourse, as Jonathan Schorsch has observed for a slightly later period, was simply not that interested in black people.[45]

The Golden Legend

Hagiography, the lives of the saints, is another path by which the classical inheritance on color and ethnicity came to the Middle Ages. The best known medieval collection of saints' lives, the *Golden Legend* by Genoa's later archbishop the Dominican friar Jacopo da Varagine, was compiled in the 1260s and drew upon a vast array of Latin sources.[46] Since most of the saints were martyred under pagan persecutions in late antiquity, Jacopo in effect repackaged and popularized, through hagiography and its canons, attitudes toward color. This thirteenth-century source hence revitalized the classical inheritance and granted it an enduring influence on later values.

For example, Jacopo re-presented the life of Saint Anthony from the fourth century source by Athanasius. In both texts the devil appeared to the desert saint as a black boy (*puer niger*), a most vile type of human.[47] The life of Saint John the Almoner contained a vision of scales weighing good and bad deeds, presided over on the good side by the whitened (*dealbati*) and on the bad side by the Mauri (the Moors). This is another proof that ethnicity and color had very early associations; the source here was the ancient collection of the lives of the desert fathers. A life of Saint Julian by the sixth-century author Cassiodorus had occasion to comment on the apostate emperor Julian, and in this work the demons were black and the great Ethiopian was Satan himself. The life of Saint Jerome noted that deformed flesh was Ethiopian flesh, and Saint Mary of Egypt was made black by the sun—more proof of the standard latitude theory.[48] The combined weight of these examples makes the case that early Christian connections among sin, evil, the Ethiopian, the devil, and blackness, found a new and even wider audience in the Middle Ages.

There is a coda to this story, and it concerns a path not apparently taken: the set of pagan values that included ethnocentrism but nothing approaching racism. Whatever these values actually were, no one has claimed that they were part of the classical inheritance conveyed to medieval people. Arnobius of Sicca, a recent and ill-informed convert to Christianity, wrote around 302–5 a kind of intellectual autobiography, which denounced paganism, a subject this North African rhetor knew quite well.[49] Arnobius had some unusual ideas that must reflect his former pagan values and education, and they convey some sense of what might have been a different tenor to the classical inheritance. He wrote an unusual bit of dialogue in which a sacrificial animal speaks to Jupiter. The beast makes a plea for its life on the basis of a common spirit between animals and mankind. Humanity, unlike the beasts, was responsible for many evils, including slavery. Arnobius also observed the foolish pagan belief that it was necessary to sacrifice white animals, a cheerful color, to the gods above and dark ones, a sad color, to the gods of the underworld.[50] Part of the pointlessness of pagan practices results from the fact that even black beasts have white bones and teeth (neither Arnobius nor his editor make any reference to Aristotle here). This text conveys a nice sense of color symbolism as it occurred to at least one former pagan, but this symbolism has much to do with animals and nothing at all to do with people. Far from noticing any divisions among people, Arnobius seems to have clung to a common identity among the mammals!

Some monotheistic beliefs and the classical inheritance prepared peoples coming to the eastern Mediterranean to privilege their own creeds, languages, skin color, and cultures over others encountered in the region. Classical Islam presents a puzzle. The Quran raises none of the issues that engaged Jewish and Christian exegetes and is free of color prejudice and racism.[51] Muhammad taught that anyone might change by accepting his message, so there was a strong measure of universalism in this religion. As Islam spread beyond Arabia, it encountered the same cultural influences that early Christians and Jews found in places like Egypt. Numerous encounters among Muslims, Christians, and Jews in the eastern Mediterranean from about 1000 into the era of the Crusades continued to shape in complex ways ideas about color and mixed relationships. At the same time, the Mongols were following the grasslands of central Asia toward the west and the shores of the Black Sea. Mongol conquests profoundly affected the Christian and Muslim spheres of influence but also radically challenged entrenched assumptions about religion, color, and human difference.

Early Encounters with the Mongols

The Mongols (known north of the Black Sea as Tartars) appeared in the early thirteenth century as new people in western Asia and eastern Europe. For the first time since antiquity, old civilizations in the eastern Mediterranean encountered new religions, languages, skin colors, and physical appearances. These unfamiliar variations of humanity challenged Christians and Muslims to rethink their standard discourses about human differences. The first witnesses—merchants, missionaries, and envoys—needed a broader perspective to explain what they were observing in the East.[52] Their reports provide precious evidence about how the presence of the Mongols unsettled received truths about nearly everything. New mixed relationships flourished on every level, from slavery and commerce to religious conversion and conquest. Mongols, Christians, and Muslims needed to devise strategies to preserve their own senses of supremacy in the face of so much mixing.

Around 1235, two Dominicans, Brothers Gerard and Julian, set out from Hungary on a circuitous journey to the northern shore of the Black Sea via Constantinople. Their aim was to learn more about the mysterious Mongols, who were threatening Hungary and other Christian lands in Eastern Europe. The friars never got much past the Volga, and a Brother Richard preserved an early account of Julian's impressions of the East. (Gerard died there.) Julian knew Hungarian, German, and a language he called Saracen, more likely Persian than Arabic. His findings on the Tartars were superficial, vague, and terrifying—the basic early impression held by Europeans. Julian had little to say about their appearance (and nothing on their color) except for the distinctive way the men shaved their heads in front, leaving a longer fringe in the back. The Tartars had slight beards, and according to Julian had no god, or even idols, and lived like beasts. They did not farm but lived off their horses, drinking their blood and milk. Above all the Tartars were excellent fighters who massacred all who resisted. They drank from the skulls of their enemies and were not allowed to marry until they had killed someone. Although Julian never seems to have come into direct contact with the Horde, he began the process of portraying the Mongols as truly dreadful opponents and an uncivilized people.[53]

Julian recorded a somewhat more detailed and considered version of his views in a letter to the papal legate in Hungary in 1237. The Tartars had replaced the Cumans, and this was an important fact about the northern shore of the Black Sea. Julian possessed a confused account of the rise of the Tartars; he had no correct names and only knew that they had conquered the lands of the Cumans and Persians. He made no mention about Chinghiz or China here. He did know that the ruler was called Khan and that the Horde, comprised of people from different nations with their own languages, was organized into units of ten, one hundred, and one thousand. Those who submitted to the khan had to fight for him or be killed, and if they died fighting for the Tartars, no one cared. The Tartars aimed to conquer Hungary, then Rome, and then beyond—in other words, the world. What is new in this document is Julian's knowledge of a letter that eventually reached the king of Hungary. Julian wrote that this letter was in a pagan script, which must be Uighur, but as it was in the Mongol tongue no one could read it. Eventually a Cuman interpreter was found to translate this message, which was probably from Batu as representative of Ögödei, then the khan of all the Mongols. Julian's account sounds like a real Mongol letter. The message was a terse command to submit to the Mongols and account for some missing emissaries. Batu warned the Hungarians that they lived in houses, castles, and cities and would not be able to escape his hand.[54]

Julian concluded by providing an important and early explanation of the word *Tartar*. He claimed to have learned this story from a Ruthenian cleric, the Archbishop Peter. The book of Judges contains a notice of the Midianites, a fierce people defeated by the children of Israel. Judges 6:5 refers to the Midianites as a "innumera multitudo hominum," and it is probably this sense of the Mongols as a vast number of people that fixes this story. According to Peter, in simple terms, the fleeing Midianites came to the banks of a river called Tartar and hence became known by that name. This river naturally evokes the better-known Tartarus, and another image of the Mongols was surely that they were from Hell. It is interesting that this river Tartar, which does not appear in the Bible, allowed Julian and others to connect the Mongols with a powerful and numerous enemy of the children of Israel—and one that was eventually defeated. Julian reported that the Mongol army consisted of 135,000 of their own skilled men and 260,000 slaves, numbers dwarfing western armies.[55]

A third early witness to the Mongols appeared in the curious testimony of Archbishop Peter, who turned up at the Council of Lyon in 1245. Peter claimed to be a Russian/Ruthenian archbishop, but he did not know Latin, Greek, or Hebrew, and the western clergy with difficulty found an interpreter to communicate with him.[56] Whoever this fellow was, he knew very little practical, useful, or accurate information about the Mongols. However, the questions posed to him at the council provide a nice image of western, clerical ethnography at this time. Peter was asked to provide news on nine topics concerning the Mongols: their origin, mode of belief, rites, way of living, strength, multitude, intentions, way of observing treaties, and way of receiving ambassadors.[57] These questions represent an effort to fathom the ordering of Mongol society, even as their conquests began to disorder Europe. Although Peter's useless answers must have frustrated the clergy at Lyon and perhaps even Pope Innocent IV himself, the questions themselves reveal an astute set of concerns about a new people. Better observers, sent from Lyon, would fill in the details.

Brother John from Plano de Carpini near Perugia wrote a *History of the Mongols,* a full narrative of his trip east in 1245–47. As an official emissary of Pope Innocent IV, John, along with his fellow missionary Brother Benedict the Pole, took up the task of developing useful information about these new people. At the beginning of his history, he listed nine topics he proposed to explore, and they provide an interesting parallel to the questioning of Archbishop Peter, an episode John likely witnessed. John's ethnographic inquiry proceeded in this order: the land, the men, rites, morals, the Mongol empire, its wars, subjugated lands, how the Mongols wage war, and the route traveled to the outskirts of Karakorum.[58] These topics, reflecting the same concerns raised in Lyon, highlight the missionary and military aspects of the Church's interest in the Mongols. As there was as yet nothing to read about the Mongols, the answers would have to come from direct observation, and Brothers John and Benedict proved to be astute students of the Mongol people.

Coming from relatively urbanized and fertile northern Italy, John was surprised that not one-hundredth of the Mongol lands were fertile and that his journey across Asia passed through no cities. Again the issue of a multitude surfaced: how was it possible for the Mongols to be so numerous amid so much desolate land? The country struck John as a terrible place—savage enough to match the fierceness of its people, who looked unlike any he knew. The Mongol face was broad between the eyes and cheeks, with small eyes and eyelids close to the eyebrows. The men were narrow at the waist, had almost no beards, and shaved their heads in a distinctive fashion. It is important to note that John wrote not a word on the color of the Mongols' skin. Of far more interest to him was their practice of polygamy and their habit of marrying women quite closely related to them. John did not label this practice as incest; perhaps he was aware of the radically different conception Mongols had of this matter. John understood a bit of Mongol family life and described their gender division of labor. Women made everything and were also skilled in archery and riding. The men made nothing but arrows and did nothing in peacetime but tend their flocks. John also supplied copious details on their dress and dwellings, and was struck by the amazing numbers of animals, especially horses and mares, they possessed.[59]

As a Franciscan, John took considerable interest in the spiritual beliefs the Mongols. According to him, the Mongols believed in one god but did not offer prayers or praises to him or practice anything that John recognized as worship. Yet he noted the presence of many idols and wrote that the Mongols venerated the sun, moon, fire, water, and earth. Because John could not find any religious laws among the Mongols, to him their cult of god was not a religion. As the Mongols had no recognizable concept of sin, John was forced to skip this familiar topic and spent a lot of time describing their traditions and behaviors. Even stranger from his perspective was that the Mongols did not force other peoples to change their faiths; his own category of person, the missionary, did not exist among them. Worse, they knew nothing of eternal life and damnation (in John's terms), so, like many future ethnographers, he was forced instead to write at length about Mongol funerary practices. Nevertheless, the Mongols had their own sense of another world, where they ate, drank, tended their flocks, and pretty much carried on as they did in this one. John must have understood that the Mongols would prove impervious to the claims of his religion and that his prospects for finding converts would be slight. Perhaps he knew enough to see that Islam would find more fertile ground among them, especially where the Mongols ruled majority Muslim populations, as in Persia and much of central Asia.[60]

John divided his discussion of Mongol morals, examining their good and bad habits, their customs, and food. At first the Mongols sounded surprisingly good, as John described how crime-free and respectful their society was. The people were tough, friendly, and had an incredible capacity for suffering. He saw no lawsuits among them, and they showed a lack of discord and envy. But then John warmed to the task of enumerating their many bad qualities. They were extremely proud and honored no other people. By nature angry, indignant, and fraudulent, they were liars and dirty eaters, constantly drunk, avaricious, mean, and homicidal. (And yet lacking discord and envy?) To the Mongols killing meant nothing. It was hard to explain just how bad they were; in his view there was certainly nothing civilized about the Mongols. John, who described himself as corpulent, was struck by how the Mongols ate anything, including lice, mice, and even human flesh when necessary.[61]

The rest of John's long history concerns the rise of the Mongol empire, and he did have much to write about Chinghiz, though he knew nothing about China. As he understood it, they called their land Mongol and themselves Tartars after one of the main branches of their people.[62] The rest of this long work is a military analysis of the Tartar threat and is concerned with the prospects of invasion for Poland and Hungary. The most valuable part for current purposes is when John finally discusses his informants, translators, and the problem of language in dealing with the Tartars. In this context, language is like the skin in the sense that it is a mediating membrane sensitive to external and internal influences. A monogenesis theory of language origins, the Tower of Babel, also explained how languages came to diverge. Language came into being inside a person, and in a medieval context it was "shaped to thought rather than causing understanding."[63] Hence, to some extent, differences in language reflected different thinking, and so these observers knew the Mongols were Others.

Like many a missionary before or after him, John set forth in linguistic ignorance of the problems of communicating in the east. Brother Benedict, who joined the mission in Poland, claimed in his own brief account to have served as an interpreter, and it is likely that he had the Slavic necessary to speak to the Russians farther east.[64] Since Kiev was now in Tartar hands, Slavic languages provided one possible way to contact the Mongols. Officials from the heartland of the western church seem not to have known Slavic languages and communicated with their eastern brethren in Latin—which could never serve as a bridge to the Mongols. Hence, even the relationship between the two Franciscans John and Benedict was mixed, despite everything they had in common as members of the order.

John understood the basic fact that the Mongols, lacking an alphabet of their own, used Uighur letters to write down their language. Somewhere between the Don and Dnieper Rivers, John and his party met for the first time a Mongol force, one commanded by Corensa from Batu's horde. Serious language problems surfaced. Another interpreter, whom John had hired or purchased at Kiev, was unable to translate the pope's letter, and no one else in the camp was able to do it either. This Latin letter was meaningless here, and John had to travel farther east to Batu's camp. Batu, the first khan of what was to become the Golden Horde, was able to supply interpreters who, working with the Franciscans, were able to translate the pope's letter into Ruthenian, Persian, and Tartar (Uighur) script on Good Friday, 1246. Ruthenian was probably the bridge the westerners used at last to communicate with the Mongols; John later referred to a Ruthenian convert who was their interpreter at Batu's camp. Mongol interpreters did the real work of putting the pope's letter into a written language that Batu could have read to him. Whatever he heard in this letter convinced Batu that the wisest course was to send this group on to the heartland of the Mongol state, where Güyüg, Ögödei's son, was now in charge of the empire.[65]

The mission reached Güyüg's camp on July 22, 1246, the first official western party to visit a great khan, and they witnessed the ceremonies surrounding his installation. At the Mongol camp John found an adept translator in a knight named Temer, in the service of Duke Jaroslav. John presented the translations of the pope's letter to the Mongol court, where there were many skilled notaries and interpreters, but none of them knew Latin either. Temer was invaluable here in helping John explain what had happened at Batu's camp and in answering the questions raised by Güyüg's officials. The khan wanted to respond to the pope, and we look at his remarkable letter below. John provided a precious glimpse at the real problems in communicating across these immense cultural barriers. The khan's people wanted to know if anyone with the pope understood Ruthenian, Persian (Farsi), or Tartar. John admitted that no one knew these languages (including himself) and that it would be best for the Mongols to write their letter in Tartar (Uighur). Then the Mongols could interpret and translate (John was careful to use both words) their own letter, and John's people would write it down in their own language, presumably Latin. The three Mongol notaries at hand translated their own letter in what must have been the common spoken language here—Mongol—and then John's people, with Temer's help, got the letter into Latin, perhaps with some help from Ruthenian. At least six people—the three Mongols, Temer, John, and Benedict—were needed to manipulate the languages in play. The sensible final step was that the Mongols wanted the Latin letter translated back to them to be sure there were no errors. They then compared the two written letters in Latin and Tartar, and had a third prepared in Persian on the chance that someone at the papal court could read it. John took back three versions of this letter, two of which, in Tartar and Persian, were created by the Mongols, who could not believe that no one in this West, wherever it was, could understand the great common language of the Mongol state, Persian. Cuman, a Turkic dialect known to peoples in the east and west and the language of the people the Mongols were replacing around the Black Sea, could not serve for this diplomatic exchange apparently because it was not a written language.[66]

Plainly the Mongols did not trust the Latin version of their letter, and John was careful not to take any of Güyüg's representatives back with him, for he recognized from the provocative letter itself that it was dangerous to let Mongols see western defenses. Perhaps John understood the true nature of Güyüg's letter, which was soon circulating in the west upon John's rapid return in 1247, because he did not include it in his written narrative of the mission. An early surviving copy appears in Brother Benedict's brief account. The letter itself starkly reveals the wide gap that made it practically impossible for Mongols and westerners to comprehend one another at this stage.[67] Güyüg, introducing himself to the pope as the strength of God, the ruler of all men, wanted the pope to know that this letter was most certain and true (a real tribute to the translators who had labored to create it). The tenor of the khan's message was made clear in three simple points. First, the pope and the western rulers were welcome to come to the khan's court, submit, and learn what they should do. Second, the pope had asked Güyüg to become a Christian, and he answered that he did not understand. Third, the pope had asked about the slaughter of the Poles, Hungarians, and Moravians, and again the khan responded that he did not understand.

So as not to appear silent, uncommunicative, Güyüg elaborated on these points. Because the peoples asked about had not obeyed Chinghiz Khan and had killed his envoys, God had handed them over to be destroyed, and they deserved it. Clearly, the khan could not fathom why the pope had failed to understand this most basic aspect of Mongol policy: failure to obey a command to submit meant destruction. In what must have amazed the missionaries and perhaps even the pope, Güyüg did not understand why the westerners believed that they alone were Christians—for he knew all about the Nestorians. Moreover, the khan did not see "how could you know to whom God sees fit to confer His Grace?"[68] The Persian version, even more forcefully expressed, showed that the khan could not grasp this level of religious arrogance. The

Latin version crisply observed that the power of God was clearly with the Mongols. The pope's request that Güyüg convert was a stunning insult to the Mongols, who concluded that it was perhaps best simply to claim not to understand it. Lastly then, Güyüg observed that the pope and these rulers in the west should certainly come and make peace. If not, then God only knew what would happen. To Güyüg, however, the sequel must have been fairly clear—these people needed to be smashed. Recall that John had concluded that the Tartars were an arrogant people despising all others, yet even they 'did not force others to deny their faith or religious law and obey the Mongols'. Güyüg could not fathom a call to abandon his faith by a distant, minor power claiming a monopoly on revealed truth. In a profound way, these internal senses of God's grace, and how and to whom it was bestowed, constituted at this stage the real difference between these peoples.

Simon of Saint Quentin, about whom almost nothing is known, was one of the early Dominicans to return to the West with an account of the Mongols. His report ended up incorporated in the *Speculum historiale* of Vincent of Beauvais and received wide attention. Simon spent two months in 1247 with the horde of Batu around the Don River, never venturing farther east or crossing paths with John's party. Hence Simon observed Mongols but never saw their homelands in Central Asia. He considered the Tartars, as he called them, to be a small and very ugly people. They had big eyes hooded with lids that made their eyes appear smaller, and they had flat faces and noses. The Tartar men were beardless except for the upper lip and a few hairs on the chin. They shaved the tops of their heads and wore their hair long in the back like a horse's mane. Both the men and the women rode well. Simon found their way of speaking to be noisy and horrible, and they sang from the throat and sounded like wolves. The Tartars drank a lot, lived in tents, owned many animals, loved to hunt, ate poorly, and on top of all this had no bread. He wrote much on the appearance and customs of the Mongols but not a word on their color. Still, Simon was among the first to draw a sharp physical difference between Mongols and westerners.[69]

The Mongols had invaded Poland and Hungary in 1242, and they posed a serious threat to the rest of Europe. However vice ridden or appalling they might seem to missionaries, the Mongols were too much of a military threat to be dismissed as inferior beings. Still, the level of knowledge about them could be very low, as the memories of Jean de Joinville demonstrate. Having accompanied Louis IX on his crusade to Egypt in 1248, Jean was called upon in his extreme old age in 1309 to set down his recollections of the saintly king. By then, or even by the 1290s when the process of canonizing Louis was well underway, Jean's memory may have been contaminated by reports about the Mongols subsequent to his adventures. Jean's account of the crusade to Egypt, so detailed and lacking in references to subsequent events, can be used as a gauge of common knowledge about the Mongols. What Jean reported was mostly nonsense. According to him, the Tartars had defeated the mighty Christian ruler Prester John and the Persians, but he knew nothing about Chinghiz or China.[70] The few scraps of ethnography he possessed about the Tartars suggested that they were a fierce, meat-eating people overwhelming in their strangeness. They were not central to Jean's account of the crusade, but he noted that Louis was interested enough in them to send out envoys to seek additional information.

Louis IX's crusade in Egypt and his search for allies against the Muslims also provide the context for the most perceptive of medieval ethnographers, William of Rubruck, whose travels took him all the way to China. He knew about John of Plano de Carpini's previous mission, and Rubruck's journey in 1253–55 resulted in a monograph on the Mongols, a new ethnic group not likely to be easily conquered or converted.[71] The most useful thing about William's rich work is his vocabulary of ethnographic difference. Skin color did not interest him. A northern European Franciscan friar writing in Latin, he used the old words mainly in their traditional meanings but in a more global context than any Roman. In the East, William felt that he was in another world. Yet he held onto the idea that there was a *humanus gener*—a phrase well translated as the human race, the only race there was. This race consisted of various groups called gentes (*gens*), by this he meant a people *(populus)* or nation *(natio)*. The Armenians were a good example, they were a *gens*, a *natio*, and they also had a *terra*, a land. This or any land might also be defined more expansively as a place that had a language and writing, things the Mongols also possessed. Once a Mongol had warned William not to say that a certain prince was a Christian because he was a Moal (Mongol). From the Mongol perspective, Christians were a *gens*, so for a Mongol to be called one *by William* meant that he was no longer a member of his own people. For Mongols, creed did not define a people, but they had picked up the idea that to the westerners like William, creed might mean something different. From William also comes the concept of the *gener*, the human race, and its *gentes*, the subunits that breed true.[72]

William's account provides several avenues into his thoughts on ethnicity, languages, and women, useful topics for any ethnographer to consider. As a well-trained Franciscan, William's mind naturally turned to the Bible when he searched for ways to describe the novelties of the East. For example, at the very beginning of his prologue addressed to Louis IX of France, William, presumably reflecting on all his adventures, turned to a passage from Ecclesiasticus. This part of the Bible evokes the atmosphere of a scholar's wisdom and his place in society. The author of Ecclesiasticus mentions the law, wisdom, prophesies, proverbs, and even riddles as elements of wisdom. He goes on to remark of the scholar, "The great avail themselves of his services, and he is seen in the presence of rulers."[73] This passage, silently on William's mind, probably recalled his experiences at the court of Möngke (Güyüg's cousin and successor, khan from 1251 to 1259), as well as that of Louis. The passage William actually cites is Ecclesiasticus 39:5, "He travels in foreign countries and learns at first hand the good and evil of man's lot."[74] William's sense of his mission to the Moal comes through this verse. This distant, foreign territory was above all to William, as he studied the Mongols, a lesson in morality.

The second biblical reference worth pondering concerns a commentary on the Tartars. The context here is William's long and arduous journey to Möngke's court. He was thinking about the astonishing array of peoples and languages in the East. He astutely observed a relationship between the languages of the Ruthenians, Poles, Bohemians, and Slavs, related to the Vandals, as he saw it. These people had followed the Huns and were now with the Tartars. (A remarkable power of historical understanding rests behind this equating of the Huns and Tartars as constructed peoples.) Thinking about the Tartars, William observed that they "had been raised up from very distant regions, a non-people and a foolish nation."[75] "Populus nullus" is an attention-grabbing phrase and not easy to translate; a "nothing people" is probably just as good a way to express William's sentiments. This thought carries William to an exact quotation from Deuteronomy 32:21. The context here is a song by Moses, which concerns in part the parceling out of people across the world. This matter follows directly from what has been on William's mind: how the Mongols came to occupy their distant lands. What happened was that God divided the *gentes* and separated the children of Adam, thereby fixing boundaries between the *populi* (Deut 32:8). Here is a vision of humanity affecting William's own thoughts. There was a human race, descended from the original parents Adam and Eve, and God divided them into peoples with boundaries, in effect, into nations. So far this is unexceptional, but it skirts the Babel problem about the different languages. Moses laments that the wandering Jews have made God angry and jealous with their false god. The Lord said to them, in effect, that if he was no god, then they were a no people, a *populus nullus*. This is precisely the passage William quotes: "as the Lord said, 'I will rouse their [the people who don't keep my law] jealousy with a people of no account (*non est populus*) and with a foolish nation I will provoke them.'"[76]

The connections William makes in his chain of memory about the Mongols and the passages from Deuteronomy are complex. The passage from Hebrew scripture was even more apt (and famous) because Paul quoted it exactly in Romans 10:19, in the context of witnessing and dispatching preachers. William found this to be his own situation in the East. So he connects the circle. The Tartars were a distant people placed far away by the hand of God, yet they remained a part of the human family.

Still, they were not a people, and they were a foolish *gens* because they did not follow God's law. So they deserved to be provoked, in fact irritated, by being reminded of their low status, by none other than William himself! The Tartars were a test and trial to the true believers, another example of God's providence. William's successors would find other such peoples scattered across the globe, but not all these groups would be visited by as peaceful a missionary and ethnographer as William.

In order for William to be a successful preacher and observer, he needed to understand the Tartars and in turn be able to speak to them. Even by the end of his mission he could barely manage the latter. At the start of his journey William acquired the services of a man he refers to as Homo Dei. Most scholars have concluded that his original name was Abdullah, and it makes sense that he was a Turkic-speaker able to communicate on some level with the Tartars.[77] In his first mention of this person, William called Abdullah his *tergemanus,* close to the standard dragoman in the Latin East, but even closer to the Turkish *terguman,* hence my conclusion that he was dealing with a Turk or Cuman.[78] All these words for interpreter derive from the Arabic *turjumān.*

William's account earns respect because of his constant, frank worries about problems of language. When he first contacted the Tartars, he carried a letter in Greek from the Latin emperor of Constantinople, and he found himself in a place where no one could read the Greek and translate it for the Tartars.[79] He also wanted to preach to the Tartars and expected to rely on Abdullah. But his interpreter was not learned or eloquent, so he simply could not explain the essentials of the faith. Abdullah said to him, "Don't make me preach, because I don't know how to say such words."[80] William learned later to his sorrow that this remarkable admission was indeed correct. After William began to learn a little of the *idioma* (language) of the Tartars, he understood that when he said one thing, his interpreter said another. When he saw the danger of speaking through Abdullah, he chose rather to be silent.[81] And there were other problems. Once, in a discussion with Buddhist monks, his interpreter became tired and not able to express his words, so his incompetence made William fall silent.[82] The problem recurred when William tried to preach to his guides. The best that could be said of Abdullah was that he simply lacked the vocabulary necessary to explain the subtleties of Christianity. Abdullah's mind contained only a small subset of language; out in the wider world there was much more beyond his power of expression. For William, the experience of being silent in the face of such chances to preach was really burdensome. Since Abdullah remained William's constant companion on these journeys, the language issue was never really resolved.

William's greatest opportunities for accomplishing his various missions came in his few meetings with the Tartar ruler Möngke Khan. In William's first audience with

Möngke, his interpreter became drunk and all efforts to communicate failed.[83] William came to speak enough to have a simple conversation with Möngke, but he needed his interpreter to understand the Khan's justly famous image of the religions of the world as being like fingers on a hand, all tracing back to some ultimate spiritual unity. (This was a point similar to the one the Khan Güyüg had made in his letter of 1246.) William's debate with a Buddhist priest or monk, as Benjamin Z. Kedar notes, required two translators, from Chinese to Mongol and from Mongol to French, further increasing the chances of miscommunication. Confusion on basic terms resulted, and another contemporary source states that William made a poor impression on the Mongol rulers by preaching damnation instead of less harshly explaining his faith.[84] William's last reflections on Möngke were a bitter regret that if he had only been able to make signs (miracles) like Moses, the Khan would have humbled himself and converted.[85] This comment suggests just how little William understood about the Mongol value of religious pluralism. Meanwhile, his interpreter, never quite able to hold his own on religion, took charge of William's funds and figured out a way to make some profit by trading with the local people.[86]

William's account has rightly served as a marvelous and perceptive record of Mongol culture. One aspect of this gendered ethnography deserves notice because of William's sensitivity to the special circumstances of Tartar women. After he described the clothing of men and women, he, like John, carefully recounted the gender division of labor among the Mongols. William had a sense that the differences between peoples largely concern the things they can change—their clothing, the ways the work, even the styles for shaving parts of their heads. He was also struck that the Tartar women rode horses just as the men did, and he understood that the beauty of the women to the Tartars depended on the smallness of their noses. (He did consider these women to be amazingly fat, but it should be noted that the only personal detail he supplies is that he himself was very heavy.) William stands at the beginning of a long tradition in which male ethnographers use the standing, habits, and appearance of women as reliable methods for characterizing the entire group. This methodology has a long sequel in the annals of ethnography.[87]

The last of the Franciscan travelers to the East considered here, John of Monte Corvino, was born in southern Italy in 1247 and end up in 1307 as archbishop of Khanbalik (Beijing). John spent some time in Persia and India before reaching China in 1294, just after the death of Qubilai Khan. His accounts survive in three letters written to inform his colleagues about the status of the missions in the East. The first letter, concerning India, has nothing to do with the Mongols but does mention two subjects that help put his later remarks in context. First, John was quite aware that India possessed a climate unlike any known in Europe. A terrestrial paradise, India had no winter or fleas. Second, India was a realm of many peoples and languages, with a few Jews and Christians, many Muslims, but above all a great mass of people (Hindu and Buddhist) who predictably struck John as idolaters. John remarked that these people were not black but olive-skinned, and thus John located himself at the beginning of a long tradition of characterizing peoples in East Asia by color. For centuries skin color had become an important issue in the Mediterranean world. The surprise is that it took so long to surface in the missionary accounts. John's near contemporary Marco Polo (1254–1324), pursuing more secular interests in the East, constantly remarked on the skin color of its inhabitants. Most of the missionaries were Italian, so cultural differences do not explain the different weight given to issues of color. The missionaries were seeking converts (and news) while merchants like the Polos were looking for profits. The first valued the universality of human souls; the second were struck by human differences and needed proxies as a shorthand way to keep track of various peoples, customs, and markets.[88]

John's second letter, written in 1305, describes his accomplishments in China. A complex relationship surfaces in the case of forty boys John purchased for the purpose of baptizing them and teaching them Latin letters and the Catholic rites. Slavery was familiar enough in China and Italy. This southern Italian missionary does not seem to have given the matter a second thought, and the boys, between the ages of seven and eleven, were presumably freed. John wrote a psalter and hymnals for these boys, but he bitterly regretted his lack of music books. Even more remarkable, John studied and learned the Tartar language and alphabet, and he translated into their language the entire New Testament as well as the psalter. Khanbalik was the Mongol capital, and there Tartar was a more useful language than any dialect of Chinese. Still, John became the first educated westerner known in the surviving sources to have direct access, through the language, to Mongol thought.[89]

In his last letter of February 1306, John wrote to the vicars of the Franciscans and Dominicans in Tabriz, the Persian city holding the thread of his tenuous connections back to the West. He wanted his colleagues to understand the serious efforts he was making for converts in the face of local Nestorian Christian hostility. Not wanting to repeat his previous letter, he discussed a series of six pictures he made which must have concerned some main events of the Old and New Testaments. He needed these pictures to teach doctrine to people he described as *rudi*, common people. However, these people were not necessarily illiterate, for his pictures had captions in Latin, Turkish, and Persian letters. By "Turkish," John must have meant the Uighur alphabet used to write the Tartar language.[90]

We can leave John and the other Franciscans patiently sifting for converts among the Mongols and Chinese. The missionaries wanted a spiritual relationship with the

Mongols and saw differences as primarily concerning beliefs and not physical appearance, though they certainly commented on this. Western Christian rulers like Louis IX wanted alliances with the Mongols to fight the Muslims. Traders like the Polos wanted profits. From these perspectives, westerners pursued their self-interests in relation to the Mongols with little thought to what might benefit their hosts. Conversion to Christianity, the defeat of Islam, and new products were valued by westerners as gifts to the Mongols, who in turn seemed not very interested in them. The potential mixed relationship foundered on these irreconcilable values, reinforced by physical differences that fostered hostility. The Mongols, in close communication with ancient civilizations in China, did not need western lessons on humanizing ties, and westerners viewed the Mongols as too barbaric to be taught anything at all. For a variety of complex reasons involving fourteenth-century crises, mainly the plague, and ruptures on the trans-Asia caravan routes, by century's end western missionaries and merchants had lost touch with the East. The missions and merchant colonies vanished, and the relationships ended, except for a lingering taste in the west for female Tartar slaves and riches from the fabled East. All that survived in the West was the memory of these relationships and some neglected texts describing them. Later dreamers like Columbus remembered some of this. Polo's book about the East, however, became the equivalent of a bestseller and kept the story of the Mongols and the riches of China and India alive to western audiences. Before exploring this wonderful source, a quick detour is necessary to see how other missionaries took up the question of defining the differences among peoples.

Two Things from Horace

Another way to explore the problems of color and ethnicity is to examine how an older author serves the purposes of later ones. Small changes and different emphases can reveal which attitudes are more recent. Two examples from Horace show how this method may yield results that illustrate how concepts of blackness and skin color developed in the later thirteenth century.

In 1286 the Genoese Dominican friar Giovanni Balbi completed his great Latin dictionary, the *Catholicon*.[91] I have used this dictionary to explore attitudes toward color, and here take a closer look at the definition of *niger*.[92] Balbi's *black* is given negative associations, and he concludes his lengthy remarks with the lexicographer's most famous tool, the illustrative quotation.[93] The line he uses is from the *Satires* of Horace (I, iv, 83): "hic niger est, hunc tu, Romane, caveto" (this one who is black, beware of him, Roman). The problem is that the quotation is extracted from its meaningful context. In context, the line is slightly more benign, and Horace is speaking of someone black-hearted, a backbiter, false friend, and a liar.[94] Balbi's point, whether it was Horace's or not, is that to be black is to be bad.

Another Dominican friar, William of Tripoli, completed a work on Muhammad and the Saracens at the convent in Acre in 1273.[95] William was well informed about Islam and believed that the religion was on the verge of collapse, with Muslims eager to convert. In his *Notitia de Machometo*, William explained the genesis of the Quran, among many other things. Another book on Islam, the anonymous *De statu Sarracenorum*, derived from William's work but sometimes expanded upon it with new insights.[96]

William knew the standard story of how at the age of forty-five Muhammad began to say that he was a prophet of God and that he was receiving instruction from the angel Gabriel.[97] Afterwards, Muhammad's listeners put down his teachings in a book. Forty years after the prophet's death his followers came together to agree on exactly what belonged in the Quran. They wanted to clarify the doctrine and law of God given through Muhammad to the Arab people, who descended from Hagar and Ishmael. William followed standard medieval ethnography: Arabs are an ethnic group of common blood, Saracens are believers in Islam, an identity based on creed. It was agreed that a certain Utman should write down the authoritative text, but he was not up to the challenge. So, some poor souls (*miseri*), Christians and Jews who because of their fear of death became Saracens, helped compile the book. But these scholars had not come to this project in the lifetime of the prophet, so like ignoramuses they put in lots of errors and falsehoods. Understanding nothing about knowledge, history, or doctrine, they acted like fortunetellers. Here William's follower used the rare word *phitonici*, evoking the pythoness at Delphi, hardly a reliable source of spiritual revelation.

So, according to this source, the Quran was put together just like the crow. Here is where a story derived from Horace entered William's work. The friar's version was that there was a crow that tried to change by taking on the feathers of differently colored birds. Claiming to come from heaven, this adorned crow showed up at an assembly of all the birds. The other birds recognized a crow wearing someone else's feathers, and they laughed him out of the meeting. William's erudite allusion raises the question: Who is this crow? The answer is in Horace's Epistle I, iii, 18–20, in the appealing context of a letter about a journey to the east. Horace was thinking about famous writings kept in the Temple of Apollo on the Palatine—perhaps the pythoness brought him to Apollo and hence to this image. Horace asked after a writer named Celsus, who depended too much on other authors. So, Celsus has to be careful, and here are Horace's lines: "lest, if some day perchance the flock of birds, come to reclaim their plumage, the poor crow [Celsus], stripped of his stolen colors [his borrowed learning] evokes laughter."⁹⁸ This is all very witty, and the only colors in Horace concern the gaudy plumage of the other birds.

William takes a different lesson. For him, the Quran is the black crow. The anonymous author added that the work has all the blackness and deformity (*nigrido et deformitas*) of Muhammad, decorated with the beautiful and luminous authorities of divine scripture inserted in it. Apparently, the apostates, deluded as they were, still remained responsible for whatever good there was in the Quran. For Horace it was enough to mention the plain little crow. All the blackness came from William of Tripoli and the anonymous author, who read into Horace something more particular about the bird. They associated the bad color and all its negative traits with the "bad" religion. Denigrating Islam with the help of classical examples was a way to display erudition. Clearly, ideas of darkness were already deeply embedded in thirteenth-century culture across the Mediterranean. What could this mean for black people?

Saracens

William of Tripoli's miserable ones, those Christians and Jews helping to fabricate the Quran, stood midway in a long tradition of depreciating the origins of Islam. William certainly knew, and Muslim tradition recorded, that a Christian monk named Bahira had foretold the young Muhammad's future as a prophet. Over time Bahira played a bigger role in shaping Islam's message, and by the twelfth century he became practically the mastermind behind Muhammad's message.⁹⁹ The prophet knew a great deal about Judaism and Christianity, and some of these traditions appeared in the Quran. It seems a small step from Islam's respectful attitude toward the peoples of the book, and the strand of Christian thought that the Quran itself was a book whose good parts, as William of Tripoli believed, were written by Christians, however heretical. This belief in turn fostered the view, held by some, that Muslims were also Christian heretics. Certainly by the twelfth century, educated opinion recognized that Islam was neither paganism nor heresy but a monotheistic faith. Knowledge of Islam in the West remained fragmentary and occasionally deluded, though somewhat better than in previous centuries.¹⁰⁰ Yet even after the Quran was translated into Latin in the twelfth century, westerners continued to use their oddly misplaced name for a people more aptly though rarely called Hagarenes. Arabs did not descend from Sarah, but the old name Saracens stuck in preference to labels derived from Ishmael or Hagar. By the late thirteenth century, the Saracens were in the process of mopping up what remained of the crusader states and Armenia. Their triumphs challenged Christian thinkers to explain this perplexing and undesirable (from their perspective) outcome. Military defeat in the East was not the expected result to papally sanctioned holy war.

The mixed relationship between Saracens and Franks is a vast subject involving state formation, diplomacy, and war. The question remains how ethnic identities evolved over the course of these struggles, and how ethnicity itself came to have explanatory force in history. On the most personal level of relationship, mixed marriages between Franks or Latins and local Christians, usually called Syrians (some of whom may have been recent converts from Islam), produced a new people, called in the Frankish dialect *poulains* (from *pullani*, foals). This is an example of observable ethnogenesis in a historical context. Jacques de Vitry, an immigrant bishop of Acre in the early thirteenth century, knew that his flock were born to this land in the East. These *poulains* were in fact his parishioners, but they did not please their spiritual leader. Jacques thought that these natives were soft, totally given up to pleasures of the flesh, and not interested in his preaching.[101] This image of easterners as carnal and unwarlike would have a long life in western attitudes about the East.[102] At this point the *poulains* were the mixed breed; it would be hard to argue that the armies of Saladin and his successors had consisted of weaklings. Hence the issue of mixed blood may have been more important than religious loyalties in determining the strength of a people. Or, so it may have seemed to Jacques de Vitry. A parallel model of explanation accounted for Saracen heroes like Saladin by claiming that they were mixed bloods descending from captured noblewomen from the West.[103] The ethnic argument could count both ways in the case of individuals; it could explain special valor or effeminacy, or the sterility of a mule. This contradictory tone to the ethnic argument of course suggests that it was well suited to reflect the biases of those employing it. Authors who tried to raise the ethnic argument above the level of the individual, or who looked at groups in more complex ways than Jacques de Vitry, had more powerful analytical tools at their disposal.

A good place to look for ethnic arguments to explain history is the proposals for how Christians might recover the Holy Land. Many writers turned toward inventing strategies for new crusades to bolster what was left of the crusader states, or, after 1291, to reconquer part of the mainland or Jerusalem itself. These plans are not our subject, but they are interesting because some of them display a heightened awareness of ethnicity. Fidenzio of Padua spent some time in the crusader states from 1266 to 1291 and for a while was head of the Franciscan order there. During the later part of his stay, before returning to Italy for good, he wrote a short work on the recovery of the Holy Land. This Franciscan friar brought a northern Italian cultural perspective through which he perceived ethnic differences in the East. From the outset, Fidenzio stressed that many nations or *gentes* had taken the Holy Land, first the ancient Hebrews, then the Assyrians, Babylonians, and Romans (he skips the Greeks), and then the Christians. Many peoples had plainly lost the Holy Land—this much of a sense of history Fidenzio possessed. The question remained: why had the favored Christians lost? Fidenzio knew about the Mamluk campaigns against Armenia in the 1280s, the fall of Tripoli in 1289, and finally the loss of Acre in 1291. Decades of experience in the East informed Fidenzio's list of seven reasons behind this collapse. The first reason was inevitably sin, a lack of purity, and what more could one say about this venerable explanation for change in history? To Fidenzio's credit he did not stop his analysis at sin, but proceeded to what he called *variatio* or *diversitas,* which was eerily close to the modern concept of diversity—here of peoples or nations.[104]

Fidenzio wrote that this diversity appeared in Acre, a city he clearly knew well. The Muslim pilgrim Ibn Jubayr had observed there in 1184 a number of Christian notaries who wrote and spoke Arabic.[105] Many Christians came to this complex city from almost all nations under the heavens. These peoples did not love this country like their own; they did not take care of it like *indigenes;* they were for the most part adventitious people—a remarkable phrase. Fidenzio must have been thinking about his Padua and its region, and how people born to a land care for it more than strangers do. What can he have meant by "adventitious people"? Were they like plant seeds blown to the East and fortunately landing on the soil of the Holy Land? Or, were they simply people out for themselves, feeding off the prosperity of Acre but likely to move elsewhere when the Mamluks ended the boom economy?[106]

These diverse peoples also had different languages, faiths, rites, and ways of living. The great divide was between the Latin or Frankish people, and the Syrian Christians. All the Frankish Christians, whose families were from what we know as the vast lands of western Europe, brought with them different tongues and customs, and according to Fidenzio many quickly returned to their native lands. Many came East with great fervor and went home with even greater. (It would be worth knowing if this period in the history of immigration really produced a flow back from the eastern Mediterranean, and what effects these people had once they came home.) Even worse, as Fidenzio saw it, many came to the East without arms or knowing nothing about them. Some of these people ended up getting themselves killed while visiting holy places. Others came promising great things and accomplished nothing—(another recognizable class of migrants from other periods of history). Some were lost to lust, while others (like later tourists) spent a lot of money in Jerusalem. This wealth enriched the Saracens, who were hence better able to fight Christians. There were also Christians who sold to the Saracens arms, munitions, wood, and other things useful for war. Finally, Fidenzio claimed that *many* Christians became Saracens and ended up fighting the Franks. Presumably Fidenzio was well placed to observe the phenomenon of the renegade, whether or not he exaggerated their influence on events. Still, it was possible in his eyes to become a Saracen, while the eastern Christians never became Franks. This asymmetry points to the success Muslims had in welcoming converts as full members of their world.

Fidenzio defined as Syrians those born in the Holy Land or other places in the East. He had a short-termer's view of the locals; apparently to be a real Frank one had to be born back in Europe. On the one hand, Fidenzio seems to have admired the Syrians; once again he had enough historical perspective to observe that after all these people had been converted by the apostles themselves and other saints. On the other hand, for the most part these Syrians had the nature or character of Saracens—they ate long, flat bread and wore their hair in a local style. Some followed the Greek rite, others were Jacobites, and they did not like one another. The Syrian Christians were not warlike and did little to defend the Holy Land. Fidenzio concludes his analysis of diversity by returning to his main theme—the Christian inhabitants were so various and diverse that they were not likely to fight well against the Saracens. To drive home this point he quoted from Jeremiah 12:9 this obscure passage, "Mine heritage is unto me as a speckled bird, the birds round about are against her; come ye, assemble all the beasts of the field, come to devour." Perhaps Fidenzio was drawn to this verse because of the *avis discolor,* an adjective recalling what the sun did to the Ethiopian woman—it darkened her. Once again the issue of color becomes mixed up with ethnic identity. This image also could represent ethnic diversity in the Holy Land, the hostile birds and beasts plainly the Saracens ready to fall on their prey. Diversity, like sin itself, was for Fidenzio a problem because it revealed an impure society.

Fidenzio's last five reasons for the loss of the Holy Land are a mix of internal and external factors. They do not directly concern ethnicity but provide a context for understanding the importance of diversity. His third reason was effeminacy, a simple lack of virility, meaning that the Christians fought like women. Fidenzio blamed the Christians for imprudence because they did not fight the Saracens and instead left them alone to multiply to a great number. From the western perspective one of the great problems the Saracens posed was that they were a numerous people. Imprudence also fit the Christian policies toward the Mamluks; in Fidenzio's view his people did not know when to fight, when to make peace, and when to flee. Discord was another cause of Christian defeats, and here he notes the problems among the Venetians, Genoese, and Pisans, between the king and these communes, and among the Syrians. Furthermore, the Christians had no one recognized ruler, and he cites the apt passage from Judges 17:6, "There was no king in Israel." Fidenzio must have known that the Mamluks also suffered from divisions, but they had a strong sultan.

Another problem for the Christians was simply that help was far away across the Mediterranean. Lastly, the Saracens then controlled the main holy places Nazareth, Bethlehem, and Jerusalem. This fact seems to have been more a result than a cause of Christian defeat, but Fidenzio may have seen this as a problem of motivation. Once the holiest places were lost, local morale suffered. Fidenzio devoted the rest of his tract to a polemic against Muhammad and Islam, and to giving practical military advice for attacking the Saracens. He did not use the same seven themes for his analysis of Islam, so we cannot learn what role, if any, unity or diversity played in Mamluk victories.[107]

A closer look into the culture of the Saracens comes from a Dominican who spent years living among them. Riccoldo da Monte Croce (ca. 1243–1320) entered the Dominican convent of Santa Maria Novella in his native Florence in 1267. After his travels he returned there to write several works, including a harsh polemic against Islam.[108] In his attack on Islam, Riccoldo did not need to evoke a sense of the East or its ethnic diversity, but his travelogue is quite rich on these topics.[109] This educated friar arrived in Acre in 1288, just in time to visit Jerusalem and other holy places in a period of relative peace. Journeying north through Armenia into a land he called *Turchia*, Riccoldo wrote that the Turks lived like beasts, like moles underground. He made his way along the southern shore of the Black Sea to Ararat and then to Tabriz, where he stayed for a year and preached through an interpreter in Arabic.[110] Since Riccoldo was in Baghdad when Acre fell in 1291, he probably spent about ten years in this large city. He was certainly back in Italy by 1300, and he presumably passed the last two decades of his life writing several works on Islam, the eastern nations, and an account of his pilgrimages and time in Baghdad. Riccoldo is a valuable witness because he knew some Arabic and had spent ten years living among Muslims.

Like a good scholastic author Riccoldo was careful to present what he viewed as the positive and negative aspects of Islam. There was never any doubt about the eventual balance of good and bad, but this account is one of the most knowledgeable descriptions of Islam in a western source. Muslims, even the Turks, were to him always Saracens. He brought to life Baghdad, a great city of 200,000 Muslims, Christians, and Jews. As a missionary Riccoldo naturally focused on Islam itself, and he wrote nothing here on the appearance or physical characteristics of these Saracens; perhaps he did not consider them that important. He did see immense differences in the faiths. Beginning on the positive side, he knew and praised the seven works of perfection. Riccoldo admired Muslim attitudes toward study and was certainly impressed by their schools. He described Muslim prayer in respectful detail. Muslims were well known for their charity to the poor, and Riccoldo also noted an asylum for the insane outside the city but wrote nothing about leper houses. He stressed Muslim practices about ransoming captives and slaves who were coreligionists. In Baghdad Saracens purchased Christian slaves, took them to the cemetery, and then freed them for the sake of the souls of their deceased parents. People too poor to do this bought caged birds and let them go. Saracens also left money for feeding stray dogs and providing bread for birds. Redeeming captives and slaves, as well as emancipating slaves as a charitable act, were well-established customs back in Italy. Saint Francis may have encouraged a greater concern for animals and birds, but in Muslims' ostensibly charitable acts involving freeing or feeding birds, Riccoldo clearly saw a genuine difference between Christians and Saracens.[111]

Riccoldo respected the Muslim hatred of blasphemy. In all his time in the East, he claimed never to have heard a profane song (unlike in Florence?). The Saracens did not mock one another, and they, especially the Arabs, were good to strangers and practiced brotherhood. This mention is one of the rare times when he marked the Arabs as a people among the Saracens. The last work of perfection was peacefulness, and Riccoldo admitted that the Muslim world was safer for travelers. Saracens were also forgiving about things treated in the West as capital crimes. Riccoldo thought that the relative peace of Muslim life was because their faith was one of the sword; yet in daily life they were merciful. Christians, who had a faith of life and peace, were incredibly violent and bloodthirsty. Again we must recall that Riccoldo was a missionary; as he noted, he was not so much interested in praising the Saracens as he was in correcting those Christians who were not living according to the law of life. Still, his account of Islam was detailed and thus far reasonably accurate.[112]

Turning to the negative aspects of the religion, Riccoldo found six main flaws: it was too easy, confused, secret, dishonest, irrational, and violent. The missionary polemic need not engage us. Instead, sifting through these so-called flaws reveals more about what Riccoldo saw as the differences between Christianity and Islam, and hence the irritants in any potential relationship between the two camps. These problems did not parallel what Riccoldo knew as the pillars of perfection. First, Riccoldo thought that Islam was too easy a faith because salvation came too easily. If one believed "there was no God but God and Muhammad was his messenger," that was enough. (Apparently something like the Nicene Creed no longer sufficed for Christians, at least according to this educated friar.) Second, and here Riccoldo revealed more about his own reading experiences than about the actual text, he found no order in the Quran and its message. It was not clear what was prohibited and permitted, and this God seemed too merciful and forgiving. (These are, it must be remembered, genuine flaws according to Riccoldo.) Next, he disliked what he saw as the secrecy of the Quran, not an easy book to interpret. He noted, for example, that the text forbade usury and fornication, yet the Saracens had ways to evade these laws.

They pretended to buy slaves who were simply prostitutes and used various dodges about buying and selling to conceal interest. Riccoldo seems well informed about the kinds of bargaining and conversations that took place in the brothels of Baghdad—perhaps he learned about these matters in confession. He seems to have forgotten completely the strategies to evade similar usury prohibitions in that banking capital Florence, and about his hometown's many bordellos. It may be that Riccoldo knew well the scholastic arguments that favored reward for risk (which excused usury) or that tolerated prostitution as a vice preventing worse ones, and he saw those elegant arguments as mitigating Florentine practices. He may have assumed that the full, literal rigors of the Quran were still in force, and hence he held the Saracens to higher standards. Or, he may simply have been more interested in condemning Muslim practices than in attacking Christian hypocrisy.[113]

Riccoldo's issue with the alleged lies in Islam concerned his tenuous understanding of the "other book" of Islam, by which he must have meant the sayings of the prophet, the hadith.[114] He had picked up somewhere the idea that there were in the Quran twelve thousand words that did not contain the truth, which quickly became twelve thousand lies. He makes a big issue over the Quran stating that Mary was a sister to Moses and Aaron.[115] Whatever the accuracy of Riccoldo's reading of the Quran, he wanted to catch Muhammad in a historical error—off by 1,500 years . (He was not about to grant a divine origin to this information.) More revealing, Riccoldo rejected the claim in Quran 54:1 that the prophet split the moon, missing completely the use of metaphor in this passage. Yet in the same section Riccoldo claimed that Muslims knew only a literal interpretation of scripture while Christians understood the metaphorical, spiritual, and other ways of knowing.[116]

The first sign of irrationality Riccoldo found in Islam was that it allowed men and women to divorce and reconcile. He basically understood the complex teaching on these matters, but he thought the rules on marriage were irrational because they allowed partners to separate, which was totally foreign to his concept of marriage. Riccoldo also claimed that the Quran permitted sodomy, and he wrote that this was in the chapter called "the Cow," Sura 2. A convert whose name Riccoldo gave in Arabic supposedly verified this claim, which in fact must have resulted from a mistranslation and ignored the explicit condemnation of sodomy in Quran 7:80. Such evidence for Islam's irrationality suggests that Riccoldo did not know Arabic or the Quran very well. This example and a bizarre story about penis size in paradise indicate that Riccoldo saw sexual practices as a sharp divide between Christians and Saracens. In fact, as his near contemporary Dante showed, sodomy was hardly unknown in Florence, which was developing an international reputation for it.[117]

Finally, Riccoldo claimed that Islam was introduced through violence, but he made little of this point. In the context of nearly two centuries of Crusades in the East this is understandable. The rest of his text concentrates on "inconsistencies" in the Quran (another legacy of scholasticism?) and attacked the personal life of Muhammad.[118] Here we are on the ground of traditional religious polemic, and there is little on Saracens and Christians as individuals, as opposed to their creeds. Riccoldo ended his look at Islam by claiming that it was well known that Muhammad had three teachers, two Jews and the Jacobite monk Bahira. Once again there are echoes of the odd kinship between the three faiths. But for Riccoldo, even after so much experience, the differences often came down to ordinary aspects of life like charity, culture, and sex. These underlying traits were much more important to him than skin color or appearance.

Marco Polo

If it is true that Marco Polo was one of the first nonclerical westerners to travel through Muslim lands to the Far East, then he had the chance to see new peoples and climates with fresh eyes.[119] Polo came from a Venetian context where there were well-entrenched ethnographic conventions for describing and even commodifying people, but he saw people who had not yet been typed, and his own lack of a formal education partly freed him from the confines of the classical models for categorizing people. Polo's merchant sensibilities and Venetian upbringing affected his creative and highly revealing way of expressing his views on human differences. Joining his father and uncle on their trip East in 1271, Polo ended up spending nearly two decades in the Mongol empire, knowing and serving the great Khan Qubilai. Upon his return to the West in about 1291, Polo became embroiled in the war between Venice and Genoa and in 1298 was captured at the battle of Curzola. In a Genoese prison, Polo began his famous collaboration with fellow prisoner Rustichello of Pisa which resulted in the account of the world, in French, that made him famous. Tuscan and Latin versions soon followed. The western world learned to study differences in the East not primarily from John of Plano de Carpini or William of Rubruck but from Marco Polo, merchant of Venice. How Polo saw human differences conveyed to a European audience portraits of new peoples that were more detailed than anything the earlier missionaries had provided.

Not all differences concerned ethnicity or the environment. Polo was an astute observer of language, and to him one of the defining characteristics of a people was that they had their own tongue (*lingua*)—surely a social construction but one that, like the skin, separated what was inside the mind from the rest of the world. Religion also distinguished people, though he tended to divide the peoples of the East into two great categories—those who worshiped idols or those who followed Muhammad.

Even the use of paper money or the practice of cremation struck him as sharp markers between peoples. Many of his observations were gendered. For Polo, the beauty of a people was determined by the appearance of its women. Color was, within the wide range of cultural characteristics, the most consistent benchmark for typing a people—in this he would have been in agreement with Buffon. Even when Polo noted almost nothing else about a people, he gave their color and often their religion. His language of color was naturally not free from bias and context, which may explain why he was preoccupied with color and Rubruck was not. The more diverse Mediterranean world trained people to see human difference in terms of color.

The unstated premise of Polo's attitude toward color was his own whiteness—the touchstone for measuring other peoples. Rarely did other groups come up to his standard of whiteness. Color also served as a proxy in his mind for some well-known assumptions about what the skin revealed about the humors or temperaments beneath it. Let us now follow him to the East and briefly examine his ideas on color and language. Again, it does not matter what he actually saw. How he constructs information for a European audience reveals the commercial economic gaze in its starkest form.

The first peoples Polo met—Turks, Armenians, and Greeks—were familiar types, who needed no comment. Georgians were a traditionally attractive people (*bella gente*).[120] Just beyond the confines of Persia, Polo was still seeing good-looking women —presumably from ethnic groups he considered familiar. At Pashai, north of Kashmir, he found the first people he described as brown.[121] They had their own language, worshiped idols, were brown, and knew well the arts of the devil—altogether a bad people (*mala gente*). Yet it would be a mistake to think that for Polo being brown was always a negative trait. The Tuscan version calls the people of Kashmir brown and thin—the Latin version, closer to Polo's own thoughts, adds that they were beautiful. Yet there is no doubt that whiteness remained the standard. Polo's description of the peoples around Erguil province, on the frontier of China, proves this. These people struck Polo as quite different, according to his standards. They had small noses, black hair, and no beard except on the chin. The women were hairless except on their heads, and they had very beautiful white flesh and were well made.[122] At Tenduc Polo saw the most white and the most beautiful people of the country, and they were also the wisest and the best merchants.[123] This mingling of traits—whiteness, wisdom, and business sense—impressed this Venetian as the most thoroughly admirable mixture. Beneath the differences of language and religion, Polo saw some common human traits he valued as the best.

Qubilai Khan, whom Polo greatly respected, was the first individual he described in detail.[124] Qubilai was an attractive size, not small or big, but of medium stature. His frame was well fleshed and his limbs of the right proportions. The Khan's face was white and vermilion—a rosy (and familiar) complexion. His eyes were black, his nose well made and positioned. Of course, the face dominated this positive portrayal of the Khan. Polo no doubt had picked up enough physiognomy to know that he was describing a sanguine person, the best type, cheerful and above all familiar to Europeans. The Khan himself had concubines recruited from the Tartars (Mongols), another conventionally attractive people. These women, selected for their beauty, were called wheat faced—a very light brown color close enough to white to be considered desirable. Even in the East, it seemed, whiteness defined the canons of beauty, as far as Polo could tell. The Chinese seemed to agree.[125] Their celebration of the New Year was called the White Festival. Their dressing in white seemed to Polo to confirm the idea that white was associated with good fortune.

In southern China Polo saw other people, like those around Toloman, whom he described as beautiful but not very white, in fact, rather brown.[126] People he never saw in situ fell into conventional categories—the Japanese were white and beautiful, the Andaman islanders were like savage beasts.[127] On the Maabar coast of India, he was puzzled by local attitudes toward color.[128] Children there were born black but not as black as they could or wanted to be. These people continuously used oil to make their skins appear blacker because in this country people who appeared more black were more greatly prized. There is no doubt that this struck Polo as the reverse of the truth. He also noted that these people painted their idols black and statues of demons white as snow because they said their gods and saints were black.

What this reversal probably meant to Polo becomes clear in his comments on the people of Zanzibar. Again, he never saw this island, but a reported glimpse of a person from there prompted a negative description.[129] The people there were all black and went around completely nude. Their hair was curly and crinkled. They had large mouths, pushed-up noses, and large lips and nostrils. In other countries they would have seemed to be devils. The women were the most loathsome in the world. This conception of black Africa, so negative in every respect, reveals the preconceived ideas toward Africans which Polo helped to make more widely known.

On the issue of color Polo provided an expected continuum: white was the best, black the worst, and in the middle brown or wheat-faced people exhibited some attractive traits. Religions, funerary customs, and languages might differ, but color remained fixed. Polo saw in India that his own whiteness was not especially valued there, and he was honest enough to admit it. But this odd local opinion did not rehabilitate blackness in his mind—he still saw it as a badge of badness.

A Late Traveler

In 1470–71 Anselme Adorno made a remarkable journey from his native Bruges to his family's original home in Genoa, and thence to North Africa and the Holy Land, seeing on the way Tunis, Cairo, Jerusalem, Damascus, the Aegean, and other places. He is a good witness because he brought a slightly non-Mediterranean perspective to the complex picture we have been tracing, but his mixed Flemish-Genoese identity made him feel a part of this world as well. This wealthy merchant from an old family cast an astute but depressed eye over the peoples he visited. Travel taught Adorno some amazing lessons about human nature and the world. He concluded that the world was deceitful; nothing was durable or lasted; there was no rest. All he saw was evil and immense misery. People everywhere displayed little good faith or justice, and even less love. Instead, there was an unquenchable thirst for riches and honors. Humans were greedy and cared only about satisfying their own passions; Adorno admitted this was the case in his own life. One person was born, another died, and life continued. This gloomy view applied to people everywhere and is a good reminder that strong beliefs in a common human identity could overwhelm issues of color, religion, language, and ethnicity.[130]

After crossing to Tunis, Adorno closely observed the world of Islam and later gave a detailed analysis of what he saw, complicated by his own considerable learning. In North Africa, Adorno found people he called black, and he considered their color a reliable sign that they were Muslims. Yet he knew enough to observe that it would be better to call these people Hagarenes rather than Saracens. Adorno knew that there was no Sabbath among the Muslims, and that they did not flee from the plague because they considered an individual's death to be in God's hands. Their holidays and tradition of learning also interested Adorno, and he studied Muslim families, cemeteries, dietary rules, and even learned their alphabet. What is noteworthy about his lengthy analysis of Islam is his generally respectful tone about the religion and Muhammad. In general, Adorno did not enjoy his travels or experiences in the world of Islam, but he never confused his inconveniences with flaws in the culture he was visiting. He concluded his ethnography of North Africa by observing that the Moors exceeded all peoples in three things: fencing, swimming, and chess. He admired their general skills with all sorts of weapons, but who would have expected a fondness for swimming in a place with so few lakes and rivers? Chess was played everywhere and was no longer a cultural identifier for any particular group, but a passion for chess, and play at the highest level, were still grounds for comment.[131]

Travel seems to have reinforced Adorno's view that latitude and exposure to the sun caused variations in human color. In Africa people were dark because of the sun, but somehow he became convinced that ancient Galata, which he identified as either near Corinth or Pera, produced the whitest people, as white as milk. From whatever part of Greece these whitest people came, there was no doubt that Adorno identified with them. Adorno, like so many of these witnesses, needed the services of an interpreter, and his party first had a Moor from Granada who spoke Spanish. In Egypt they acquired the services of a monk, Brother Lorenzo de Candia from Crete, who spoke Arabic, and Adorno admits they would have been lost without him. Also in Egypt Adorno saw the distinctive yellow turbans of the Jews and the blue ones of the Copts. Color remained a useful identifier even when it was simply clothing and not skin. Adorno knew that the sultan of the Mamluks was a Scythian (as he described him) from Russia with blond hair. Slavery was unavoidable in Egypt, and there were also many Italians, Greeks, Albanians, Slavs, Russians and others enslaved as Mamluks. Finally, as Adorno prepared to enter the Holy Land through Sinai, he advised travelers not to forget to take plenty of *teriaque*, which he said was good for poisonous bites. This hashish-based drug was the traditional cure for seasickness, and it is interesting to contemplate a woozy Adorno and his stash making their way East.[132]

In the Holy Land, Adorno had the typical experience of hardly seeing the people and instead noticing only things and places. Ethnography of places like Jerusalem often suffered (and still does) from these expectations of pilgrimage. Early Christianity and strong memories of the Crusades also informed what Adorno expected to see in the Holy Land. An abandoned Acre, for example, reminded him of the city's glorious crusading history, and he also knew something about the Genoese past there. Perhaps his expectations based on historical memories were too high, for his party had such a miserable time in these Muslim lands that they felt as though they'd been there for a thousand years. One of Adorno's vivid memories of these few weeks was what he saw at a place called Jefferkin, somewhere near Capernaum on the Sea of Galilee. He was on the road from Nazareth to the lake. He noticed a slave market where men and women were exposed for sale, naked like beasts in public. It seemed to him to be the main business of this small place, in as close to the middle of nowhere as travel took him. Adorno had seen slaves throughout his journey; from Genoa to Tunis and Cairo, they had been ubiquitous. For some reason, perhaps because there was little or nothing else to see, the inhumanity of the slave trade forcefully struck him then, perhaps because these people had no clothing so that their defects would be in plain sight. Perhaps he grasped the humanity he shared with them, for he did not note their color, and in this backwater, they may well have been a mixed lot.[133]

Language and religion remained relatively fixed in the eastern Mediterranean and beyond. Mixing may have produced some pidgin dialects and the occasional spiritual syncretism, but lines between the monotheistic faiths and their languages remained pure. Self-interest in religion measured benefits by salvation and not by harmonizing differences in belief. Languages could admit new words or even be considerably changed. Petrarch and others in Italy lamented the decline of classical Latin just as Ibn Khaldûn missed classical Arabic. In their minds, conserving the language required returning to its original purity of expression. The supporters of orthodoxy in creeds also had strong opinions about the clarity and unalterability of an original revelation. Attitudes about color were also entrenched, but the eastern Mediterranean and the wider world around it revealed a broad array of human types that might mix or even change.

The classical inheritance included strong doses of ethnic chauvinism and contempt for any people who could be called barbaric. True racism, the valuing or disvaluing of people on the basis of skin color or ethnicity, pushed color symbolism and related somatic preferences into a more general categorization of people as beautiful or ill-favored, or simply good and bad. Early Christian exegesis, strongly shaped by Egyptian assumptions about color as packaged for wider consumption by thinkers like Origen, presented an image of evil that included themes of darkness so pervasive as to color all subsequent encounters with darker peoples. Yet the missionaries also inherited a strong tradition of fundamental human equality that valued each colorless human soul as worth enlightening. The arrival of the Mongols introduced radically new elements in the eastern Mediterranean mix, but over time mercantile judgments about ethnicity and color, and the values of holy warriors on all sides, overshadowed the best intentions of more generous missionaries like William of Rubruck. All types of mixed relationships, as the next chapter shows, became caught up in the general assumption that differences established hierarchies and were not grounds for pluralist or tolerant values. The very strangeness to westerners of Mongol attitudes on these matters shows that even mixed relationships resulting from necessities of all types did not foster any lasting beliefs in human equality, as the pervasive slave systems in the region also demonstrate. Encounters with the Mongols also established patterns of dealing with the Other.

The writers surveyed here put forward the entire spectrum of possible ways to explain difference. Exotic foods, new drugs, and aphrodisiacs delight the senses and might enrich the intrepid. Inside the body, the four humors responded to climate, and latitude and the stars shaped behavior and color. Marco Polo crossed more longitude points than any previous westerner, but he could not incorporate this factor into his way of seeing ethnic difference. In many cases curiosity and travel must have preceded any possibility of new relationships. Travelers found that the venerable science of physiognomy provided vital clues for deciphering the faces they discovered. What remained constant in the perception of ethnicity outside the middle climate was, of course, color, however the arbiters of color chose to define it. The consequences could be grave for those whose color strayed too far from the ideal. For the theologians and missionaries the paramount thing beneath the skin was the soul, and their belief in a common humanity tended to downplay differences based on skin color, at least at first. Of course these people noticed color differences, but they tended to be more struck by differences in creed. When commercial ambitions shaped the ethnographic gaze, color became a much more important marker of value and temperament. Placing an economic value on relations with other people—or in the case of enslaving them, on the actual bodies—required a shorthand method of determining prices. So the merchants saw color where the missionaries and friars saw souls. This neat distinction is not always applicable; Adorno reveals how complex the traveling gaze could become when the motives for journeying were themselves mixed. Economic and spiritual reasons for mixing with other people placed different values on the skin and what was beneath it.

Finally, the theme of what is beneath the skin becomes hard to separate from the outer world and its values. According to Abelard, black skin might conceal a redeeming whiteness, down to the bones that proved the essential virtue of the oppressed. Centuries later, W. E. B. Du Bois saw things differently. He was struck by how people become used to injustice so that it appears a normal part of life. (He was thinking of poverty and slavery.) When oppression "is hidden beneath a different color of skin . . . all consciousness of inflicting ill disappears."[134] The long history of color prejudice tells how a certain color of skin during the Middle Ages became a way to justify this oppression, at least in the minds of those who inflicted it.

CHAPTER TWO

Mixed Relationships in the Archipelago

A series of settlements stretched from Caffa in Crimea down to Chios and Crete in the Aegean, and ended with Cyprus in the eastern Mediterranean. These places are like an archipelago, multicultural merchant establishments in the middle of a war-torn, violent region. In the daily life of such places, the realities of mixed relationships between masters and slaves, business partners, wives and husbands, and even the living and the dead become vivid by examining not the products of high culture but humble notarial contracts. The Genoese archives preserve the largest number of these records, but they also hint at the vast amount of missing sources generated by all the peoples of the region. Contracts make it possible to reconstruct daily life from the ground up, from the humblest personal concerns that usually escape history. Records by people trying to make or break relationships reveal how assumptions about identity ran up against practical necessities, motivated by a love of gain or simple emotional ties. Life was fragile in the archipelago, and none of these places has a modern culture directly descending from the medieval world. But the provisional nature of these places makes the signs of mixing even more important, as they were to some extent survival strategies in a challenging world. Purity in the archipelago was a convenient strategy at times but was meaningless in daily practice.

Crete

This large island at the base of the Greek archipelago experienced the longest period of foreign domination; the Venetians occupied Crete from 1211 to 1669. One of the first places in the eastern Mediterranean to come under durable western rule, Crete is the archetype of the island colony. Here a Greek and significant Jewish minority lived under Venetian, largely urban rule for centuries. Crete supplied valuable agricultural commodities like grain, wine, and wool, and served the navies of Venice as a vital way station for destinations to the east and south. The island was worth having, and the Venetians were fortunate to pick up this spoil from the wreckage of the Byzantine Empire in the aftermath of the Fourth Crusade of 1204, and wise to defend it against Genoese interlopers in the earliest phase of its rule. The main urban center, Candia, provided a base for Venetian merchants and a capital for the Venetian feudatories who came to dominate the countryside. Venetian rule left behind many good sources that have been exploited by historians, most notably Sally McKee, who wrote a fundamental work on ethnicities and cultural exchanges on the island.[1] More lasting than the crusader states, Crete is the archetype for the colonial outpost in the east, a model certainly for subsequent Venetian ventures in the Aegean and Black Seas. McKee has looked closely at mixed relationships on the island and offers a testable hypothesis on how ethnicity can explain or distort our understanding of what happened in these complex places.

The reason for looking at these places is to investigate mixed relationships of all types in a complex, multicultural context. Crete, with its mix of Italian, Greek, and Jewish inhabitants is an ideal environment for such a study, as McKee clearly understands. McKee's main theme, clear in the subtitle of her book, concerns what she calls "the myth of ethnic homogeneity." Ethnic categories, so malleable and changeable over time, are, according to McKee, best studied as tools used by contemporaries to accomplish certain ends. From this perspective the Venetian rulers of Crete had varying conceptions of what it meant to be a Latin, and this category, for example, served their purposes when it came to establishing status on the island. Greeks and Jews had other ideas about how their religions and languages forged identities in the face of Venetian rule. So, along with most scholars of medieval ethnicities, McKee opposes an essentialist understanding of ethnicity and is especially interested in problematizing medieval and contemporary ideas on ethnic purity. For Crete, other fault lines like urban versus rural, new versus old families proved to be as important as the slippery notions of Latin and Greek. McKee found, for the central part of her study that the fourteenth-century peoples of Crete engaged in a wide array of mixed relationships, from business to sex. Many of the island's inhabitants were bilingual at least in speaking Venetian and Greek, while written records were kept by notaries working mainly in Latin but also Greek and Hebrew. Hence, there developed what McKee calls "shared cultural attributes," mainly in names, language, and customs, even as the major groups retained some sense of separate identities.[2]

Like the other places studied here, a Creole identity on Crete, if indeed it existed in the medieval period, did not survive late medieval and modern transformations, in this case the long centuries of Ottoman rule. The surviving source materials, overwhelmingly from the Venetian legal and linguistic context, may well misrepresent the experiences of Greeks and Jews on the island.[3] The rich evidence, still not completely collected or analyzed in statistical form, suggests a focus on slavery, marriage, bilingualism and interpreters, and business ties as the areas of life where peoples found their senses of identity to be forged and challenged. McKee's findings for Crete, where there were so many intermarriages and cross-group business ties, prove her case that any sense of ethnic purity was at best a self-serving myth and at worst a gross distortion of social and cultural life. This conclusion conceded, there remains the issue of how contemporaries used the tools of ethnic difference in their legal relations. Ethnic purity aside, people still had identities that helped determine the kinds of lives they were able to have on Crete and elsewhere. Rather than simply catalogue instances from the rich notarial records of how individuals crossed ethnic lines in business or family life, a close look at one issue, slavery, can illuminate the range of relationships and help to set up a way to investigate these issues on the other places not benefiting from studies of McKee's depth. Slavery in the archipelago shows that the tie between master and slave, besides being unequal in status and volition, often crossed one of the big boundaries of creed or ethnicity.

The notary Benvenuto de Brixiano was active in Candia, the main city on Crete, for much of 1301.[4] Although it is perilous to use the work of one notary to generalize about broader economic and social trends, the emphasis is warranted here because his focus is sharply on slave sales and the activities of one big slave trader, the Genoese merchant Vasallino Belegerio. Brixiano's records contain notices of the sale of fifty-eight slaves, nineteen men and thirty-nine women. The women usually brought a price between twenty and thirty hyperpers—a little more expensive than a cow, a lot cheaper than a horse.[5] These contracts do not always supply the ethnicity of the slave, but those that do reveal Greek (eight), Tartar (five), Cuman (four), and Turk (two), as well as individual Bulgarian, Alan, and Russian slaves. The presence of slaves from the Black Sea regions and beyond indicates the complicated ethnic mix of peoples and languages on Crete. The buyers and sellers of these slaves were mostly Italian and Greek men, with a sprinkling of women active in the market. The slave merchant Vasallino first appeared in the records on August 3, 1301, and over the next seven weeks he sold a total of twenty-four slaves in Candia.[6] He sold no Greeks and his cargo was from the Black Sea, so perhaps his original purchases were made in Caffa. There are several interesting aspects to his activities. On August 5, he sold fourteen slaves to all sorts of local buyers, perhaps something of a record and testimony to the appetite for slaves on Crete. His wares were mostly women, twenty versus four males—a pattern similar to the kind of feminized slavery increasingly practiced in Genoa. The few male slaves he sold seem to have been children—two were sold along with their mothers, and one went for the small price of five hyperpers. So this slaver perhaps controlled his presumably unwilling victims by arranging a cargo of women and children. These non-Greek foreigners entered Cretan society at a time when landlords were still able to buy and sell Greek peasants, called *villani*, at considerably higher prices—five were sold for 212 hyperpers—which would have purchased twice as many slaves.[7]

A local dealer, Hemanuel Vergici (possibly Greek) was expert at buying Greek slaves from the Turks, probably at nearby mainland ports like Smyrna. The Greeks ending up in slavery on an island predominantly Greek tell an interesting story. In a few cases, the sellers specifically noted that the slave was a captive (two were from Samos, and the contracts allowed for the enslaved males to be ransomed by their relatives for the sale price.[8] So the gendered nature of slavery complicates expected ethnic divisions; males captured in raids or at sea were an acceptable item of commerce on Crete, but there needed to be a mechanism by which relatives could reclaim these people. But the slave market, if one particular place in the harbor zone existed for this purpose, brought together all the diverse peoples of Crete in a rich array of mixed relationships as buyers and sellers of humans. Turks and Tartars were more likely to be slaves, while Venetians were masters and never slaves on the island. Greeks could be both, and Jews did not participate in the slave system legitimated by Christian record keepers.

Crete, a true island colony in the archipelago for centuries, has been closely examined; its surviving records illuminate ethnicities there and the "myth of ethnic purity." McKee has also investigated the status of children from mixed relationships between slave women and free men.[9] The legal status of these children, and how they were treated throughout the Mediterranean, help demonstrate the results of mixing between slave and free. The rest of the places under review here have not received such attention, so a closer look is needed to see how they varied or not from the Venetian experience on Crete. Besides slavery, marriage, business links, the circumstances of Jews, and the hopes expressed in last wills, all show mixed relationships among ordinary people. These ties existed in a context where the majority stayed home or stuck to their own kind.

Caffa

This city on the south coast of Crimea, first called Caffa by the Byzantines, rested on the remains of the ancient Greek colony of Theodosia.[10] Byzantine Caffa left no traces in the historical record until the Cumans overran the region in the eleventh century. Around 1250 the Golden Horde of the Tartars became the dominant power on the northern shores of the Black Sea. And then an amazing colonial venture began around 1275 as the Genoese established a port on the vestiges of what little remained of the previous settlements. The first Genoese Caffa was destroyed around 1314 and was refounded in 1316. From 1316 to 1475 the Genoese prospered in Caffa. Back in Genoa, the Office of the Gazaria and other institutions administered, through local agents, the port and its cluster of dependencies in Crimea. Michel Balard estimated that at its postplague height Caffa was a city of about 20,000 people, of which the Genoese were a minority amid a rich ethnic mix dominated by Greeks and Armenians.[11] In 1475 the Ottoman Empire conquered Caffa, and Turkish Kefe remained an important port and provincial capital until Russia seized the region in the late eighteenth century. Renamed Feodosia, the city lapsed into decay and obscurity.

Caffa's location at the apex of the Black Sea guaranteed the port a role in the cabotage trade that circulated grain, cloth, slaves, timber, and other commodities along the coasts. The Genoese always understood that there was money to be made in this short-distance trade, which linked Caffa to Pera, Constantinople, Licostomo at the mouth of the Danube, Trebisond in Asia Minor, and Poti in the Caucasus. Perhaps the most valuable and certainly the most precarious link was Tana, at the mouth of the Don River. This town, a true frontier entrepôt where Genoese and Venetians traded but did not completely rule, served as a main terminus for the overland trade across Asia to China.[12] In normal times fortunes were made in the grain trade, with some of the wheat and profit making its way back to Genoa. Trade in exotic commodities from the east, more vulnerable to disruptions along routes not controlled by the Genoese, has always attracted more notice from historians and has probably been overrated as a factor in Genoese prosperity in the Black Sea. The Genoese thrived in Caffa mainly because no sea power before it dominated trade in the Black Sea, a little Mediterranean. In this limited sense Caffa was another Genoa, another central place profiting from cabotage in its zone of influence.

In many other ways Caffa was emphatically not another Genoa. Whoever was the local khan of the Golden Horde controlled the region and also determined Caffa's fate. Genoa was in no position to fight the Tartars over Caffa, but a mutual self-interest based on commerce allowed this anomaly to flourish for centuries. Caffa was, like the other Genoese colonies, an odd place, fitfully governed from home by various quasi-public institutions and probably founded by private initiative. Some Genoese, mostly men but certainly some women, settled in Caffa to make a living through ordinary businesses that served the needs of Genoese, Italian, and other traveling merchants, their ships, and crews who passed through the port. The Genoese were a minority in their own city, but one that through its consul and officials governed Caffa in the Genoese interest. But the experience of being a minority in a city with Armenians, Greeks, Italians, Provençals, Catalans, Jews, Russians, Circassians, Cumans, Tartars, Lazi, Abkhazians, Mingrelians, Georgians, Alans, and others gave these settlers an experience that had almost nothing in common with the typical life of the Genoese back home.

Caffa provides an engaging setting for exploring how the Genoese defined themselves as a people in this complex ethnic mix. One approach is to examine how the Genoese defined themselves legally as "inhabitants" of Caffa, how being a Genoese citizen secured overseas privileges in places like Caffa, and how being a burgher, a property holder, established other rights. These ways of defining status are certainly important, but mixed relationships reveal more about how ethnic differences mattered in Caffa's society. Nobody ever claimed to be a Caffan in the surviving sources. People instead belonged to established groups and often experienced some sort of relationship with a person of another group. These mixed relationships helped each party to define itself by its relative standing, and by whose rules applied in a given situation. A range of relationships existed and can be distinguished by the degree of control one party had over another. For example, the bond between a Genoese master and a slave (there were no Genoese slaves) is one in which Genoese rules and power absolutely shaped the bond. Yet even here, the power of the Tartars in Crimea still mattered, and Genoese rules on slavery had to occasionally bend to accommodate them. When a Genoese man or, rarely, a woman, married outside the group, the marriage contract and the terms of the dowry followed Genoese law, but some local variations entered into these relationships.

In slavery, marriage, and other matters, Genoese currency, the lira, hardly mattered, and the Genoese used moneys belonging to other peoples. So they found themselves in a complex cash nexus over which they could not exercise control. This problem surfaced in almost all business contracts, whether among countrymen or between a Genoese and an outsider. Finally, when a Genoese or someone else contemplated death, the rules of inheritance, charitable customs, and habits of testamentary practice helped to shape a will that had to conform to Genoese law in order to be deemed valid. Every sort of contract, whether it concerns a slave, a dowry, a cloth sale, or a dying person, can and frequently does supply evidence on mixed relationships, and hence a fresh view of how the Genoese saw and defined themselves as a people.

The relationship between slave and master was a clear form of a mixed tie because it was the most likely to include two people from different ethnic groups. For master and slave the power dynamic was asymmetrical, and the genders were usually different. Of the twenty-three slave sales surviving from Caffa for 1298–99, in every case the buyer was Genoese or Italian. Twenty-two of the buyers were men and two were women (in one case two men purchased a slave). The preponderance of male buyers is not surprising and resembles the custom back in Genoa. Women did not usually frequent slave markets as customers. A closer look at the two instances in Caffa is revealing. In one case an Italian or Genoese woman sold to another woman a small white boy from Sevastopol aged four years. Another Genoese woman purchased a ten-year-old girl from a Genoese man.[13] There are too few cases to generalize here, but nearly all the slaves were young, between the ages of ten and twenty. Close to the sources that supplied slaves, Caffa was likely to have a young slave population. Keeping in mind this market in very young children, it is worth wondering, when women appear in these sales, if they were acquiring a surrogate child? After all, what economic reason prompts the purchase of a four-year-old? These women did have the choice of adopting these slaves and maybe some did, but adoptions rarely leave traces in the records.

These slaves, thirteen women and ten men, were nearly in gender balance, unlike in the western Mediterranean, where female slaves were the most numerous. Little is verifiable about the sources that supplied these slaves, and it would be wrong to presume that they were a random population by age or sex. The youth of this sample suggests that perhaps some mature men and women were able to resist enslavement or were more likely to be killed in resisting it. Their captured children, presumably balanced by sex, need to be placed in the context of those children sold into slavery by their parents. Not knowing the motives or cultural habits of the people selling their children makes it difficult to predict if they were more likely to sell girls than boys, but this does seem to be the norm where surplus children are disposed of in the market for economic reasons. Slaves of all ages, not willingly participating in this market, sometimes may have been able to shape the circumstances of their sales by appealing to or discouraging potential buyers.[14]

The sellers of slaves were more diverse. Italians and Genoese (sixteen) were still the most numerous, but Armenians, Greeks, Muslims, and Russians also appeared in the market. Notably absent were the Tartars and Cumans, and presumably these tribes dealt with the Genoese through intermediaries. Since these sales were all individual and not by lot, the actual slave traders and raiders on the wholesale side of the market were probably not appearing in these records—which represent the end of the process of enslavement, when everything was perfectly legal. People selling their children or raiding for slaves probably did not require the services of a notary. The sellers of slaves in Caffa were doing business with Genoese or Italians in the record-keeping style dictated (literally) by the colonial power.

These methods of making contracts often required interpreters, usually called dragomans in the thirteenth century and sometimes *torcimans* or *trucimans* in subsequent centuries. (The Latin *interpres* also eventually appears.) For example, when the Armenian candle maker Xaaba sold a ten-year-old girl to the Genoese Matteo de

Predono, one of the witnesses was Andoria, called "the dragoman for the present act," the interpreter knowing Genoese and Armenian, and perhaps other languages. The notary drawing up the contract, Lamberto de Sambuceto, was fluent in Genoese and Latin, and he needed the interpreter to deal with his Armenian client. The next contract in the notary's cartulary, for the following day, June 2, 1290, records the sale of a slave by a Greek from Sinope to an Italian agent. In this case, too, one of the witnesses, Segagola, a cloth merchant, was the "dragoman ad predicta," the intermediary familiar with Italian and Greek. In a more complicated situation, a Muslim woman, Jeracharona, sold a Russian girl to two Genoese merchants. The witnesses included two dragomans, both with Italian names, so there might have been three languages at stake here: whatever the woman spoke, probably a Mongol or Turkish tongue, the Italian of the Genoese, and some other language, perhaps Greek or Armenian, known by one interpreter who knew one of the other languages! Finally, a Greek interpreter assisted at a sale in which a Greek man sold a slave to a Genoese, and the parties yet again did not share a common language. It is worth pointing out a case where no one needed an interpreter. A Russian named Johanes sold a Russian boy named Janino to an Italian. The clue here may be that the seller described himself as an inhabitant of Caffa, a long-term resident who had probably picked up enough Italian to do business with them. The slaves themselves, mute observers of their transfer as objects for sale, in most cases likely understood little about what was happening to them, except the rough fact of being sold. The occasional language barrier, itself a sign of a mixed relationship, was no obstacle to accomplishing the sale. Multilingual interpreters facilitated these market transactions. Being a dragoman was in some cases a useful side profession for a person who learned to thrive in a hybrid environment.[15]

Perhaps as early as the 1290s, but certainly by the early fourteenth century, somewhere in Crimea, probably in Caffa, a Genoese merchant or missionary began to put together the nucleus of what became known as the Codex Cumanicus.[16] This precious relic of what must have been a number of dictionaries (the classic mixed book) supplies in three columns word lists in Latin, Persian, and Cuman, the language of the Kipchak Turks. Cuman was usually written in Uighur script, but in the dictionary these words appear in Latin letters. That Persian appears right next to the privileged Latin suggests that it may have been more important as the intermediary language between Latin and Cuman. For whom was this dictionary created? The entries (alas not alphabetical) are a complex mix of religious and commercial terms, suggesting that notaries and priests used it. This dictionary begins with *audio* (I hear), a useful verb, conjugated through the tenses with subjunctives, so the compiler was educated and ambitious. The absence of the vernacular Genoese proves that its audience was small, limited to interpreters who could read. Literate interpreters, important in generating documents and converts, were not the only ones active in facilitating commercial transactions. In the markets a lot of negotiating must have taken place in a rudimentary pidgin borrowing words from other languages. Interpreters could help here, as well as beginning to supply the formal grammatical structures that in some places lead to the emergence of a truly new Creole language. As far as we know, this never occurred in Caffa; the gulf between the linguistic communities was simply too great, and perhaps the time too short. Pidgin might work for some negotiating, but the Genoese notaries continued to control the terms of contract and the Latin language guaranteeing legal force. So interpreters, literate or not, supplied the means of communication, from treaty making (see chapter 3) down to the selling of a slave.

A glimpse forward to 1381 and a surviving fragment of the registry of the chancery in Caffa provides more details on the work of interpreters. At this time, and in a small amount of material, we learn of four interpreters active in Caffa: Luchino Caligepalle, an official interpreter of the court for Greek and Italian; Filippo de Sant'Andrea and Giovanni Ricio, also using Greek and Italian; and Raffo Ceba, proficient in Turkish and Italian.[17] These interpreters were all Genoese, another proof of their power in Caffa. Yet the way to balance this power was to learn languages, and it is interesting that the numerous pieces of business involving Armenians did not require interpreters. Armenians learned languages in order to bargain and retain some control over the negotiations they conducted with the Genoese. Missionaries in Caffa, the most likely users of the dictionary, needed to preach in vernacular languages, and so they too functioned as interpreters, in this case of Christianity itself.

Even someone who knew the languages could find him or herself in circumstances that made business difficult. Another theme in other places is illness and how it prevented normal communications in a variety of situations. On January 7, 1382, a Muslim named Coia Aysse, an inhabitant of Caffa, found himself mostly confined to his house because of gout.[18] Since he could not go out, he needed to appoint a representative, an Italian lawyer from Pavia, to collect some money owed to him. Raffo Ceba interpreted these details for Coia and his lawyer, and the consul's vicar and some Genoese officials were the legal witnesses to the arrangement. Coia found a way to continue his business, but the method left him entirely in the hands of people using Latin and Italian. Incidentally, we learn that a Muslim lived in Caffa in 1381 but at the lowest rung of legal significance.

This brief excursus on interpreters helps to place in a broader context the linguistic issues surrounding the relationship between an owner and a piece of property that could speak. The relationship between buyer and seller was a temporary one, and both parties must have planned for it to be short and sweet. Let us begin with the broken relationship, for however long it had lasted, between the seller and the slave who was being sold for good. A last sale from 1290 shows the complexities that might arise. The Russian Ivan sold another Russian named Little Ivan—the boy was thirteen. Some of the slaves sold to Genoese would remain in Caffa, while others might swiftly find themselves on a ship bound for Pera or Genoa. So the severed relationship between master and slave might mean a move down the street or across the Mediterranean. Many of the people mentioned here must have carried memories of their former relationships, part of the rich context of every life in a place like Caffa. Little Ivan too may have picked up some scraps of Genoese, and he would have needed them to communicate with his new master, who was unlikely to know any Slavic tongue. The Slavic speakers, probably in the same boat as the Armenians, needed to learn the language of the Genoese in order to function in Caffa. Thus even their names had to be placed into a recognizable form for the Genoese to understand them.

A broader look at all the slaves sold reveals the diversity of the broken tie. The twenty-three slaves noted consisted of seven Circassians, five Lazi, three Russians, two Cumans, two Hungarians, a Greek, an Abkhazian, an Indian (!), and one of unstated ethnicity. Their average age was 13.3 years. None were older than twenty-four or younger than four and a half. No Tartars appeared among them—a sign that perhaps the recent conquerors of the region were not yet offering their own people as slaves. These slaves came into Caffa from the north and east, mainly the wild areas between the Black and Caspian Seas. The vulnerabilities of this ethnically diverse and divided region made it a prime supplier of slaves. The Genoese especially valued Circassians from the eastern shore of the Black Sea.

Sales contracts reveal only the slaves' ethnicity, names, and, rarely in Caffa, color. Since the heyday of Roman law, sales contracts required the notice of a slave's ethnicity because people believed that this was an important fact affecting the slave's temperament and value.[19] One type of ethnic label in the east was tribal. Abkhazians, Lazi, and Cumans were recognizable peoples with a specific territory, language, and other customs. Being a Greek in Caffa might mean almost anything, and the category of Russian was probably expansive as well. These labels served the Italian buyers and sellers as conveniences. How the slaves might have identified themselves is unknown, but they may not have been mute and passive witnesses to their own sales.

Some names clearly imply an ethnic origin but once again probably meant more to the Italians than to the bearers of the names. Three male Circassian slaves were called in Latin Circasso, or Zico in the Italian spoken in Caffa, and there were also two women named Zica. Of course these were not the slaves' original names, they were Italian contrivances. At a certain point there would have been too many slaves from the same ethnic group to name them all after it. Another common feminine name,

Archona, appeared across ethnicities: Russian, Indian, Hungarian, Circassian, and Lazi. Only one female slave's previous name turns up in the record, but it is a curious reversal; a Russian slave once called Margarita now carried the name Tinaia, perhaps a master's whim. Few slave names in Caffa were Christian, and none of these contracts mention whether the slave was baptized or not. Religion does not seem to figure as a useful way to identify a slave.

Only a few of these contracts note the slave's color. Of the men, a Lazi, Circassian, and a Greek slave were called white. Of the women, a Circassian was labeled brown, and a rare slave from India was by local standards black. Inexplicably, black was the only color defined in the Codex Cumanicus: *nigredo* in Latin, *síay* in Persian, *charamac* in Cuman.[20] There is not enough evidence to suggest what the difference between white and brown meant in Caffa, or indeed how the Italians would have sorted themselves out along this abbreviated spectrum. Being black in Caffa must have been unusual; there are no traces of Africans there, and a slave from India had traveled a long distance across Asia to end up in Caffa. Her story would be worth knowing.

In these mixed relationships, Italian owners lived with slaves who were younger than the purchasers, unlikely to be Catholic Christians (at least at first) and who probably spoke only a smattering at best of any language most Genoese knew. Odd names and exotic ethnicities also distanced these slaves from the Italians. A slave was the "other," and custom and the law rigorously subordinated these women and men. Most buyers seemed to need the slaves for their own local purposes. Smiths and armorers bought male slaves for heavy physical labor; families acquired women to work as domestic servants. These documents pass over less excusable motives and forms of abuse and exploitation that occur in any relationship, like slavery, that rests upon violence to create and maintain it.

A final and late vignette on slavery in Caffa ties together some of the themes on the relationship between master and slave. On Saturday, June 19, 1473, less than two years before the fall of Caffa to the Ottomans, and at a time when the sea voyage through the Bosphorus and Dardanelles had become virtually impossible for the Genoese to make, Angelo Squarciafico agreed to take back to Genoa by the land route eleven female slaves belonging to Battista Giustiniani (two) and Carlo Lercari (nine).[21] The owners agreed to pay Angelo twenty-five Venetian ducats per head to cover his salary and the expenses of the trip, including food, tolls, and horses. This venture is astounding on several levels. The ride from Caffa to Genoa, a difficult enterprise across the war-ridden steppes of eastern Europe, was the only way to get these eleven slave women back home. Even so, the contract provided Angelo with incentive to prevent runaways: he had to return his fee for each successful escape. What Genoese wealth there was in Caffa would soon belong to the Ottoman Turks, and the economic reasons for remaining there must have seemed increasingly tenuous. Yet these slaves remained Caffa's most lucrative export, as prices continued to increase in Genoa in the face of contracted supplies from the Black Sea. So this risky contract made sense to all parties, and presumably Angelo had his own reasons and profits to make by escaping to Genoa. The contract does not provide the names or ethnicity of his cargo, and no records back in Genoa reveal that he arrived there.[22] The slave trade may not have been the thing first drawing the Genoese to Caffa in the mid-thirteenth century, but at the end of their time there, it was the business or relationship that outlasted all the others.

Marriage provided another opportunity for Genoese in Caffa to enter into a mixed relationship. Evidence about marriages survives in the one extant notarial cartulary, itself a tiny fragment of all the business that transpired there in 1289–90. Marriages left behind documentary evidence only because there was enough wealth at stake to make worthwhile writing down the details. Other peoples, especially the non-Italians, married without engaging the services of a notary. So, that notices of only five marriages survive is not so surprising because dowry agreements were not common acts in notarial cartularies. These five marriages took place according to Genoese law, as expected, since they were redacted by a Genoese notary for at least one Genoese partner to a dowry contract. By 1290 the colony had existed for about fifteen years, so few Genoese women had migrated to the new city, and there was hardly enough time for the families who had moved to Caffa to have daughters of marriageable age born there.

In the first marriage, an Ugolino from Piacenza accepted a dowry of 3,000 aspers (one hundred lira, a decent Genoese dowry) to marry Franceschina, a woman of Russian stock. All the witnesses to the contract were Genoese. This model of the mixed form of marriage, where an Italian man settled down to family life with a woman and some money from the region, makes sense in a new place like Caffa. Another Italian immigrant, Lanfranco from Pavia, agreed to marriage with a woman named Xeri, the daughter of Saldorino de Vangrari; these people were locals, not Italians. The other pattern that should be noted here is that prospects in Caffa attracted men from across northern Italy, not just Genoa and Liguria. Even in distant Caffa, however, not all marriages were mixed. Vassili from Trebisond agreed to marry Agnesina, the daughter of Constantino from Simisso. These two cities were formerly Byzantine ports on the coast of Asia Minor. This marriage looks like a happy meeting of two immigrants in a foreign city. Agnesina's dowry was provided by her former master; she had worked as a servant (*famula*) before her engagement. The master Giunta from Bologna was exceptionally generous to provide any sort of dowry at all, but the sum he volunteered, 600 aspers or twenty lira, was about as small a dowry as the records in Caffa or indeed Genoa ever recorded. Still, Giunta's mixed relationship with his ex-servant led to a marriage that reunited two people whose roots were the same. In a similar vein, Guirardo Cattaneo from Genoa agreed to the marriage terms that Bonanato from Camogli, a small port east of Genoa, arranged for his daughter Margarita. Apparently these people, neighbors back in Liguria, found a suitable marriage far away in Caffa. Finally, Guadagnino de Castelliono, possibly Genoese, married Simonina the daughter of a Genoese tailor in Caffa for a respectable sixty-lira dowry.[23]

Generalizing from this small sample is perilous, but at least the notary Lamberto de Sambuceto supplied evidence for a range of relationships, some of which were indeed mixed. All the husbands were Genoese or Italian. The future wives were more diverse—two Genoese, one Greek, one Russian, and one other local, perhaps Armenian. What wealth was at stake in such marriages flowed from the family or sponsor of the bride to the husband. Hence, the Italians profited in yet another way from their relationships with the local people. No local man acquired a Genoese wife—a possible mixed relationship worth hunting for in other colonial contexts.

The Genoese sources remain the only real way of recovering details about daily life and mixed relationships in Caffa. Most likely other communities, like the Muslims, had their own notaries, producing records that have not survived. A stray reference from 1382 in the chancery records reveals a Muslim merchant living in Caffa and appointing a Christian burgher as his legal representative. Back around 1332, that formidable Muslim traveler Ibn Battuta had visited the place he called in Arabic al-Kafa. Ibn Battuta described Caffa as a great city on the coast of Crimea, inhabited by Christians, mostly Genoese. This observation, neglecting to notice others like the Armenians, may reflect the limits of his ethnographic gaze rather than the facts of life in Caffa. He claimed that he and his party stayed at the mosque of the Muslims, and he recorded an engaging story about reciting the call for prayer from the mosque's minaret. The local *qadi* was alarmed at possible local reactions to hearing the call—this implies that it was not easy to be a Muslim in Genoese Caffa. Ibn Battuta safely toured the local bazaars and saw two hundred ships of all types filling the harbor, which he called "one of the world's celebrated ports." Yet he leaves some confusion about the population of Caffa by saying that all the inhabitants of Caffa were infidels. H. A. R. Gibb rightly wondered whether there was a Muslim presence in Caffa or not. Maybe Ibn Battuta recognized that none of his fellow Muslims could be called citizens and that their legal rights were protected only by the sultan of the Golden Horde.[24]

None of the sources considered so far, even Ibn Battuta, hint at the existence of Jews in Caffa. For this evidence we must turn to the obscure record of how Genoese officials auctioned off the possessions of a deceased notary in 1371. Among the ninety-five men who purchased land, goods, and slaves from the estate was Salamonus Iudeus, Solomon the Jew, who bought an old cape for a woman for ninety aspers, a very small purchase from the nearly 20,000 aspers worth of things sold. Laura Balletto has looked closely at the rest of the buyers and found that they were overwhelming Genoese and other Italians, with few Greeks, no Armenians, a couple of Georgians and Tartars, and one Jew.[25] The ethnic minorities mainly picked up the small, inexpensive items. It may be that they felt uncomfortable participating in an auction no doubt held in the language and at the convenience of the ruling Genoese. Armenians and Jews should have had little trouble bidding in this environment, yet they preferred not to enter into another mixed relationship between auctioneer and bidder. Records of Jewish, Muslim, and Armenian notaries, had they survived, would tell a more complex story about mixed relationships in Caffa. The Tartars of the Golden Horde no doubt also saw things in their own way. Perhaps their copy of the treaty they made with the Genoese in 1387 would have provided some alternative to the Latin version the Genoese preserved for themselves, the only surviving copy.[26]

Chilia

To the west of Caffa, the Danube enters the Black Sea in a swampy delta with few good ports. Medieval ships did not need deepwater ports, however, and the river systems around the Danube served a large and attractive hinterland with valuable crops and commodities. Hence the cabotage trade of the Black Sea included the Danubian basin, and the Genoese were also there to insinuate themselves into the local trading patterns. The major cities in the region were Chilia, which most scholars agree was also called Licostomo, and Maurocastro (Black Castle), at the mouth of the Dniester, which oddly became Cetatea Alba (White City) in the local dialect.[27] The major ancient port Constanta was well south of the delta. In the fourteenth century the Danube marked a politically hazy but geographically well-defined frontier between the lands of the Tartars to the north and the kingdom of the Bulgars to the south. Straddling the frontier, some portion of the indigenous population clung to its Romance language, the ancestor of Rumanian, or Cuman, or some type of Slavic language brought by the Vlachs (Wallachs). At the mouth of the Danube, where no outside power appeared to predominate, the opportunities for foreign merchants were best. The few fragments of notarial records created in this region suggest that supplies of commodities, especially grain but also honey, beeswax, and slaves drew merchants there. The local monetary system relied on weights of silver called *sommi*, and the ubiquitous aspers based on the old Byzantine coinage.

A Genoese consul had been present in Chilia since at least 1322.[28] The consul served as the official head of the Genoese community and its representative to whatever sovereign power actually ruled the place. The records of the Genoese, which begin in 1360, are the only meager source documenting commercial life. Chilia is an excellent place to explore mixed relationships because a number of different communities came there as equals to do business. Genoese and Venetians were the main groups of Italians present, and their names and contracts reveal wider contacts with merchant colonies in Pera and especially Caffa. Chilia was off the beaten track of long-distance trade but thoroughly integrated in the cabotage cycles of the Black Sea. The Genoese there were putting down roots; a will from 1383 contains the reliable sign of the local community's durability—the existence of a church called San Francesco de Licostomo.[29] Wherever the Italians settled for long, the Franciscans would follow.

Six sales of slaves reveal the special mixed relationships existing in Chilia. All the buyers were Italian men, but what is most interesting about the sellers is that Tartars came to Chilia to sell slaves, who were also Tartars. On February 11, 1361, a man identified himself to a Genoese notary as Thoboch the Tartar, from the one thousand of Coia, the hundred of Rabech, the ten of Boru.[30] Thoboch was a true member of the Horde who knew his exact place in its military formation. The other two Tartars selling slaves also named themselves in this precise manner. Thoboch came to Chilia to sell a thirteen-year-old girl, Bayrana, also called a Tartar. The practice of slavery among the Tartars is not well understood; nor is it clear exactly what it meant to be a Tartar in the fourteenth century. How strong did the Mongol element remain, and how many people from different ethnicities had joined the Mongols to become Tartars? Among the military men, the Mongols were still in force, but was that true among their slaves? In Bayrana's case, her youth and the specific notice that she was a Tartar, suggest that she was indeed one, sold by a people who freely practiced slavery and had no scruples about selling off one of their own to outsiders likely to export her to Italy. This sale took place in the house of a Genoese moneychanger from Voltri and was witnessed by him, a messenger of the consul, and two Tartars. The contract does not mention an interpreter, so perhaps the parties were satisfied that two Genoese and two Tartar witnesses sufficiently guaranteed that everyone understood what was happening.

Another sale in April did require the interpreter Giovanni de Clarence, perhaps indeed from the Morea in Greece, but here called a Venetian and an official in Chilia. Here the witnesses were all Italian, so the seller, Themir, may have wanted matters explained to him clearly, since his customers were also Italians, two brothers from Piacenza. For sale was a twenty-two year old Tartar woman named Ianecotolo. The final such transaction in this record concerned the Tartar Daoch, who sold to a Greek from Constantinople a thirteen-year-old Tartar girl named Taytana, a daughter of one of his own slaves.³¹ An interpreter with a Greek name was present among the witnesses, so the languages may have been Tartar (Mongol) and Greek. Two other sales were among Genoese and one Venetian, and the last one, between a Genoese and a local man not a Tartar, needed an interpreter. All the slaves sold were women; the oldest was Ianecotolo, and the others with ages given were twelve or thirteen.

Slavery in Chilia appears pruned down to a simple trade—the suppliers were Tartar men selling their own female slaves; the buyers were all Italian men. The contracts usually required an interpreter who was a person from the east or someone who had been there for a long time. The languages of commerce were Genoese, Mongol, Greek, and whatever was the lingua franca in Chilia itself. Other contracts, especially those concerning honey and beeswax, show a wider need for interpreters; there was an Armenian from Caffa active in the local trade.³² A document from 1373 hints at a complexity regarding ethnic labels in Chilia and what they meant. A man describing himself as Giorgio de Genova, once Tartario, promised to work as a servant to a Tuscan for five years in exchange for food, clothing, and a salary of seven florins a year.³³ (By this date any sort of money passed in Chilia, even florins.) This simple contract for hiring a servant hints at the fluid nature of identity in Chilia. Giorgio wanted a new name, and he took Genoa's own as a way to identify himself with important people. It seems that he was once a Tartar, perhaps even an ex-slave who was now on his own. The women the Tartars were selling were identified as Tartars, but perhaps they too were recent ones, plundered from local populations and easily reassigned another identity. Still, the Italians did not practice this style of enslaving one's own people.

Chilia served the Genoese and other foreign merchants as a place providing opportunities to prosper in the grain trade or other commodities. Genoa was not going to rule in Chilia; the place was simply too exposed to be taken over as a formal colony, and the Tartars were nearby on the frontier. Better to leave the bother of ruling such places to others. What the Genoese needed in Chilia was personal security, and the markets they brought to local people seem to have benefited the self-interest of all parties. The Genoese were in no position to impose political or even ethnic superiority. But by controlling the languages of contracts and negotiations, they were in a good position to impose some of the rules most important to them in the markets.

Chios

Chios is a sizeable island in the Aegean barely separated from the coast of Asia Minor. Opposite the island, at a place called Phocaea, substantial alum deposits had for some time been attracting merchants who exported the chemical back to cloth towns where dyers used it to fix colors. Chios itself was the unique source for mastic, a gum harvested from a shrub cultivated since antiquity. This fragrant gum was used for chewing and as a base for ointments, and was the reason for possessing Chios and monopolizing its most valuable product.[34] The weakened Byzantine Empire attracted various predators in the early fourteenth century, and the Genoese admiral and entrepreneur Benedetto Zaccaria occupied the island in 1304 and was also active in Phocaea.[35] Chios remained in the control of a private family rather than under Genoa itself until 1329, when the Byzantines reestablished their authority. The story of how a Genoese fleet, frustrated in its desire to attack Monaco, ended up seizing Chios and Phocaea in 1346 is a remarkable tale.[36] Chios became the main Genoese colony in the eastern Mediterranean until 1566, when the Ottoman Empire occupied it in a relatively bloodless conquest. (Phocaea on the mainland was lost in 1455.) Chios actually belonged to the investors in the original fleet, and Genoa was never in a position to redeem the island by paying its debts to the ship owners. Hence Chios was a unique venture, a privatized colony that usually could not count on much help from Genoa itself. This venture or company, called the Maona of Chios, changed hands and was renegotiated periodically in its early decades. In the late fourteenth century many of the shareholders in the original Maona adopted the common name of Giustiniani, in the style of a Genoese *albergo*, or family clan, in order to foster a sense of common purpose among the island's owners and to claim the monopoly of the mastic crop and its export. These Giustiniani became increasingly powerful as a large clan on Chios and back in Genoa. They were not the only Genoese on Chios, but they were the most important influence in defining what it meant to be Genoese, strengthened in their case by family solidarity.

As an economic asset, Chios's value derived from the local monopolies over the raw materials mastic and alum, as well as local products like timber, salt, cotton, and sugar, among others. The well-defended port city of Chios was a safe harbor for the cabotage trade in the Aegean and a useful way station for long-distance travel along routes like that from Pera to Famagusta to Alexandria. Chios was not a convenient terminus for the caravan trade, and it was a modest outlet for products from the Turkish-dominated parts of Asia Minor. By 1415 the Maona found it expedient to pay tribute to the Ottoman Empire.[37]

The island's population, difficult to estimate, was reduced by the plague of 1347 and was probably in the neighborhood of 20,000—nearly all Greeks.[38] An indigenous Jewish population was present at the time of the Genoese conquest. The Jews remained a tiny percentage of the population, though their numbers would increase as refugees arrived from other parts of the Mediterranean, especially Spain, in the late fifteenth century. The importance of these Jews lies in their absence from Genoa and most of its colonies. No Jews were permitted to live in Genoa in this period, and they rarely appear in Caffa either. Coming upon an established community, the Genoese decided to tolerate the presence of Jews on Chios, and so it was one of the few places under Genoese rule where Christians and Jews regularly interacted.

Chios was, in 1346, a settled and prosperous place that the Genoese had desired for some time. Some members of the original fleet settled for good, partly displacing the Greek nobility, but the island remained substantially Greek, with a few Jews. Notarial records from the time of the Genoese conquest tell how mixed relationships developed there. As with Caffa, documents concerning slavery, marriage, and death provide the most details on what mixing occurred, but here there is also information on how shared work experiences and even diseases created relationships never seen back in Genoa. Again, the few surviving sources reflect the values of the colonial power and show only a tiny fragment of what contracts were made on the island.

There are only a few published recorded slave sales from Chios, some from the 1350s, a few more from the 1390s, and eighteen scattered across the fifteenth century, making a total of thirty-five.[39] As expected from the origin of these sources, Genoese and Italians predominate as purchasers, especially in the fifteenth century, when only one Greek appeared as a seller. All the buyers were men, including the Latin bishop of Chios in 1483.[40] The sellers, in a temporary relationship with the purchasers, were much like them—thirty-one Genoese or Italians, three Greeks, and one from Germany. One of the sellers was a Genoese widow named Catalina, who sold to the noble Odoardo Fieschi in 1359 a Tartar woman named Margarita and her eight-month-old baby boy.[41] In such cases the father of the child remains a mystery, but still, the widow was trying to get a problem out of her house.

The slaves, again as expected, were more heterogeneous—six Circassians, seven Tartars, five Russians, five Bulgarians, three Greeks, two Turks, and one Armenian, Abkhazian, Goth, Albanian, Bosnian, Hungarian, Wallachian, and even a woman identified as an Assyrian, perhaps a Kurd. A well-educated notary called one slave Getic, someone from the Danube area and not a Greek, so perhaps another Wallach. The slave notices from Chios come from a later period than those from Caffa, so it is not surprising to see Tartar and Turkish slaves on Chios. Circassian slaves demonstrate that Chios was part of the wider world of the slave trade, and these people, as nearly all others, came there by sea. In the fifteenth century, Bulgarian slaves from the Balkans, probably caught up in the Ottoman conquests, began to turn up on Chios. This Genoese island in the Aegean became a very cosmopolitan place. Fifteen men and twenty-two women (a few slaves sold in groups) again show a relatively balanced slave population, unlike in Genoa, and this sample was also young. The oldest man was forty, and nearly all the slaves were in their teens or twenties, down to a child of nine.

On Chios a population of Genoese and Italians largely sold slaves among themselves, as other communities may also have done in contracts that did not survive. For buying and selling slaves, the Genoese did not need interpreters, but other business between local Greeks and Italians required them. When Ihera Michelina sold part of a house in 1381 to Georgio Virmilia, she needed a Genoese galley captain, Vassalo da Sestri, to translate from Greek into what the notary called "locucio latina," which was in fact Italian.[42] Interpreters mentioned in the notarial records on Chios come from Italy as well from the Greek east, places like Clarence in the Morea, and Phocaea. Two more interpreters appear in an interesting transaction in 1398. The governor of Chios needed them to communicate with the Greek ambassador from the local Turkish ruler in Teologo.[43] One interpreter, Simone Perello from Voltri in Liguria, knew Greek and Italian; Niccolo de Portofino, another Ligurian, presumably knew Greek and perhaps Turkish. On Chios itself, the colonial Italians easily communicated among themselves with their own notaries. Interpreters were necessary in a few instances where business took place across linguistic boundaries, but more often no interpreter was needed. This suggests that in many contexts ordinary people were bilingual, and there are some interesting examples of this on Chios.

The Greek sellers of slaves owned two Turks and a Circassian woman named Xeni, baptized according to the Roman rite.[44] The only Greek buyer, who was from Crete, purchased a Circassian. The two Greek slaves, both men and the first to appear in the records from 1359, may have been born into slavery or have fallen into it as a result of the conquest in 1346 or more recent Genoese wars against the Byzantines. A Greek girl, twelve years old when she was sold in 1450, was named Rhoda, perhaps for the island of her birth.[45] The Genoese were not going to rule Chios for long if they made it their business to enslave the Chiots, who had, however, an ongoing slave system of their own. Better for both Genoese and Greeks to import slaves from the Caucasus or Balkans.

Another type of notarial contract from Chios, the manumission of a slave, illuminates the mixed relationships between masters and slaves. Like the sale of a slave, a manumission marks the end of a relationship, at least in a legal sense. The master had the right to set the terms, which sometimes included continued service or indeed a cash payment. The sixteen manumitters known from Chios were fifteen Genoese and a Diego from Seville, and all but two were men. All appear to be from prominent families: a de Negro, a Franchi, a Zoagli, a Spinola, and two Giustinianis, two Paterios, and two Pelavicinos. Owning a slave was usually a sign of some wealth in the fifteenth century, and freeing one as an act of charity or economic calculation usually cost something and was not lightly done. One interesting introductory formula, used by the notary Antonio Foglietta, ascribes to the manumitters a sentiment that may have been too loftily expressed to match their real feelings, Still, even if they only dimly understood it, the formula must have prompted some thoughts on slavery and the human condition. At the beginning of the contract, after his customary "In the name of God amen," Foglietta wrote, "Since by nature all people are born free and slavery had been introduced by the law of nations against natural law, through the said law of nations was introduced the benefit of manumission to extinguish it."[46] Probably very few slave owners appreciated the difference between natural law and the law of nations, but some, more likely these manumitters, would have agreed that there was something unnatural and possibly wrong about slavery. But both types of law, as well as the third, divine law, spoke in this context about all people, not the subgroups of humanity. Law appealed to the concept of a common humanity, while daily life on Chios and elsewhere concerned relationships where people dealt with differences as well. One manumission took place on Christmas Eve of 1403, also New Years Eve in this Genoese colony, a date that might prompt some reflections about slavery and equality.[47]

Three of the freed slaves were identified as Circassians, two were Abkhazians and two were Russians, and even a Moor found himself a slave on Chios. There were five men and eleven women in the sample, reflecting the general balance of the slave population there. In two cases a few details about the mixed relationship survive and help explain the manumissions in their contexts. Tomasso Spinola owned a thirty-seven-year-old Abkhazian woman named Hanasta.[48] He freed her according to the conventional formula, namely, that Hanasta had performed many services and good deeds for her master. Also, Hanasta had wet-nursed Spinola's granddaughter Isolta, described as the daughter of his son-in-law Napoleone Vivaldi. Isolta's mother, unnamed here, was presumably deceased. Hanasta established what anthropologists call a milk relationship with her master's kin, and this type of mixed tie evoked the gratitude prompting the manumission. In the second case, Diego from Seville, a dyer, freed the slave he called Manolo, who seems to have called himself Varentino from Achaea in Greece.[49] This Castilian, from the other side of the Mediterranean world, called his slave by a name familiar in his language, but Varentino's Greek roots eventually prevailed. In the next notarial act the newly freed slave promised to work in Diego's dye shop for one-third of its profits, a sure sign that the work kept these two men together in a relationship that transcended slavery. Diego must have expected better conditions and profits from working alongside a free man laboring for a share, rather than with a slave whose incentives to work were always problematic and who might simply run away.

Another manumission suggests how a slave's relationship with the master could become a reason for eventual freedom. Isabella de Negro freed her Circassian slave Caterina, provided that she remain a Roman Catholic.[50] In order to understand the severity of this condition, it is important to see that in Chios in the 1450s, it had become standard practice to renounce the ancient Roman legal rights of patron over an ex-slave. Roman law still governed these fifteenth-century contracts, and the legally minded knew that a master retained certain rights over an ex-slave. The most relevant of these customary rights at this time concerned ingratitude. If a slave displayed a lack of regard for a former master, the law returned that person to slavery and the offended owner. Proper gratitude was probably a difficult concept to define in legal terms, and so most manumitters renounced the rights of patronage and in some cases the explicit claim resulting from ingratitude. Much of this probably depended on the notary's education and habits, and the manumitter's experiences as a slave owner. In this example the concern was Isabella's. Caterina, a Circassian and hence from a place not practicing the Roman Catholic version of Christianity, had converted to Catholicism. Isabella must have worried about the sincerity or durability of this conversion. So, she stipulated that if Caterina changed her faith, she would once again become a slave. On Chios the majority faith was Greek Orthodox, closer to the Georgian, Armenian, and other Christian rites of the Caucasus. The mixed relationship between the Genoese slave owner and Circassian slave was hierarchical, and as the slave Caterina also had the duty to accommodate her mistress. The accommodations of slavery were endless; no doubt Caterina had the duty to learn the language of her owner. Another way to bridge the asymmetries of the relationship was to share a faith, and there certainly seems to be a connection between Caterina's decision, ostensibly voluntary, to do this and her eventual freedom. In any mixed relationship where power was not evenly shared, some acts like adopting a new language or religious practices could change the balance of forces separating the parties and bring them closer together.

Marriage contracts do not appear in the earliest notarial records surviving from Chios, probably because many of the original members of the fleet were already married. It took some time for those deciding to settle on the island to establish what passed for regular family life. The earliest marriage contract contains just a hint of an unusual mixed relationship. Nicola Franco son of the late Giorgio Cavegno, simply an inhabitant of Chios and not a citizen, agreed to marry Marieta de Costa.[51] Her relative Cristoforo de Costa, called a burgher of Chios, acted on behalf of the orphaned

Marieta. The curious feature of this contract is that it required an interpreter, Lazzarino Niccolo de Rapallo. The languages at issue here are not clear. Marieta's family was clearly Genoese and well established as legal residents of the city of Chios. The clue may be in Nicola's low status as a mere dweller on the island. The names are not much help, but perhaps Nicola was Greek, and thus a rare male from the occupied population acquiring a wife among the colonial elite. The dowry, a modest 250 hyperpers, also suggests that Marieta's prospects were limited, so a marriage to a rising Greek subject was perhaps the best she could do.

Three other marriages indicate another type of mixing that occurred. A burgher of Chios married the daughter of a burgher of Pera, the Genoese colony near Constantinople, and part of the dowry was a house in Pera.[52] These two Italian or Genoese families found potential spouses as a result of the regular traffic and trade between Pera and Chios, and those relationships in turn solidified the ties among the colonies. Pera fell under the control of the Ottoman Empire in 1453 and quickly dwindled under Turkish rule. A document from October 1453 reveals two refugees from Pera, a husband and wife, establishing the legality of their marriage by recording the dowry terms on Chios.[53] This couple, who do not appear or claim to be Genoese, would not have found life on Chios to be very different from that in Pera. A final marriage from 1457 shows the more familiar pattern of an Italian male, Raffaele de Costa, marrying a local Greek woman, Anna, whose dowry consisted of a house and lands on Chios.[54] More than a century after the Genoese conquered the island, this marriage still required the presence of an interpreter, Antonio Florio.

The dense networks created among the colonists and other people are demonstrated in a complex insurance claim from 1454.[55] Andrea from Naples, an inhabitant of Chios, appointed the Genoese citizen Gregorio Magnono as his representative to find a slave named Margarita, whose ethnicity was left blank in the document. Margarita had been purchased on Chios by Bernardo de Ferraris, as agent for Ottaviano de Costa, from Gabriele Giustiniani—all Genoese. Margarita's intended fate was to be shipped back to Genoa on a vessel owned by Oberto Squarziafico, and Bernardo had prudently insured his cargo, in Ottaviano's name, through Andrea. Margarita disappeared somewhere in this process, presumably during the eastern part of the trip, as we learn all this from a notarial act redacted on Chios. Andrea paid off the claim and now had title to the slave, hence his attempt to recoup the loss by finding her through Gregorio Magnono, a finder or slave catcher. Margarita may have jumped ship before it sailed and was loose somewhere on the island. The prospect of crossing the Mediterranean all the way to Genoa might prompt flight, which would have been much harder once she was in Italy. Here freedom was just a short step away across the straits to the Ottoman mainland. The mixtures here are fascinating. One of the oldest and most characteristic Mediterranean businesses, selling a slave, is combined with a relatively recent Italian, perhaps Genoese innovation, the insurance contract. The slave was caught in a web of Genoese and Neapolitan merchants. The slave catcher, probably a local Greek, had no physical description of Margarita, and once away from the Italians, one wonders just how enthusiastic the local Greek population was about finding lost Genoese property. Gregorio's financial incentive to find Margarita is not clear in the document, but it must have been worth his while.

The old pre-conquest Jewish community on Chios appears in the notarial records in ways that show the relationship between them and the much larger Genoese population, themselves embedded in the Greek majority. Why did the Jews use Genoese notaries, and what does this reveal about the internal structure of their community, as well as the relations Jews had outside it? Among Jews, laws and enforcement mechanisms based on reputation helped guarantee contracts, written or oral, made according to Jewish customs.[56] For many purposes Jews had no need for Christian notaries and their Latin contracts. As in the Christian kingdoms of Spain, there were occasions when a Christian version of a contract, if we can call it that, added legal force to an act that might eventually require the laws and courts of the Genoese, in this instance, to enforce it.[57] When the Jews dealt with the Genoese or Greeks, they probably lost control of the system enforcing the contracts, so they were compelled to participate in the notarial system of creating legally valid documents.

Given these circumstances, most matters internal to the Jewish community would not ordinarily appear in Genoese or Greek notarial cartularies. When Jewish business surfaces in the records of these other groups, it is probably because the Jews wanted to add an additional layer of legal weight to their own sanctions enforcing contracts. For example, in 1398 a Jewish agent for three other Jews, who had shipped from Salamis trade goods that ended up in Chios, went to a Christian notary to record that he had taken these goods into his custody.[58] Another Jew, Callo Pangalo, styled as an inhabitant of Chios, stood as guarantor of the custodian. Three burghers of Chios, Italians or Genoese, witnessed the notary's document. In this instance, perhaps because the Jews were from different parts of the Aegean, but more likely because the issue was securing goods in Genoese Chios, it made sense to create a local, legal record of the arrangement. Also, the goods had arrived on a Genoese ship. The absence of interpreters suggests that the local Jew, able to communicate with a Genoese notary, was simply taking an extra step to make sure that the property of his coreligionists would remain safe.

Another piece of business concerns something internal to the community and reveals a great deal about its wider relationships. Jhera Melica, the wife of the late physician Ismael, gave a house, gardens, and certain other lands to her son-in-law

Eliseo Calachi, also a physician.[59] From its first line this remarkable document departs from the ordinary. Notaries began each act with the conventional "In God's name Amen," and occasionally, as in wills, added formulaic Christian sentiments about the spiritual aims and benefits deriving from the purpose of the document. Jhera's donation begins with an original comment in notarial Latin reflecting Jewish beliefs about the purpose of good deeds: "In the name of God who created heaven and earth, by whose example the human race, His shining mercy appearing manifest in written words, daily finds the teaching that through good deeds rewards and favors are graciously bestowed . . ."[60] This Genoese notary must have found it interesting, if not refreshing, to begin a standard donation in this unique way. The three houses Jhera was giving away were located in the Jewish quarter, itself placed inside the fortress of Chios in the heart of the city.[61] Jhera also owned an orchard in the district of the soap makers, and there her neighbors included the Genoese Ambrogio Vegio and a Greek Chiot. In another place she owned lands bordering the properties of two Greek priests. Jews by custom lived in the fortress under the protection of the Maona but still owned lands elsewhere in the city and vicinity. The title to property depended on the power of Genoese authority, so it made sense for Jhera to ratify this gift in a valid notarial contract. Five Genoese or Italian men, including two notaries, witnessed the act, as well as an interpreter Lazzarino de Rapallo. He was likely needed to mediate between the Greek known by the local Jews and the legal Latin of the notary and the Genoese of the witnesses.

How Jews interacted among themselves on Chios helps explain their relations with the wider communities. A routine notice of an obligation to pay the silk tax shows that Jews had mandatory ties to the main power on the island, the Maona.[62] Jhera Chamesti added a codicil to her will in 1394 partly to fix a defect in it; she had forgotten to leave anything to the Maona.[63] This obligation suggests that the Jews were, as elsewhere, a special property belonging to the ruling authority, in this instance a body of stockholders, who imposed a kind of death tribute on "their" Jews. By subordinating Jews in this way, the Maona signaled to the rest of society that this was not a mixed relationship between equals. That the Jews were huddled under vigilant eyes in the citadel reinforced the obvious hierarchy in the relationship.

Commerce provided the most regular grounds for Jewish and Christian merchants to interact. In 1450 two arbiters, Angelo da Rimini and Tobia Mosera the Jew mediated a dispute over money for buying grain between Lazaro Catalano and Micael de Nicosia the Jew. What is interesting here is that the necessary process of arbitration, so vital to avoiding expensive law suits, worked across religious and linguistic boundaries. A Christian and a Jew, disputing the terms of a contract, turned to another Christian and Jew to amicably settle the problem, which they did. It appears that this matter brought together someone from Rimini, a Catalan, and a Jew originally from Cyprus. Another document shows that Angelo da Rimini also served as an interpreter capable of explaining an insurance problem concerning terms in Greek and Latin.[64] The existence of multilingual people on both sides of the divides, and the use of arbitration to settle disputes, show that Jews and Christians did some business based on reputation, trust, and common business practices.

A loan reveals some of the complexities of doing business across the religious divisions of Chiot society.[65] In May of 1394 Raffael the Catalan borrowed 200 ducats from an agent of the prominent Genoese noble Domenico Cattaneo, and he promised to repay 350 ducats within two years. This apparently simple transaction reveals two distinctive features not typical of ordinary loans. Raffael "swore upon Hebrew writing, according to the custom of the Jews" to repay the loan.[66] The problem was the oath, which sufficed when Christians did business among themselves. How was a Christian creditor to have faith that a loan to a Jew would be repaid? Swearing on Hebrew scripture, physically present, seemed to meet the requirement. It was efficient to have confidence in enforcement mechanisms based on reputation and not rely on courts to resolve every loan's problems. So Cattaneo's representative accepted a Jewish oath, and Raffael must have supplied whatever text in Hebrew he needed to do his business. Also, a mixed loan like this freed the parties from their usual spiritual qualms (if indeed they had any) and economic obfuscation on the issue of usury. Rules governing the proper rate of interest to take from a brother were out the window when it came to this sort of loan. The rate of interest here, seventy-five ducats a year, or 37.5 percent, is very steep by late fourteenth-century standards and must indicate an especially risky or desperate situation for Raffael. Notaries usually concealed the true rate of interest in order to avoid accusations of usury. Here the parties were free to be frank and exploitative. A useful study would take a careful look at mixed loans versus those inside communities. Maybe this research would generate a number revealing the premium or cost of doing business across boundaries, however defined. This contract needed no interpreter, raising the complex question of what was the common language between a Catalan Jew, a Giustiniani on Chios, and the notary. A good guess would be Genoese, not Greek.

A superficially straightforward sale of a house between two Jews raises issues about the wider Christian world on Chios and the need for interpreters. Master Eliseo bought a house from Elias and his mother for 225 ducats. In this sale among themselves, the Jews also swore on Hebrew writing, in the presence of two Christian and two Jewish witnesses, with no interpreter required. In the next act in the cartulary, Eliseo generously gave Elias the right to reclaim the house within the next four years for the same price plus expenses and also allowed Elias's mother to live in the house during the interval for free. The witnesses to this agreement, which also occurred before vespers on the evening of May 29, 1394, were the same two Christians who witnessed the sale, but there were no Jews. Simone Perello of Voltri acted as interpreter. Other documents in which Master Eliseo conducted complicated affairs with the Genoese do not record interpreters and strongly indicate that Eliseo must have spoken Genoese well. Why, then, did the Jews not witness the second act, and why did it, unlike the first, have an interpreter? Eliseo and Elias were certainly able to communicate with one another, so the interpreter must have been there to make sure that the Genoese witnesses *really* understood the arrangement they were legally ratifying by being present and named.[67]

A final piece of information concerning the Jews on Chios reveals something about the complexities of life there. A routine matter sets the context. On July 7, 1404, the Jewish physician Benedetto de Ologar, in order to reward the good service of his wife Druda, decided to give her one hundred gold florins of Barcelona, beyond what he owed from her dowry and what she could expect in his will. This act of generosity, or the trip to the notary, or the recent event he was about to narrate, caused Benedetto to make an unusual formal declaration before the notary, who recorded it right after the donation. Here is what Benedetto had to say.[68] On the previous Saturday evening, the fifth of July, in the early morning hours between one and three, while Benedetto was sleeping, it appeared to him (presumably in a dream) that two Christian youths came and said, "Get up and let's go to the garden of Francesco Giustiniani, where we'll find some good beehives and fresh water." Benedetto agreed to go and arose, still asleep, and went to a nearby well in front of the synagogue of the Jews. Although he was at the well, he thought he was in the garden to see the beehives, and so he ended up falling into the well (which cannot have been very deep.) Down in the well he awoke from his dream. Amazed to find himself there, he cried out for help. A number of Jews in the vicinity heard his cries and helped to extract Benedetto from the well and return him to his house.

At first glance this episode of sleepwalking seems to have prompted Benedetto to make a generous gift to his wife. This is not surprising; Druda may have been a long-suffering woman. Still, Benedetto's dream was exceptionally vivid and detailed, down to these beehives in a particular garden. And then there are the Christian youths: why introduce this mixed relationship? Why were they the ones to initiate this adventure? On a more somber note, what Benedetto has to explain is how he ended up in a well in the middle of the night and disturbed the sleep of his neighbors in the Jewish quarter in the fortress of Chios. So, he comes up with this vivid dream to explain his predicament. The story may have been as Benedetto told it, and we are left to wonder about the Christian youths, and why he went to the trouble and expense to have a notary make a legal note of the incident. And what connection did this have to the one-hundred-florin gift?

People brought together by their work might see each other as rarely as the partners to commercial transactions. The employer-employee relationship need not be close, especially if the employer did not need to supervise workers' activities. The best way to ensure hard work was to make the laborer in effect a partner by paying him or her a share of the profits rather than a daily wage.[69] Across the medieval Mediterranean the best way to regularize this type of working tie was the *societas* contract. Familiar to students of commerce as an investment tool, the *societas* also served more humble purposes. For example, the wealthy Niccolo Giustiniani committed to a local Greek a herd of 140 goats. The Greek did the work of tending to the animals, the Genoese supplied the capital, and they presumably split the profits from the milk, cheese, meat, hides, and other products. The Giustiniani had been on the island for a long time by 1451, but they had not come there to herd goats. The division of labor between the Greek who knew the land and its pastures, and the Genoese diversifying his investments, allowed the colonialist to benefit from intimate local knowledge he did not possess. Of course, the indigene profited from working a large herd that he could not afford to own. Whether he would have given up this opportunity to see the Genoese off the island is unknowable. The local Greeks also worked for the Genoese as servants, a relationship where contact was far more regular and close. Theodora Greca contracted herself to Jacobo de Andora for two years for a meager seven ducats plus food, clothing, and a place to live.[70] Inexpensive servants, one of the benefits of colonial rule, brought people from different ethnic groups into a typically hierarchical relationship that reinforced local patterns of subordination.

A more equitable work tie formed between the Genoese Lodisio and the Greek Manoli, both goldsmiths, who formed a partnership in 1466.[71] They agreed to open a shop together, work at their common trade for six months, and share expenses, especially charcoal. Since the partners split the profits, this looks like a typical *societas* contract. Rather generously, Lodisio also agreed to supply fifty ducats to buy gold and silver, and the profits from this would be shared as well. Manoli must have brought some real smithing skills to this work for the Genoese to make him a partner on such favorable terms. The market on Chios for gold and silver wares must have been small and mainly Genoese, so Lodisio may have been the partner expected to draw in the bulk of the business. The parties needed no interpreter to make this contract. All signs, even the brief but customary trial period, point toward a successful collaboration across ethnic and religious divides. The Maona would not have been able to rule Chios for so long had there not been some easy working ties between the two main groups.

Another matter concerning work returns us to the world of slavery and its peculiar mixed relationships. On March 31, 1381, the notary Giovanni de Goasco borrowed from another notary a Tartar slave, Cristina.[72] Cristina's job was to provide milk and other services to Giovanni's little son while on a trip back to Genoa. Once there, Giovanni would return the slave or pay forty lira if he did not. For some reason, perhaps his wife's death or inability to give milk, he needed a wet nurse for the long voyage from Chios to Genoa. Cristina was still lactating, and for her owner this loan represented a free trip back to Genoa and expenses for his slave. And so another Tartar woman ended up in Genoa, and her work was to establish a milk tie with a Genoese child.

An unusual final document from Chios provides a glimpse of another type of mixed relationship—the experience of suffering from a common disease. The great event across this world was the plague of 1347–48, which in parts of the West resulted in massacres of Jews, lepers, and others.[73] One of the best-known tales concerning Caffa is its possible role in being a point of entry for the plague to begin spreading beyond the Black Sea in 1346.[74] Unfortunately, records from the Genoese colonies in the East shed no real light on the course of the plague there and how it affected minorities. As most contemporaries understood in their calmer moments, and as was known across the Muslim world, the plague was a universal event afflicting all people. For Muslims, who were encouraged to believe that the plague was a mercy and martyrdom from Allah, there was no desire to seek scapegoats or punish the sick.[75] Maybe on Chios they learned something of this point of view. Chios provides a small piece of evidence on another pervasive illness—leprosy.

In November 1471 the Greek Siderus Lunatha needed to obtain some evidence concerning the testament of Gavatiano Calica, a leper, whose last wishes were taken down by a Greek notary and priest.[76] To learn what he needed to know, Siderus went to the house of the lepers, San Lazzaro, where it seems he must have shouted to the witnesses from outside the front door. There were four witnesses, one Lombard shopkeeper from Biandrate and three Greeks, all lepers. The Lombard swore on the Bible, and the Greeks on the figure of Jesus, presumably an icon or a crucifix, concerning the details of this oral will. The terms of the will are not the issue here, nor is the fact that no one needed an interpreter—neither the Latin notary nor the witnesses, a Greek priest and another man who seems to be an Italian. What life must have been like in the leper house of Chios can only be imagined; it may be that in these grim circumstances the lepers became bilingual. Genoese and Greeks shared this institution, where the leveling experience of disease broke down most barriers.

The range of mixed relationships on Chios, from marriage and work to illness, shows the complexities of life on this colonial island. Some Genoese enriched themselves, the Greeks and Jews survived the occupation, mastic continued to be harvested, the cabotage trade thrived, and goats were herded. Chios was in some respects another Genoa, but there the Genoese compromised on some issues and experienced some things unthinkable back home.

Cyprus

This island's geographic position assured that it would play a major role in trade and communication across the eastern Mediterranean. Cyprus remained part of the Byzantine Empire until 1191, although there was a long period from 688 to 965 when Muslims and Greeks exercised an unusual condominium over the island. Richard I of England conquered Cyprus in 1191, but he had no plans for it other than selling it. After first selling Cyprus to the Templars in 1192, Richard creatively sold it again to Guy of Lusignan, the former ruler of the Latin Kingdom on the mainland. The Lusignan family and its heirs continued to rule Cyprus until Venice formally took over in 1489.[77]

Cyprus's indigenous population consisted of Greek Christians, with an increasingly important overlay of a French-speaking military and religious class after 1191, when a Latin Church also began to establish itself. Thirteenth-century foreign merchants also found the main port, Famagusta, to be a convenient way station in the eastern trade. The Genoese received their first commercial privileges in 1232.[78] Two facts determined the foreign merchants' standing in the kingdom. Cyprus was a crusader state, and so it naturally played its part in the complex political situation in the Latin Kingdom and its main city, Acre. To follow one thread among many, Genoa's relations with Cyprus and its rulers were generally bad because they were mostly on opposite sides of the grander struggles involving papacy and empire, or more locally, Genoa's series of wars with Venice. After 1291, when the last crusader cities on the mainland fell to Mamluk Egypt, Cyprus became even more important to western merchants as the easternmost (along with threatened Armenia) Christian state in the Mediterranean. Also, refugees from Acre, Tripoli, Beirut, Gibellet, and other cities settled on Cyprus, reinforcing the French colonial elite who dominated the island's economy. Although Cyprus was an independent kingdom, from the perspective of the indigenous population it was also a colony (in this sense resembling Chios). Thus it cannot be an accident that the first surviving Genoese contracts redacted on Cyprus come from 1296, around the time the island's economic role became more significant. Even as the Mamluks extended their rule from Egypt through Palestine and Syria to Armenia, western merchants still proposed to trade in the eastern Mediterranean. More severe papal interdictions of commerce with Egypt might have diminished open trade in munitions and materials useful in war, like timber. But trade in the east had endured throughout the crusading era and it would continue on into the fourteenth and fifteenth centuries, when Muslim powers were even stronger in the region.

All of these major issues provide the context for the evidence on mixed relationships of all types on Cyprus. This evidence comes mainly from the pens of Genoese notaries, especially the active Lamberto de Sambuceto, working intermittently on the island from at least 1296 to 1307. In these years and for some time after, Famagusta on the east coast was the main center for Genoese residents and merchants on Cyprus, whose kings generally favored Venetians, Pisans, or nearly anyone over the Genoese. After a complicated series of events, a riot, mainly by the Venetians, after the coronation of Peter II in 1372 resulted in a ruinous sack of the Genoese community.[79] From the Genoese perspective this insult required a response, and a large fleet attacked Cyprus in 1373. A speedy victory allowed the Genoese to occupy Famagusta, a city they de facto ruled from 1373 to 1464. Eventually, Famagusta became a colony, as the Cypriots were never able to come up with the money to pay their debts to the Genoese and redeem the city. The first fifteen years of significant Genoese presence on the island, from 1296 to 1310, provide the best evidence for mixed relationships. By a stroke of luck, the records that survive in Genoa are virtually the only good set of documents that sheds light on the other communities in Famagusta and the other major cities, especially the capital Nicosia. Of course, from a Greek or colonial French point of view, it is a pity to see Famagusta only through the contracts of Genoese and Venetians active in the city. Yet without these sources almost nothing would be known about the richness of life in this ethnically and religiously diverse city. The phase for which the most evidence survives is the period in which the Genoese jostled with merchants from Barcelona, Languedoc, Italy, and elsewhere to find ways to make money under the watchful eyes of a monarchy with its own hostile relations with neighboring Muslim states. Cyprus was always a place the Venetians and Genoese would have preferred to subvert to their own rule, but the entire island was beyond their power to absorb until Venice took over in the late fifteenth century. Venetians were not in charge of Famagusta, a place they definitely wanted to have.

A slave passing from one owner to another shows the temporary connection between buyer and seller, as well as the slave's broken tie to the former owner and the uncertain bond with the new one. Forty-four slaves appear in the earliest records (to 1310), twenty-six men and eighteen women. The balance in favor of male slaves conforms to the familiar patterns observed in Caffa and Chios. The ethnic diversity of these slaves was, if anything, even more pronounced than elsewhere. For women and men local origins were most prevalent, but with a different emphasis. Turkish and

Saracen slaves were most numerous among the men (thirteen of twenty-six). How these people entered slavery remains mysterious, but the relative youth of the population suggests trading and raiding rather than capturing prisoners of war. Echifor, a ten-year-old white boy, was described as coming from Turkish and Greek stock.[80] A mixed relationship somewhere in Asia Minor produced a slave who himself embodied a mixture arousing comment in Famagusta. The surviving documents preserve the local sense of the unusual. The notary Lamberto de Sambuceto twice noted that male Muslim slaves were circumcised. Most of the time records of these sales included little about the physical appearance of the slaves; only color was regularly supplied. Circumcision was not a reliable way to identify a particular slave, so perhaps these notices testify only to the curiosity some Christian merchants had about foreign practices. Women slaves' ethnic balance in some respects was the reverse of the males; Greeks comprised nearly half (eight of eighteen) of the sample, and there were only two Turkish women. Slavery was quite international on Cyprus. One male slave from Spain, described as black, might be sold together with a Circassian from the Caucasus. A Mongol woman turned up as a slave on Cyprus, as did a Cuman from the north shore of the Black Sea and a Hungarian from farther west.

Among the thirty-seven sellers (less than the number of slaves because of lot sales), there was only one woman. All the buyers were men. Nearly all the sellers and buyers were Genoese or clearly Italian. This is a little surprising even though a Genoese notary kept the records. Lamberto wrote many contracts for merchants who hailed from across the Mediterranean, so this record suggests that the Genoese were the most active participants in the slave trade. The only other people who appear at all in this admittedly small sample were those who migrated to Cyprus from the lost crusader states on the mainland, from places like Acre and Tripoli. There, too, people were familiar with the slave trade. A few Catalans appeared among the buyers, and one Jew sold a slave in 1301. Moses the dyer sold to a Genoese an unusual slave, a fifty-year-old Muslim man named Abrain, who originated from the Garbo area of North Africa.[81] Abrain was one of the oldest slaves in the sample, as well as one of the most expensive at 130 white bezants. Moses sold this slave according to the legal conventions the Genoese imposed in their markets, and no Jews formally witnessed the sale. He sold a Muslim slave, the only type, besides a Jewish one, which he could probably legally own on Cyprus. Abrain was a valuable slave, but the contract is silent on what skills he possessed, and his purchaser did not list an occupation. Apart from this one case, however, the buyers closely resembled the sellers, but not the slaves.

The records, however, permit a few glimpses of men who owned many slaves or who were repeatedly in the market for slaves, and so they may be dealers. The vast majority of purchasers seem to have been casually in the market for a servant. A stray reference from 1302 in an exchange of currencies shows that Pasquale di Pasquale, a Genoese citizen, was able to pledge eleven Mongol slaves as surety for 350 gold bezants.[82] He was clearly dealing in slaves, but most people operated on a smaller scale. For example, in 1301 Giovanni da Voltri, a Genoese, bought in a lot three Greek women aged thirteen, seventeen, and twenty, and a thirteen-year-old boy, all for 150 white bezants. Four days after this sale, his supplier, the barrel maker Antonio da Noli, another Ligurian, split the proceeds with his two partners, also Ligurian. These people seem to be investors who formed a temporary partnership to trade in these slaves acquired somewhere in Anatolia. Their customer Giovanni Rex was more experienced. In March he had purchased a Turkish man whom the seller had originally bought in Armenia. This slave cost Giovanni only thirty-one bezants, and he had quickly acquired five more slaves. In June Giovanni sold a white male named Brusco, a fourteen-year-old described as a Russian from Gazaria, the Genoese Crimea.[83] Giovanni received 125 white bezants for this boy, so he handled at least six different slaves during a few months in 1301 and appears to have known how to make a profit in the trade.

Ugolino da Portovenere (another Ligurian) also seems to have been a slave dealer. In 1302 he sold three Turkish men, very anonymously, with no ages, color, or names listed, for 280 white bezants.[84] His supplier Lionardo, a ship owner and merchant, may have been yet another regular Genoese slave dealer. Another potential dealer, Giovanni de Pando, from Messina, in 1300 sold a black slave from Spain for 120 white bezants, and in 1301 he purchased a forty-five-year-old from Alexandria for the high price of sixty-five gold bezants.[85] Sicily was another place with active slave markets, so it is not a surprise to see a merchant from there trading in slaves in Famagusta. A last potential dealer, again with a Ligurian toponymic, Bernardo da Quiliano, paid the high price of 181 white bezants for two Turkish slaves, a female aged twenty-four and a male aged thirty.[86] The one hint about the Genoese side of slave dealing is the prominence of people from the smaller towns of Liguria, places like Noli, Portovenere, and Voltri, with no signs of big merchants from Genoa itself. These sources from Famagusta are so fragmentary and so slight a percentage of the hypothetical original number of contracts that caution is in order. Still, as a marker for further inquiry, and a sign of yet another mixed relationship, there was great wealth and power concentrated in Genoa. With the partial exception of Savona, the other places in Liguria could not rival the capital in any sense, even though its people usually enjoyed Genoese citizenship and its valuable rights in a city like Famagusta. Maybe the kinds of men who were more likely to fill the niche of slave dealer were entrepreneurial types from the smaller places. Back in Liguria the slave population was certainly concentrated in Genoa, but perhaps the dealers were not.

There is not enough information from which to draw firm conclusions about the average price of slaves in Famagusta or, more important, about the main factors affecting price. All that exists is a few clues. The oldest male slave, already seen as sold by Moses the dyer, commanded the highest price of any male slave. Age alone, for men, reveals little about the slave's value. The most expensive female slave sold for 200 white bezants, and she was a twenty-two-year-old brown Saracen named Maria. For the women we may suspect that age influenced the price and that younger women appealed more to buyers who might be motivated by sexual interest. The usual price of a female slave ranged between thirty and one hundred bezants. The oldest woman, a Christian named Maria aged sixty, sold for one hundred white bezants, but she was sold as a lot along with her son Ballaba, a Saracen. The parties made no attempt to distinguish the individual prices of the slaves. The mother, probably commanding the lower price, was still able to remain in the same household as her son. At twenty Ballaba was at the high end of the average age—most slaves sold were in their teens. The youngest appeared alone in the market at the age of eight; this little Axia sold for a substantial fifty white bezants. This child was white, and color was yet another factor undoubtedly affecting price, but with too little evidence from Famagusta to be certain just how. The contracts generally specified color—Turks were always white, Greeks nearly so, with only one described as brown. The one Armenian woman slave recorded was labeled "de medio collore," perhaps between white and brown.[87] The one black slave listed was from Spain.

Since the buyers and sellers were overwhelmingly Genoese and Italians, and none of the slaves were, all the slaves were unfamiliar on several levels to the buyers. In looking for broken relationships, we need to focus on the sellers. Occasionally, a sale reveals something about the relationship to be ended or commenced. In October 1301 Nicola da Ancona sold his fifteen-year-old slave Maria for one hundred white bezants.[88] He imposed exceptional conditions on this sale. Maria was to work in the buyer's household for the next four years, and the buyer was not to sell her or to commit any violence or abuse against her. After the four years had elapsed, or before if the terms of the sale were violated, Maria was to receive her freedom. Nicola obviously cared about this slave but not enough to set her free on the spot, and he pocketed a tidy sum for her four years of work. Still, very few slave owners ever expressed worries about the violence of slavery. In 1307 Ansaldo da Savona sold his twenty-year-old Greek slave Maria for only thirty white bezants, quite a low price.[89] The purchaser, Berthozio, immediately loaned this slave to his newly married niece Donna Gemma. Maria became part of a dowry, and she was to work for the couple for as long as the buyer wanted. This type of present, probably seen as a thoughtful use of a slave, reveals how at times the relationship between buyer and slave might be casual, and Maria's new tie to Donna Gemma was the one that now mattered. Gemma's use of the slave was at her own risk, which meant that if Maria ran away or died as a result of maltreatment or turned out to be a thief, the problem and any losses were Gemma's, not the owner's. Berthozio retained the right to recall his slave at any moment, so Maria's ties were precarious all around.

The other main ways to break a relationship with a slave were manumission and emancipation by testament. In the first case, the owner was often healthy, and so there was the prospect of a new tie between free persons. Testators in Famagusta were usually ill, so to free a slave by will generally implied freedom sooner rather than later for the slave. Soon it would be illegal in Genoa and its colonies, however defined, to free a slave by will, lest the slave hasten the owner's death and his or her own freedom.[90] Through manumission the owner presumably earned the slave's immediate gratitude. Fourteen manumissions survive for Famagusta, ten by men and three by women (one man twice freed slaves). Most of these slave owners were Genoese, and they all appear rich; freeing a slave was an expensive charitable act. In Famagusta the owner rarely expected anything in return, so the impulse was genuinely merciful. Since Lamberto de Sambuceto wrote all these documents, there is a familiar ring to most of them. Nonetheless, the common motive of nearly all the owners, the slaves' good service and the desire by the owners to gain spiritual rewards for their souls, appears heartfelt. Ten men and six women obtained their freedom this way. Gregorio Niger freed his slave Jacopo with no strings attached.[91] On the same day Jacopo acknowledged to Gregorio that he owed him two hundred white bezants for items he had purchased, and he intended to pay this debt at an unspecified date in the future. What is striking about this loan is that it is a rare instance of a former owner taking a real interest in how his or her ex-slave began a free life. Although the other owners seldom demanded anything for manumission, they did not give their slaves a thing, except presumably the clothes on their backs.

A person owning slaves and facing death made a will in order to deal with issues of salvation, family, and property that extended beyond the narrow issue of the tie between master and slave. Forty wills survive from Famagusta between 1296 and 1302—a good sample. A will represented a last chance to make choices. One possible choice was, of course, to pass the slaves on to the heirs and continue the relationship into the next generation. Ansaldo da Sestri's will revealed that he owned three slaves; he left Fatima to his wife, Archona to his daughter, and the third slave, Tommaso, seems to have ended up in the residual part of the estate left to his sons.[92] Fatima, like nearly all slaves mentioned in wills, was not described with the level of detail common in a sale or even a manumission, but her name indicates a Muslim origin and hence a mixed relationship, in this case an enduring one. Pietro Piloso's will of 1296 reveals him to be a farmer, and he listed his goods in this way: one male slave, Nicola; two female slaves, Cali and Catalina; one horse; two cows; one calf; thirty-eight goats; and one ass.[93] The slaves appeared at the top of the list and had names, but they were in the animate part of the estate. Pietro singled out Cali for special notice. She was to be freed after two years' service to his wife and children. The other two slaves were simply part of the estate, along with the goats. This was another choice a testator faced—free this slave and not that one. Hence, the wills are complex sources on mixed relationships. The slaves need not be mentioned at all, let alone freed, so these documents do not provide a complete portrait of slavery. Thirty-six of the forty-six wills were made by men and ten of these freed a slave. Of the four women, one freed a slave. Since men and women die in equal numbers, the numbers by sex here do not seem right and they suggest that the early settlement on Cyprus was still largely male. Maybe the women were simply younger, or lived longer. Of the testators, people with some property, one-quarter owned slaves, a higher percentage than back in Genoa. This is another sign that mixed relationships between owners and slaves were more common in Famagusta than back home.

The advantage of the wills as a source on relationships is that they sometimes yield a wealth of information on personal ties, far more than occurs in a sale or manumission. Gianuino de Murta placed his life and relationships on display when he made his will on December 21, 1300. Listed among Gianuino's many and generous charitable bequests was his former slave Mariono and her daughter, to whom he left a house in Famagusta and fifty white bezants each. This exceptional generosity naturally raises the questions of whether he was the father of Mariono's child. The answer will never be known, but a look at the rest of the legacies will help put these in context. Gianuino owned a female slave, Anayma, whom he left fifty white bezants for the good of his soul. He also owned a black slave, the only one whose color is noted, named Margarita, and he wanted her to serve his wife for four years and then be freed. He also left her fifty white bezants. Gianuino then made provision for his stepchildren, leaving them four hundred white bezants he was owed, and he also excused them and their mother from considerable sums they owed him. He left his small house in Famagusta to the daughter of his former slave Catalina, and he ordered that no person should stand in the way of this bequest. He also left to Catalina and her daughter a furnished bed. This kind of legacy usually indicates some special tie, spiritual or familial, between the giver and receiver. Besides the two houses he gave to ex-slaves, Gianuino wanted his other houses and possessions in Famagusta to be sold and the proceeds used to fund the rest of his estate, which he left to the poor. On the same day, in a separate act, Gianuino carefully freed his slave Catalina, here described as white and twenty-four years old, in a manumission to take effect after his death. This notarial act did not mention Catalina's daughter, and Gianuino took pains to address this in yet another piece of business conducted on the morning of December 21. In this manumission Gianuino freed a number of slaves—Catalina's brother Jacobino, and her unnamed daughter, whom he was raising for the love of God. He also freed Anayma who was mentioned in the will and who was only eleven years old.[94]

Giovanni's will reveals that he had a wife, Isabella, and some stepchildren; he left them money and was done with them. He made sure that they could not interfere with his other families, his slaves. One group was Catalina, her brother, and daughter, whom Giovanni was supporting and who may very well have been his own child. Mariono and her daughter made up another family, and they also received a house and cash. Little Anayma received her freedom and some money. Giovanni left the remainder of what still looks like a substantial estate to the poor, and nothing obliged him to act this way except the claims of conscience. He was, even by the standards of his time, a very generous man. With no legitimate children of his own, it still seems as though he contributed to the ethnic mix on Cyprus.

On August 20, 1301, the rich widow Piacenza Flexono made her will. Her late husband Ugheto Flexono must have dictated a will but it does not survive. He did leave behind some engaging problems, which his wife addressed. She asked to be buried in the same pit (*fovea*) where her husband lay in the church of San Michele in Famagusta. So this marriage, which had produced no surviving children, still meant something to Piacenza. She also left ten white bezants, a small sum, to Salvono, the natural son of her late husband. To the mother of this boy she also left ten white bezants. Piacenza owned a slave, Agnese, whom she freed and left thirty white bezants and a mattress, some sheets, and other bed furnishings. Piacenza bequeathed the rest of her goods, which included a house and a fair amount of jewelry, to the poor—again, a generous act of charity. Piacenza was dead by September 12, when the notary recorded that Lady Isabella, a friend of the deceased, and her former slave Agnese, acknowledged that they had received their legacies—Isabella ten white bezants, and Agnese the thirty white bezants and the bed. Agnese rather quickly gained her freedom, some cash, and a bed. On September 14, Anna, mother of Salvono, the late Ugheto's natural son, declared that she had received the monies Piacenza had left them in her will. Something unfathomable is revealed by Piacenza's not naming Anna in the will, and we learn this woman's name only by the chance survival of a later piece of business. Anna had no family name or public identity of any kind except for her status as Salvono's mother. If Anna were Genoese she would have claimed the status, and if she were a former slave that probably would have been noted as well. What Anna and her son received in Ugheto's will, if anything, would certainly be worth noting.[95]

Occasionally, a testator placed conditions on a slave's freedom in an effort to change what was a mixed relationship. In 1302 the wealthy Jacopo Porco freed his slave Fatima by will, but he insisted that she first be made a Christian.[96] Whether or not he could have compelled Fatima to convert during his lifetime is a separate issue. By stipulating conversion before freedom he offered Fatima an incentive to appear a voluntary convert. The main barrier between Fatima and the Genoese community would vanish. The more frequent condition was that the slave continue to serve the testator's relatives for some period of time, usually a few years, and then be freed. Such a condition satisfied the testator's charitable impulses and also maintained the master-slave relationship for at least a while into the next generation.

The realities of slavery probably required the slave to learn the master's language as a matter of survival. As we have seen for Chios and Caffa, people sometimes needed interpreters. Notices of *dragomani* were rare in Famagusta. Tommaso from Gibellet, a lost crusader (and Genoese) city on the Syrian coast, made his will in Famagusta in 1299.[97] Tommaso claimed to be Genoese. Although his family may have been in the east for generations, the claim to be Genoese was still important for legal and social reasons. When making a will Tommaso needed the interpreting skills of the priest Robert, a master chaplain of the church of Famagusta. Most likely Tommaso spoke only the version of French prevalent in the crusader states and among many westerners on Cyprus. Robert helped to make sure that the testator communicated correctly with the notary who was taking down these last wishes in Latin. None of the witnesses said they were Genoese, and certainly only the notary and the priest knew Latin. Business rarely required the services of an interpreter because people in Famagusta generally shared a common tongue—usually Genoese, often French. A complex and important contract worth over 4,000 white bezants between Giovanni, son of Iosepe, probably a Greek citizen of Nicosia, and Ricco Manfredi of Florence in 1301 needed two interpreters, Giovanni de Porta, of Genoa, and Viviano, a moneychanger who lived in Famagusta.[98] Giovanni lived in Nicosia as well, and it seems likely that the language issue here was Greek, and so two translators were necessary to bring a Florentine partner and a Genoese notary fully into the details of settling the contract.

An early mixed marriage also required an interpreter, and again one of the parties was a refugee. In 1297 Pisanello from Messina married Benedetta the daughter of the late Omodeo from Tripoli, a city that fell to the Mamluks in 1289.[99] Benedetta brought her husband the huge dowry of 2,400 white bezants in a house, goods, and a slave. As befitting a marriage between a Sicilian and a woman whose family came from the

Latin East, the contract was drawn up according to the laws of the kingdom of Cyprus, a place where they were both in some sense foreigners. Pisanello spoke an Italian dialect and Benedetta French, and so the interpreter, Jacobino, son of Passarota, helped the bride and groom communicate.

Seventeen marriage contracts survive from Famagusta, and more than half of them involve mixed relationships. Their pattern conforms to the one that needed an interpreter: marriages between Genoese or Italians and women from the East, old crusader possessions like Acre, Tripoli, 'Atlit, or the beleaguered kingdom of Armenia. The dowry Benedetta brought her husband was the highest recorded in Famagusta. The second-highest belonged to Agnese, whose family came from Acre and who married a Genoese man according to the laws of the kingdom of Cyprus and Jerusalem.[100] Only one man who appears to be a refugee, a Giovanni who was from Beirut, entered a mixed marriage, and he married a Genoese woman named Catalina who had a smallish dowry of 400 white bezants.[101] Another man from the East—a Manuele with the toponymic "de Romania," a Greek from the Byzantine lands—in 1302 married a Genoese woman with the tiny dowry of 133 white bezants, the smallest in the sample. If a pattern can be discerned in these marriages, it is Genoese men marrying into well-off families originating in the East, and some eastern men marrying Genoese women with quite modest dowries. In the rest of the cases Genoese married Genoese in familiar ways according to their own customs. The Genoese residential community of Famagusta in the 1290s was large and old enough to have enough young people of marriageable age find one another in the East. Their dowries occupy a middle range between the two types of mixed marriages. This pattern makes sense, given the premium the Genoese expected—less for their daughters who married locals, more for their sons who married locals.

On Cyprus, as on Chios, the Genoese and the customers of a Genoese notary occasionally witnessed business connected to Jews, which would have been invisible to them back in Genoa. Jews were on Cyprus before Richard's conquest, but they had their own ways of making contracts and rarely appear in the records controlled by the Genoese, who did not rule in Famagusta in this period. On Cyprus there was a connection to the more substantial and active Jewish communities on Sicily. Some of their business brought them to Famagusta and the notary Lamberto de Sambuceto. Raffaele from Palermo appointed his son to collect some debts from another group of Jews, who promised to pay what they owed in Crete, yet another Mediterranean island with an old Jewish presence in a complex colonial setting.[102] These Jews for the moment in Famagusta found it desirable to record their business according to local laws, and two sets of Italian witnesses, in one case three men from Ancona, added legal force to these contracts. In only two other contracts did mixed relationships between Christians and Jews appear. A Genoese merchant named Domine borrowed one hundred white bezants from a Jewish physician named Elia, an inhabitant of Famagusta.[103] Domine promised to repay this gratis loan within the long term of six years, and he handed over as pledge for the repayment his Turkish slave named Fatima, who must have been a Muslim. Fatima, who was to stay with Elia, was a kind of living interest payment, whose work and services during the interval constituted the real but hidden premium on the loan. Domine did plan to repay, however, because the contract did not stipulate that Elia would get to keep the slave for good if he did not. Finally, Mussa of Messina appointed a representative to collect from three prominent Genoese his share of the seven hundred white bezants that were the price of some Jewish slaves they had sold to Raffaele of Palermo, presumably the same one seen before in Famagusta.[104] This deal looks like a ransom where some Jewish slaves the Genoese owned ended up being rescued by their coreligionists. Episodes like this cannot have increased the trust between Jews and Genoese.

Work, apart from the many labors of slaves, does not seem to have brought many Genoese regularly into a relationship with those outside their community. A common pattern reveals itself in the apprenticeship agreement made in 1301 between Raffa from the Porta Vacca neighborhood of Genoa and Giovannino, also from Genoa. Raffa agreed to teach his pupil over the next six years how to be a shoemaker, and the apprentice promised to work hard and loyally during the term. These two Genoese in Famagusta pursued the same craft, probably with compatriots as their main customers. Sometimes refugees crop up in mixed work relationships. Giovanni, whose late father came from Gibellet, promised to become a servant and to stay with Alessandrino da Zaragossa, perhaps an Iberian, for the next ten years in exchange for food, clothing, and shoes. Alessandrino promised to teach him something, but the contract did not specify the trade or skill. The general impression from Lamberto's records of the Genoese is of an insular group of immigrants interacting with the wider communities only when there was money to make.[105]

The notary Nicola de Boateriis, originally from Mantua, worked for Venetian merchants in Famagusta from August 1360 to October 1362.[106] Only 185 acts survive from this period, so Nicola was not a busy notary, but he does provide a glimpse of the city in the relatively peaceful years before the Genoese takeover of Famagusta. Nearly all of his clientele were Venetians, Genoese, or other Italians, so the view of mixed relationships is limited. Still, there are some signs of how ties among the various communities on Cyprus evolved after the plague.

At twenty-five contracts, slave sales comprised a good percentage of this business and suggest that slavery was more important in the labor-starved Mediterranean in the 1360s. Only one woman appeared as a buyer and one as a seller, again suggesting that men, here nearly all Italians, predominated in this trade. Among the sellers we find some prominent Genoese names like Spinola and Doria, signs that Venetians had no problems with buying slaves from their rivals. This sample of slaves included seventeen women and eight men, just a hint that the gender balance of slavery tipped toward women after the plague—a familiar pattern. Unfortunately, Venetian sales contracts were not as detailed as the Genoese, so these always omit the slave's color and frequently the age. Ethnicity still counted for a lot when buying a slave, and here the Venetian contracts were specific—twelve of the slaves were Greeks from Romania, ten were Tartars, and two were Bulgarians (one slave was sold twice). Prices averaged about 175 to 180 white bezants, a considerable increase from the earlier part of the century. Some of the buyers intended to emancipate the slaves, and so ransoming Greeks played a significant part of this trade.

Eighteen manumissions appeared in this sample, and there are a few more from the wills. Seventeen of the manumitters were men, and this makes sense because the overwhelming majority of the purchasers were also men. In theory women might inherit slaves and then have the chance to free them, but men made the five wills in this notary's record, so we cannot be sure this happened. The freed slaves were twelve women and six men, an interesting reversal from the gender pattern of their owners. All these slaves appear to have been Greeks, many from Negroponte. An interesting example from July 1361 sheds some light on the relationship between master and slaves and the motives behind manumission. Constantino de Priore, from the Cypriot countryside, came to Famagusta to free his slave Dimitri, the son of Giorgio from Negroponte.[107] This act of manumission contained several statements to the effect that people were happier who enjoyed the benefits of freedom and that originally all people were born equal—two powerful motives to free a slave.[108] This manumission did not explicitly claim that Constantino was also motivated by a desire to atone for his sins by this act of charity and by the 160 white bezants he received, called frankly the price of redemption. Since one of the witnesses to this act was a Marco Dulcebono, called the ambassador to the king of Cyprus from the community of Negroponte, this manumission looks more and more like a ransom.

In a similar case, on November 11, Paolo Colonna from Crete bought the slave Maria de Negroponte from a citizen of Famagusta for 130 white bezants and freed her the same day.[109] Paolo had little to say about his motives, but he did receive 130 white bezants from Dimitri de Callafati of Negroponte, Maria's father. Dimitri and the now freed Maria acknowledged that they still owed Paolo sixty-five white bezants (half the price), but more importantly they recorded the precious fact that Maria, who had been previously called Irene, had been captured by Genoese and then brought to Cyprus to be sold. Paolo appears as the useful intermediary not profiting from this ransom, and the Genoese as villains, seizing Greek Christians and selling them, apparently legally, in Cyprus. The original seller had the unusual name Missauth, son of David, perhaps an Armenian, certainly a Christian. Why did not Dimitri directly approach this person in order to recover his daughter? The dry notarial records do not contain the answer, but we may suppose that a father and the owner of his daughter might not have been able to transact an amicable sale and so they required a broker.

Nearly all the business written down by this notary took place among Venetians, and so his cartulary and two marriage contracts reveal nothing about mixed relationships. What they show instead is a Venetian community that might be in the process of becoming more insular. A sign the other way, that what we are seeing is the narrowness of the notary rather than of the community, appears in the will of the wealthy Venetian noble Nicola Coffin, made on June 23, 1362.[110] Nicola was married to Isabella de Laiazzo, princess of Armenia, a state long lost to the Muslims, and he clearly loved her, referring to Isabella as his beloved (*dillecta*) and very lovable (*peramabilis*) wife. Nicola left half of his goods to be distributed for the benefit of his soul, and the other half (except his slaves) to Isabella, who had children, but not with him. This looks like a prestigious, colonial marriage, bringing Nicola a fine princess, but probably not a big dowry—the will is silent on this point.

Nicola Coffin is also interesting as a slave owner, and his will put his slaves in the half of his estate to be disbursed according to his wishes. First Nicola freed his female slave Crusi de Romania and left her the considerable sum of 100 white bezants and a small silver belt. Then he freed Maria de Romania and left her fifty white bezants, and Irene de Negroponte, to whom he bequeathed twenty-five white bezants. All in all, Nicola calculated his affection, if that is the accurate term, for his slaves in a precise, scaled way. He ordered these slaves to be obedient and remain under the authority of his wife for her lifetime. So, he freed them and was generous, but he imposed a condition on their liberty that stretched out into the future, for the lifetime of this Armenian princess. It was better to free them now, however, rather than keep them as slaves for his wife's life, for this would have given them a motive to make that period as short as possible.

There is a final detail to note in this will concerning the mixed marriage. The notary asked the testator unusual questions, probably in order to make sure the will was legal and that it exactly reflected Nicola's last wishes. First, the notary asked: If Isabella married again, should she remain an executor of his estate? Nicola answered that she should only be in charge of the part left to her. Second, the notary asked: If Isabella married again, was she still heir to half his estate? To this Nicola answered yes; he was quite firm in the body of the will and in responding to this question that he was not using his estate as a bribe to force his wife to remain single. Finally, the notary asked why did not Nicola make provision (as was common in wills) for the possibility that his wife was pregnant? A posthumous child in theory would have become Nicola's heir. To this question Nicola gave a remarkable reply: "I surely know that she is not pregnant nor is she in the process of conceiving, since she is now of an advanced age."[111] So, Nicola did not provide for any posthumous child because it was not necessary. The bond between Nicola and Isabella did not rest on a common heir, but on love clearly stated, a possibility not to be denied to a mixed relationship.

Cairo

Old Cairo (Fustat) was not part of this archipelago; it was engulfed in a large city, the capital of Fatimid, Ayyubid, and Mamluk Egypt. Cairo and its peoples lived under continuous Muslim rule, and western merchants were largely confined to the seaport of Alexandria, which they never turned into a colony. The Geniza (storeroom) of the Jewish synagogue in Old Cairo became a repository for all sorts of discarded papers bearing the name of God and hence not to be treated like garbage. In practice every type of record, from personal letters and accounts to entire books, was deposited here, and the collection, which was rediscovered and dispersed in the late nineteenth century, has proved to a treasure trove on medieval Cairo, especially the Jewish community.[112] These Jews had business and other contacts stretching from Spain to India, and they mixed with their Muslim and Christian neighbors to the extent that most of the records are in Arabic written in Hebrew characters! Cairo provides a useful point of contrast to places like Famagusta or Chios, where Christian powers made the rules and boundaries. Summarizing this vast material is not the aim here, except in the narrow area of what S. D. Goitein has called "interfaith relations," which in Egypt mattered the most.

Since the surviving heterogeneous mass of random documents and papers mostly concerns Jews, information on mixed relations was, according to Goitein "less conspicuous" than it would be in actual daily life. Rules of the Jewish and Christian communities prohibited mixed marriages, but Muslim men were free to marry Christian or Jewish women. Non-Muslim men and women also could not convert to any religion other than Islam, unless they intended to flee. For a Muslim to convert was a capital offense. Although Jews and Christians suffered from bouts of interfaith strife and sporadic hostility and discrimination, they enjoyed wide economic freedoms and could work at whatever trades and professions they pleased—except, in theory, for the government. All the communities engaged in many types of business as partners and customers. Neighborhoods tended to be mixed, though the vast majority of people in the city were Muslims. Arabic was the lingua franca for all, and in these records there is no evidence for sustained ethnic prejudice of any kind. Jews owned female slaves who mainly worked as domestic servants and in the best of circumstances were treated as members of the family and were, despite the law, often converted to Judaism. These slaves mainly came from Nubia and Europe and were very expensive. Goitein believed that all these ties fostered tolerance: "For as soon as people of different allegiance mix closely, they discover that the invisible republic of decent men stretches beyond the barriers of religion, party, and race, a discovery incompatible with the claim of absolute superiority of one particular group."[113] This humane opinion resulted from an intimate and sustained study of these records. His sources inevitably privileged religious differences; after all, in medieval Cairo even marriage between a Rabbanite (the majority, accepting rabbinical teaching) and Karaite (the minority, believing the Bible alone) Jews counted as mixed marriage. Still, even allowing for discrimination, the poll tax, and the permanent status as second class minority, the climate in Cairo before 1250 seems more tolerant than in the Christian eastern Mediterranean. After that date, when the Geniza records begin to become thin and the corresponding information on the archipelago becomes thicker, the circumstances seem to converge and minorities everywhere experienced more difficulties. Centuries of religious warfare have their consequences.

The records of the archipelago show that the relationship between master and slave was often gendered and also colored by ethnic differences. Slavery was perhaps so entrenched because ethnic differences between master and slave strengthened the tie and the means to enforce it. Some masters freed their slaves, and some slaves found ways to help shape that desirable outcome. Both master and slave crossed the boundaries, though of course the rules left little choice to the slaves. The polyglot nature of the archipelago favored those who were bilingual and required such skills in the smaller and relatively powerless groups, such as Jews everywhere and Armenians living outside their homeland. Interpreters found useful employment, and those whose language became a lingua franca enjoyed advantages that doubled if they became bilingual in another such tongue. A pattern of asymmetric marriages emerged where westerners like the Venetians and Genoese men profitably married into the local elites. Despite all their differences, some people found ways to work together that seem relatively harmonious when compared to religious warfare surrounding the region. Cities like Caffa and Famagusta seem as multicultural as anywhere else in the world. Still, each of these places had special features not reproduced elsewhere. Venetian rule on Crete was direct and lasting, the Tartars affected Caffa, refugees from the Latin crusader states washed up in Famagusta, and Chios had a distinctive and probably ancient Jewish community. But in all of these places, a hierarchy, based on received truths concerning the human family and its varieties, was imposed by the predominant people, who were usually never slaves. Only the Tartars willingly sold their own, apparently including kin, to people they regarded as inferiors.

The search for monetary gain in a slave sale, marriage, or commercial partnership sometimes affected the hierarchy, as the subordinated had a chance to use their economic leverage to improve their status. Kate Fleet concludes her study of Genoese and Ottoman trade by observing that "money largely formed the basis of the relationship between the Genoese and the Turks and this, rather than any religious scruple, dictated relations."[114] Outside the realm of buying and selling commodities, ethnic and creedal differences played more complex roles in decisions on marriage, emancipations, and testamentary bequests to children of mixed relationships. Ordinary commerce may have been at arm's length and may have taken place solely out of self-interest. More enduring ties also existed and helped people understand who and what they were. Treaties show that citizenship counted for a lot, but mixed relationships of all types challenged any purist definition of a people, no matter how narrowly or broadly defined. Yet these mixed relationships were precisely the ones troubling the makers of neat categories.

Notarial records used in this chapter were sources biased in favor of those ordinary people willing to enter a mixed relationship—except for the slaves trapped involuntarily. People in places like Caffa or Famagusta were already, in a sense, preselected to be more open to all the experiences the East offered. Individual judgments on self-interest led some free people to cross barriers when many private activities seemed to profit from mixing with the other. The surviving records privilege the activities of the colonists, whose daily life took place in a vast context of more homogeneous yet less documented populations. Their mixing with indigenes was not always positive; the brutal facts of concubinage or the racist assumptions of slavery were not humane exports back to the West. Besides all these personal decisions about self-interest, rulers or governing elites had the opportunity to forge new ties, and treaties are also records of these activities.

CHAPTER THREE

Treaties and Diplomacy

Individual people formed mixed relationships of all types, but other circumstances forced them to act in groups to foster their self-interest. Instructions to ambassadors, diplomatic letters, drafts, and treaties in ratified form tell parts of the story of how rulers and peoples created ties. Vast numbers of these documents survive. The few discussed in this chapter concern mixed relationships and are not limited to commercial or military considerations. A treaty enables two peoples to create a relationship that may or may not be mixed, depending on their similarities and differences. Since the focus here is on mixed relationships, the treaties that best serve the purposes of this analysis are those made between two very different states. Such treaties usually had to cross such boundaries as distance, language, religion, and ethnicity. By attempting to forge a relationship based on some common goal, the parties created a bond whose durability and sincerity might have been initially questionable.

A treaty reflects the results of a negotiating process that is usually lost to history, so caution must guide any efforts to infer the stages of negotiation from the agreement itself. Letters and other diplomatic exchanges fill in the stories of relationships that foundered before the stage of treaty making. Unless copies of a treaty exist in the languages of both parties, questions about what exactly the text meant may be raised. These are typical problems facing historians using documents whose context was often intended to be secret. Yet, with all these caveats in mind, treaties and other types of texts can serve not simply as standard sources for political or diplomatic history, but as evidence for mixed relationships not very different from marriages between people of different backgrounds. The advantage here is that the treaty, for example, is much more detailed than a marriage contract, and the contexts of its parties, usually sovereign powers, much better understood.

Treaties

The treaty as a contract defined the terms of a mixed relationship, so how did the rules of the treaty, and the broader context, shape its content? For decades before the first surviving treaties were made, trading states like Amalfi, Pisa, and Venice sought commercial privileges from foreign rulers. The resulting documents or charters, which were basically prototreaties, also established at times a mixed relationship. However, these economic concessions do not naturally lend themselves to a broader context establishing all aspects of a relationship. A treaty, which is closer to a true contract, reveals more about the economic and political aspirations of both parties. Treaties establishing a mixed relationship raise the issue of how the parties communicated. For a long time in the eastern Mediterranean, Greek remained the language of treaties, though westerners always wanted an immediate Latin translation of the original. Various vernacular languages—including Greek, Italian dialects, Persian, Arabic, and Uighur—served the negotiators and interpreters, but the earliest surviving treaties written in these tongues date to the fourteenth century. The power in the eastern Mediterranean with the longest tradition of making treaties, the Byzantine Empire, established rules or protocols for making treaties that affected western and Muslim subsequent practices. Governmental archives do not survive from the eastern regions until the rise of the Ottoman Empire, so we depend on the chance existence of copies in official western archives in city-states like Venice and Genoa.[1]

The standard form of a treaty made by an eastern power sometimes began with the date but more often started by invoking God's name and blessing.[2] Even in a treaty between western and eastern Christian states, let alone with a Muslim power, the invocation struck right at the heart of the issues surrounding a mixed relationship. Mutual self-interest enforced a treaty's terms, but the parties also depended on solemn oaths to guarantee that people would do what they promised. A treaty presumes an initial lack of trust, so enforcing its terms across confessional boundaries required a mutual recognition that oaths were binding according to different rules. Still, the monotheists assumed some transcending deity who was not to be offended by breaking an agreement. In Turkish treaties and some other types, the next section of the treaty contained the ruler's sign or seal (*tughra*) to establish the authority of the document. Then an introduction supplied the names and titles of the parties, the date the treaty became effective and its duration, and sometimes a *narratio* or explanation for why it existed. The main body consisted of specific clauses or terms. A treaty usually concluded with an oath to keep its terms, and in Byzantine and Turkish treaties the ruler's seal or sign validated the document. According to established Muslim law, no peace treaty was possible with infidel powers, only truces for a fixed and usually short duration.³ In other matters, Muslim practices drew on Byzantine precedents and were also careful to distinguish agreements made directly between rulers (rare), between a ruler and another's representatives (common), or between the representatives (less common). In practice the rulers of Genoa and Venice never traveled to the east to negotiate, so the vast majority of treaties were negotiated by western representatives. This asymmetry in the relationship produced documents that looked like concessions by eastern powers, but we must be careful not to mistake the true nature of the tie.

Three side issues about treaties establish the contexts for using these documents as sources. Treaties regulated military as well as commercial ties. The experience of fighting together, another mixed relationship worth studying, has left few traces in the records. Hence the balance here is much more on the side of trade. Second, another part of the classical inheritance (pagan and monotheistic) and a subtext of trade was that commerce with foreign peoples was viewed as corrupting and a cause of decline.⁴ This decay mainly resulted from the greed and love of luxuries that trade encouraged. Treaties regulated trade, but this did not necessarily mean that the states viewed commerce as completely positive, or as a morally neutral way to benefit from comparative advantages. Parts of the treaties may instead reflect old suspicions about mixing with foreigners and their corrupting goods. Finally, some adventurers always operated well outside the boundaries and rules set in treaties. Intrepid merchants like the Polos and their successors established trading links with China that were not regulated by formal agreements. Some states tried, for example, to legitimize pirates by turning them into semiofficial corsairs or by compensating their victims. But piracy too was hard to fit inside the rules. On the fringes of the orderly world, a treaty presupposed or endeavored to create zones where rules governed exchanges. Informal actions and even other treaties always complicated the hopes of the rule makers. Still, a commercial treaty or even a military alliance was a tie that often required the parties to put aside, at least temporarily, their own self-regard and claims to purity.⁵ Habits of thinking in extremes of right and wrong, us and them, were not useful when self-interest required a bilateral approach.

The Byzantine Treaties

These generalities about the opportunities treaties present to students of relationships become clearer when we interrogate a specific, early document: the pact of 1155 between the Genoese and the Byzantine emperor Manuel Comnenus.⁶ An unusual feature of this treaty is that the emperor's representative, Demetrius, came to the West to find allies and that this agreement was made in Genoa. The Genoese had to believe that he was fully accredited to make promises in the emperor's name. They also had to understand these promises, and because maybe only a few Genoese understood spoken Greek, these promises were made in Latin and perhaps were negotiated in that language. The basic terms of the treaty guaranteed the Genoese peaceful trading access to Byzantine lands and promised that they would pay taxes no higher than those of the Pisans, old allies of the Greeks. Demetrius also promised that the emperor would give the commune a gift of 500 hyperpers and two decorated cloths (*pallia*) a year; the archbishop would receive sixty hyperpers and one cloth. Demetrius carried sufficient cash to pay to the commune on the spot the first fourteen years' installments, 7,000 hyperpers. The agreement also promised the Genoese a commercial establishment in Constantinople—a merchant quarter for their traders.[7] Finally, Demetrius stated the emperor would have his signature or seal (in practice both) placed on the document, binding Manuel and his successors in perpetuity to observe its terms. So, even though Demetrius was empowered to make the treaty in the emperor's name, the Genoese recognized that the official, sealed copy would have to be delivered from the capital.

In a parallel agreement the consuls of the Genoese commune promised to keep the peace with the emperor and not to assist his enemies, and swore that those Genoese inside the empire would provide help when it was attacked. They also suggested a number of refinements to the terms, which clarified, to the benefit of the Genoese, exactly what the emperor promised them in Constantinople, among other things. The fragmentary nature of the surviving record suggests that the Genoese may never have received a final, ratified copy of the agreement, though clearly both parties believed that an alliance had been established.[8] This would be the last time that a Greek envoy came to Italy in a position of strength. In subsequent treaties with eastern Mediterranean powers, and always with the Muslim ones, western envoys, empowered to negotiate, traveled to the East. This reversal of positions reflects the growing shift in the balance of power between the parties, especially between Latins and Greeks. In all mixed relationships, the power, prestige, or wealth of the parties would never be exactly balanced. Over time, as the balance of strength shifted from one party to the other, the negotiations and terms of the treaty reflected the altered context. A small matter to note here is the emperor's cash gift to the commune and the bishop of Genoa. From the Greek perspective, Manuel Comnenus was certainly not paying tribute to the Genoese or even hiring them in advance to defend his empire. More likely, the donor was establishing a superior position over the party receiving a gift. The *pallia* reinforced this impression; they were beautiful silk weavings far beyond the skill of the Genoese and thus another token of who was the dominant force and culture. Yet the Genoese were a proud people not eager to be patronized by anyone. Perhaps from their perspective the gift symbolized that Manuel recognized their growing stature in the world, a view that the more valuable gift of a merchant quarter would confirm. Gifts were the one part of the treaty that the parties understood in their own quite different cultural contexts.

More than a century later, the pact negotiated between the Byzantine Empire and the commune of Genoa in 1261, the Treaty of Nymphaeum, reveals the radically altered circumstances of the Greek state.[9] The context for this treaty encompasses the story of the thirteenth-century Mediterranean world and is far too wide for present purposes. Since this was not the first agreement between the two powers, they were in a way renewing their vows rather than forging a new relationship. A few basic facts help clarify the parties' goals. Since the Fourth Crusade and the conquest of Constantinople in 1204, the eastern empire of the Greeks had been shattered. A Latin (French) emperor ruled in Constantinople, and the Venetians had acquired valuable territories, like Crete, in the Aegean. The Greeks ruled a small state in Anatolia hemmed in by the Latin empire and the Turks. These developments had harmed Genoese trade and made access to the potentially lucrative markets of the Black Sea more difficult. Genoa had fought a disastrous war with Venice in the 1250s that had damaged Genoese interests in the eastern Mediterranean, particularly in what little was left of the crusader states. It made sense for Michael Palaeologus, by far the most powerful of the remaining Greek rulers, to try to recover Constantinople, but he thought he would need help, particularly naval assistance. These facts were enough to draw Genoese negotiators to Anatolia, and in the spring of 1261 they returned home with a deal and Byzantine ambassadors empowered to ratify any mutually acceptable changes to the terms.

Given the nature of the negotiations, it is not surprising that the actual original treaty does not survive. Changes and the distance between the principals made it hard for there to be a formal, final document, and in fact the rulers of Genoa and the emperor Michael never met. What survives is an authenticated copy in Latin of the Genoese copy. No drafts or instructions to ambassadors have been found, and the official contemporary historians had good reasons to be vague about the document and its terms. The treaty takes the form of a set of promises, beginning with what the Byzantine emperor offered the Genoese for their help. The second part of the treaty presents the Genoese conditions and the exact nature of their military assistance. A final section takes up two changes the Genoese government wanted in the final agreement. Close reading of the Latin text reveals some part of the effort to forge this relationship between Genoese and Byzantines, Latin and Greek Christian peoples. It is also quite clear that the art of treaty making had considerably improved over the century since the first pact.

The first thing the emperor offered the Genoese was an amicable and perpetual peace, or, a warm peace. In particular he agreed to fight with them against their mutual enemy Venice. Both parties agreed to make no truce or peace with the Venetians without the consent of the other. This is a classic case of peoples brought together by a mutual enemy that had harmed them. Everything separating the Byzantines and Genoese did not matter when faced with the desire for revenge. On any scale measuring differences between peoples, the Venetians and Genoese were much closer to one another than either was to the Byzantines. Already it is clear that the Genoese were the ones working hard to cross differences and ally themselves to a truly foreign power. When this level of asymmetry exists in a relationship from the onset, there is likely to be a similar imbalance in the perceived rewards from the risky strategy. It may be that what the Genoese got was not as highly valued by the Byzantines as what they needed from the Genoese, but what each party valued in its tie with the Other remains the key issue here.

The second item in the treaty supplies the first taste of what the Genoese wanted and is also a sign of a problem they posed for the Greeks. Michael promised that the Genoese would be safe in his domains, secure in their persons and goods, especially in cases of shipwreck. To a state whose prosperity derived from trade, such assurances were always highly welcomed. But from the Greek perspective there was a problem about just who counted as a Genoese. In the East to be subject to the emperor and to live in his state defined his people. Genoa was a kind of aberration; it was a commune or city-state that ruled other cities and villages along the coast of Liguria. Genoa was subjected in a vague way to the western emperor, but it lacked a true lord and hence was often offensive or at least inexplicable to monarchs dealing with it. So it was natural for Michael to wonder: to whom, exactly, was he making this promise of safety? From the Genoese perspective it was an equally intriguing question: who was a citizen of Genoa? The emperor apparently shrugged and left this vexed matter for the Genoese to decide. The treaty stipulated that Genoese officials must certify by letter just which people in Romania were indeed Genoese, or from the district of Genoa. This notion of a district, a kind of mixed Genoese domain where all sorts of people lived, was included in nearly every reference to the Genoese in the treaty. For simplicity the broad definition of the Genoese need not be repeated every time they are mentioned, but it needs to be kept in mind that all the people from Ventimiglia and Savona in the west to Camogli and Rapallo in the eastern Riviera benefited from the treaty. In dealing with an outside power, the Genoese were able to subsume all their own mixed relationships with the occasionally rebellious communes of Liguria into a common identity when in Romania, the Greek east. The Byzantine emperor was practically asking for a passport centuries before such a thing was invented. He also feared that some interlopers would claim to be Genoese and seek his protection without having contributed to the Genoese effort in the relationship. For the Genoese in the east, this issue of who deserved the label Genoese would no doubt cause headaches to harried officials expected to certify the matter on the spot.

The third term of the treaty shows why it was important to know just who was Genoese. The emperor promised that the Genoese were free to travel throughout his territories and that they would be free of all taxes when entering and leaving his empire. This freedom from customs taxes was a prized privilege the Genoese merchants wanted above nearly everything else. It separated them from lesser peoples who had to pay such taxes. The problem here, and the internal sales taxes further complicate the issue, is that the Genoese were operating inside the empire on more favorable terms than the emperor's own Greek subjects, who were not immune from all of his taxes on markets.[10] This privileging, in its literal sense, of Genoese traders may have fostered animosities in the Byzantine lands. The principals were undoubtedly aware of this irritation, but other considerations predominated. The mixed relationship created by the treaty was among elites who were not above sacrificing some interests for the sake of other advantages. Harmony among Greek and Genoese traders did not matter as much as other things.

The fourth promise also went to the heart of what the Genoese wanted, in this case a spot they could call their own, a merchant colony (*fondaco*). These places, as defined by the emperor, contained a loggia, a combination of an inn and market, a palace or a building where the Genoese official lived, a church, a bath, an oven, a garden, and sufficient houses for resident merchants. This self-contained unit was a kind of Genoa away from home; it was a place the Genoese owned outright, and more importantly, a place where their law prevailed. It was not a colony in a grand territorial sense, but it embodied the privileges the Genoese wanted as traveling and resident merchants. Michael promised the Genoese *fondacos* in Anea, Smyrna, and Landrimiti, cities he ruled, and by God's grace in Constantinople and Salonika, cities he hoped to conquer. He also promised the Genoese quarters on the islands of Lesbos and Chios, already his, and the hoped-for (but never realized) prizes of Crete and Negroponte (classical Euboea). These territorial acquisitions represented the fullest expression of what the Genoese wanted and were able to get, in addition to their personal safety, which was more certain in a place they owned. These colonies make clear the limits of the mixed relationship; on the ground the peoples would remain distinct.[11] And it is worth noting that the Greeks acquired no *fondacos* back in Italy.

In item five of the treaty, the emperor promised that the Genoese would not be subject to Byzantine justice but would be handed over to their own authorities for punishment. The most specific misdeed on Genoese minds was *rapina,* a broad category covering thefts and extortion. This provision continues the process of carving out a privileged niche for the Genoese inside the Byzantine state. What developed in future centuries into diplomatic immunity covered every Genoese operating inside Byzantine territory. Other treaties provide more detailed evidence on what constituted this guarantee about justice, and we explore the topic in other contexts. But this issue of justice went to the heart of the question of what rules governed the mixed relationship. The Genoese insisted that when they were far from home and in another country, they would not submit to local justice. They did not trust Byzantine law or judges to protect their interests, and this view must have resulted from a frank assessment of how Greek merchants would fare in Genoese courts in similar circumstances. When overseas, merchants needed a reliable mechanism for settling disputes, and the best one they knew was their own. Today sovereign states would not submit to this kind of glaring exception to their own legal systems. States in the Middle Ages were no less proud, but enforcing local rules on foreign traders simply drove them elsewhere and prevented any sort of relationship from developing. Western merchants insisted on importing their own justice along with their goods. Almost always, and certainly in Genoese relations with the Greeks, the rules on justice were not reciprocal. The few Byzantine merchants lucky enough to reach Genoa did not have the right to have their disputes settled according to their system of law. Justice was not equal under some agreed-upon system of universal merchant law, even among Christians, but depended on who had the power to make the rules.

The next provision in the treaty continued this thread of concern for Genoese safety. Michael guaranteed that no other power would be allowed to arm itself in his lands in order to fight the Genoese. In effect this clause meant that no enemies of Genoa would be allowed to provision their fleets or resupply in Byzantine ports. This naval context becomes clearer in the next sentence, which denies trading rights to all of Genoa's enemies except Pisa. Genoa was not at the moment actually at war with Pisa, but the neighboring city-states enjoyed a cold peace at best and frequently fought. Byzantine ties to Pisa, however, were even older than those with Genoa. In this case the emperor held the line at breaking one old relationship in order to strengthen another. This matter marked the limit of Genoese leverage on the Greeks.

The treaty as a document, as a faint *pentimento* of the negotiating process, occasionally shows exactly how one argument or thought lead to another in the complex balancing act of establishing this new relationship. In the treaty's seventh provision, the Byzantines, having denied the Genoese something about Pisa, gratified their desire for revenge against Venice. The Genoese may have begun to nod and smile at this point. Michael promised the Genoese all the rights they once had in Constantinople, a place denied to them since the crusader and Venetian conquest in 1204. In particular, the Genoese would receive the church of Santa Maria and its precincts and cemetery, now held by the Venetians. Cemeteries remained significant features of treaties because the mixed relationship did not extend to the grave. People wanted to be buried in their own soil, even if it was far from home. They wanted to rest with their own kind, interred according to their own rites. By receiving as well the Venetian fortifications in the city, the Genoese were being invited to displace Venice in the capital. This alluring prospect, combining revenge and future profits, neatly compensated the Genoese for their prospective efforts against their mutual enemies.

Being reestablished in Constantinople was not enough for the Genoese, probably because they still had to sail or row there through the dangerous, largely Venetian-controlled Aegean Sea. So the emperor in the eighth clause gave the Genoese all the rights he had in Smyrna, in effect making them lords of the city and its port. Smyrna had already appeared in the list of cities where the Genoese would receive a merchant colony, but the negotiators revisited this place and came up with something more. Here Michael had to concede his own rights and a piece of his empire. His loyal subjects in Smyrna got to keep their possessions, as did the Greek Church, but they would now be subject to Genoese authority. This concession was probably the most difficult for the Greeks to stomach and points to the high price the Genoese were able to command for their services. Coming as it does right after the details concerning Constantinople, the gift of Smyrna points at the heart of what the Byzantines wanted at any price, their former capital. (This is the great irony of the treaty, already known to some readers. The Byzantines by military chance soon recovered Constantinople on their own, without Genoese help. The Genoese insisted on their rights in Smyrna and elsewhere anyway, a galling result for the Byzantines.)

The ninth item in the treaty represented an act of cultural memory, even mnemohistory, in the changed context of the century that had elapsed since the first treaty between the Byzantines and the Genoese. Back in 1155 a representative of the emperor Manuel Comnenus had granted the Genoese their first commercial privileges in his state. In this older agreement Manuel too had been seeking Genoese naval help against his enemies, but he had to offer a lot less for it. As an aspect of Byzantine diplomacy the emperor had promised to give the commune 500 hyperpers and two *pallia* a year. By 1261 the value of these sums had eroded, but Michael Palaeologus promised the same annual gifts. In these changed circumstances it is harder to evaluate the context of this gift on both sides of the relationship. Byzantine power was a shadow of what it had been in 1155, yet the renewal of their grant might have appeared to them to be a restoration of a relationship that implied Genoese subordination as a recipient of largesse. For the Genoese, these gifts were not about sums or their status in the Byzantine hierarchical view of the Mediterranean world. The Genoese were punctilious about debts, and perhaps they saw the Byzantines as a lesser power well behind in their payments. The resurfacing of the original gifts also demonstrates a strong sense of historical memory by both parties, even in the changed context where the meaning of the original gift no longer mattered.

The last five provisions of the treaty concern commercial matters vital to Genoa. The emperor promised that he would never embargo grain exports to Genoa and that the Genoese would be free to purchase and export grain throughout his empire without any impediment or tax. No Genoese ship would be detained for any reason. No new taxes would apply to Genoese businesses. Among the Latins, only the Genoese and Pisans were permitted to enter the Black Sea, as well as those who paid for the right and were not prohibited by the Genoese. Here again the emperor was not prepared to abandon his old friends the Pisans, or his own merchants. Access to the Black Sea was something the Genoese had wanted for decades. The Venetians had closed off this potentially lucrative market for grain, slaves, and other valuable commodities. The Genoese wanted the right to sail there freely without tolls, and the pleasure of excluding the Venetians. Finally, the emperor promised to release all Genoese held in his prisons and allow them to leave his domains. This kind of wiping the slate clean was a customary way to begin a renewed relationship.

The rest of the treaty concerns the reciprocal promises the Genoese made to Michael. There is no need to repeat all the details here, only to emphasize the treaty's initial balance. So, the Genoese made the same promises in the first three clauses about a perpetual peace, no truce with Venice, and the safety of Byzantine ambassadors and merchants in their own territories. But the Genoese promised nothing equivalent to what they had received in items four and five. They made no territorial concessions of any kind to Byzantium, and offered no *fondacos* to its merchants. Nor did they exempt any Greeks from Genoese justice. The fundamental fact about this relationship was that the Genoese were coming east and expected to stay there; there was no equivalent welcome for the Greeks in their part of Italy. After this section, the treaty resumes its balance. The Genoese promised not to allow the emperor's enemies to arm themselves in the commune's territories and not to prohibit Genoese from fighting for the emperor. Genoa did insist, however, that they could leave Byzantine service whenever they wished.

Clause seven begins the process of specifying exactly what military help the Genoese were prepared to offer the Greeks. If a Venetian or Pisan fleet threatened the empire, all Genoese merchant vessels in the region would be available for the emperor's hire for a specified period of time. This was what mattered to the Byzantines the most, since they apparently lacked any credible naval power at this time. Genoese ships in the Aegean would be mostly galleys, with large crews of perhaps 140 men or more heavily armed. Any merchant craft in this period was always prepared to fight pirates or enemies of Genoa, so placing the average trading vessel on wartime status was not complicated or unusual. What the Genoese promised was to put all these private ships at Byzantine disposal but not for free. The Genoese constrained their citizens to stop normal commerce and fight for the Greeks, and be compensated for it. In practice Venetian or Pisan ships in the region spelled trouble for the Genoese anyway. The concession to the Byzantines was apparently modest, the right to hire a wartime navy, but it was what they most wanted.

The heart of the Genoese promises to the Byzantines involved making available up to fifty war galleys, a huge fleet, to serve in the East. The treaty provides minute detail on the payments to the officers and crews, as well as generous provisions of food and drink. These galleys were to serve against the emperor's enemies, except the Roman church and those peoples (*communitates*) and barons with whom the Genoese had existing treaties. We return to this item after briefly noting the rest of the Genoese promises. Genoese merchants would not carry the goods of others in order to evade customs taxes. They also had the right to export from the empire all merchandise except gold and silver bullion. The Byzantine authorities were not going to give up their profits from minting, even to establish this vital relationship. Finally, the Genoese agreed that when they claimed the promised concessions in the cities and on the islands, they would make sure that only Genoese benefited from the immunities from taxation. The parties ratified this treaty in Nymphaeum, near Smyrna, on March 13, 1261, and the emperor empowered some ambassadors to take the agreement back to Genoa for formal ratification by the commune.

The commune's committees and neighborhood representatives gathered in Genoa on April 28, 1261, to consider and ratify the treaty. Genoa formally swore to the agreement with two exceptions. The first goes to the heart of this new, mixed relationship between Byzantines and Genoese. The government wanted a more explicit list of those powers against which it would not fight on Michael's behalf, and so a new clause listed all the communities with whom the Genoese had agreements. The list is long, but it preserves the Genoese sense of its preexisting relationships, which at the moment counted as prior and more weighty obligations. This is the set of Genoese friends: the Roman church; the western emperor; the city of Rome; the kings of France, Castile, England, Sicily, Aragon, Armenia, Cyprus, and Jerusalem; the counts of Toulouse and Provence; Philip de Montfort Lord of Tyre and his heirs; all the barons of Cyprus, Jerusalem, and Latin Syria; the Hospitalers and all their houses; the city of Acre; the King of Tunis; the Sultan of Cairo, Damascus, and Aleppo (Mamluk domains); the Sultan of Turchia; the Marquis of Montferrat and all the other Lombards; the city of Pisa; and finally Guillaume de Villehardouin, Prince of Achaea, and his heirs. This list is so comprehensive, covering so much of Christendom and the Muslim world, that the question naturally arises: Who has been excluded? Who are the emperor's enemies the Genoese will fight? Michael's major enemy was Venice, and the Genoese made it clear they would fight no one else except that city and the weak French crusader figure currently holding the city of Constantinople. Even Pisa, even the Ottoman state, fell outside the list of potential enemies. Genoa was, of course, honoring its treaties and attempting to preserve its trade in places like Egypt where it may not have had a formal agreement at this time. Genoa's list therefore contains real and hypothetical relationships. The presence of the Hospitalers is notable because the Genoese had long and deep ties with the Hospital of Saint John, in Jerusalem and as San Giovanni, one of the largest charitable institutions in Genoa. The Genoese were hostile to the Templars, so much so that they did not include these fighting monks among those they would not fight. As a last point, the Genoese promised the imperial ambassadors that in their own zone of influence they would act against rebels and pirates who threatened the Greeks.

The Genoese knew well one likely cost of this treaty with Michael. The official city chronicle succinctly tells the story. The Genoese wanted revenge against Venice, so they made an alliance with the emperor of the Greeks, obtained many concessions and the city of Smyrna, and sent a fleet to the East.[12] In his first year as pope, Urban IV excommunicated the Genoese, saying that the city's treaty with the Greeks worked to the prejudice of Christianity and the Roman Church. The pope ordered the Genoese to send ambassadors with full authority to his court within a month, or he would excommunicate the city's officials and place it under interdict, in effect a church strike. Genoa sent representatives to the pope to defend the city and make clear that they would not follow the mandate of the Church against the Greek emperor. So the excommunication and interdict remained in effect. This is how the anonymous city annalists told the story, not an easy one to place in context, as Genoa, usually a loyal friend to the Roman Church, was now officially cut off from it. It is likely that the local clergy remained loyal to the commune. With all its potential advantages, the new relationship in the East carried this price, which the Genoese anticipated and were prepared to pay. Meanwhile, the Byzantines by themselves took Constantinople on July 25, 1261. The ups and downs of Genoa's efforts to restore relations with the papacy are not relevant here, but the excommunication and interdict were not lifted until 1267, in a quite changed international environment.[13]

The Genoese-Greek relationship was based on a mutual calculus of self-interest. Michael gave up taxes and pieces of his own empire to find the resources to fight the Venetians, and the Genoese were willing to endure being pariahs in Latin Christendom for a chance for vengeance against Venice. Plainly, Venice controlled the terms under which the mixed relationship between Genoese and Greeks would continue to work, or not. Michael soon tried to balance his dependence on Genoa by negotiating a treaty with his former enemy Venice in 1265, but the Venetians refused to ratify the pact.[14] So Genoa remained Byzantium's most reliable ally, and in 1267 Charles of Anjou, now firmly ruler of the kingdom in southern Italy, began a fifteen-year struggle, with many allies, to conquer the Greek state. During most of this period, leading up to the famous Sicilian Vespers of 1282, Venice tried to remain cautiously neutral, but it was dragged into one alliance against the Byzantine Empire in the early 1280s. An alliance against the Angevins, including Genoa, Aragon, and the Greeks, fostered the revolt on Sicily and changed the balance of power in the Mediterranean. All these great events provide the context for exploring the developing nature of mixed relationships in the East. By the late thirteenth century the Greeks, the Genoese, and the Venetians were a familiar triangle, and they had a firmer grasp of one another's language and culture. Still, hostilities and gaps of comprehension remained.

A truce to last five years between Michael and the doge of Venice in 1268 casts light on how the Venetians attempted to restore their position in the revived Byzantine Empire. This agreement survives in the form of a sixteenth-century Latin copy of the Venetian ratification by the doge Raineri Zeno, so it is not possible to closely understand the negotiations or the language issues surrounding the creation of the original truce.[15] Venice's promises came first, and they were brief but valuable. By promising not to attack the Greeks and to release all prisoners, the Venetians committed themselves to stay apart from western efforts to conquer the empire. This was much less than the kind of help the Genoese were still providing, but it was a tribute to Michael's skills that he had more or less taken off the board the two most powerful navies in the Mediterranean. What the Venetians wanted in return was to be readmitted to a favored trading status within Byzantine territories. Given the long period of hostility between the two powers, and that Venice still controlled major parts of formerly Greek territories, places like Crete and Negroponte, restoring economic relations would take some doing.

Michael promised much to the Venetians, and probably the most important things were a merchant quarter in Constantinople (for which the Venetians would have to pay) and safe access to the Black Sea. He would not expel the Genoese from his empire or harm them (something the Venetians would have liked), but he promised to make sure his allies would not interfere with Venetian access, and this meant safe passage through the Dardanelles and Bosphorus. In addition, he guaranteed that he would not disturb Venice's extensive colonial empire in the Aegean. The truce also granted Venetian merchants all the usual commercial privileges for safe trade, reliable weights and measures, freedom to buy and sell with no taxes, and protection of the rights of deceased and shipwrecked Venetians and their goods. Michael recognized a generous measure of autonomy for Venetian *baillis* (like the Genoese consuls), who had wide jurisdiction over Venetian subjects throughout the Greek empire. In exchange, Venice promised to make efforts to rein in those pirates under its authority, but this excluded some beyond anyone's control. Venice promised not to break the truce if it were violated but instead to seek to solve the problem, a remarkable effort to avoid war. Byzantine merchants were promised safe access to Venice, but they would have to pay taxes there. All in all this was a good but not great deal for the Venetians, and it was much better than their former relations with the Byzantines would have predicted. Michael secured the peace and a potential counterweight to his troublesome Genoese allies.

There is one thread worth following through Venice's subsequent tangled relations with the Byzantine Empire. A renewed truce from 1277 survives in early Greek and Latin copies.[16] This truce, to last only two years, closely followed and refined the details from the 1268 agreement. The one striking new provision, clause five in this and subsequent documents, was that the emperor Michael Palaeologus promised that Venetian *guasmuli* (*gasmouloi* in the Greek text) and their heirs would be free and "*franki,*" just like Venetians.[17] The defining authority here was the *podestà* of the Venetians, and the time frame concerned their period of control over Constantinople, which ended with French rule there in 1261. Over the course of more than half a century in the capital, Venetians had children with local women, and the fruits of these mixed relationships were called *guasmuls*. This name *guasmulus* (with variants *vasmullus, gasmullus,* and *vassamulus*) had at its core the word for a mule, the nonreproducing product of breeding a horse and a donkey. The mixed Venetian children were, of course, not sterile and had heirs of their own.

The Venetian ratification of the treaty called these people *vassamili* and repeated the exact text of the original clause, and similar terms appeared in the Venetian and Greek texts of a ten-year truce made in 1285.[18] Many concerns arise in this simple clause, but the main issue seems to be Venetian citizenship. As in other cases, because these truces and treaties overwhelmingly concerned economic advantages, the question inevitably became: just who had these rights? Defining Venetian citizenship was a matter for the Venetians themselves, but these mixed people were partly Greek. Hence, the emperor had some rights to determine their position, but he freely conceded them. Two familiar words defined the status of mixed persons; they were *liberi* (free) but also *franki,* and in an eastern context this meant westerners, non-Greeks. Freedom must have become an issue because some of the mothers of these people were slaves or people of some other ill-defined status. Ordinarily, children followed the status of the mother, but the Venetians wanted freedom here to be unambiguous regardless of parentage.[19] Like the *poulains* of the crusader states, *guasmuls* were principally a colonial people, but this category also was too vague in the thirteenth century. They needed to be legally defined as Venetians but also as westerners. Their Greek or eastern heritage was overwhelmed by the male Venetian ingredient in their makeup. Elsewhere, long-standing colonial societies on places like Crete and Cyprus also produced people of mixed ancestry, but in this case some Venetians found themselves retaken by a temporarily robust Byzantine Empire. Where westerners ruled, they would not need treaties to fix the status of mixed breeds.

The Aegean Treaties

Byzantine treaties dealt with Aegean matters (among others) in the thirteenth century, and, in the fourteenth, western powers like Aragon, Venice, and Genoa continued to make treaties with the Greeks. But as the Byzantine state became increasingly debilitated, the Aegean Sea, the first archipelago, in the fourteenth century became an amazingly complex contested region. Greek states, French principalities, Turkish emirates, Venetian and Genoese colonies, the Hospitalers on Rhodes, Catalan adventurers, Serbian and Bulgarian kingdoms, and others established mixed relationships and fought among themselves to control the shores of the Aegean. No other region of Europe or the Mediterranean became a cynosure of so many ethnicities in such a small place. The big story between 1300 and 1500 was that one emirate, belonging to the house of Osman, turned the Aegean into an Ottoman lake, with only a few islands like Crete, Chios, and Rhodes still resisting. To know only the end of this story is to ignore how unlikely this outcome was, especially since Tamerlane's forces demolished the Ottoman State in 1402 and for a time seemed to reshuffle all the powers in the Aegean. Certainly, western powers like the Catalans and the Venetians worked hard to make the Aegean their lake, and the Greeks never forgot who had been the first people to dominate its coasts.

Such a contested sea provides abundant examples of efforts to establish truly mixed relationships by treaty. Greek remained the language of diplomacy, and so those with a good working knowledge of it, especially the Venetians and Turks, continued to enjoy advantages. A few key events frame the context for how relationships developed in the Aegean. The transfer of the knights of Saint John to Rhodes in 1306 marked the Aegean as the main battleground between Muslim and Christian powers.[20] The crusade that captured Smyrna on the Anatolian coast in 1344 showed that western forces had taken the initiative from the Greeks in fighting Turks for control of the Aegean. Westerners continued to hold Smyrna until 1402, and Genoese enclaves on the coast lasted beyond that. When the Ottomans crossed the Dardanelles in force for the first time in 1354 and thereby pierced the traditional boundary between Asia and Europe, it became clear that all the southern Balkans were now threatened. The second half of the fourteenth century witnessed a dramatic Muslim advance on the northern and western shores of the Aegean. Tamerlane's victory in 1402 was a calamity for the Ottomans, who struggled for decades to reassemble their hegemony in their own domains as well as over independent emirs like the rulers of Menteshe and Aydin. Throughout the fifteenth century the number of players in the Aegean diminished as the Ottomans conquered the remnants of the Byzantine state and the Frankish principalities. It was during the period of maximum complexity, the fourteenth century, that the possibilities of relationship were richest. The variety of peoples in the Aegean suggests that language was a complicated issue, even given the dominance of Greek. Treaties between Venetian Crete and the emirates of Menteshe and Aydin provide the first context for exploring the issue of how language affected relationships.[21] These treaties survive in official Venetian copies and thus are nearly all Latin translations of Greek originals; only late in the relationship (1358) is there notice of an official Turkish copy made for the emir of Menteshe.[22]

Oaths between Christians and Muslims, in the broader context of the Crusades, complicated the issue of treaties between them. A wonderful example of this problem occurred in the disasters Louis IX of France encountered during his invasion of Egypt and merits a brief digression. By the spring of 1250 Louis and many nobles of his kingdom, including the eyewitness for this account, Jean de Joinville, were prisoners of the newly established Mamluk rulers in Egypt. Lucky to still be alive, the French needed to talk and purchase their way out of captivity, and the Mamluks were in the end willing to let them go in exchange for an enormous ransom and the return of Damietta. Yet how were these warring parties to believe that the other would fulfill their part of the bargain? An oath would suffice, if it were the right one. Joinville remembered, after more than half a century, the precise form of the oath.[23] The Mamluk emirs swore that if they broke their promise, they would be as dishonored as a person forced to go on pilgrimage to Mecca with an uncovered head, and as shamed as men who leave their wives but then take them back. (An aside here informs us that according to Muslim law this was truly disgraceful.) In the third part of the oath, the emirs said that if they violated the terms of the pact they would be as bad as a Saracen who ate pork. Nicholas of Acre, one of the captives who knew "sarrazinnois" (Arabic) assured the French that these oaths were the strongest a Muslim could take. Whether or not these oaths were written down, they satisfied the French.

But the emirs wanted Louis to take an equivalent oath, and they wrote down, on what Joinville said was the advice of renegade priests, three guarantees. Louis agreed to swear that if he broke the treaty he would be as dishonored as a person who denied the Lord and his mother, and also be outside the company of the apostles and all the male and female saints. The third part of the oath stipulated that if Louis did not keep his covenant with the emirs, he would be in the same state as a Christian who renounced God and his law, and trampled on the cross. This last point was too much for Louis, and he refused it. Using Nicholas as the interpreter, the emirs, who had sworn as the king had asked, said that they would kill all their captives if Louis did not swear. Louis said he would rather be dead. In an interesting move, the Mamluks began to make an example of the venerable patriarch of Jerusalem, who then offered the king loud assurances that he would take the guilt on his own soul for whatever oath Louis took. Joinville did not know in the end just what oath was taken, but the emirs were satisfied and the problem was solved.[24] Louis knew, as did everyone, that oaths taken under duress could be explained away or absolved later, and the main task here was to get the king safely out of Egypt. Still, Louis was punctilious about paying to the penny the first part of his ransom, and honor as well as an oath, written or oral, could bind parties in the midst of bloody war.

Language shaped the relationship between Turks and Venetians in the Aegean and taught each party about the other when it was necessary to swear an oath. An exemplary oath occurs in the middle of a treaty made between the emir of Aydin and Venetian Crete in 1348.[25] Since these treaties take the form of promises from the emir to the Venetian ambassadors, this oath taking was one-sided. The emir swore by the God who made heaven and earth, the sea and everything in it, the God who had power over life and death forever. Nothing was like this God, who never died and was not begotten (*generatur*). Up to this point the Latin translation of a Greek oath reflecting a Turkish oral statement would not give the Venetians any pause. But now the clear values of Muslim religion were coming through, about Allah who was eternal, always one, and never appeared on earth in human flesh as the Venetians believed Jesus did. This oath speaks clearly in Muslim terms, ones the Venetians knew and understood to be valid for their partner in this treaty. Such words taught westerners much more about the true values of Islam than the propaganda usually put forward about the idolaters worshipping Muhammad.[26]

The emir also noted that his all-knowing God had created writing and the quill, the instruments necessary for creating documents like this one. He swore by the God who made angels and archangels and the 124,000 prophets, beginning with Adam and concluding with Muhammad, to whom the faith of the Muslims was first made known. Next the oath provided phonetically in Latin letters some of the many names of God in Arabic. The emir swore in the name of this God, who was known through four texts: the laws of Moses, the psalms of David, the teachings of Jesus, and the law of the Muslims from Muhammad. Finally, the emir swore with his hand placed on the Quran, written in Arabic, while reciting the core of his creed, that there was no God but Allah and Muhammad was his prophet.[27] Doubtless this statement was needed to satisfy the Venetians, for they did not have to read one of the rare Latin translations of the Quran or be lectured by Franciscan missionaries in Morocco about the essentials of Islam. They knew what mattered to the emir, and they wanted to see him with his hand on the Quran. They were probably pleased to hear (and read) him say that if he broke his oath he would have to walk to Mecca barefoot but still be damned with the worst villains of Islam. Among many other things, the texts of these treaties containing similar oaths prove a good working knowledge of Islam not only among scholars in Oxford or Paris, but among merchants and diplomats in Venice and Genoa. For example, despite endless literary confusion about the Muslims in some way worshipping Muhammad, the Venetians never would have accepted an oath taken on his name, for they knew it would not obligate the taker to anything and would in fact seem blasphemous. These ordinary commercial agreements hence reveal a much deeper understanding about culture than might be expected from this type of document.

Now, to turn to the pacts themselves. The emir of Aydin ruled a territory centered upon the port of Teologo, near the ruins of ancient Ephesus. Emirs of Menteshe had their capital at Palatia, a port near Miletus. These states in southwest Anatolia inevitably became important to the Venetians, who owned nearby Crete and smaller islands like Karpathos and Kasos. The Venetian government left the burden of making treaties with these Muslim powers to the man on the spot, the Duke of Candia, the Venetian-appointed ruler of the island. The basic task of these treaties was to establish the rights and privileges Venetian merchants needed to conduct business in the emirates. By now these are familiar enough: the Venetians wanted their merchants and ships to be safe; and they wanted low customs duties, reliable weights, a merchant quarter with a church, and the right to have a consul who would look after Venetians and judge their disputes. These treaties were supposed to set up a rather one-sided commercial relationship, in which Venetian ships had the right to dock, provision themselves, and debark merchants and their goods, while at the same time promising Muslim merchants in Crete nothing at all. Hence, the one-sided character of the surviving documents—promises and oaths from the emirs, nothing from the Venetians. If we read between the lines of these pacts, we recognize that the Turkish states expected to benefit from this trade by collecting taxes, usually 2 percent each on imports and exports, and by enriching their own people who sold to the Venetians. These traders in turn supplied the Turks with items they wanted, like wine and soap.

Both parties conducted this trade in the context of frequent warfare and insistent papal demands that no war materials of any kind be sold to the Turks. The number of treaties is testimony to how frequently they were broken or needed to be restated.

Beyond the usual terms of trading concessions, these pacts provide details on the special relations between Crete and the Venetian homeland, and the emirates. The first treaty with Menteshe guaranteed the customary customs rates but exempted the key Turkish exports of grain, vegetables, cattle, horses (particularly prized on Crete), and slaves. Specific taxes were levied on these items, such as the high duty of ten aspers per slave.[28] This list reveals what goods the Venetians wanted in Menteshe, especially slaves. In turn the emir had first call on the luxuries Venetian merchants brought to his shores. The Venetians were most interested in limiting Turkish sea power, and they did this by extracting concessions that the emir would not put any armed ships (usually galleys) in the water. The 1337 treaty with Aydin recognized the precarious nature of the relationship by allowing each party one month's notice to withdraw, hence giving Venetian merchants enough time to sail away.[29] In the same year a treaty with Menteshe contained the first detailed provisions concerning slaves. The unique conditions of traffic in humans required special notice in commercial treaties. The emir promised that if any slave fled from one of the parties to the other and took stuff, the emir would restore the property and the slave would be free.[30] Context here is vital. The emir is presuming that it will be a Muslim slave who flees to his territory. He will return the stolen property, but he would never turn over a Muslim runaway to Christian ownership. (He might sell such a slave, but runaways were another matter.) It was probably inconceivable that a Muslim would flee to the Venetians, for it was certainly common knowledge that such a slave would not fare well and was bound to be exported. Turks owned many Christian slaves, however, and the treaty made an oblique reference to this issue. If any Venetian ship owner or sailor dared to take away a slave knowing him to be a slave, he ought to pay the slave's owner twelve florins.[31] In effect, the Turks would allow Christian slaves to run away to the Venetians, but they intended to collect a respectable price for each head. These Turks probably had a large supply of such slaves, whom the Venetians would not hesitate to purchase by one means or another.

A 1358 treaty between Crete and Menteshe made specific reference to the slave issue from another perspective. The emir promised to return ten Cretan slaves (*emalota*) currently in his domains, one woman and nine men, as well as others, including twenty-four who had been taken in a raid on Sitia in Crete.[32] Despite these pacts, the Turks occasionally launched galleys to raid Venetian possessions and carry away valuables, like people. Here the Venetians used their trading leverage to get the emir to work to return these slaves at no expense. In a later treaty from 1375, this emir also promised more explicitly to offer no help at all, not even by words, to other Turks who might be at war with Venice.[33] The state in question here was no doubt the Ottoman emirate, which was growing in power in Anatolia and soon would be in a position to absorb Aydin and Menteshe. The problem for the Venetians and others became that the Ottomans were not interested in making treaties or mixed relationships but instead were eager to carry the battle to them. Treaties became temporary truces or agreements to pay tribute—a far cry from these advantageous commercial links.

A Genoese-Mamluk Treaty

Thus far the subject has been mixed relationships as revealed in treaties in one core area of the Mediterranean, the Aegean. Stepping back to the broader context of Muslim-Christian interactions, we can see how other relationships affected how these peoples perceived one another. Egypt, the great economic power of the eastern Mediterranean, was often in a stronger position than the Byzantines to negotiate with western merchants. A brief look at a characteristic Egyptian treaty shows what form Muslim-Christian relations took when powerful, equivalent economic self-interests temporarily overrode other concerns.

The fall of Tripoli in 1289 left Acre as the major Christian-controlled port in what remained of the crusader states. Although the western naval powers and Cyprus made gestures in defense of the coast, all eyes were turning to the inevitable—the loss of Acre, which occurred in 1291. Merchant states like Genoa had to devise a way of continuing trade with the East. The Black Sea and Cilician Armenia provided possible venues, but the Mamluk state, soon to encompass the entire coast from Alexandria to Antioch, was the power able to set the terms of trade. After the loss of the crusader states, the papacy took an even dimmer view of commerce with the most powerful enemy of Christendom. Yet the navies of Venice and Genoa were essential to any proposed recovery of the Holy Land, and these states consistently argued that embargoes against Egypt weakened them more than they harmed the Muslims. Whatever the truth of these assertions, Italian merchants and others were going to devise ways of maintaining this lucrative trade despite hostilities and wars in the eastern Mediterranean. Genoa's alert diplomats approached the Mamluk Sultan after Tripoli's loss but before Acre's, and looked for ways to maintain a Genoese trading presence in the most profitable eastern markets.

The interest here is not in the economic details of the pact made between the Genoese and the Mamluks in May 1290. Instead, the focus is on the tenor of the relationship between these two powers intending to profit from trade while not pretending to be at peace. The surviving texts provide the best evidence about the linguistic and cultural differences that made it difficult to establish this kind of wary mixed relationship. The Muslim chronicler Ibn 'Abd al-Zahir gave a good account of the context for the agreement and some excerpts from the oaths ratifying it.[34] It is curious and revealing that he was more interested in the guarantees than the terms. Perhaps from the Muslim perspective any disputed terms were details that could be resolved by people of good will, provided that both sides were morally committed to the pact. The Genoese archives contain a Latin translation of the original (missing) Arabic text of the agreement, and this document is long on economic details and much briefer on the ratifying oaths.[35] So, in some respects the surviving sources are at cross purposes; the practical Genoese were more interested in the details; the Muslims wanted to know why they should believe the Genoese about anything.

The Genoese envoy Alberto Spinola traveled to Egypt with the power to conclude this pact, and he brought back a document that is clearly a translation of an Arabic text—the detailed and respectful list of the sultan's titles could only come from such a source. The Arabic account of the oaths states that the agreement was in Arabic with an interlinear version in Frankish, which must be Latin. Unfortunately, this interesting document no longer exists. The Genoese version in Latin, perhaps preserving the flavor of the interlinear translation, contains a great deal of information useful to the economic history of the Mediterranean. For present purposes, a few details are important. The pact was made between Spinola and an emir representing the sultan, and this conformed to Muslim rules about agreements made between representatives. Also according to Muslim custom was the provision that the pact lasted for the life of the sultan and his heir, and the lives of the captains of the people in Genoa; on both sides in practice this meant that the pact's duration would be rather short. Above all the Genoese needed to feel safe and secure in their persons and goods in Egypt, and this the sultan promised. The Genoese had a consul in Alexandria who was empowered to settle disputes brought by a Saracen against a Genoese. When a Genoese had a claim against a Saracen, a Mamluk official heard the case. This mixed and equivalent procedure respected Muslim justice on its own territory. The Genoese paid customs duties in Egypt and conducted much of their business in the Mamluk customs house, where they clearly needed notaries and interpreters. The Genoese made sure that they would not be forced to buy or sell anything against their will, and so they escaped Mamluk habits of forced sales, so lucrative to the emirs and costly to merchants.[36] The Genoese had a traditional claim on one church in Alexandria, and this pact secured it. Finally, the Genoese obtained the useful condition that if any of their ships reached the East and learned that war had broken out, they would still be safe and secure as during peacetime. Innocent traders would not suffer from being out of touch with the news. Basically, this pact offers what terms Genoa could obtain from a great power over which it had little leverage. Still, both sides benefited.

The other area where the Latin and Arabic versions overlap concerns the special promises Alberto Spinola made to the Mamluks. These stipulations, no doubt demanded by the Muslims, guaranteed the sultan's subjects equivalent safety in the lands of the commune of Genoa. The unstated principal of this mixed relationship was that Muslim merchants were not coming west; it was the Genoese (and Venetians, Catalans, and others) who had this right, by virtue of their navies.[37] The Muslims were forced to accept this inequality until their naval power could match that of the westerners, which did not happen in this period. Both sides knew that Egyptian and Syrian merchants did not sail to Genoa, so this zone of safety probably really meant the Genoese colonies in the eastern Mediterranean. Even if this promise meant nothing in fact, it showed that the agreement was equal, that the sultan's negotiator would not yield to the Genoese anything they were not prepared to reciprocate.

The Latin account contains the oath that the sultan's emir Husām al-Dīn swore to the Genoese. According to Peter Holt, it resembles Muslim oaths to other treaties in this period.[38] Husām invoked the name of God three times and swore according to the law that God gave the Saracens. There is a clear, respectful sense here that this God is no idol or Muhammad but a God to whom valid oaths are taken. Across the great religious divide separating thirteenth-century Muslims and Christians, this comes as close to recognizing the similarity of their gods as any document ventures. Alberto Spinola's full oath, which only appears in the Arabic account, invoked the name of God three times but also included references to the cross, the Gospel, the Gospel writers, Mary, the Holy Spirit, and other significant parts of his faith. Then the Arabic account provides a slightly more detailed version of Spinola's stipulations, and it lists the Genoese witnesses in Alexandria to his promises. This version also notes that Spinola signed the interlinear Arabic and Frankish copy, and it names the writer of the Latin translation, Jacopo Pellegrino, secretary to the Genoese ambassador.[39] Only the Arabic account notes that the Melkite bishop of old Cairo, Peter, administered the oath to the Genoese ambassador and that this act was also witnessed by some Coptic clergy. Clearly, the Mamluks wanted their own Christian subjects to confirm that the oath taken by this westerner was valid. Finally, the Arabic writer makes clear that the Muslims were careful to translate the Genoese guarantees from Latin into Arabic. Three Muslim interpreters collaborated to make sure the translation was valid, and it is useful to know that the Mamluk officials had notaries capable of reading Latin and checking the different systems of dating—eastern Christian, Muslim, and western Christian—involved in certifying the pact.

This treaty shows a developing sense that mutual economic interests could provide good reasons for pacts between hostile powers. Muslim and Christian knowledge about what constituted valid oaths for those of a different faith was steadily increasing. By the late thirteenth century, envoys were capable of negotiating in a number of languages, and people on both sides of the divide had mastered writing in Arabic and Latin. The Mamluk Empire in 1300 was the most powerful and sophisticated of the Muslim states, but elsewhere mixed relationships with Muslims operated according to different rules.

The Black Sea Treaties

The Black Sea was a vital trading zone for Italian merchants and also one of the places where the Mongols, in the form of the Tartar Khanate of the Golden Horde, affected the Mediterranean world. From the time of Batu and William of Rubruck, the Golden Horde's capital was at Sarai, originally an encampment on the lower Volga. Later, it was at New Sarai farther upstream.[40] Crimea, attached to the mainland by a narrow and swampy isthmus, posed an administrative problem solved by establishing, in effect, a sub-khan to rule at Solgat. This place, more of a camp than a true city, sat in the middle of the peninsula about as far as possible from the sea. Mongol power depended on rapid movements by horsemen, and on the Black Sea they showed no real interest in controlling coasts or ports. Over the middle decades of the thirteenth century, the Tartars replaced the Cumans as the rulers on the northern shore of the Black Sea, and Genoese and Venetian merchants began to establish themselves along the southern shore at Caffa, and even in the Sea of Azov at Tana. Agreements or treaties, oral or written, may have existed in the first century or so of contact, but they no longer survive. The nature of Tartar society and rule seems to have precluded the possibility of their archives surviving, though we know from other sources that its rulers kept documents redacted in Uighur script. For copies of treaties between the khans of Crimea, the Golden Horde, and other states, we must turn to western sources, in particular the Genoese archives.

Venetian and Genoese merchants ventured by land all the way across Asia, but the Black Sea remained the place they could still reach by ship, their safest and by far most efficient means of transport. Still, the Black Sea was filled with warring peoples who spoke a bewildering array of languages. Potential relationships drawing the Italians to this part of the East were bound to be mixed as well as dangerous. Some people must have believed that it was easier to make money, despite the risks, in this region than it was in Genoa or Venice. Making money was the reason for the Italians being there, but what did that matter to the Tartars? What benefits did they gain from the relationship? There is an almost wistful effort to answer this question in a set of instructions the Venetian government issued in 1383 to its ambassadors going to the Tartar court. The first specific piece of advice concerned the nature of the relationship with the Tartars. Above all, the Venetians wanted the khan of the Tartars to understand that his relationship with Venetian merchants in Tana and elsewhere benefited his own empire. Their ambassadors were to do him the courtesy of saying they believed he knew this, but they were told to reiterate this main point. These advantages of commerce were not enumerated, and the Venetians admitted that they too gained from this trade. (The advantage that the Venetians wanted to discuss was the level of the customs duty, an issue where the Tartars could very well see their self-interest.) What comes out of this document is the clear worry that the Tartars did not understand that they benefited from trade as much as the Venetians. Not only would love and perfect friendship emerge from buying and selling, but the Tartar empire would also be the winner, as would the Venetian state.[41]

The task here is not to explore economic history or the comparative advantages of trade between the Tartars and the Italians but rather to understand this trade as the reason for the relationships that developed between them. Analyzing efforts to cross the big cultural divides between these two peoples makes it possible to see what each party wanted and understood about the other. The problem of common languages remained central to early peaceful attempts to establish relationships. The many languages—Mongol, Uighur, Persian, Greek, Latin, Genoese, Venetian, Armenian, and Slavic, among others—used in the Black Sea create a rich context for understanding the role of language in relationship. In order for people to use language in a meaningful way in such a complex context, they needed interpreters. These indispensable people were especially useful in treaty making, for without clarity here all other contracts would founder.

The Venetians and the Genoese had been fighting in the eastern Mediterranean since their first war in 1258, which concerned rivalries in the crusader states.[42] Their second war, which started in 1294, again concerned trade in the East and this time started in Cilician Armenia and Cyprus. A third war, began in 1350 as a struggle over the remains of the Byzantine state and access to the Black Sea. The earliest surviving treaties concern Venetians' efforts to establish for themselves a place to rival Genoese Caffa.

Andreas Zeno negotiated what appears to be the first Venetian treaty with the Tartars in 1333. Venetian merchants had been coming to Tana to trade for some time, but clearly they wanted to regularize their rights there. The surviving copy presents a linguistic puzzle. The official copy presented to the Venetian government contains the statement that it was translated from Persian into Latin.[43] The original treaty concluded with a coda by a Dominican, Brother Domenicus the Pole, who stated that he had translated the treaty word by word from Cuman into Latin in August 1333, presumably at the time it was negotiated on the banks of the Don River. The early dictionary from this part of the world was trilingual for Latin, Cuman (Turkic dialect), and Persian (Farsi); the second two were official languages known at the court of the Golden Horde. But there is no mention here of Mongol or the Uighur script in which it was written, and how could the treaty be in both Cuman and Farsi? Unfortunately, the treaty does not mention any interpreters, so we cannot know in what languages—Cuman, Farsi, or both—it was negotiated. Surely, Venetian and Latin were not much used (yet) at the Tartar court. A document in either eastern language never appeared in Venice, where there were, at least since the time of the Polos, a few people who knew Farsi, the lingua franca of trade in central Asia. A fair guess here would be that the Venetians negotiated in Farsi through interpreters with the khan's representatives who spoke Cuman. Mongol was not an issue here because there never was a copy of the treaty in that language. As the form of this treaty is a list of grants or favors that Khan Uzbeg (1313–43) made to the Venetians, it was perhaps not so important for the Tartars to have a copy. After all, the Venetians promised them absolutely nothing. In this sense the treaty resembles a typical medieval charter, and it was always more important for the recipient rather than the grantor of favors to have a copy. What sense this distinction made to the Tartars may become clearer when we look at the actual terms of this relationship.

Most importantly, the Venetians wanted a place where they could build houses, dock ships, and conduct their business. They wanted a merchant colony in Tana, and the Khan Uzbeg granted them a place on the shore of the Don River. He also set the tax they would pay on their transactions at 3 percent, a fairly low duty that would have little effect on prices. Still, the khan exempted precious stones, pearls, gold, silver, and gold thread from any tax, as had been the custom in trade with the Venetians, who were presumably supplying these luxuries to the Tartar elites. This was one of the benefits of the relationship from the Tartar perspective. The khan went on to make an agreement on weights and to set rules for the brokers, whose fees would be fixed and not subject to change. These brokers provided an invaluable service in trade, since they facilitated commerce by accepting deposits; they were also bonded and probably served as interpreters as well. Uzbeg also allowed the Venetian consul to sit with the lords of Tana, his own officials, to settle any disputes. Most important for merchants was the promise that no Venetian would be held responsible for the misdeeds of others—a frequent style of justice in the Tartar domains. Finally, the khan promised the same tax on ships as before, without troubling to state what it was. The document was sealed with his red sign (*tamoga*) in the Year of the Monkey, on the fourth day of the eighth moon, which Brother Domenicus gave as August 7, 1333. It is interesting that the Tartars, by now Muslims, still used this East Asian system of chronology. This very basic treaty gave the Venetians the minimum assurance they needed to conduct business in Tana, and the khan, as the local sovereign and certainly the superior power, as an act of grace conceded these privileges, which cost him little.

A plan to send out a consul to Tana in 1344 noted that he should travel with an interpreter, but the languages required are not supplied.[44] Among the duties of the consul was to determine who was Venetian, but the instructions specifically denied him the power to make anyone a citizen "who was not by origin and tongue a Latin."[45] Whatever the nature of their relationships with Tartars and others in Tana, the Venetians intended to hold their citizenship close and restrict it to Latins by birth and language, in effect Venetians from back home or from the well-established colonies in the east like Crete. Children of Venetian men by local women may have prompted this concern that the consul in Tana not hand out Venetian status to just anyone.

In 1342 or 1344 the Venetians were careful to seek a renewal of their privileges from the new khan, Gambek (1342–57), at exactly the time when Genoese possessions in Crimea were coming under threat.[46] These concessions, also in Latin, are more verbose than the first ones but repeat closely the terms of the earlier grant. The one difference concerns the clarified grant of land to the Venetians; here it is noted that their place is to be separate from that of the Genoese, a clear sign that by now the Genoese too were established in Tana, though no list of privileges for them survives. Gambek, however, added three new items to the previous terms. He allowed the Venetians to purchase large and small leather (hides) at the very high duties of 50 and 40 percent, respectively, the same rates the Genoese paid.[47] Here is an interesting cultural aspect of the mixed relationship. The Tartars lived off their immense herds of horses and other animals and presumably had leather to sell. It would be worth knowing what the market for leather was back in Italy just before the plague, when population levels were still high and animals fairly expensive. The khan was willing for his subjects to sell hides, and there were presumably still takers at these exceptional tax rates, which filled the ruler's treasury. There is certainly close calculation of economic self-interest behind these Tartar terms of sale. Finally, the khan allowed the Venetians to supply themselves in the same way as the Genoese, presumably in provisions, and he granted them the right to recover their goods from Venetian shipwrecks. These two modest grants did not really change the balance of power between the Tartars and Venetians.

These years witnessed a flurry of letters between Genoa and Venice as the two powers warily and ultimately unsuccessfully explored the possibility of making common cause against the more aggressive Golden Horde. A draft of a treaty between Andrea Dandolo, doge of Venice, and Giovanni de Murta, doge of Genoa, in 1345 begins with a vehement denunciation of Khan Gambek for his many misdeeds.[48] The khan and his people are compared to a disease, and, inspired by the devil, have robbed and harmed Venetian and Genoese merchants, endangering their very souls as well as their goods. The khan, styled as a "princeps Agarrenorum," (prince of the Hagarenes, a Muslim ruler) was perceived as a monstrous infidel and enemy to the Christians about whom something must be done. Back home these Italians were free to vent their real feelings about the Tartars, and these were far from love and perfect friendship. In reality, the Tartars were a disease needing a cure, "according to the words of the Evangelist [John 21:17] feed my sheep, not eat my sheep, not graze my sheep, did the lord command."[49] Whatever the exact meaning of this puzzling sentence, the Italians clearly saw the Tartars as predators on the innocent merchants, who instead deserved a good shepherd.

The Venetians and Genoese failed to make common cause against the Tartars, and in 1347 Venetian ambassadors negotiated another set of privileges from the khan Gambek.[50] The surviving copy of this treaty is in Venetian dialect, which is closer to the actual language in which it may have been negotiated than the other languages in which treaties often were written. Again, in keeping with the style of agreements with the khan, the treaty takes the form of a list of grants to the Venetians. This document concludes, however, with the name of the Muslim scribe, Yman Iussuf, who redacted it, though probably not in Venetian. Once again, the Venetian records are not clear on who translated this document into dialect and what other languages were used. The khan Gambek made his words known to the one thousand, the one hundred, the ten—all those who served him in the Horde—in a Tartar style that must reflect the work of his own scribe. The scribe dated the pact in a syncretic way, writing that it was made in the Muslim year 748, on the twenty-second day of Ramadan, but also in the Year of the Pig! Gambek was well aware of the favors his predecessors had conceded to the Venetians, as well as of his earlier grant. The khan guaranteed the safety of the Venetians at Tana, but now they paid a 5 percent tax on transactions, perhaps a penalty for recent hostilities. Otherwise, this list repeats the previous one and contains the same commercial privileges, down to the matters of shipwrecks and high taxes on hides. It is interesting that in the Venetian dialect, their piece of land in Tana was called a *bagno* (bath). This durable word eventually came to mean any ethnic enclave, even a prison. Only at the very end did the khan grant a new favor, that the Venetians were not obligated to pay the Genoese anything; this was perhaps another sign that the Venetians had charted a less hostile course in their relations with the Tartars. Gambek concluded his commands to his people to honor these terms with a warning: if they did not obey, they should be afraid. It was a nice echo of Mongol in the Venetian language.

Genoa and Venice ended their debilitating war in 1355, but rivalries in the Black Sea naturally continued. In 1356 the Venetian ambassador Andrea Venier made his way to the court of Ramadan, who was ruler in Solgat and representative of the khan of the Golden Horde in Crimea. This region was the core of Genoese interests in the Black Sea, so the relationships were now becoming triangular as Venetians, Tartars, and Genoese each looked for advantages against the others. In these circumstances it would have been natural for the Tartars in Crimea to play the Italians against one another, a strategy that seemed to work well in Tana. The Venetians obtained the usual trading privileges from Ramadan, including a 3 percent tax rate and a fair method for settling disputes.[51] Two unusual provisions appear in this pact. Tavern keepers were exempt from what appear to be local taxes; the Venetians had no formal merchant *fondacos* here and were probably depending on their own inns for lodging. Traveling merchants always wanted a familiar place to stay among their own people, and this was the best the Venetians could manage in Crimea at this time. The second term suggests what they were doing there. When ships were loaded at the little ports the Venetians were allowed to use, a Tartar and a Venetian official were supposed to check the cargo to ensure that no fugitive or runaway slave was there. The Venetians were certainly in the business of exporting slaves, and this trade suited the Tartars, but it was in the interest of both parties to make sure that the slaves had been "honestly" acquired in the markets.

The Venetians were also careful to reestablish better relations with the new khan, Birdi Beg (1357–59). Ambassadors journeyed all the way to his court on the banks of the Volga to finalize a new pact on September 24, 1358, corresponding to the eighth of Sival in the Muslim year 759, as recorded by the khan's scribe Sabadin.[52] Again, this pact took the form of directions from Birdi Beg to his officials, ordering them to implement these favors to the Venetians. The khan also rehearsed the history of these pacts, going back to the time of Uzbeg and noting that problems had occurred in the time of Gambek. Birdi Beg observed that the tax rate had climbed to 5 percent as a result of these troubles, and he proceeded to confirm in exact detail the privileges the Venetians enjoyed in Tana. This summary of the old concessions concluded with the familiar warning to his Mongol subjects that they should not commit acts of violence against the Venetians or otherwise violate these orders, or else they should be afraid. Six of his Tartar lords witnessed this act, which the khan had sealed with his red tamoga. At about the same time the lord of Solgat also renewed his grant to the Venetians, and the khan began a process for compensating the Venetians for one of their galleys, which had been plundered.[53]

For about the next twenty years, the Genoese and Venetians tried to carry on ordinary commerce in the more challenging circumstances of anarchy and plague. Genoa's circumstances in 1380 were quite difficult.[54] During its fourth major war with Venice, which had begun in 1378, the Genoese suffered a catastrophic defeat at Chioggia, losing thousands of men and ships. By 1381 both sides, exhausted, made a peace that maintained the status quo in Italy and the East. The Genoese colony at Pera had withstood attacks from Venetians, Greeks, and even Turks, and on Cyprus Genoa clung to the favorable position it had held there since 1373. Birdi Beg, the last of the descendants of Batu, had died in 1359, and anarchy prevailed in the domains of the Golden Horde until Toktamysh (1376/77–1395) began to restore order.[55] The new khan at first needed to rely on local leaders at Solgat to deal with the Genoese. By 1380 the Tartars and the Genoese would be looking to restore working relations, and for the Genoese in particular it was necessary to preserve some area of strength against the increasingly dominant Venetians.

The first treaties to survive, from 1380 and 1381, found a circuitous route to preservation. Only the part of Caffa's records that eventually came to Genoa had a chance to survive Caffa's fall in 1475. In 1383 the Genoese consul in Caffa had copied two agreements made in 1380 and 1381.[56] A note on the back of the first treaty calls it a copy and translation. The amazing thing about the copies is that they are in Genoese dialect and not the Latin almost always used for official documents in Caffa and Genoa. (The Venetian switch to the vernacular had occurred earlier, as we have seen.) The dialect is very rough and the spelling awful, and the language here truly reflects what the people negotiating with the Tartars spoke at the time. Even better, what the Genoese had was an original copy of the treaty written in Uighur, and their task was to put the document into the "Latin" tongue, which was what they called their dialect. Three notaries cooperated in this task. Giuliano Panizario wrote the true Latin introduction and explained that what followed was a faithful copy of a Uighur exemplar. The two other notaries were Francesco de Gibelleto, who seems to have been the real expert in Mongol language and script, and Luchino Calligepalle, whom we saw earlier as an official interpreter for Greek in 1381.[57] Like the other two notaries, Luchino was an expert in Genoese, but what seems to have happened is that Panizario and Calligepalle used their dialect (and perhaps scraps of spoken Mongol) to put into written words what Francesco, who could read Uighur script, said the treaty meant. What is important here is that Tartar power dictated the primary written language of the treaty, Uighur. The Tartars had their own interpreters who could speak to the Genoese but certainly not in Latin! In this case, so unusual in Genoese diplomacy, it made sense to leave the treaty in Genoese dialect, the only type of copy that could be confirmed with the Tartars.

These linguistic realities on the frontier of Christendom created a unique setting for the Genoese, clinging to a coastal strip of Crimea in the face of the Golden Horde, to reestablish a relationship with the Tartars. Only out there would a treaty in Uighur make any sense. Some Genoese who could speak and perhaps even read Uighur must have made it back to Italy, but as far as we know not one scrap of paper in that script found its way back to Genoa or Venice to survive in the archives. People have looked hard, for such a piece of paper would be a unique record, like the trilingual dictionary in Latin, Persian, and Cuman. Precious indeed would be a Genoese-Uighur dictionary, and we would love to know if these three notaries had one at hand. More likely, the information existed in the minds of these quite valuable multilingual people. Perhaps as a result of the different Venetian and Genoese styles of making treaties, the Genoese documents are much more preoccupied with issues of language and translation than are their Venetian counterparts. Or, perhaps, the Genoese, great makers of dictionaries and speakers of a little-known dialect, were simply more aware of language problems.

The first treaty, dated November 27, 1380, was negotiated by Ellias bey on behalf of the ruler of Solgat, Inach Cotoloboga, and Giannono de Bosco, the Genoese consul in Caffa.[58] Cotoloboga's envoy, his own son, made it clear that the treaty was in the name of the person the Genoese text called "emperor," the khan Toktamysh. The parties negotiated the pact in the palace of the commune in Caffa, and four Tartars participated in making the agreement along with the ambassador Ellias bey. The treaty stated that Antonio Mazorro would make a copy in Latin (whether in true Latin or Genoese we can't say, for it did not survive), and Francesco de Gibelleto wrote the copy in Uighur to which the seal of the commune was attached. The interesting detail emerging from the legal statements about the literal act of treaty making is that apparently the Tartars relied on a Genoese notary to make a copy of the treaty for them in their own script! Nevertheless, six other Tartars actually witnessed the treaty, including their interpreter, incongruously named Giovanni Rizo. It appears that the Tartars could communicate with the Genoese only through Genoese who spoke their language; presumably they hired Rizo for this task. No member of the Tartar military hierarchy needed to speak Genoese. Still, the Genoese who helped to interpret this treaty and write it down in Uighur script were careful to date it in a respectful manner—in the Saracen era 782, the twenty-eighth day of the month written here as Sochada. Their Muslim Tartar guests, as the superior power in the region, presumably insisted on this courtesy.

The interesting mixed relationship created by the effort to come to terms is just as important here as the actual details of the treaty. The Genoese consul and officials of the commune, on behalf of its entire people (called in the treaty *franchi*) promised to be loyal and faithful to the khan. They would be friends to his friends, and enemies to his enemies, as the treaty put it. The Genoese rarely made this kind of promise to a foreign ruler, and their remarkable concession was required in order to maintain their footholds in Crimea. Additionally, they promised not to open their cities or fortifications to his enemies, and also pledged "to increase the reputation (name) of the empire according to their power, as they did for past Khans."[59] This too is a novel promise in a treaty, committing the Genoese to respect and publicize the Golden Horde. So careful were the Tartars to preserve their rights, even in territory ostensibly Genoese, that they stipulated that a Tartar official and any merchants be allowed to enter Caffa and have a market there similar to ones in the rest of the khanate. However, the Genoese consul had the right to govern the affairs of the inhabitants of Caffa, and this was an important concession of self-rule to the merchant colony there.

For his part, Ellias bey made promises to the "Grand Commune of Genoa" and Caffa, indicating that the distant Genoese capital was the power with which the Tartars were actually dealing. In this treaty, Crimea was called "Gotia." (Hence, we have an echo of historical memory, no doubt Genoese, stretching back to a homeland of the Goths in late antiquity.) The Tartars promised the Genoese that they could keep what they had in Soldaia and Cembalo, smaller ports along the coast, in the same manner as what they had in Caffa. The promise included sufficient lands and water rights, which showed a recognition that a hinterland was necessary to support the crops, animals, and possessions the Tartars agreed to permit. Water was important in Crimea, and the cities needed some lands to make them not totally dependant on imported supplies. Genoese merchants were to be safe throughout the domains of the khan; this valuable guarantee permitted traders access to a huge market. The next clause reveals a key commodity the Tartar lands supplied. Any male or female slave who fled from Caffa and went to Solgat, or who fled Solgat for Caffa, would be returned, with a fee of no more than thirty-five aspers, a kind of reward for covering expenses. Both parties practiced slavery and did not intend for either side to provide sanctuary for the other's runaways, regardless of the religion of the slaves—a subject that would be even more important in the next century as the prices of slaves continued to rise.[60] Finally, if the Tartars had any disputes with the Genoese, their own officials in Solgat and Caffa would settle them.

Ellias bey took this treaty back to Solgat, and a few months later, on February 24 1381, another representative, Iharcasso, came to make basically the same agreement.[61] One slight change in the second treaty is that the Genoese refer to Crimea by their preferred name, Gazaria, a word evoking the now distant Khazar domination of the region. The real difference here is that this treaty was witnessed by four Genoese, including their interpreter Giovanni da Camogli, and Giovanni Rizo assisted the Tartars in confirming the pact. Five new Tartars witnessed the act; their names were written down and authenticated by Sichassan Scrivan, clearly a Tartar notary. The Tartars obviously had thought about the agreement for three months and then sent back ambassadors who brought the khan's assent. In effect, the treaties are mirror images, one copy for each side, but the second rewritten for style. One immediate result of these treaties is that the Genoese in Caffa would be able to export greater numbers of Tartar and highly prized Circassian slaves.

The Venetians were not inactive in this period, but no treaty survives between them and the Tartars. A set of instructions to ambassadors sent out to the khan in 1383, already noted for its suggestions on how to extol commerce, at least provides a general sense of what Venetians expected from their relationship with the Tartars.[62] The ambassadors were authorized to spend up to 1,000 ducats (and possibly up to 1,500, in a nice mix of frugality and avarice) on gifts to the khan and others in order to accomplish their mission. Treaties tend to omit this aspect of relations, so it is useful to be reminded that presents helped smooth the way. The main tasks of the mission were to secure a reconfirmation of existing privileges and to make sure that Venetian merchants were compensated for any injuries they had suffered out there. Since the instructions do not mention any interpreters or funds to pay them, perhaps the ambassadors knew enough languages to see them through the mission.

On August 12, 1387, another treaty between the Tartars and the Genoese revealed that previous attempts to put their mixed relationship on a sounder footing had not succeeded.[63] Once again the linguistic context of the treaty is more revealing than the actual matters the treaty addressed. This treaty survives in the Latin original and is a much more formal document than the previous ones. An inhabitant of Caffa, Ivanixio de Persio served as the interpreter for his city and translated this document from the Tartar language (*lingoa tartaria*) into "Latin," likely Genoese. There are no signs here of Tartar interpreters, so once again the Genoese enjoyed a linguistic advantage. Three negotiators represented Toktamysh, designated as emperor of the Tartars. They were Oglan Sounihi bey, Boia bey, and the familiar Cotoloboga, now styled as "Lord of Solgat and Right Arm of the empire of Gazaria," the khan clearly in charge of Crimea.[64] These ambassadors had written credentials in Uighur, sealed with Khan Toktamysh's *tamoga*—the same authentication (*tughra*) used by Turkish rulers. Francesco de Gibelleto translated these documents into Genoese for the notary responsible for redacting the treaty. It was now vital for the process of treaty making for both sides to establish in writing that they had the power to make agreements. The Genoese party had similar letters from the capital and were accompanied by the consul of Caffa, two officials, and a doctor of laws—another sign of the increased formality surrounding these procedures. The Tartars managed to get on without legal advice, but, as we have seen, Muslim tradition established the parameters of treaties with infidels. This time the Tartars hosted the negotiations, which took place under a pavilion belonging to one of the ambassadors in a great field outside Solgat.

Previous treaties in Uighur script, marked with the *tamoga* of the khan, were present, and these documents must have been the two pacts just considered. Both sides agreed to ratify these pacts, another sign that they were not entirely effective. Oglan swore in the Muslim way, and the Genoese swore on the Bible. Next the parties agreed to put aside any claims for homicides, arsons, robberies, and damages of whatever type, and no one was permitted to make any claims for compensation. The list of offenses is standard fare but hints that the previous six years had seen their share of problems between Tartars and Genoese. The only exception to this amnesty is again revealing: any male or female slaves, other beasts (*sic*), and merchandise found could be claimed by the rightful owners, and Cotoloboga and the Genoese consul in Caffa would be the judges of these matters. (A treaty between the Ottoman ruler Murad I and the Genoese, also made in 1387, contained similar detailed provisions about runaways.[65]) Once again, slaves appear at the top of the list; they were the great common interest and source of profits for Tartars and Genoese, who always rose to defend the rights of owners. Finally, Cotoloboga promised, no doubt at Genoese encouragement, to supply a good and sufficient coinage at Solgat and his other territories. The conduct of trade required a sound currency, and adopting coinage marked another step the Golden Horde took to becoming a more regularized state. The relationship between these two parties, founded on slaves and silver money, ultimately experienced great stress as a result of Tamerlane's conquests in the 1390s and the early fifteenth century. After this last great Mongol conqueror's death in 1405, the Golden Horde and the Ottoman states gradually reasserted their authority, and Genoese Caffa faced new problems (which we explore later).

At the western margins of the Horde's territories, what was Bulgaria had collapsed into a group of fluid principalities, the most important of which from the Genoese perspective was Dobrugia, which controlled the coast from the Danube south to what remained of the Byzantine Empire.[66] The same basic issues of the 1380s, rivalry with Venice and the need to secure trade in the Black Sea, prompted the Genoese authorities in Pera to deal with Ivanko, prince of Dobrugia and the son of the despot Dobrotiza, the founder of the line. This trading zone, familiar to Genoese merchants for about a century as a reliable supplier of wax, honey, grain, and slaves, was just as important to Caffa as Pera. In this case, Bulgarian, Greek, and Ottoman issues made Pera the logical point of connection. The Genoese *podestà* in Pera was their most important official in the eastern Mediterranean, and Giovanni de Mezzaro struck a favorable deal with Dobrugia on May 27, 1387.[67] This treaty demonstrated what the Genoese really wanted when they were in a strong enough position to dictate the terms.

This lengthy treaty regulated many economic matters not germane to a discussion of a mixed relationship. The initial point to observe about the terms of the relationship is that perhaps 10 percent of the treaty concerned what the Genoese would do for the Bulgarians, while the other 90 percent described in detail what they wanted in return. Both sides remitted all claims and promised to keep the peace. Genoa promised Ivanko's subjects safety in the commune's lands and swore that its galleys would not attack Bulgarian territories. That was the extent of what Genoa was obliged to do. In return, the treaty lavished attention on the specifics of how Ivanko would protect Genoese traders and merchandise in his realm. Genoese consuls could settle according to their own procedures any disputes between their people and Bulgarians in criminal and civil matters. This extensive right to their own justice gave the Genoese a very privileged position in Dobrugia. These Genoese consuls operated in merchant colonies with their own loggia and churches. Here, the Genoese would be safe from bother and harm. The treaty makers went to extraordinary lengths to set no limits to the security of the Genoese—their innocence and rights to self-defense would not be disturbed even as much as children were when their parents gave them sour grapes for teething problems![68] Such was the state of Genoese innocence and protection from local laws and customs.

The treaty also established rules for what would happen if Ivanko broke the peace; these would surely have been difficult to enforce but were yet another sign of Genoese hegemony in the region. If war broke out, Ivanko promised to give the Genoese a reasonable amount of time to remove themselves and their goods to safety. The Genoese had one month to move light, easily transportable merchandise and a full six months for heavier items, presumably grain shipments. The treaty stipulated an immense penalty—100,000 gold hyperpers—for any party breaking its terms, so even in wartime, a violation of these rights would establish a huge claim to settle later. Another real advantage for the Genoese was the Bulgarian promise not to embargo the export of any goods, except in time of famine. In practice, this gave the Genoese the right to export as much grain as they could purchase. In a time of shortage, Ivanko had permission to prohibit all exports; if anyone was allowed to ship, so were the Genoese.

The Genoese imposed a limit on the customs duties of 1 percent on exports and the same on imports, an extremely low figure that was not going to enrich Ivanko's treasury. Gold, silver, pearls, and jewels were exempt from all duties; such was the common interest among Bulgarian nobles and Genoese merchants to protect the luxury trade. Ivanko promised to free all Genoese with their wives, concubines, and legitimate and natural children—a comprehensive definition of the Genoese overseas family. Excluded from this liberation of captives were slaves; both sides were careful to ensure that no person could escape slavery by this amnesty. A final striking provision affecting the issues around relationships was that the Genoese consuls had the right to determine just who counted as Genoese in any situation.[69] This provision highlights the value attached to Genoese citizenship and also the comparative generosity in handing it out; any local official could in effect make citizens. The concubines, no doubt local women, deserve notice here. This status was illegal in Genoa and represents the rougher attitudes toward women in the East. Yet the treaty itself protected the status of concubines and their children, and with a wave of the hand a consul could declare them all Genoese and eligible for the protections of the treaty.

Both sides in Pera swore to uphold the treaty, and Ivanko's ambassadors committed him to ratifying it within one month of receiving it. The Genoese swore according to Latin customs and the Bulgarians according to the Greek rite—a sign that at least one recognizable bond, Christianity, united the parties in this relationship although they remained separated by language, ritual, and much else. The agreement took place in the palace of the *podestà* in Pera, across the Golden Horn from Constantinople, still precariously held by the Byzantines and close to the Ottoman state. Apparently Ivanko's representatives, Coste and Iolpani, benefited from the services of public translator Bartolomeo Villanucio, a notary and witness to the treaty. Whether his language was Greek or Bulgarian hardly mattered; the Genoese were able to dictate the terms of this treaty and flex their muscles in the Black Sea. Their naval strength, shattered by the Venetians, still could overawe Dobrugia, and their perceived economic self-interest could be imposed on these Bulgarians. Having the upper hand, the Genoese made the treaty in Latin and worried little about interpreters. Language too was a problem for the Bulgarians, who probably needed to learn enough Genoese to bargain away their wheat and honey at low prices to people who would not even pay a meaningful customs duty. Everything about this treaty smacks of condescension. The Bulgarians did not even receive the courtesy of a guarantee of safety in Genoa, so unlikely was it that any number of them would ever make it there, except as slaves.

The Tartar Diplomatic Correspondence

In chapter 1 we looked briefly at the letter Güyüg sent to Louis IX of France in 1246. Our interest now is in how westerners and Mongols failed to make treaties in this period, how the mixed relationship, confined to letters often at cross-purposes, never developed as parties hoped or planned. Letters exchanged between khans in the East and the papacy and the kings of France in the West have attracted a great deal of scholarly attention over the years.[70] The loss of eastern archives means that the Mongol letters are scattered across western libraries and collections, and, while the papacy kept good copies of its own correspondence, the royal letters back to the Mongols do not exist. What this fragmentary correspondence can reveal is how the parties, so far apart in space and culture, explored their own self-interest while attempting to fathom the aims of the other. Güyüg's early effort to contact Louis IX, itself an attempt to answer his own (missing) letter, raised three basic points that remained a leitmotiv through the correspondence. The great khans in the East, or the later khans of the Golden Horde or the il-khans of Persia, ordered western rulers to submit, refused to convert, and explained away western queries about massacres. The Tartar rulers never abandoned their sense that these petty western rulers should behave as all others and submit, and they never quite understood the missionary zeal of the Franciscans and Dominicans who served as bearers of this correspondence. For a time in the later thirteenth century, Mongols and Christians saw in the Saracen world, especially Mamluk Egypt, a common enemy that might draw them together. But even on this point the vast distances as well as different aims prevented the parties from establishing a formal alliance against the Muslims. The value of the correspondence rests in what it reveals about what the parties intended, and what little they actually understood about one another.

An early letter shows that the relationships were indeed triangular and that the Muslims recognized the threats they faced. In 1260 Hülegü the il-khan of Persia wrote to Qutuz the Mamluk sultan of Egypt.[71] This letter, preserved by the Muslim historian Al-Maqrāzā, was a stark Mongol threat warning the Mamluks to submit or be destroyed. The khan knew that the Mamluks were once neighboring people; they were slaves mostly from the Caucasus or Central Asia. The framers of this correspondence understood enough Muslim culture to quote the Quran against Egypt's rulers, and they ended the missive with this ominous verse:

Say to Egypt, Hülegü has come
with swords unsheathed and sharp.
The mightiest of her people will become humble,
he will send their children to join the aged.

What is important here is the response: Qutuz killed the ambassadors who delivered the letter and led his armies into Syria to battle the Mongols. He knew that these acts made any negotiations impossible, and that there would be no peace between Mamluks and Mongols on terms dictated by the il-khan.

Hülegü wrote to Louis IX in 1262 through a scribe, who was able to compose the letter in Latin while remaining true to Mongol habits of expression.[72] The khan needed to provide the context for his own letter, since he seems to have assumed, probably correctly, that Louis would not be well informed about the latest events in the Middle East, at least their significance from a Mongol perspective. This letter, consisting of four basic parts, helps to provide the context Louis needed to understand and presumably obey the khan's commands. First, Hülegü carefully traced his lineage back to the great Chinggis, claiming the powers that proved his domains extended everywhere. Again, this opinion removed much of the possibilities of normal diplomacy, since an uncontrolled area, like France, was a place that had not yet properly submitted to them. Then the khan in effect introduced himself to Louis, as his friend, and in respectful tones reminded the king that the khan was a genuine and effective enemy of the Saracens. Still, there is no doubt that from a Mongol perspective the khan was ordering the French to join him in the worthwhile activity of devastating the Muslims.

Hülegü next boasted of his many recent conquests, giving special prominence to the destruction of the main Assassin fortress at Alamut in 1256 and, of course, the dramatic conquest of Baghdad in 1258. Louis, who had returned to France from the Holy Land before these events occurred, perhaps knew all this, but the khan treated these matters as news. More recently, the khan noted, he had taken Aleppo and Damascus in Syria in 1260, claiming to have freed many Christian slaves from the Mamluks.[73] The khan neglected to mention that Prince Bohemund VI of Antioch (ruled 1252–75) had ridden with the Mongols when they captured Damascus and received some lands for his support.[74] The khan's general Kitbogha was a Nestorian Christian, and this alliance between a Mongol army and the much-weakened principality of Antioch left behind no written treaty or agreement. This mixed relationship probably existed along the lines Mongols demanded; Bohemund made a kind of submission to the khan and fought alongside his forces as a faithful ally. The rulers of Christian Armenia also saw advantages to allying themselves with the Mongols, but again this happened according to Mongol practices. These farsighted rulers were gambling on the only power in the area strong enough to halt the advance of the Mamluks through the Holy Land and Syria. The khan also did not mention that the Mamluk sultan Qutuz had defeated the Mongols at 'Ain Jalut in Galilee in the autumn of 1260.[75] He had no reason to assume (yet) that this was a serious problem. But this reverse may have made the khan more interested in writing to the king of France.

The last issue in this letter concerns the khan's attempt to lure Louis back to the East in person or at least secure his military assistance as in some way the overlord of lesser powers like Antioch and Armenia. The closest the khan came to an actual concession was the promise to return Jerusalem, a city he briefly controlled in 1260, to the king. Announcing that he intended to proceed against people he called "Babylonian infidels" (the Mamluks), Hülegü wanted Christian powers to hold the coast and provide half of a trap that would catch and presumably destroy the Mamluks. This plan made sense, but Louis was too far away to contribute, and the local Christian powers too weak to hold up their end of the strategy. The khan was not offering to make a treaty with any of these powers, so we are not looking at an aborted treaty so much as an order not obeyed. This Mongol perspective on events shows their sense of the mixed and highly subordinate relationship they expected with these petty rulers in the West. Bohemund may have thought his best option was fighting alongside the khan, but in the end his efforts gained little, and Antioch fell to the Mamluks in 1268.

The Christian perspective on the Mongols, besides the early comments by Joinville and the missionaries, comes through clearest in the many letters various popes from Innocent IV onward sent to the East. These letters collectively reveal that the papacy, like the Tartar khans, had its own preconceptions about how the world worked. The tone of these papal letters is not diplomatic in the ordinary sense; instead, they summon the recipients to hear and obey. A good example of this type of papal letter is one John XXII sent in 1318 to Uzbeg, khan of the Golden Horde.[76] Although Uzbeg later became a Muslim, at this moment he was about eighteen years old and probably seemed up for grabs. By now the il-khans in Persia had converted to Islam, and the prospects for Tartar allies against the Saracens had dimmed. John XXII had to find supporters where he could, and most of this letter explained papal powers to the young khan. The pope had heard that the khan favored the Christians, so his time was not wasted in pointing out that his power over the keys to the kingdom of heaven granted the pope authority over salvation and eternal life. Therefore the khan should oppose the enemies of Christianity and allow the religion to be practiced. One specific issue the pope had to raise concerned his desire that local Christians be allowed to use their bells, a custom that had evidently lapsed, perhaps a sign of Muslim influence on the Horde. The pope resent this letter in 1323, adding a special request about the plight of Christians in Soldaia in Crimea. There the Christians had been expelled, the bells thrown down, and churches turned into mosques.[77] The Genoese had only recently reestablished themselves at Caffa, and the situation in places like Soldaia was probably still wild. So they were in no position to enforce religious tolerance there and were probably lucky to enjoy the use of church bells in Caffa itself. John XXII promised Uzbeg many spiritual rewards if he helped these people, which of course points to the heart of this mixed relationship. Uzbeg was not a Christian, and while the pope may have hoped for his conversion, he had little leverage over Uzbeg's behavior until that happened. It is unlikely that the khan ever wrote to the pope, and he confined his diplomacy to the Genoese and the tangible benefits they brought his people.

The pope wrote in 1322 to another Tartar prince, Abusca, who had been converted to Christianity by Girolamo the Franciscan bishop of Caffa.[78] John XXII was delighted by this conversion, and his letter consisted entirely of praise and blessings. Although this prince was a son of a khan, his conversion was no harbinger of favorable developments from the papacy's perspective. Although missionary efforts continued even in China, the plan of fighting Islam by converting the Tartars never worked. The papacy continued to send to the East Franciscans and Dominicans who pursued this agenda, but they were not really attempting to establish a relationship with local people. Instead, the policy was to press for a submission as rigorous as what the khans demanded from the defeated. The delicate maneuvering that characterized treaty making satisfied neither popes or khans.

The treaties discussed here were contracts outlining the terms by which the parties planned or simply hoped to accomplish their specific ends by satisfying to some degree the needs of a partner. More cold blooded than a marriage agreement, a treaty that crossed one or more of the big barriers of religion, language, or ethnicity compelled the parties to agree on what was crucial to their relationship. Hence, treaties have been rewarding to explore in detail because they are the lingering records of deeply felt self-interest by vanished peoples and states. When the original negotiators pruned away the inessentials, they found an irreducible core of wealth and war. They understood comparative advantage but frequently yielded to protectionist impulses, especially as they concerned Others. Ambassadors, translators, and merchants were in the best position to see across the barriers and possibly find between them a small area of common ground. Diplomatic correspondence sometimes preceded successful treaty making and at other times signaled a mutually frustrating failure to communicate.

A major theme in treaties was the collective search for justice—for fair treatment through a process that served self-interest and honor even as it acknowledged the needs of others. Threatening letters or favors dispensed as acts of grace implied hierarchical relationships that were not between equals in any sense. Treaties were sometimes between roughly equal partners but also might subordinate weaker powers to stronger ones. Even in the most unequal treaty some claims to justice survived. This justice often amounted to simple fairness in terms of power exercised or economic exchanges. Hence, even the idea of a treaty recognized the rights and claims of others, which may be why at times some cultures completely rejected the concept.

Even a short truce posed the same issues of fairness to both parties and represented a relationship.

Treaties, and failures to make treaties, reveal how mixed relationships may or may not have developed. In the Far East, Mongol China eventually accommodated itself to diplomacy, and in the Far West kingdoms in Iberia figured out how to make and break treaties according to some rules.[79] In the middle ground, the area stretching from the Black Sea through the Aegean to the Holy Land and Egypt, treaties crossed linguistic, confessional, and ethnic frontiers that forced parties to confront their own senses of identity by negotiating with Others. Defining who was Genoese or Venetian in the East fostered clearer thinking about the legal and ethnic identity these labels signaled. New types of people, like the *guasmuls* or the *poulains*, were the fruit of mixed marriages and sexual relationships and created new categories that needed to be fit into existing concepts of identity. Sometimes distance and a rigid sense of otherness prevented peoples from coming to terms in a treaty or even prevented their grasping foreign concepts of identity, like strict political or religious subordination. Treaties forged mixed relationships in which each party tried to gain economic advantages over the other and seldom recognized any benefits to equitable trade. On a more personal level, details about slaves reminded everyone that the common practice of slavery further complicated identities because people, now considered to be legitimate items of commerce, passed across the frontiers. As a Tartar passed from the Golden Horde through Caffa or Cyprus on her way west, her identity was as complex as that of a Genoese or Venetian ambassador passing in the other direction.

Military plans loomed large in treaty making or the search for allies. Great empires like the Byzantine, Mamluk, Mongol, and Ottoman were preoccupied with wars and needed to take occasional notice of peoples like the Venetians and Genoese whose navies were important. However powerful the fleets of the maritime republics were, they could not conquer or absorb any eastern state. Hence, these relationships were always at cross purposes. People did fight together, and it would be worth knowing more about the experiences of Bohemund of Antioch riding with the Mongols.

Trade supplied another common ground where the self-interest of both parties overlapped. Venice and Genoa had strong fleets because they needed to carry back to the West the grain, slaves, spices, cotton, honey, hides, and all the rest for which markets far away rewarded the intrepid with big profits. Much of this trade occurred across major barriers of faith and language, and was viewed with suspicion by the pure of heart because it fed a taste for debilitating luxuries and enriched potential or actual enemies. Yet, in and outside the rules of treaties, such trade continued and flourished. Ordinary relationships that facilitated such relatively peaceful exchanges did not stop wars, crusades, or fanatics on all sides from trying to end it in the name of political or religious purity. Trade rewarded realists familiar with the gray zones of life and those who saw how their self-interest sometimes coincided with those of an ostensible enemy. This type of person, not just merchants but the whole range of people who mixed with the Others at all levels, exemplified the benefits of an open mind. Sometimes people went too far in these endeavors or came to identify with the Other so closely as to want to join them. Such people, often judged to be renegades, pushed all types of self-interest to an extreme beyond the more constrained aims of officials making treaties.

CHAPTER FOUR

Renegades and Opportunists

The mixed relationships considered thus far existed across a spectrum from the purely voluntary on both sides, like a treaty between two sovereign states, to the completely involuntary on one side, like the bond between master and slave. (There seem to have been no mixed relationships in which both parties are unwilling.) It is time to take this medieval context of mixed relationships and examine it from another perspective by looking at the phenomenon of the renegade. As a category, the renegade might define an individual or an entire people; one member of a relationship or all of them. The term naturally implies a judgment, usually by the group feeling betrayed, that the renegade is some sort of traitor, a person who has left one group for another, usually an enemy. Treason will figure in this analysis but not medieval treachery in its entirety. Temporary or strategic renegades need not detain us either. Sometimes, especially in the age of holy wars, one Muslim or Christian state found it temporarily convenient to become allies with the "infidels" against their coreligionists. These strategies for survival often involved treachery and accusations of bad faith, but momentary military necessity rather than a long-term impulse to change identities drove these decisions. A temporary mixed alliance did not form a genuine relationship between the parties.

The subject here is not the Florentine betraying his city to the Sienese but the renegade who crossed one of the big boundaries of faith, language, ethnicity, or color. A renegade is a person who willingly or unwillingly breaks a strong tie and then attempts to forge another. Hence the subject is partly motive, which is always difficult for the historian to fathom. A person may become a renegade at the point where a feigned or insincere loyalty becomes impossible to sustain, and the person moves from private hypocrit to public renegade. It is also important to keep in mind the push-pull aspects of the phenomenon. Some people may be unwilling renegades, pushed out of their group by personal worries or a perceived lack of fit by one's ostensible people. On the other side are the attractions, actual or illusory, that a person may feel when looking across the boundary. Some traitors fit these categories

—voluntary or coerced, compelled or lured, as do some marriage partners, apostates, and other transgressors of the so-called rules. Given the nature of relationship, the renegade seems different to those he or she has betrayed, and to those who benefit from the switch. But the test of loyalty to the new group was often stern for medieval renegades, and they found it hard to shed a reputation for unreliability. Hence to be a renegade was an identity formed in an act viewed with repugnance by some and grudging admiration by others. By forging the identity of renegades in the context of mixed relationships, the people under review here, by crossing the boundaries, help explain how permeable these barriers were and how they defined those on one side or the other.

Identity formation occurs in a cultural context that sets the rules for self expression, and the context changes across the spaces and peoples in this study. In a broad sense the common features of Islam, Christianity, and Judaism define the apostate in such a way as to make this person a distinctly western phenomenon. Not all cultures demonized the creedal renegade in this manner. "Because Africans did not see their traditional religious understanding as complete and unerring, they were open to practices and beliefs from elsewhere and to new revelations that might come to individuals from the spirit world."[1] For these Africans, and animist Tartars, becoming a religious renegade would make little or no sense, while Muslims, Jews, and Christians, drawing on their sense of particular, exclusive revelations, were intensely preoccupied with apostates. Miguel Cervantes defined *renegar* (to become a renegade) as "to give the soul to Satan" and this pithy remark, literally demonizing the Other, highlights loyalty to one's creed as the core value.[2] Because so much depended on one's perspective about the person and the act, it is useful to expand the concept of the renegade and see this person as being on a continuum ranging from involuntary through a gray zone into voluntary acts of betrayal. The best way to proceed with this analysis is to examine some archetypal people and place their types along the continuum, and to keep in mind that this method also categorizes relationships, broken and new. Hence, the renegade may be at the same time a hero and a traitor; it is a question of context, dates, and places. Since these relationships were not static but changed over time in a historical context, it is no surprise to find the renegade in the gray zone as a potential or actual harmonizer. The renegade, whose complex identity often included new language and cultural skills, could become a bridge between the two worlds and shed his or her status as traitor to either one of them.

The involuntary renegade may at first glance appear to be an oxymoron, but this is true only if choice is fundamental to the act of becoming a renegade. Consider the figure of Moses, not just as the character in Hebrew scripture but also as a historical type whose meaning changed over time.[3] According to the standard version of events, he was abandoned as a child, rescued from the Nile, raised as an Egyptian, and achieved a position of prominence in that culture. All the time, he was an unknowing renegade, a person whose daily life was a constant sequence of betrayals of his Hebrew people and faith. Although this was not his fault, he had become an enemy to his people, only to be awakened to his true heritage and mission. This Moses, the involuntary (and temporary) renegade stands in stark contrast to Moses as a true Egyptian prince who betrayed his own people by leading their Hebrew slaves to freedom.[4] Moses the prince was to his fellow Egyptians a true traitor.

The exile justly or unjustly expelled from his or her native land is another type of involuntary renegade. The wandering exiles, unlucky individuals like Dante or entire peoples removed from their homelands, comprise a set of renegades on which the proper perspective is vital. An exile was unlikely to accept the fairness of the assigned status, so to this person the exilers may have seemed the true renegades, the betrayers of the cause or people. Exiles also had to form sustaining relationships with their new hosts. For my purposes, the exiles wandering farthest are the most interesting because they had to learn new languages and cultures in order to survive, and these acts can leave traces in the historical record. Dante would be more valuable to this study if he had gone off to the Golden Horde of the Tartars instead of Verona to write his poetry of revenge, and how different that poetry might have been.

Since the idea of betrayal necessarily involves a moral perspective, there is naturally a gray zone where choices and morality conflict or are ambiguous.[5] As Primo Levi's telling analysis of this part of the continuum reminds us, perspective and moral choice can become quite confusing when those not faced with the dilemma presume to examine those who were. The best example in the heart of the gray zone is the mercenary, the man who fights for money. The mercenary could be neutral, betraying no one, not his own people, his opponents, and certainly not his employer. The Vikings (Varangians) who had traveled from Scandinavia to Constantinople to fight for the Byzantine emperors were so far from home that their becoming mercenaries betrayed no one. But this is a lucky mercenary, and a rare one to expose himself to no reproaches from any quarter. The question to be asked here is of course: who is the mercenary fighting, the friend or foe of his own people? A good example of this problem has already appeared in the case of the Catalan Grand Company, that band of Catalan mercenaries originally coming to the Aegean in the early fourteenth century to fight for the Byzantine emperor against the Turks. At first there was no problem here from the Christian perspective; Catholic Catalans traveled far from home to earn money by fighting for other Christians, admittedly Orthodox ones, against Muslims. Back home in Aragon-Catalonia no one considered these adventurers to be renegades; they were pure opportunists. But the Catalans under Roger de

Flor eventually turned on their employers and became renegades from the Byzantine perspective. Even worse, they began to attack the Venetians and the local French heirs of the original crusaders. When the Catalans crossed the line and left the Turks alone to take over lands controlled by fellow western Christians, they would appear to the Greeks to be renegades and even worse enemies than the Muslims. And yet from their own perspective, these Catalans no doubt had ample justifications for their acts. Even worse were those individuals who openly fought for one's enemies—the clearest case here would be Christians who fought for pay for Muslim powers, or vice versa, whether or not these people eventually decided to convert. In this case fighting for the enemy of one's people pushed the mercenary out of the gray zone and into clear treachery.

At one extreme of the renegade continuum are the true voluntary traitors and apostates. Like individuals, groups were capable of this extreme act: witness those Hebrews at the foot of Mount Sinai who betrayed the God who had delivered them from Egypt, as well as Moses. Their exemplary punishment served as a warning to all potential traitors, and the names and fates of Dathan and Abiram in particular became a proverbial curse in the Middle Ages on those who broke agreements.[6] This type of renegade deserved the fiery pit, in this case the punishment of many besides the ringleaders. In a Christian context, the classic traitor was Judas, the man who was guilty of betraying an innocent Jesus to his enemies who put him to death. These archetypal acts of betrayal define the renegade at the extreme, but they do not present the kinds of opportunities available to ordinary people in daily circumstances. So the classic traitors, or an apostate like the fourth-century Roman emperor Julian who left Christianity to become a pagan, do not fit my purposes here. But the type needs to be kept in mind—not all traitors or apostates, but those crossing the line into voluntary treachery by betraying across the boundaries of religion, language, ethnicity, or color. Dante's categories of the worst sinners at the bottom of Hell are a useful guide to finding these renegades. Judas joined Brutus and Cassius as the worst traitors of all time down there, but again these spectacular renegades are not the main concern. For Dante the line between being a common if archtraitor and being a renegade seems to be crossed at three points: those betraying their own kin, their country, and their friends and benefactors.[7] Looking for potential renegades in mixed marriages, among those who fight for the enemies of their own people, and among those who make money at the expense of their group are useful ways to deepen understanding of the true renegade.

Finally, before exploring some medieval renegades in the eastern Mediterranean, it must be acknowledged that the status of renegade was often gendered. For example, wherever fighting determined the possibilities to be a renegade, as with mercenaries, these were basically male activities. For women and nonfighting men, the assigned roles of their sex and the hold of faith shaped their potential experiences as renegades. Being a captive put women and men in the position of becoming renegades if they became comfortable in their status and joined up with their captors. There are many examples of women and men, slaves and captives, not seeking to escape or be ransomed in the long run but instead choosing, with varying degrees of liberty, to become a member of the dominant group. At the other extreme, few women held enough power to become meaningful, voluntary traitors. So, there were fewer women in the gray zone as fighters but possibly more in positions aiding or preparing to take revenge on the enemies of their people. Women were not often formally exiled for the same reasons, but as captives and slaves they figured among the involuntary renegades. Marriage and apostasy gave women an equal chance to become renegades, and their economic activities also posed the same moral challenges faced by men. In brief, the spectacular renegades were more likely to be men, but in the continuum of renegades in daily life, women should be well represented.

The eastern Mediterranean proves to be fertile ground for finding renegades. All types of sources need to be exploited in searching for renegades because they often operated behind the scenes, and the group they left behind had no reason to celebrate their acts or even remember them. The core areas of the Mongols, Muslims, and Catholic Christians were more likely to produce garden-variety political traitors, who are not the subject of this book. Some examples help show how the continuum of types of renegades reveals further subtleties in mixed relationships of all kinds.

Digenis Akritis

Digenis Akritis, whose name in Greek means "Double Descent Frontiersman," was a main character in a Byzantine epic or series of tales about a legendary hero who may be placed in the ninth or tenth centuries.[8] This epic concerns the heroic deeds of Digenis, but as his name suggests, the main interest is in his parents. (Digenis clearly evokes Monogenis, the only begotten Jesus, who was descended from God, but also half one thing and half another.) The hero's father was a Muslim emir, himself the son of a Greek father and an Arab mother. This emir, usually called in the poem an *ethnikos*, or heathen, fell in love with a Greek Christian woman captured in a raid. The emir converted and married the girl, thus becoming in the eyes of the Muslims, especially his mother, a renegade. His mother sends a letter containing a very good analysis of what it meant to be a renegade. The question of course is: whose values are actually reflected in this text? For the moment, let the values be as nonspecific to any faith or ethnicity, instead reflecting a deeper stratum of common beliefs about honor among Muslims and Christians.

> How could you renounce your kinsmen and faith and country
> And become a reproach to all Syria?
> We are abominated by all men
> As deniers of the faith, as law-breakers
> And for not having observed well the Prophet's words.
> What has happened to you, my child? Have you forgotten these things?
> How could you not remember your father's deeds,
> How many Romans he slew, how many he carried off as slaves?
> Did he not fill prisons with generals and toparchs?
> Did he not plunder many of the themes in Roman territory
> And carry off beautiful high-born girls as prisoners?
> Was he not pressured, like you, to become a renegade?
>
> . . . .
>
> But he kept the Prophet's commandments,
> Spurned renown and paid no attention to wealth,
> And they hewed him limb from limb and took away his sword.
> But you, not even under compulsion, have abandoned everything at once,
> Your faith, your kinsmen and me, your mother.[9]

The emir's mother introduces many new issues into what it meant to be a renegade. Given the nature of this source and its transmission, the relative importance of these factors remains uncertain, but the order in which they appear in this work must reveal something about their relative weight. From the beginning the mother's lament privileges three loyalties—family, faith, and country. But her entry into these subjects takes place in the overall context of reputation, of honor, because that value is the one the loyalties all have in common. Peregrine Horden and Nicholas Purcell have proposed that honor might be one of the particular values (along with shame) of the Mediterranean microecologies because it is a finite resource, in a way like water, and hence strongly nurtured and protected.[10] Certainly, the emir's mother conveys a strong sense that honor is a precious commodity to be hoarded and, once lost, impossible to recover. The emir has become a reproach to his own people in Syria, and his reputation and that of his family has been destroyed. To be a denier of the faith in Islam was of course also a serious charge—to break the Prophet's laws and deny his words by becoming an apostate carried a sentence of death. Oddly, the emir's mother brings up his father's noble deeds, but of course it must be remembered that his father had himself become a renegade by converting to Islam. Still, the mother's point is that she did not care for the family's reputation in Byzantine lands, but instead about what honor meant in Syria. There, the emir's father was remembered for his conquests and booty, for his valor as a warrior and the esteem it brought his family. Hence, the mother's most important question, "Was he not pressured, like you, to become a renegade?" She refers to his being surrounded and threatened by loss of possessions and death, but he remained loyal to his faith. By contrast, the emir has succumbed to love, in a way, but also to the attractions of power and wealth that accrue to him as a member of Byzantine society.

One of the many ironies here is that soon enough the emir's mother willingly converts to Christianity and flees Syria for Byzantine lands. Her own conduct contradicts all her views about being a renegade; such is the appeal of faith in this instance, even though the poem has several instances where characters renounce faith for love. From the Byzantine perspective of the poem, the emir's mother is now a heroine and has increased her honor. Still, family counts as a primary loyalty, and the desire to keep the kin together produces several conversions to foster that goal. Being a renegade to one's faith only seems less serious here because the other side of the story is absent; from the Muslim perspective the emir is a damned traitor. Being loyal to one's territory counted for something, but less than it did under the Roman state, perhaps because frontiers were so fluid and the state itself weaker than it had been.

Now that the family has been reunited the emir and his wife have brought Digenis into the world. Their marriage has resulted from love (Eros) bringing two people of different races into one faith.[11] The word for "different race" here is a hybrid of *allo* and *phylon*, implying a strong difference between the two groups, Greek and Arab. A few lines later the poem also observes that many have changed their faith because of desire (love).[12] There is no doubt that the marriage between the emir and the Greek woman is a mixed relationship, here brought about by love. Even loyalty to religion might succumb in the face of this strong force in peoples' lives. Somehow the power of love does not make marriage dishonorable in this context where people recognize that attraction and calculations of wealth crossed the boundaries between Greek and Arab. It appears that love and honor trump religion and ethnicity.

The story thus far set the stage for the appearance of Digenis Akritis, the hero of the tale. His role as frontiersman, the lonely defender of Cappadocia against all enemies, is not the main concern. Rather, his double descent, an "ethnic" (heathen) on his father's side and a Roman on his mother's, determines his unique status in this frontier society in eastern Anatolia. Still, whatever his mixed heritage, the poem is careful to note that he has a white and rosy face, and that his eventual bride, also Roman, has a face like snow.[13] Canons of ancient and medieval physiognomy declared these white faces as the best to have, so their appearance here is not surprising. But in contrast the poem states that Digenis's main opponents, the Arab Muslims, are awful Ethiopians and descended from slaves.[14] In a roughly contemporary source, the tenth-century novel *The Life of St Andrew the Fool*, Ethiopians appear several times as black demons, even the devil himself is a huge black man.[15] This poem considers the Ethiopians to be a terrible and shameful people; their dishonor seems to result from their faith, since someone like the emir could cast off this demeaning status. It is also curious that Ethiopians, admittedly dark, do not appear so in this poem, and thus they were capable of changing. It could be that the term *Ethiopian* is simply a learned synonym for *Arab*.

These Ethiopians are said to descend from slaves, and this opinion must derive from the old story about Hagar and Ishmael. If the ethnographic gaze of this poem sees the Arab people as coming from Abraham through his wife's slave Hagar, then it was possible to insult the entire race as unfree and hence profoundly dishonorable. A fine balance dictated not pushing this point too far, for to demean these enemies meant that the accomplishments of heroes like Digenis also paled. And if these enemies converted and came over to the Romans, they became suitable parents for the very same heroes. Hence this poem encourages a close look at honor in mixed relationships as well as the things people could change, like their faith, and the things they could not. In a remarkable passage from Byzantine hagiography, Saint Andrew the Fool rejects a gift of dates from a eunuch slave who received the fruit in exchange for sodomy. Andrew believes that this slave should have been willing to submit to any punishment or persecution rather than commit this act. "Thus if the slaves do not bow to the abominable sodomitic passion of their masters they are blessed and thrice blessed, for thanks to the torments you mention they will be reckoned with the martyrs."[16] Honor required a slave to rebel against this sin, but the master still had the right to punish the slave. In the East the occasionally competing claims of slavery, color, and religion complicated loyalties.

Obadiah the Norman

The chance survival in the Cairo Geniza of a few pieces of an autobiography make it possible to reconstruct this remarkable tale of a spectacular renegade.[17] Making sense of this story requires considerable conjecture, but at least here the convert Obadiah controls the record; his own words provide nearly all the details.[18] Shortly after 1071 in Oppido, a small town near Bari in southern Italy, a woman named Maria (nothing is known about her but the name) gave birth to twins Roger and John—the future Obadiah. She was married to a Norman knight named Dreux, who may have been in charge of the town. This possibly mixed marriage between a newcomer to the region and a woman who may have been from old inhabitants (Greek, Lombard, or indigenous Italic—the choices are numerous) was a common means by which the Norman mercenaries turned themselves into a settled power in the area, eventually, under their heroic leaders like Robert Guiscard, establishing states in the Mezzogiorno and Sicily. At first the Normans, true outsiders, fought for whatever power could pay them, whether Lombard princes or Roman pontiffs. But these mercenaries soon saw opportunities to establish themselves as the true rulers in the region. This Dreux was now a noble player in this game, and his son John was destined for a career in the church. John, a product of a Christian marriage, was maybe of "double descent" like Digenis. Unfortunately, the sources do not reveal what languages he spoke, but he must have known Norman French and Latin at least, and he certainly learned Hebrew well.

What little John tells about his youth concerns a story about Andreas, the renegade archbishop of Bari. The rumor eventually reached Bari that this Andreas fled to Constantinople, converted to Judaism, was circumcised, and then went to Cairo. Joshua Prawer has looked closely for the seeds of truth in this rumor and found a captured archbishop of Bari named Urso in Egypt around the time of the First Crusade (1095–99) who had converted, presumably to Islam.[19] There was indeed an Andreas archbishop of Bari who went to Constantinople in 1066 and was never heard from again.[20] These stories may have become conflated in young John's mind and set an example that it was possible to entertain doubts about Christianity, convert, and then flee to the only safe place for such a person, the world of Islam. John believed that Andreas had become a Jew, not a safe decision for any Latin or Greek Christian in southern Italy to make. Also as a youth, John dreamt that he was officiating in a church and was addressed by someone; the text breaks off at this point and the content of the message is unknown but was striking enough for Obadiah to recall and write down years later.

As a young man in the church at the time of the preaching of the First Crusade, around 1096, when John was probably in his mid-twenties, he relates that he had developed a fear of the uncircumcised.[21] What could this have meant in a place where John would have feared his fellow Christians, even his father and twin brother, and indeed his own body? Perhaps John was somehow drawn to the covenant with Abraham and its promise of God's protection. In the context of local excitement about the crusade, in which the Norman Bohemund of Taranto, Guiscard's son, would take a prominent role, John's fears became more generalized. He became fixated on a passage from Joel (2:31), which he later quoted in Latin: "Sol convertitur in tenebras et luna in sanguinem antequam veniat dies Domini magnus et horribilis" —and in his text John, who later became Obadiah, quoted it in Hebrew as well.[22] All students of this conversion have closely scrutinized this passage. S. D. Goitein believes it showed that his conversion was a personal, Christian matter in the sense that no one converted him to Judaism.[23] Prawer looks at this passage because it is a key to studying John's motives for his eventual conversion to Judaism. A standard translation is, "The sun shall be turned into darkness and the moon into blood before the great and terrible day of the Lord comes."[24] The prophet Joel, another witness to a troubled time, interested Christians because he seemed to foretell the coming of the messiah and the descent of the Holy Spirit. Joel was the kind of prophet people turned to in times of signs and wars, a good description of the Christian west at the beginning of the First Crusade.

For John the day of the Lord was the Day of Judgment and the coming of the messiah; if Prawer is right, John saw Joel as predicting a future that was coming true in his own time, in the late 1090s or soon thereafter.[25] John did not accept the standard Christian exegesis that Joel predicted something that had already come to pass in the time of Jesus. Because John began to see things differently, he also viewed the crusading movement in a novel way, as a sign that the coming of the messiah was imminent. Norman Golb has also noted that eclipses around the time of the first crusade may have given special meaning to this passage from Joel as John understood it.[26] These Normans in Italy, cultural transplants who frequently married local women, seem to have been especially fervent crusaders, willing to journey even farther east to recover Jerusalem. More travel and new experiences would have been particularly appealing to a certain sort of adventurer in the next generation. A younger son training to be a member of the clergy, John directed his sense of Norman adventure toward a novel understanding of scripture, and a new life in the East apart from the path taken by the crusaders. It is also clear that John was aware of crusader hostility (and worse) toward Jews. In his memoirs the convert remembered that the crusaders were hostile to the enemies (presumably Jews) they were leaving behind while going to Jerusalem.[27] John was becoming a renegade by sympathizing with the faith of these victims of crusader violence. Some combination of his own prophetic understanding and a highly unusual identifying with oppressed people compelled John to become a renegade.

A surviving fragment of a prayer book colophon in Obadiah's own hand dates his conversion to 1102, and an ingenious reconstruction of another fragment strongly suggests that this conversion took place in Italy.[28] Where the name "Obadiah" (Servant of God) came from is not clear, but it fits the bearer's sense that he was a witness to stirring events who acted upon them. Benjamin Z. Kedar rightly points out that none of this explains why the conversion and flight were delayed from the time of the preaching of the first crusade (1096), and he suggests that messianic concerns and crusader difficulties in the East may have prompted a spiritual crisis in 1102.[29] Eventually, Obadiah learned enough Hebrew to write down the circumstances of his life, but again it is not known where he mastered this language. What is clear from Obadiah's account is that he somehow traveled to Baghdad, where the local Jewish community supported him, and where he presumably advanced his education in Judaism and the Hebrew language.[30] Obadiah counts as a spectacular renegade because he made his way, again by unknown means, across the violent world of the Holy Land at the time when crusaders were establishing their Latin Kingdom, and settled in the great capital of Islam. He did all this apparently by himself and with few resources, since his account stresses the charity of the Jewish communities supporting him. In Baghdad, Obadiah joined the circle of orphans who studied Hebrew and sacred texts, and thus this mature man, already learned in Latin and other religious texts, began a new life.

Obadiah wrote in detail about the discrimination Jews suffered under Muslim rule in Baghdad. He must have been struck that the group he joined was not much better off than it was in southern Italy, and he must have known about the destruction of the Jewish community in Jerusalem in 1099 and the ban crusaders placed on their living in this city. Still, the basic fact was that he would have been executed back home but was allowed to practice his new faith in Baghdad. Obadiah was also sensitive to any news about the coming of the messiah, and he reported a message announcing the imminent gathering of Jews to Jerusalem where the messiah would appear.[31] Obadiah notes that nothing in fact happened and that the gentiles (in this context Muslims) and the uncircumcised (Christians) mocked the Jews over this. It is not surprising that Obadiah remained alert to the imminent coming of the messiah, and his new faith seems to have survived this disappointment. Obadiah spent some time in the second decade of the twelfth century in Aleppo and then Damascus, where the local community of Jews again maintained him as an act of charity. Obadiah never mentions work (perhaps not the focus of his autobiography), but he is careful to note the groups who made his life possible. It is clear that he copied a manuscript, perhaps for hire, and his handwriting has been identified in some songs, so he may also have been a conduit for western church music entering the world of Hebrew liturgy.[32] Perhaps Obadiah was for all these reasons a source of pride to the other Jews, a kind of celebrity convert and renegade who bolstered their confidence during difficult times. At any rate Obadiah passed these years along the eastern borders of the Christian

Latin Kingdom; in the surviving text he says he never reached Jerusalem itself but spent time in Dan among Jews, at Banyas, a Muslim fortress east of the Jordan.[33]

The last event Obadiah discusses, and this would be around 1122, concerns his time in Dan, among the poor Jewish community. While Obadiah is there a man named Solomon the Karaite arrives and announces that God is going to gather all the Jews to Jerusalem within the next two and a half months. Obadiah sensibly asks Solomon how he knows this, and Solomon answers that he is the man people were waiting for, the messiah.[34] Obadiah and Solomon then conduct a curious conversation in which Obadiah reveals detailed knowledge about the messiah's proper lineage and asks for a sign to prove this claim, and Solomon expands on his plans and diet—claiming not to eat bread or drink water. The text breaks off at the point where Obadiah announces he is going to Egypt via Tyre (still in Muslim hands and hence safe passage for him), after the so-called messiah warns him it is a waste of time since the gathering in of the Jews is coming so soon. Since this text ended up in Egypt, scholars assume that Obadiah made this journey, but nothing more is yet known about him.

Obadiah's experiences in the East reveal a renegade especially attuned to messianic rumors who finds a warm welcome in the Jewish communities there. Himself perhaps the product of a mixed relationship, Obadiah's life was a testimony to the multicultural experiences available to an intrepid person. Converting to Judaism and flight were rare experiences in the medieval West, so Obadiah did not lead a typical life on any level. At the time of the crusades, Christian clerics did not ordinarily become renegades because of messianic visions. This life serves as a reminder that the renegade's chances of entering the historical record were small, yet his mere presence in Baghdad and Damascus must have affected Jewish morale there in stressful times. His highly idiosyncratic experiences also serve as a reminder that the more that is known about the circumstances of individual renegades, the less typical they appear. By way of contrast, another Jewish conversion became public as a result of a dream Samau'al al-Maghribī had on the night of November 8, 1163.[35] Intellectual and spiritual concerns prompted Samau'al to change religions, but he joined the majority community and was welcomed into Islam, with no changes for his flourishing career as a scientist and physician. For Samau'al dreams too played a role in his decision to become a learned renegade to his family and fellow Jews. He did not have to flee and change his life (unlike Obadiah); he wrote a polemic against his former coreligionists and became famous. Religious apostates are only a small part of the story of renegades in this chapter, whose focus remains on the relationships made and broken as a result of these decisions. Obadiah and Samau'al were notable because they could write; others needed to have their stories told by others.

Firuz

At the same time that Obadiah was experiencing his religious awakening, the armies of the first crusade were also being spiritually transformed by their difficult march and battles across Asia Minor.[36] After the massacres of Jews in the Rhineland and the first battles with the Turks, the depleted main force arrived at Antioch in October 1097. The ensuing siege of Antioch produced a notable renegade whose name in the western sources, Pyrrus, may have evoked in the learned a recollection of costly victory in the time of the ancient Greeks and Romans. More plausibly called Firuz, his role in ending the siege on the night of June 2, 1098, provides a glimpse of how an apparent act of treachery appeared to a number of witnesses and subsequent commentators. Multiple accounts from Muslim and Christian sources make this renegade an especially well-documented example of how context determines the perspective on the traitor's motives. A close look at Firuz takes the story of renegades beyond apostasy to treason; yet to some he was a hero.

The complex narrative of what exactly happened at Antioch, where the army knew dissension and heightened spiritual tensions, has been frequently and well told.[37] Various writers explained Firuz's treachery differently. Probably the best known of these accounts is the anonymous *Gesta Francorum* (Deeds of the Franks), a work providing source material for some later versions and one with wide readership in the west.[38] In this narrative, a Turkish emir named Firuz, commanding three towers in Antioch, became the friend of Bohemund, one of the crusade's leaders. This mixed relationship somehow crossed battle lines and linguistic barriers. The source provides no clue as to how a friendship developed in these circumstances, but the parties exchanged messages, and Bohemund enticed Firuz into promising to betray the city and to become a Christian. Bohemund used this secret to extract from his fellow commanders an agreement to turn over the city to whoever succeeded in breaking into it. The besiegers also knew that a large Turkish relief army was making its way to Antioch, so it was desirable to take the city quickly. Bohemund then called on Firuz's help, and, as a token of his sincerity, the Turk sent his son to Bohemund as surety that he would actually allow the crusaders into the city. On the appointed night Bohemund's forces scaled the wall where Firuz was in charge, and as they appeared on top of the wall Firuz was alarmed at the small size of the force, fearing it would fail. So he exclaimed in Greek "We have few Franks" (the author provides this comment in phonetic Latin letters for the Greek and then the Latin translation). Then a larger number of men scaled the walls, eventually opened a gate, and proceeded to take the city, slaughtering many Saracens and Turks along the way, including Firuz's own brother.

This source provides no real motive for why Firuz became a renegade, apart from an implausible friendship with the Norman leader from southern Italy. Firuz had a son who played the role of pledge in this account. Finally, Firuz spoke Greek, which suggests that his own ethnicity was more complicated than this source, where he is simply a Turk, allows. This author found nothing more to say about Firuz, so how he might have benefited from his treachery remains unknown.

Another well-known account of the first crusade, by the eyewitness Fulcher of Chartres, tells a similar story, though it never names the faithless Turk.[39] What is striking here is that Fulcher provides a clear motive for this Turk's acts: Jesus appeared to him and told him to give Antioch back to the Christians. The Turk then gave his son to Bohemund and the city fell; this account is close to what the Gesta supplied but does not have the Turk speaking any Greek. A more complete account by yet another witness, Raymond D'Aguilers, a chaplain in the service of Count Raymond of Toulouse, offers more details on some of the key issues.[40] Raymond provides more of a historical context, and he knows that Antioch had been in Byzantine hands only fourteen years before and that many Greeks and Armenians remained in the city. Some of these people became Turks and took wives. Raymond suggests that these were the people who were in constant communication with the Frankish besiegers, who knew that a relief force was on the way. One of the Turks (and Raymond is careful to distinguish Turks from Saracens) in the city sent word to the crusaders (not just Bohemund) that he wished to hand over the city.[41] Raymond does not name the traitor, nor does he give any special prominence to Bohemund in initiating this plan or the attack. His account of the conquest of Antioch resembles the others and emphasizes looting and the slaughter of its inhabitants. Unable to cite an explicit motive for this act, Raymond, who also had no desire to exalt Bohemund, left an ambiguous portrait of his renegade.

Abbot Guibert of Nogent, the famous autobiographer and astute analyst of relics, also wrote, at some distance in space and time from the actual events, a history of the first crusade, but he was well placed to interrogate returning veterans.[42] Guibert's longer version of Firuz's story emphasizes the relationship that slowly grew between him and Bohemund. Not claiming to know the actual terms of their agreement, Guibert stresses that Bohemund gradually convinced Firuz to turn over Antioch and also become a Christian. Guibert has Firuz send his son to Bohemund to guarantee that he will surrender his towers to the crusaders. Here too Firuz speaks Greek, again suggesting that this Muslim may be a recent convert. As the Franks come over the walls, Guibert has them shouting "God wills it" (*Deus id vult*), a clear sign of how the participants, not party to any deal between Firuz and Bohemund, saw instead the providential nature of their entry into Antioch. Perhaps this fervor explains another aspect of the account, the mistaken killing of Firuz's brother, as well as something Guibert makes much of, the slaughter of the Turks and Muslims of both sexes, with not even the elders spared. Later in his account Guibert mentions that Firuz did indeed convert and was at the siege of Jerusalem.[43] But this traitor proved treacherous yet again, deserted Christianity, and returned to his faith.

Guibert mentions Fulcher's account in order to cast doubt on his explanation for why Firuz became a traitor in the first place.[44] Guibert does not believe Fulcher's story that God appeared to Firuz and encouraged his conversion. Guibert instead agrees with other witnesses who do not say this. The issue here is again the motive for treachery. This discussion occurs in the context of Guibert's analysis of the discovery of the Holy Lance (which he also doubts) and other so-called divine interventions in the crusade. Guibert concedes that Firuz existed, that he was a real person in the history of these events, but he was not motivated by a divine command. Instead, Guibert sees the roots of this treachery in a human relationship with Bohemund. Rejecting any supernatural explanation for this betrayal leaves Guibert resting his argument on an improbable mixed friendship.

The *Chanson d'Antioche* is part of a cycle of French poems, *chansons de gestes*, on the crusades. Reworked by many hands and relying on a number of sources, this poem is about the conquest of Antioch. Conceived originally by Richard the Pilgrim as a romance set in the realities of 1098, this imaginative tale was meant to appeal to a French courtly audience, with all its expectations about the East and treachery. This poem is not a reliable historical source on the battles for Antioch, nor did its authors intend it to be. The *Chanson* illuminates European perceptions about the events in Antioch, and it is clearly attuned to the common beliefs of the French warrior class. The historical Firuz disappears in this poem, but this fiction shows how his treachery came to be understood in a context that naturally reflected well on the crusade and its collective leadership, not simply Bohemund as a friend.

In the *Chanson* Firuz goes by the name Datien, and he is a real Muslim, a change necessary to how this version of the story unfolds. The basic account remains the same; Datien is in charge of his tower and is in touch with Bohemund, and a large Turkish relief force is approaching the city. Datien's nameless wife, a loyal Muslim, berates her husband for contemplating treachery in handing over his fortifications to the Franks.[45] He talks too much to the Franks, and she fears that he wants to become a Christian. In order to prevent this "very great treachery" from occurring, she tells her husband that she will reveal to her father, brothers, and the ruler of Antioch everything about his plans. The text calls her a pagan and states that she is loyal to Muhammad. Datien answers his wife's arguments by pointing to the obvious power of the Franks, and by saying things that make it clear that he is already in some sense a

Christian. His wife disagrees, so he puts her to death in such a gruesome manner that her body is dismembered into twenty pieces, a fate she predicted and is willing to endure for her beliefs. Yet this wife is no heroine to the authors or audience, and the text betrays no sympathy for her or her beliefs.[46] Datien is perhaps not exactly a hero either, but he is clearly doing the right thing for a French courtly audience, even to the point of killing his spouse to protect his betrayal of the city. As in the case of the stories told by Usamah (discussed in the next section), Muslims would have judged the wife to be the honorable partner. In the *Chanson* the devil takes her soul, and she ends up extinguished, along with her broken body.

The *Chanson* tells the story of the city's fall in a fanciful and detailed way, making sure to mention favorably as many members of the French warrior class as possible. Datien resurfaces in the account of his brother's death, another event of the story of Firuz that entirely changes here. Datien calls on his brother in the name of God and Holy Mary to renounce Muhammad and his sorcery.[47] This pagan brother condemns Datien as a traitor, and so Datien washes his hands of his brother's fate. Robert of Flanders obligingly cuts off his head, and once again Datien has readily sacrificed a member of his family to foster his plans to betray the city. In the aftermath of the Christian victory, Datien is baptized, and this is probably all the audience needed to know about his motives, which would have made perfect sense to them.[48] Wrenched from its original complex and multicultural context, the story of Datien became a straightforward tale of how a higher loyalty to a new faith excused, indeed justified, the way Datien helped the crusaders. Back in France this version of events was more clear and understandable, especially in a romance where the realities of life in Antioch were irrelevant. The new actor, Datien's wife, makes claims of honor and loyalty that were not persuasive in this French context, yet seem deeply rooted in Mediterranean conceptions of honor.

Two Muslim accounts provide short and completely different explanations for the betrayal of Antioch. Ibn al-Athīr (d. 1233) simply stated that the Franks made a deal with Ruzbih, a cuirass maker, and gave him money and lands to hand over the tower he worked in.[49] From this perspective, no relationship other than giving and taking a bribe accounted for this renegade's acts. Ibn al-Qalānisī (d. 1260) briefly explained that some armorers plotted against Turkish rule in Antioch because they had been badly treated, so they sold one of the towers to the Franks.[50] Here the renegades were plural and anonymous but also in the business of making protective gear for the troops. No hint of religious or ethnic motivation appeared in these sources, where bribery was a sufficient cause. If a loyal Muslim wife had become a martyr in these events, these sources would have certainly remembered and related this honorable act.

Who betrayed Antioch, and for what cause, may never be established. What emerges from these disparate accounts is that from a Christian perspective the just cause of holy war required acts that in other circumstances were dishonorable crimes. Actual ethnic and religious loyalties in Antioch were too complex for participants in holy wars to admit as causative agents in the unfolding drama. No one was as yet prepared to find any honor in one's opponents, and lessons about honor from a Muslim woman fell on deaf ears. The conquest of Antioch required a legend that fit God's purpose, from either a Muslim or Christian perspective. Yet there seems to be at the base of this event a renegade, inexplicable in a Christian context except as friendship, plausible in a Muslim context only as an act of bribery. Whoever Firuz really was, violating some religious loyalty was plainly something he did. Firuz plainly broke some ties and made new ones. But where his soul was in the first place, and whether he took it back from Satan, remains unclear.

Faithless Franks

The crusader states in the Latin East formed a frontier region whose fluid boundaries and loyalties in a sense created renegades. Obadiah circled the Latin Kingdom, but for him to enter it would mean certain execution. His near contemporary, the Muslim Syrian Usamah Ibn-Munqidh (1095–1188), left behind a unique account of this complex world in the early twelfth century. Usamah's stories reveal how his society accommodated itself to a long period of warfare against the newly established crusader states. These memoirs are not primarily about the Franks or renegades; Usamah was interested in the story of his own family and Muslim efforts to expel the invaders. But there are a few nuggets of information in his text concerning warriors who crossed from one side to another. Sometimes religious conversion was a necessary part of the act of becoming a renegade, but occasionally some other factor, often a desire to survive, prompted switching allegiances.

The first story concerns Ali the far-sighted, whose acute vision made him an especially effective raider of caravans.[51] When Ali's Muslim lord was killed, Ali "passed into the service" of a Frankish lord in the principality of Antioch and helped his new master attack and loot Muslim caravans. The Franks held his wife as a captive, but Usamah does not claim that this was what prompted Ali to betray his own people. In fact, Ali's wife did not approve of this raiding and tried to talk her husband out of helping the Franks. Eventually this wife, with the help of her brother, murdered Ali and fled to Usamah's camp. According to Usamah, the wife was prompted by anger against the harm her now infidel husband was inflicting on Muslims. Usamah concludes this edifying story of religious loyalty trumping marital ties by noting that this woman was "treated with special regard and respect." Ali became a renegade in this account not because his wife was being held (after all her flight was easily accomplished) but because he loved this way of life, whoever the victims were. This story appears in the context of notable women who attack the enemies of Muslims. So, far from the marital tie enforcing a specious loyalty to a traitor, part of the moral of this story was that it was this woman's duty to kill her irreligious husband—a recourse that might have saved the life of the fictional Datien's wife.

Usamah knew about the Franks partly from his peaceful and warlike encounters with them, and from knowing Frankish captives in his father's household.[52] He concluded that the Franks were "an accursed race, the members of which do not assimilate except with their own kin." In another story, an attractive Frankish captive preferred to escape and marry a shoemaker rather than remain with the Muslim lord who was the father of her child. To Usamah her choice proved that the Frankish woman preferred her own kind to a luxurious life as a captive in a castle. Religion was not the issue here; for Usamah it seems to have been class. He could not understand why a woman would rather be married to a cobbler than a lord, regardless of the circumstances. Another captive, Raoul, converted to Islam and seemed to prove by his religious practices that he was a sincere believer in his new faith. Raoul eventually married a Muslim woman and had two sons. After at least a decade of living as a Muslim, Raoul took his family and possessions and fled to the Franks, where he and his boys became Christians (apparently the wife did not). It was Usamah's hope that God "would purify the world from such people!" yet he surely knew that such instances occurred in Muslim and Frankish society. The thread seems to be that people, especially the Franks, wanted to be with their own kind even more than they wanted to practice their original faith. In Usamah's thinking, honor and loyalty should overwhelm any desire to mix outside one's own group. Whether or not Usamah is right about Frankish exclusivity depends on what the motives of subsequent renegades were.

A contemporary notice from a Christian source confirms that the problem of mixed marriages in the Latin East was general. In 1166 or 1178–79, Pope Alexander III wrote to the archbishop of Tyre in response to a question about what to do, as so often happened there, that someone willingly or unwillingly became an apostate—literally left the Christian religion—and then married.[53] The archbishop's letter, not preserved, must have asked whether a Christian could remarry after being abandoned by a renegade Muslim partner (who could freely marry). This person, loyal to the faith, was tired of hoping for the spouse's return and was not willing to wait any longer and wanted to marry again. As the context of this letter suggests, this was not an uncommon situation. The pope's reply was firm: people in this situation could not marry again. Such a marriage would be like fornication, so instead these people should reconcile (easier to advise than to accomplish) or live chastely (the same). Christian spouses, no doubt mainly women, abandoned by renegades, were stuck with their fates. This unfortunate situation was not grounds for dissolving a union, presumably because the renegade might one day return home, as Raoul actually did.

Usamah made one other famous ethnographic comment that shows the open minds occasionally found in mixed relationships. He told the story of a Muslim friend invited to dine in Antioch by a Frankish host, who was proud that he employed Egyptian cooks and never had pork in his house.[54] From this anecdote, as well as the way this Frank intervened to protect his guest in a Christian town, Usamah concluded that "among the Franks are those who have become acclimatized and have associated long with the Moslems. These are much better than the recent comers from the Frankish lands. But they constitute the exception and cannot be treated as the rule." This opinion has a venerable tradition in colonial literature: over time a few invaders become seasoned and not as bad as the recent arrivals nor the majority of settlers who remain true to their culture. In this case the real test was diet; a Frank who picked up a dislike for pork was clearly not one who invariably preferred his own kind and their ways. In Usamah's long experience, such Franks, really cultural renegades, were exceptional. From a Muslim perspective the local dry and sunny climate perhaps was responsible for improving the Franks.[55]

The battle of Hattin in Galilee occurred on July 4, 1187, when Usamah was still alive to be cheered by the news that Saladin and his army had crushed the forces of the Latin Kingdom, capturing its king and the true cross. Soon important strongholds like Acre and Jerusalem fell, and the kingdom was lost, except for the port of Tyre. Expert studies have illuminated the dramatic pivotal role this battle played in ending the first phase of the kingdom's existence.[56] The great themes of crusader history are not the subject here. What matters to the analysis of mixed relationships are the small instances of insider knowledge and betrayal permeating accounts of Raymond III, count of Tripoli (1140–87). This interesting figure, sometimes viewed by contemporaries as the arch faithless Frank, provides a thread to follow through the tangled history of the Latin East in this period. Two episodes before Hattin show the roots of suspicions about his loyalties. Raymond had the misfortune to be captured and spent ten years (1164–74) of the prime of his short life as a prisoner in Aleppo.[57] This decade among the Muslims may have provided Raymond a chance to study and perhaps learn to speak Arabic. But it also may have sharpened suspicions about the count upon his return. Was he completely reliable? Had he become too dovish and sympathetic to his captors?[58] In 1186, after the death of its child king Baldwin V, leading nobles became rivals for control of the Latin kingdom's affairs. Raymond was outmaneuvered by an alliance of nobles headed by Guy, soon to be king. In these circumstances, fearing an attack from his enemies, Raymond sent to Saladin for military help, and Saladin was happy to provide it.[59] This temporary alliance with the most powerful Muslim ruler in the region probably fostered the opinion that Raymond was a renegade. By the next year Raymond and Guy were reconciled, at least on the surface, and Raymond fought at Hattin on his side. Still, recent memories of some bitter opponents were strong and no doubt colored accounts of Raymond's acts before and during the battle. Apart from all its other meanings, Hattin also seems to be a place where problems about renegades were stark.

A fresh account discovered by Jean Richard presents two important stories.[60] During the heat of the battle, a knight named Jean, who had fought with the Turks and knew everything about them, advised King Guy to attack Saladin, his standard, and those forces surrounding him in the center. If Saladin was defeated, Jean claimed that victory would ensue, probably on the theory that the Muslims would lose heart and flee if they saw their leader taken or killed. The leaders of the Frankish forces, agreed with this plan, except Raymond. (It is important to remember that Raymond's advice to Guy is always suspect because of their past quarrels and Raymond's complex relations with Muslims.) Raymond noted that Jean had sworn loyalty to the Turks and then had broken it, implying that he was not the sort of man to be trusted; in other words, he was once a renegade and might be so again. This Jean may be the Jean Gale who, having defected to Saladin to escape charges of murder, eventually betrayed Saladin too and returned to the Christian fold.[61] Although Raymond had been a captive among the Muslims and his own loyalties were suspect, this Jean had twice voluntarily become a renegade and seemed to Raymond to be entirely incredible. In this account, Raymond urges the king to move up to the heights of Hattin, a course of action that leads to disaster. Every phase of this battle and the advice given during it have been hotly contested in the sources and by historians ever since. What is important here is to note that the Frankish army included at least one knight who had fought with the Turks and knew their ways. Jean's intelligent advice was not taken because a prominent leader did not trust the source. Both armies probably included men who knew well the tactics of their opponents from the personal experience of having fought at their side. What should have mattered about Jean was where he was on this day. Of course, the story assumes that Jean is real and not some made-up detail accounting for the drama of this defeat. Richard, Prawer, and Kedar accept Jean and his advice as a genuine part of the battle's story.

The second story in Richard's source starts off with a known fact: Raymond of Tripoli and a small contingent around him escaped the defeat. It seems likely that even Jean made his way to safety.[62] What is of interest here is how this account moves from a plausible means of explaining Raymond's escape to an entirely fanciful story of his death. This text assumes that Raymond was a traitor (*proditor*). By a prearranged signal his small force was allowed to pass through the Muslim lines and find temporary safety in the castle at nearby Safed. An excellent account of the battle explains Raymond's escape as a Muslim strategy to let his charge, ordered by the king, pass harmlessly through their lines while they proceeded to destroy the Frankish main army.[63] The Old French chronicle simply observes that Raymond and some other nobles, having seen the king captured, fled the scene of battle.[64] Another version of how Raymond and some others escaped has Raymond simply observe that the time had come for anyone who could flee to do so.[65] The most detailed account has a far more sinister explanation, making Raymond a true renegade.[66] To hammer home the point, the author of this version claims that as he lay dying, Raymond was circumcised and became a Muslim. Supposedly, Raymond had always been surrounded by Saracens and Turks by family tradition (*ex paterna se traditione*) and had had a pact with Saladin all along. According to this source, Raymond of Tripoli had become one of those acclimatized Franks, in his case crossing the line into treachery and even conversion.

Marshall Baldwin sensibly has observed that no Muslim source claims Raymond's conversion, and it is most unlikely that this supposed coup would escape all notice.[67] Muslim sources give a mixed view of Raymond, with one author observing that only fear of his fellow Christians kept him from converting to Islam.[68] The contemporary English chronicler Ralph of Coggeshall records another story that Raymond of Tripoli, having planned to turn over his lands to Saladin, was found dead in his bed.[69] In this telling Raymond was intending to be a renegade, but a mysterious death interrupted his betrayal. The Old French chronicle provides the fullest contemporary account of Raymond's death.[70] By August 1187 Saladin had entered the county of Tripoli itself and taken Botron. Raymond returned by sea to his capital at Tripoli and immediately took to his bed. He had no direct heir to take up the task of defending the county against the Muslims, so he turned to his godson Raymond, the eldest son of his friend Bohemund III of Antioch. The father had other plans for his first son, so he sent a younger son, Bohemund, to take over in Tripoli. Raymond, by now aware that he was dying, had no choice but to leave the county to Bohemund and shortly thereafter expired. This source, consistently favorable to Raymond, considers his death a great loss to Christians, and there is again not the slightest hint of any deathbed conversion, simply a search for a successor. Other observers, however, searching for a scapegoat for the loss at Hattin, found it convenient to brand Raymond as a renegade. His period of captivity and temporary alliance with Saladin cast just enough doubt on his motives to make such an accusation plausible to those far from the scene. Also, he had the good fortune to survive a disaster, and such people are often envied as well as censured. In 1186 it could be argued that Raymond had committed an act of treachery by becoming Saladin's ally, but he was no renegade.

Genuine renegades at Hattin can be found in several contemporary accounts that note that some warriors actually switched sides during battle. One version of the Old French chronicle mentions five knights from Raymond's contingent who, just before the battle, crossed over to Saladin and urged him to attack the Christians, who were in a state of disorder.[71] A letter purporting to come from the Genoese consuls to Pope Urban claimed that six knights (three are named) were inspired by the devil to go over to Saladin.[72] Even worse, they converted to Islam (became Saracens) and told Saladin everything about the Christian plans and dispositions. These faithless Franks were another means of explaining how the battle was lost. Whether such an amazing event could take place during a battle is unclear—the three names lend credence to that report but are also precisely the kind of detail likely to be added to a rumor to make it more plausible. The common thread throughout Hattin accounts seems to be that knights born in the kingdom were trying to save their lives by any means necessary, and some of their methods struck distant observers as treacherous. These western authors were perhaps more likely to see Muslim-Christian interactions as sharply hostile, with no room for occasional cooperating across the lines. Anyone who deviated from this strict test of loyalty by establishing any sort of mixed relationship with the enemy became a renegade. In the realties of life in the Latin Kingdom in the 1180s or on the field of battle at Hattin, the choices were not so simple. Renegades, actual or imaginary, were perfect scapegoats for disaster, especially if they died in mysterious circumstances.

The thirteenth-century jurist John of Ibelin, in his *Livre des Assises* finished around 1265, took up the legal issue of who had standing as guarantors in the high court of the Latin Kingdom of Jerusalem. Among the excluded he listed perjurers, deniers of the faith, traitors, bastards, and all those who served the Saracens for a year and a day against Christians or Greeks.[73] Ibelin's definition of Christians meant those who obeyed Rome, and generally excluded Greeks, Syrians, Armenians, and Jacobites. Hence, converts were naturally renegades, but local customs placed a traditional time limit on simply fighting for the Other. A few months on the Muslim side did not count as treachery endangering legal status, and one might spend a lifetime with them fighting the Mongols. Conversion, however, probably struck both Christians and Muslims as treasonous, and a renegade was a "despicable traitor."[74] Still, the Latin East witnessed conversions between Islam and Christianity at all social levels from slaves to knights, with only rare signs of any local people converting to Judaism.[75] Franks living near the heart of Islam faced ever-mounting defeats and found ways to survive capture and enslavement. Sometimes they joined the victors—a venerable palliative to the sting of defeat.

Möngke's Goldsmith

Among the more ambiguous renegades were captives who somehow established lives among a new people and never returned home, for one reason or another. These are interesting renegades because they were likely to be ordinary people caught up in great events. Unlike Raymond of Tripoli, they were not to be ransomed for huge sums. A small group of such individuals appear in the Franciscan friar William of Rubruck's account of his mission to the Mongols in 1253–55.[76] This text reveals western attitudes toward the Mongols as an ethnic group, and William also imparts in passing information about westerners he found at the Mongol court in Karakorum in East Asia. Note that William had only one companion by this time, his unreliable interpreter Abdullah. So his gaze naturally turned to any familiar people he found so far from home, and it is likely that he recorded every such person he met. However, it was not William's purpose to write about these people, so they are mentioned as useful in facilitating his larger purpose of meeting the khan. Pulling these stray references together shows an interesting collection of people thousands of miles from their original homes.

On first arriving at the Mongol court, William met a woman named Paquette (Pascha), originally from Metz.[77] She was attached to a Christian Mongol lady at court and was married to a Ruthenian with whom she had three young boys. William thought that she was doing well, and she helped his small party by feeding them, always a major issue on the friar's mind. Paquette had originally been captured by the Mongols in Hungary, so she was already far from her original home. She had given up living among her own people (however defined) in a Christian land, and she found a husband and a good life in the East. It is not clear whether Paquette was free to leave; yet did her decision to remain mark her as in some sense a renegade? It might be better to see Paquette as an opportunist making the best of a potentially disastrous situation—captivity, which placed special burdens on women. Instead of ending up a slave or worse, Paquette found a life and was raising a family. Her other value to William was that she told him about a master goldsmith from Paris named Guillaume Bouchier. This person was working on a big commission from the khan, so he was well connected at court, and he had a boy, someone he raised, who was an excellent interpreter. William immediately wrote to Guillaume asking for help, and he received a response promising assistance in a month.

Soon Guillaume regularly appeared in William's account. The goldsmith was a great friend of Bulgai, the khan's chancellor, and this connection was valuable in gaining access to Möngke.[78] Guillaume also told William about Korea and the great area of China to the south still free of Mongol rule.[79] This casual reference suggests that the goldsmith was the source of much of William's information about China, a land he never actually saw. William describes in detail the work Guillaume did for the court, including a silver crucifix for Bulgai and a remarkable fountain that dispensed mare's milk; wine; cosmos, a honey beverage; and beer to the khan's guests.[80] This apparatus took the form of a great silver tree, and at the top was the figure of an angel with a trumpet, able to summon the drinkers through the device of a person hidden in the tree's base. This remarkable and expensive work of art impressed William as something truly amazing, out of his experience yet created by a French master goldsmith from the Petit Pont in Paris. The goldsmith's service to the Mongols did not make him a renegade because these luxuries gave no military advantages to the enemies of his king.

William dined with Guillaume, probably frequently, as getting adequate supplies of food was a perpetual problem for these western visitors to the Mongol court. The friar used the occasion of one of these dinners to provide more details about Guillaume, some time after his initial appearance in the narrative.[81] Guillaume's wife was from Hungary, the daughter of someone originally from Lorraine. She spoke French and Coman well. Another person at the dinner, Basil, the son of an Englishman, was also born in Hungary and knew the same languages (*ideomata*). Basil, Guillaume, and his wife had all been captured in Hungary, one of the westernmost points the Mongols reached, and apparently a profitable venture. These captives spoke the local language and seemed comfortable living among the Mongols, their status as captives apparently unimportant if not entirely forgotten. By successfully integrating themselves into the Mongol community, they were proving themselves to be survivors, not renegades.

Guillaume provided a useful service to the friar by making for him an iron griddle for baking the host needed for Mass.[82] William dryly observed that Guillaume had some vestments he had made for himself and carried himself like a cleric, though he knew little of letters. Presumably he was illiterate in Latin, but was he able to read the original letter in French that William sent him? There was something odd about Guillaume's behavior, but one of the advantages of being an opportunist/survivor was that there was no one to reproach him in the Mongol East, certainly not a Franciscan priest so dependant on him. Guillaume made a statue of the Virgin in the Gallic style, a silver pyx, and a cart with decorations, which the friar used for traveling services. William also noted the time his benefactor fell gravely ill and nearly died as a result of an overdose of rhubarb.

During a discussion of Möngke's brothers William wrote that one of them captured Master Guillaume in Hungary at Belgrade, where there was a Norman bishop.[83] (Again, this part of Guillaume's biography comes late in the account, some time after the wife's story.) Presumably the goldsmith had been in the service of this bishop at the time, which would account for his presence in Greater Hungary. Guillaume was given (the fate of captives) to the khan's mother and after her death passed to another brother, Arigh Böke. The khan noticed Guillaume's work and paid his brother for these expert services. Hence these French captives opened the minds of Mongols about new styles in the decorative arts, and this lowering of barriers may have lessened fear of the "other" on both sides.

Master Guillaume also told William the story about the demon, summoned by a pagan Mongol priest, who betrayed a Hungarian woman hiding in the goldsmith's house.[84] This tale was part of William's account of Mongol beliefs and the powers of demons, and William did not doubt that demons played a big role in their spiritual systems. Again, Guillaume served as his informant about local practices, another sign that the Parisian had deep roots in the culture. It is hard to figure how long he had been in the East, but a safe guess is that it was about a decade since the Mongol forays into Hungary. In this time Guillaume had risen socially; William noted that he served as a cupbearer at Möngke's feast.

William's last notice of Guillaume occurs at the very end of his narrative, when he discusses his plans to return to King Louis IX of France.[85] The goldsmith secretly solicited the gift of ten *iascots* of silver that made it possible for William to return in style, at least at the beginning of his trip. Half the sum went toward the friar's expenses, and the other half to Abdullah, who, as noted in chapter 1, did not make the best use of it. Master Guillaume, "once your subject [*civis*]," (here William directly addresses Louis) sent the king a present—a piece of leather decorated with precious stones, possibly an elegant belt. The Mongols carried such belts to avert thunder and lightening, and it is odd that Guillaume should consider this an appropriate gift and that the Franciscan did not criticize it. Guillaume also sent along many greetings and prayers to the French king but apparently did not express any desire to return to his domains. William concludes that he was extremely grateful to this goldsmith, leaving the strong impression that the mission would have failed without him. In fact, William's companion Brother Bartolomeo of Cremona remained with Guillaume, not as an ostensible renegade, but perhaps as the spiritual adviser to the small group of foreigners living at the Mongol court.

These five people—Paquette, Guillaume and his nameless wife, Basil, and William's companion Bartolomeo—comprise a set of westerners known to be resident at the Mongol court in 1254. Four started out there as captives, and one looks like a volunteer. After his return, there would have been no reason for William to conceal any unhappiness among them when he prepared this report for the French king. There is no sign that any of them were seeking ransom or rescue—the usual hopes of the captured. The absence of any feeling stronger than greetings suggests that these westerners were happy to live among the Mongols, and Guillaume in particular may have been practicing his profession at a level and with resources impossible to obtain back in France. It is hard to imagine the abstemious Louis commissioning the great tree of drinks. This small group did not marry locals but instead sought refuge among their own "kind," their fellow captives at the end of the world. They were also quite free to continue practicing Christianity. At best economic opportunists, at worst small-time renegades, they appeared to be thriving in ways unknown to the western world until William returned to tell their tales. It seems that from the Mongol point of view these people were no longer captives but had become expatriates—living peacefully and productively far from home.

Segurano Salvaygo

The Genoese merchant Segurano Salvaygo appears in a justly famous notice imbedded in a plan for recovering the Holy Land written by Guillaume Adam sometime between 1318 and 1322–23 (when another source records Segurano's murder). Guillaume's main goal was to promote a crusade to defeat or even destroy the Muslims, and he wrote from the vantage point of his position as bishop of Sultaniyeh, the Mongol capital of what was by then the Muslim khanate of Persia. Guillaume was a well-educated Dominican who had visited Egypt and had thought hard about the big picture of Muslim-Christian relations in the East.[86] His views on Segurano Salvaygo portray a man who went far beyond the bounds of economic opportunism and had become a traitor to all Christians. Whether or not this extreme view is fair to Segurano depends on this contemporary's judgment, as well as a few scraps of information preserved in Genoese notarial records and Muslim sources.

Guillaume's case against Segurano drew upon the former's great hatred for the way some Christian merchants were trading with Mamluk Egypt and strengthening that enemy of Christendom which had recently destroyed the crusader states. Guillaume had a keen eye for the economic motives and consequences of trade, and he also understood how the Mamluk rulers of Egypt depended on a steady supply of young slaves from the Black Sea region to replenish their ranks of slave warriors, the Mamluk ruling class. It made no sense to Guillaume that the men he called false Christians and great sinners would help the enemy by supplying slaves, because he knew that by themselves the Mamluks did not have the ships or merchants to get to the sources of supply; for this they needed foreign merchants. As part of the standard litany of disparaging remarks on Islam, Guillaume also stressed that in his view the Mamluks also purchased these boys to gratify their own libidinous purposes. But he reserved his greatest ire for the Genoese purveyors of these slaves, especially Segurano Salvaygo.[87] This Genoese called the sultan his brother and friend, and Guillaume thought the merchant was actually a promoter and defender of Islam. With his own eyes Guillaume saw (presumably in Alexandria) Segurano's ships flying the banner of the sultan. This "sinful" merchant was engaged in selling boys acquired from the Tartars, as well as wood, iron, and other raw materials for munitions. Segurano was alone responsible for importing ten thousand boys into Saracen hands in Egypt, and all this naturally augmented Muslim military power.

It is worth expanding the context in order to understand the bishop's overall sense of the economic underpinnings of Muslim-Christian relations in the east. Guillaume also sharply censured Christian pilgrims to the East because the money they spent and tribute they paid only strengthened Egypt, and he wanted such travel stopped.[88] He understood that Egyptian merchants controlled as middlemen the fabulously profitable trade with the Indies, and western merchants buying pepper, ginger, silks, and other commodities were also simply enriching the enemy.[89] Guillaume's plans were grandiose but perceptive; he wanted Christians to get their own ships into the Indian Ocean, most likely by collaborating with Persia, in order to disrupt this trade. Guillaume knew that Persia was now a Muslim power, but he thought its self-interest in breaking the Egyptian monopoly of the eastern trade would be enough incentive for Persia to work with the Christians. Remarkably, Guillaume also knew that sometime in the 1280s the Genoese had been negotiating with the ruler of Persia to send galleys down the Euphrates into the Indian Ocean, but their own civic strife had prevented them from accomplishing this feat. Guillaume obviously understood enough about economic motives to see how they might affect state policy, but with Segurano he saw nothing other than selfish treachery. Guillaume's real anger against people like Segurano seems to have derived from his sense that the Tartars were drawn into supplying slaves and even possible alliances with Egypt as a result of Genoese intermediaries. He sensed that, because of naval deficiencies on both sides, the Black Sea and Alexandria would not come together without the ships, crews, and, above all, men like Segurano Salvaygo.

There is no easy way to make a just appraisal of Segurano's motives solely from the information the Dominican bishop provides. For example, he may not have known that the Mamluk sultan Qalāwūn had made a treaty with the Byzantine emperor Michael Palaeologus in 1281.[90] One aim of this agreement was to make sure Egyptian merchants had safe access to Crimea, presumably to buy slaves. Perhaps the Genoese had later insinuated themselves into this trade as middlemen taking a share of the profits. If so, they were simply filling a power vacuum and strengthening themselves by driving up costs for the Mamluks! Guillaume was usually well informed about the Genoese; he had only good things to write about the Zaccaria family on Chios in the Aegean because he saw these people as interested in disrupting commercial links between the Black Sea and Egypt.[91] So, not all Genoese were evil. But he also knew all about Genoa's famous Officium Robarie, which kept a fund to compensate victims of unlawful Genoese piracies, and he was incensed that this policy extended to Muslim and Jewish victims.[92] Again, on some level the bishop probably understood that enlightened economic self-interest prompted the Genoese to indemnify victims of pirates the state could not control, but it did not make any sense to him that this policy could trump religious loyalties. For a bishop this was consistent thinking, but it was not the way Segurano reasoned.

Benjamin Z. Kedar has gathered a few other pieces of information that supply the context for Segurano's activities.[93] Kedar persuasively demonstrates that Segurano and the Genoese merchant Sakrān who appears in Egyptian sources were the same person. At first glance the new sources seem to confirm all Guillaume's suspicions that Segurano was working closely with the Muslims. The Genoese merchant first appeared in the East bearing precious gifts, including cloth and birds, in 1303–4.[94] Segurano was able to intervene to have Egyptian envoys to the Tartars released from their captivity by the Genoese on Chios. Several times Muslim sources recorded how Segurano either arrived with envoys from the Golden Horde or helped maintain communications between the two powers. In one notable endeavor Segurano seems to have helped transport a Tartar princess who was to marry the sultan of Egypt. Supplying slaves was clearly part of Segurano's purpose as far as the Mamluks were concerned, and he was quite successful. Egypt was becoming increasingly reliant on Circassian as well as Kipchak Turkish slaves, and the Genoese were invaluable intermediaries in this trade through Caffa and the Black Sea.[95] None of this would have surprised Guillaume, but there was more. The Mamluk official in charge of the sultan's treasury invested the large sum of 60,000 dinars with Segurano and supplied him with sugar and other goods worth 40,000 dinars "for commerce."[96] Kedar rightly questions the terms of this contract. Were the Mamluks actual business partners with Segurano, placing some capital with him for a share of the profits along the usual contractual basis of Genoese commerce?[97] Certainly 100,000 dinars was valuable capital from which Segurano would also draw profits. If the average male slave destined for the military cost between one and two thousand dinars, and if Segurano was in the business of importing thousands of them into Egypt, then he was certainly rich enough to own a small fleet in his own right and be an independent power in the eastern Mediterranean.[98]

Evidence from the Genoese notarial records also proves that Segurano and his family retained their commercial ties to their home city and extended their commercial reach as far as the cloth-producing regions in the Low Countries.[99] Hence, their interests in alum and wool helped to tie together the North and Black Seas and crossed several zones of the world system. Segurano probably benefited from flags of convenience, and it makes sense that he would put himself under the sultan's banner at times when the Golden Horde was hostile to Genoa, as when it destroyed Caffa in 1308. Segurano must have been well aware of papal opposition to his type of trading, and even back in Genoa there must have been people who shared Guillaume's view that Segurano was going too far. And there was his violent end. Caught up in a period of tensions between Egypt and the Golden Horde, the khan seized the merchant's goods and murdered him. This killing, which a Muslim source dates to 1322–23, was not mentioned by Guillaume, which helps to date his work, for there is no doubt he would have relished recording what would have been, in his view, Segurano's well-deserved fate.[100]

Bishop Guillaume Adam, though living deep inside the Muslim khanate of Persia, would never have considered himself a renegade but rather a missionary well placed to advise western Christians on how to reconquer the Holy Land. No activity of his could be construed as aiding Islam, and he was even in a way a spy gathering information on how to defeat his enemies. The bishop's grasp of the economic realities of the East served his larger purposes of crusade and mission, but he had fathomed the value of trading connections in the region. He understood that Mamluk Egypt depended for its existence on a reliable and large supply of slaves and that its control of Indian Ocean trade routes enriched the state. For all this, and his knowledge of commerce that extended to a good sense of what the Venetians, Pisans, Catalans, and above all the Genoese were up to, he singled out by name Segurano Salvaygo as a merchant whose pursuit of self-interest had transformed him into a promoter of Islam—by Guillaume's standards a renegade.

From a less partisan perspective, where does Segurano fall on the continuum of renegades? Everything about his career suggests, as Kedar has pointed out, that he fit the pattern of intrepid Genoese merchants of the late thirteenth and early fourteenth centuries, and his sphere of activity encompassed the delicate ties between Crimea and Alexandria. As someone whose efforts to remain on good terms with the sultan and khan eventually cost him his life, Segurano must have understood the risks of his activities, including censure by church leaders. Coming from a city riven for decades by splits between the papacy and secular rulers, whose own family usually supported the Guelf allies of the popes, Segurano was probably inured to ecclesiastical condemnations. Church-declared embargoes against Egypt permitted exemptions based on individual claims that their activities were in the greater interests of Christendom, despite appearances to the contrary. Segurano's self-justifications remain unknown, but any trade that enriched a Genoese added to the naval power of what was, along with Venice, the leading navy in the Mediterranean. Segurano had not converted to Islam, as others had, so he was not an apostate but rather an economic opportunist with different standards than the bishop. After all, Karām ad-Dīn, the Mamluk official who had placed 100,000 dinars at Segurano's disposal, was part of a regime steadily hostile to Christian interests in the East but still profiting from western merchants coming to Alexandria to buy spices. No doubt this Mamluk calculated the profits from Segurano's ventures as compensating for a temporary commercial alliance with an infidel, and the wealth would only make the sultan stronger. Spiritual arguments on all sides stressed an ideal of holy war that now included an economic component; making a living, and a profit, required different standards.

Venetian and Genoese Witnesses

In the fifteenth century, Venetian merchants and ambassadors remained among the most intrepid and frequent visitors to the eastern Mediterranean and beyond. Official and private accounts of their travels show how Ottoman conquests created fresh opportunities for people to become renegades or simply take advantage of what opportunities for freedom came their way. The Venetian noble Iosafa Barbaro, in a chatty account of his travels and experiences at the Persian court, told a few stories about people who crossed, voluntarily or not, some sort of line that changed their status. He recalled an interesting event from 1455, when he was visiting a wine shop on the Rialto in Venice and saw two men in chains, whom he immediately knew to be Tartars.[101] He asked the shop owner about them and learned that they were supposedly slaves of a Catalan and that they had fled in a small boat and were captured at sea by a merchant. Barbaro sensed something was not right about this story and immediately complained to the *signori di notte*, officials with jurisdiction over instances of unjust captivity. These officials came, freed the slaves, and condemned the shop owner. Taking the men to his house, Barbaro questioned them (in their own language) and learned that they were from Tana, where he had been, from a family he knew. In fact, he recognized one of the slaves, who soon realized that Barbaro had once saved his life during a fire! So now Barbaro had saved him twice—this time from the death of slavery. These Tartars stayed with Barbaro for two months, and as soon as the next convoy was departing for Tana, they wanted to leave Venice and never see it again. These Tartars were improperly enslaved, by their own people or some foreign merchants, and were likely to be sold again had they not been lucky enough to be rescued by a kind-hearted and vigilant activist like Barbaro. The slaves were involuntary renegades stuck in a wine shop, then guests in a noble's palace, and then free passengers on a galley homeward bound. It was in Venice's interests to remain on cordial terms with the Tartars controlling Tana, which may explain the alert response of the officials.

Another Venetian traveler, the ambassador Ambrogio Contarini, met at least one returned slave on his adventurous travels to the court of the Persia in the mid-1470s. (Traveling through Poland and Russia to reach Tabriz via the Caucasus, he was looking for help against the Ottomans, who had sensibly closed more direct routes to Persia.) Passing through the land of the Mingrelians near the eastern shore of the Black Sea, he came across Nicolo Capello, from Modon, a Venetian colony in southern Greece. Nicolo had been captured and converted to Islam but was now living contentedly beyond the confines of the Ottoman state.[102] He did not seem eager to be anywhere else, having found a haven and a new faith. Contarini also met a woman named Marta, a Circassian who had been the slave of a Genoese, and a Genoese (presumably another one) had married her. No husband was apparent now, and the Circassian, perhaps originally a slave in Caffa, was now living an independent life in her home region, running an inn of sorts. Contarini stayed with her for four days and pronounced her to be "buona compagnia." On his return, Contarini stayed with Donna Marta again, and this time she nursed him back from a nearly fatal fever.[103] Marta cured him with a sack or charm containing oil and herbs, and Contarini was extremely grateful not to be left to die in these lands. People like Nicolo and Marta were probably everywhere, just beneath the radar of the kinds of records kept by the majority population or the ruling powers. Runaway slaves were safest in areas like the eastern Black Sea, for the moment not controlled by the Ottoman Empire, Venice, or Persia. In a gray zone like this, the definition of renegade was at best vague, and in reality there was no one to ask difficult questions about status. But these refuges were not easy to reach, and a woman like Marta was especially intrepid.

Barbaro was ambassador in Tabriz from 1473 to 1475, and he collected the following story from his guest Pietro de Guasco, who was originally from Caffa, which had been conquered by the Ottomans in 1475. Chozamirech, a rich Armenian merchant, had a goldsmith shop in Tabriz.[104] One day a Muslim (considered a saint because he had made the pilgrimage to Mecca) came into the shop and told the merchant he should "rinegar la fede di Cristo" and become a Muslim. (In this story there are numerous misperceptions of Islam; this Muslim is not like a western saint, and a

Muslim is called a Mohammadan.) The merchant responded humanely because he did not want to embarrass his visitor, but the Muslim persisted. The merchant then showed him some money, but the Muslim said that he did not want money but he wanted him to convert. Chozamirech responded that he did not want to convert but wished to remain a Christian. This rogue (as the tale considers him) then took a sword from the sheath of someone standing nearby and struck the merchant in the head, killing him. The murderer then fled. The merchant's son, who witnessed all this, began to mourn and speedily went to the gate of the *signore*—the local government official—to tell him what happened. Very angry, this *signore* ordered an immediate search for the culprit, who was soon found two days from Tabriz. When the man was brought before the *signore,* the official took out a knife, killed him on the spot, and had his body thrown to the dogs in the piazza. The *signore* explained his act very simply: "What? Islam should grow in this way?"[105]

This story appeared in a part of Barbaro's account devoted to explaining religious hypocrisy and how Christians were mistreated in the East. The episode is complex and credible. Armenian Christians existed under Ottoman and Persian rule, but their situation, even as a people of the book, was precarious because there was no outside Armenian power to guarantee their safety. A Genoese or Venetian merchant in Tabriz was not likely to face the choice this goldsmith had to make. From the Italian perspective, the choice offered the Armenian was to become a renegade, literally, with this verb *rinegar,* to deny the faith. He chose to resist, in the mildest and most polite way, even hoping to pay or bribe his way out of the situation. The fifteenth-century Mediterranean world was filled with instances of mass or individual forced conversions, even when official Christianity and Islam prohibited the practice. Still, this Armenian had no quick recourse to the *signore,* and one word of acquiescence would have put him in the dangerous position of a lapsed Muslim should he ever return to his faith. So, an angry Muslim, acting in a private capacity and perhaps further provoked by the offer of money, struck out, not even having his own weapon at hand to commit the murder. Naturally, from a Christian perspective this Armenian was a martyr and, if not a candidate for sainthood, surely he was holy and blessed.

But the end of this story is also interesting. A Persian official recognized the injustice and with summary severity punished the murderer. His final comment recognized that Islam did not condone forced conversion, and there is also a hint that this sort of pressure and violence was harmful to legitimate efforts at converting nonbelievers. The Italians were honest enough to include this part of the story, but they probably considered the justice here to be exceptional. Just as the gray area between empires had places of refuge, the empires themselves were places where minority status was perilous and refusal to become a renegade not safe.

A final story from a Genoese source, this one originating in Caffa, shows how persons moved across ostensible frontiers. Manfredo de Sauli was the consul or governor of Caffa in 1420–21.[106] A Tartar fled to Caffa and converted to Christianity, presumably from Islam. Manfredo gave this fellow back to the khan (where he certainly faced a grim fate) but asked for mercy for him. The consul's conduct was subsequently investigated, and he said that he did not want to be in conflict with the khan, a situation that certainly would have meant trouble for Genoese commerce. Both sides to this delicate relationship tried to respect where possible the claims of purity on both sides; in this case loyalty to creed was at issue. Manfredo also insisted that the Tartar's conversion was forced, which perhaps made him feel better about his decision to repatriate the Tartar. Back in Genoa this decision looked bad, and Manfredo was heavily fined for it. The usual relations between Caffa and the Golden Horde required that runaway slaves should be returned or the owners compensated, but this was a case of a free man. On the spot, Manfredo knew that the khan was not going to stand for Caffa becoming some sort of haven for renegade Muslims, and he weighed the benefits of continuing trade as more important than defending a recent convert he viewed with suspicion. By other rules in a different context, he should have protected the renegade, but Manfredo probably thought that any fine was worth enhancing his status among the Genoese traders.

Montaigne's Opportunistic Renegade

Michel de Montaigne spent part of the summer of 1581 taking the waters near Lucca. While there, he heard the story of a man he clearly tolerated as an engaging rogue but still the kind of renegade no one should trust. This fellow was a soldier or sailor named Giuseppe, who lived near Montaigne and was a kind of quasi convict, kept in chains but commanding the oarsmen on a Genoese galley.[107] At this time the Genoese galleys primarily used Muslim captives and Italian convicts to do the arduous work of rowing into battle. These unfortunate men were likely to be worked to death within a few years and comprised a difficult crew, to say the least. Someone in the crew needed to communicate with the rowers, and somebody of Giuseppe's background was ideal because he could undoubtedly speak Turkish and Italian. But some of Giuseppe's experience made him an even more appropriate choice, which helps explain why the Genoese needed to keep him in chains. As Montaigne relates, Giuseppe was captured at sea by the Turks, and to save his skin he became a Turk, which required that he be circumcised. Circumcision on adults was in a way a bar to conversion; it was a dangerous, irreversible operation and a visible sign that a person had become a renegade. Still, the Muslims were rightly suspicious of any convert who would not submit to it, and above all Giuseppe wanted to stay alive, so it seems. He also got married, which would have reassured his new cobelievers. So, for an unknown length of time, Giuseppe lived among the Turks, presumably somewhere along the Barbary Coast in a place like Tunis or Algiers, where thousands of Christian captives languished (including, for five years, Cervantes). Giuseppe was, however, no longer a captive waiting to be ransomed but a renegade who had joined up with the Turks.

Giuseppe's activities as a renegade extended to joining Turkish raids, which were a real problem to Christian Mediterranean lands in the sixteenth and seventeenth centuries. On one such expedition, usually intended to yield booty and above all captives to be ransomed (a lucrative business for the Turks), Giuseppe found himself in his native land near Lucca. Isolated from his comrades, Giuseppe was captured by the local people, promptly claimed that he had intended to surrender all along, and became a Christian again. This volte face cannot have surprised his fellow Turks if they had any idea of his character, and it was a wise move if he wished to avoid an early death at an oar or inquisitional charges of apostasy. Because it was so difficult for ordinary people to be ransomed or escape from the Turks, Giuseppe's captors were likely to believe his intention to surrender at the first opportunity.

Some aspects of Giuseppe's subsequent life interested Montaigne enough to record them in his travel journal. There is the predictable story of encountering his mother, and the shock of seeing Giuseppe again, whom she did not recognize at first, soon killed her. The local church was happy to receive Giuseppe back into the fold, and although Montaigne does not describe these ceremonies beyond receiving the Host, the church had by now well-established rites for reintegrating ostensibly involuntary converts back into the fold.[108] Not everyone was made of the stuff of martyrs, and a returned captive was not an unfamiliar sight; Montaigne claimed that there were many in the hills around Lucca. (Falling between the navies of Genoa and Tuscany, this part of the coast would have been good hunting grounds for Turkish raiders, and the mountains often harbor interesting people.)

What most struck Montaigne's fancy was his conviction that Giuseppe remained at heart a Turk. Having conversed with the fellow, Montaigne was in a good position to believe this, but there was more proof. Giuseppe was in the habit of slipping off to Venice and mixing with the Turks there. This is an entrancing image: Giuseppe, lonely for the company of Turks, went to a city where he was likely to find a number of congenial people—captives rowing for Venice, slaves of both sexes, emancipated slaves likely to be at least nominal converts, and even occasional envoys or merchants from the Ottoman Empire. Venice was one of the cities in Italy most influenced by the culture and art of the eastern Mediterranean, and so it is no surprise that Giuseppe went there rather than Genoa, where he was much more likely to be recognized.[109] The way Giuseppe mixed with the Turks somehow meant that he ended up resuming his travels, perhaps as a stowaway, for Montaigne does not leave the impression that Giuseppe somehow resumed raiding. In any case Giuseppe ended up being caught again; how many times this happened is unclear. The Genoese could use a man of his experience, yet when in their service he was wisely fettered. Montaigne met Giuseppe during one of his stays in his native land, and his ultimate fate is unknown. There were many captives all across the Mediterranean in this century, but the vast majority of them did not become renegades, and even fewer would have figured out how to switch back and forth as neatly as Giuseppe.[110]

Giuseppe comes across as a genial renegade, at worst an opportunist looking to survive. It would have been the rare ex-captive who missed the company of Turks as much as he did. Exactly what he missed he apparently did not explain to Montaigne, and any effort to fill this gap is pure speculation. By this century, enough of Turkish culture—soon even its tobacco and coffee, carpets and book covers, music and dress—was readily available, and the watchful eyes of the Genoese no doubt prevented Giuseppe from fraternizing with their crews. So the suspicion is that he missed the people, their language, and ways, but not enough to return to someplace like Algiers. Giuseppe had truly become half one thing and half another, and so by his lights he was probably not a renegade at all.

Throughout the story of the renegade, the runaway slave has appeared in a variety of contexts, usually as a humble person trying to escape capture and, consequently, notice in the surviving historical records. The successful runaway slave may have been judged a renegade by his or her former owner, but that self-interested perspective does not warrant labeling slaves or indeed captives as renegades, no matter how their instinct for self-preservation may have motivated them to accommodate to what their owners expected. Slaves entered their state through birth, an act of violence, or a selfish sale by parents; captives by definition were formerly free people with the prospect of ransom or some type of rescue. Behind the renegade there must be some act of volition, some intention to cross a boundary by choice or to push someone else across it. The crossing of one of the big boundaries of creed, ethnicity, or color created a new, mixed relationship in a fresh context where the renegade faced suspicions and new tests.

Renegades' motives have turned out to be contingent on circumstances, as they should be. For a person to take on or have imposed the identity of renegade was the beginning of new problems. When states were well organized and strong, their frontiers helped to define the renegade. Assimilated captives ran the risk of alienating their original people and failing to sufficiently impress their new group. Loyalty to one's creed and beloved forced some people to create relationships over the boundaries of faith and ethnicity. An apostate may seem the arch renegade, but the realities of changing religions were complex, and some people appeared to be traitors without actually converting. The imaginative powers of the poets who told the story of Digenis sustained the drama of a tale that placed the demands of honor and love at occasional cross-purposes. Honor was the bedrock of belief throughout the eastern Mediterranean, and much opportunism could be excused or forgotten if honor had been maintained or if tragedy intervened, as in the case of Datien's wife. Obadiah's spiritual angst led him to apostasy, Raymond of Tripoli sought political survival at the cost of his reputation, and Segurano, along with others, wanted to make money. These were lonely enterprises. Obadiah became a wandering Jew, Raymond died unloved in his bed, and Segurano was murdered. Yet they risked much, perhaps because the alternative, a coerced or feigned loyalty to a creed and its rules, or a state with its taxes, was even worse.

It may seem that there were as many motives as there were renegades. Religion and homeland were easier to change than ethnicity and physical appearance. The new relationships forged by renegades inevitably reflect these facts of life. After ancient Rome, few states were yet able to command a patriotic loyalty. Emotions, like plain fear and love for a mate, or money motivated some renegades, as did the miraculous or divine providence itself. Hoping for profits or bribes cannot be discounted as encouraging some to venture across the frontiers, and friendship and family ties pulled some people across the big barriers. Honor and revenge were part of many renegade stories. Defeat, or even its prospect, caused some people to go over to the winners. One could not necessarily tell renegades by their faces, but everyone knew they were no angels, at least not the good kind.

CHAPTER FIVE

Human and Angelic Faces

Medieval people had no scientific raciology or indeed any ideology to conceive anything like miscegenation—a word that did not yet exist. Stray evidence about mules and human hybrids in the Venetian colonies did not constitute a conceptual framework or any sort of theoretical stance toward mixing. Beliefs about faith-based purity did not admit any tolerance of religious syncretism. Rather than leave the story there, we can analyze a few things medieval Mediterraneans did and see the possible connections among them. First, they looked at people and judged and ranked them according to venerable rules sanctioned by immemorial practice and the science of physiognomy. Second, all these cultures privileged the face and especially the eyes as the real clues to deeper knowledge about people. Third, they literally looked up to angels and feared the fallen ones. The reader is not being asked to step through the looking glass into another book on physiognomy, or one on angels, but to explore the admittedly speculative connections between these two traditions of ancient and medieval culture in the eastern Mediterranean.

Physiognomy was an ancient science claiming to uncover deeper truths about a person by interpreting his or her complex surface. Angels, also a legacy from ancient belief systems, were not human; they were pure beings, often appearing in human guise with remarkable faces. Angelology and physiognomy became more sophisticated and nuanced in the eastern Mediterranean in the Middle Ages as Christian and Muslim cultures employed these beliefs for many purposes, including comprehending and explaining human differences. Facial features and angels were intensely practical matters, yet these manifestations also taught important spiritual and theoretical lessons about equality and the search for purity in this world and the next. Along with honor, perhaps no other value occupied the western religions more than purity. Saints and holy people were indeed pure, and ordinary folk certainly wanted favors from them and relationships with them. Saintly visages have already appeared in this book. People, and especially artists, could project upon angels types of faces that reflect the findings of physiognomy and, by extension, the panoply of explanations for human variations.

Physiognomy

The ancient science of physiognomy taught its practitioners that physical traits revealed temperament, emotions, and character. Causes of physical variations among people and between species remained mysterious and connected to other theories; one might believe that the ways the stars and planets moved or the manner in which the four humors of the body were in balance actually determined how traits manifested themselves. Whether these external influences operated beneath the skin—for example, too much black bile caused melancholy and mournful features—or outside it—Saturn exercised the same baleful effect—the result was the same; these influences affected a physical feature or sign that adepts could interpret. In antiquity and the Middle Ages, people certainly understood the causes of some traits; it was no mystery that the heavy drinker had a red face and burst veins. For most traits, however, the causes were not so obvious. Aristotle understood the reciprocal relationships between changes in the body and changes in the soul.[1] Some changes in the spirit or soul obviously had no effect on the body. When a person became a doctor or a musician, none of this stored knowledge left any signs for the physiognomist to study.

By common agreement this science allowed its practitioners to see the inner person by observing physical traits. Self-diagnosis was possible, yet how people applied the principles to learning about themselves is an intriguing subject for which no evidence exists. Apparently, no one was interested in studying the soul or its emotions to determine how they sometimes affected the body's characteristics. The inheritance of physical and temperamental traits baffled observers, and few commentators tried to understand and explain to others in terms of physiognomy why children had some paternal and other maternal traits, or, indeed, mixed ones. A curious passage from the Babylonian Talmud, perhaps from the third century, in the context of discussing those physical flaws that barred people from serving in the temple, briefly considered types of mixings.[2] Here a rabbi expressed the view that tall should not marry tall, short not short, very white not very white, and very dark not very dark, because the children would turn out like the parents and hence be ineligible to serve in the temple. In the case of color, he feared that the children would be white like albinos or black like pots. Similar parental influences reinforced the trait in question, but it needs to be kept in mind that all the possible parents involved were Jews, so the mixes took place within the varieties of that particular people. Indeed, the message here seems to be that marriages that mixed these traits would produce children not barred from serving in the temple!

Another old theme related to physiognomy concerns the dark child born to white parents or the reverse. This fabled situation has been, across the centuries and the globe, an occasion for suspecting adultery or some mysterious intervention because the outcome, the color of the child, did not follow the expected pattern of like begetting like. One venerable theory had roots in the biblical story of Jacob's deal with Laban concerning the dark or spotted sheep (Genesis 30:31–43). Jacob figured out that if his ewes conceived while looking at streaked or spotted rods, they would give birth to lambs with the same trait and, by agreement, increase his share of the flocks. By this theory of inheritance, any woman bearing a child darker or lighter than anticipated could claim that some visual influence at the time of conception explained the result. Even past the end of the period covered here, Tommaso Campanella, writing his utopian work *The City of the Sun* in 1602, noted that by "magical means" paintings of colored horses, cattle, or sheep by visual suggestion affected the color of children born to women gazing at them at the right moment.[3] These bits of evidence suggest that somatic and nonsomatic forces shaped heredity in ways that no one really understood or could reconstruct. Was it the man or woman looking out the window at a brown or white cow that ended up affecting the child? Physiognomy, by studying the actual manifested traits, offered a surer path to understanding human difference.

One medieval thinker who tried to unify a grand theory of physical traits and features and heredity was the noted translator and astrologer Michael Scot, who for a time at the end of his life worked for the emperor Frederick II in Italy. Scot wrote a work on physiognomy sometime around 1230, and his research drew on a number of ancient sources. He was exceptionally interested in the question of mixed parentage. Scot took a holistic approach to physiognomy and treated it as a branch of medicine as well as one of the useful predictive arts. At the beginning of his text, he discusses in a fairly conventional manner the issues surrounding male and female seeds and how they contribute to the makeup of the embryo.[4] Among other issues, he puts forward the known fact that if the seed of the male is more powerful than that of the woman, the fetus will be like him in skin and strength in sex, which here must mean the sex of the child rather than its socially constructed gender.[5] To illustrate this point Scot notes that when a white woman has sex with an Ethiopian she produces a white daughter. A black woman having sex with a white man would have a black son, as was apparent all the time.

It is not clear what observations Scot is actually making about the issue of inherited skin color. What he has in mind seems to be a hierarchy of gender and color differences, complicated by racial prejudice. So the black man, apparently weaker in his sex, cannot overcome the superiority of his white partner, who will determine the sex (female) and color (white) of her child. A white man, however, will apparently always have a son with a black woman, as his gender is more powerful, but her seed must be stronger with respect to color. This was the only way to impose some order on the prevailing rules as Scot saw them; it may be that his thinking is simply implausible and inconsistent. The important point remains that Scot sees all these children, no matter what their parentage, as either white or black. His system of thought needs to preserve a sharp color line, just as clear as the one between the sexes. Hierarchies in gender and color complicate any logical effort to fathom the system here, but the consequences for the black son are interesting, as he apparently proves that black women may have only black children, and likewise white women, mating with white men, have white children. This line of reasoning would reinforce any tendency to have children follow the condition or social status of the mother, as mattered so much in slavery.[6] The problem for physiognomy is that skin color carried so many messages to the astute observer that its practitioners, like Scot, needed to preserve meaningful distinctions among even the many subtle gradations in human skin color. As a science, a body of knowledge capable of making testable predictions, physiognomy did not go far in helping people understand the inheritance of human differences. But this science, like others, revealed that certain traits were more common in particular ethnic groups and helped to define them. Aristotle had taught that certain ethnicities (*ethne*) in humanity shared common features.[7] It will be no surprise that color loomed large in this analysis. The classical inheritance here was not good for darker-skinned peoples, especially Africans.[8]

Physiognomy was not limited to cataloguing and analyzing physical traits. Analysis of gender explained physical differences and also stressed how men and women behaved differently.[9] Only women were capable of suckling children, only men had beards, and the sexes obviously differed in their genitals, a subject on which physiognomy texts were usually brief. Temperaments and physical characteristics shaped most of the analysis of gender. Still, even here, color might matter, and once again Scot offers an opinion that may reflect popular rather than learned traditions. He was certain that milk from black or brown women was always better than that from women he called white and red.[10] Why this should be the case is not made clear, and it is, of course, complicated by the fact that the milk itself, whatever the source, remained white. Perhaps Scot believed that darker women were closer in color to the goats and cows who also provided healthy milk for people. Somehow the white woman, closest in color to milk, did not produce the best type. Scot's opinion may have encouraged high-status white women to allow their darker slaves to nurse their offspring and believe it was better for the children. But most types of behavior were not so gendered.

Observing behavior closely was a skill necessary for understanding how traits were expressed not only as static signs but also through movements and gestures. How a person walked or how the eyes moved revealed a great deal about character and emotional states. In physiognomy, the sense of a person was holistic and included every way the body existed in time and space. Hence, the physiognomist was really a detective, and, once the object in question was sufficiently known, it was possible to predict the future behavior of such a constructed being. One of the most interesting features of physiognomy is that it did not privilege humans but instead looked for commonalities in the animal kingdom; a big head could be a sign of sensitivity in people and dogs.[11] Still, Aristotle was suspicious of equating people and animals; although he loved to catalogue similarities, he knew that no people were truly like animals.[12] He also understood that there was no point to a detailed analysis of a single person, where the traits would in a circular manner confirm the temperaments, and vice versa. The science was well positioned from the start to study people in groups.

The learned who believed physiognomy's claim to be a science knew the story of Philemon, whom scholars know to have been Antoninus Polemon (ca. 88–ca. 145), the rhetor, friend of Hadrian, and skilled author of a text on physiognomy.[13] In a well-known version of this story the students of Hippocrates drew a picture of their master and showed it to Philemon to test his skills.[14] Philemon looked at the portrait and concluded that the person was a crafty liar and a lustful man given to fornication. The students naturally were angry because Hippocrates had such a wonderful reputation, and their first impulse was to kill Philemon. But since the physiognomist had only read the picture as he saw it, the students returned to Hippocrates to tell him about the diagnosis. Their master was stunned and freely admitted that he had struggled his entire life to control these traits. The lessons here were several. First, physiognomy was proved to be an accurate science. Second, a person through reason and discipline had learned to control his bad traits. Thus, physiognomy did not invariably dictate destiny but left creatures the opportunity to be better or even worse than they were inclined.

This indeterminacy subsequently allowed Christians to practice their skills in applying this science in the real world. Roger Bacon had observed that the grace of God could help people overcome a bad disposition of the body, and physiognomy could reveal natural tendencies toward good and evil. Hence the science really concerned the ways people were inclined to behave and not necessarily their actual conduct.[15] But its predictive powers should not be depreciated. Everyone knew that the predictive powers of physiognomy in individual cases were not completely reliable, but there were many instances where these powers were worth considering. It may also have been true that many standard descriptions of famous men and women catalogued precisely those traits that people knowledgeable in physiognomy would need to know in order to interpret the character of the subject. Physiognomy continued into the Middle Ages to be useful for interpreting the traits of individuals or groups. Peter of Abano provides two examples; the bloodshot eyes of the Ghibelline tyrant Ezzelino da Romano revealed his evil, bloody temperament. Closer to home, Peter also noted that the people of his native Padua had moist, red eyes, in their case revealing a taste for wine and the habit of drunkenness.[16] Once the person or group was known, predictions were possible. In theory the science could help one choose an appropriate spouse, yet there was no advice about what sort of children resulted from marriage between different physical types. Physiognomy disappointed any of its students who were looking for a sustained and coherent explanation of human mixing. But it still claimed to be the best judge of the results. The face remained the best place to look for inner truths.

Saintly Faces

The *Golden Legend,* by the thirteenth-century Genoese archbishop Jacopo da Varagine, served in chapter 1 as a touchstone for received opinions about color prejudice. This compendium of saints' lives, drawn from a variety of sources and represented by Jacopo, is also a general source for impressions of the face. Once again, the widespread popularity of this work, and its translation into many vernacular languages, allow it to stand for the common knowledge of the period. The face was a remarkable thing, the greatest miracle of God in a small matter, because no two faces were alike.[17] Few of the hundreds of people appearing in the work received any detailed description of their faces, but there was an old story about the most important face—that of Jesus. Ancient tradition recorded the desire of Abgar of Edessa to have a portrait of Jesus, who instead pressed his image on a piece of linen for the king.[18] Jacopo is vague on details but notes that this face had good eyes and brow, and was long and inclined or looked upward, a sign of maturity. (It is no accident that the first feature mentioned was the eyes.) Saint Mark was also a model of a good face, with a long nose, a raised, noble brow, beautiful eyes, and a thick beard, his head balding with gray scattered in his hair.[19] Saint Bartholomew had black and curly hair, with a white (*candidus*) face, big eyes, equal and straight nostrils, and again was a little gray-haired with a thick beard.[20] The best and most familiar type of face emerges from these positive signs, and it is worth noting that the beard, not common in the shaved thirteenth century, obscured in men some of the facial color but none of the important features. A demon's face provided the obvious contrast. Here the Ethiopian inevitably had a flashing black sharp face, with a thick beard and hair reaching down almost to the feet, large red scintillating eyes, and sulfurous flames coming from the mouth—an altogether horrifying visage.[21] The patriarchal gaze here took in only male faces, but it applied the traditional rules to separate the good from the bad.

Not all religious traditions were in theory as receptive as polytheism and Christianity to the appeals of physiognomy. Jewish sources, so alert to any hint of pagan idolatry, remained in the Middle Ages, as S. D. Goitein has noted, uninformative about physical appearances in practical or theoretical settings.[22] Hence, there was little interest in physiognomy and only rare descriptions of people. The sage of Egyptian Jews, Abraham Maimonides (1186–1237), was simply described as a "tall old sheikh of lean body" with no other details, and even this much was highly unusual.[23] Muslims, too, were hostile to anything anthropomorphic.[24] Oddly, it was a Jewish convert to Islam, Samau'al al-Maghribī (d. circa 1175) who gave a precise description of the Prophet Muhammad, whom he saw in a dream in 1163.[25] According to this source, Muhammad was dressed in white, was of average height, heavy, a distinguished-looking man whose color was medium between pale and ruddy, yet somewhat swarthy. He also had black eyes and eyebrows. This description, obviously influenced by physiognomy, is altogether positive (except perhaps for the eyes) and may have escaped censure because it appeared in a dream that had a good result. Even so, Jewish and Islamic cultures cannot be expected to yield evidence on a par with Christian sources, where images and physical descriptions abound.

Another type of face conveyed meaning to those fortunate enough to view or imagine it. Angels naturally appeared however they wished, and artists had the privilege of inventing how they appeared. People in general projected onto angels their own cultural values. Angels were in theory incorporeal beings, but there was a *vultus angelicus*, an angelic face displaying the person's holiness. (It was said that Saint Dominic could tell a demon inside simply by looking at a human face.[26]) Gregory the Great made a famous pun by commenting on the faces of beautiful English (*Angli*) boy slaves as being really angelic (*vultos angelicos*).[27] Human powers to describe this face failed and left only a sense that whatever faces angels possessed, they were perfect. Faces might trick the unwary, however, as a famous story about Simon Magus revealed. This evil man impressed his own face on a saintly character in order to evade capture and death.[28] Saint Peter could, of course, see through this ruse to the real person beneath the false face, but it is remarkable that the power to shift faces, or in this case to be literally two-faced, taught the lesson that first appearances could be deceptive.

The *Legenda Aurea* also supplies clues to decoding the face's most distinctive feature, the eyes. One of the miracles told about Saint Thomas of Canterbury concerned an English woman who wanted to have *oculos varios* (blue-grey eyes) and for her vanity was blinded instead.[29] After some difficulty she succeeded in getting her original, seeing eyes back, but the story reveals an amazing desire predating by seven centuries the invention of contact lenses. In the life of Saint Basil appears the story of a grieving father whose daughter has fallen in love with a slave, and he regrets that the sweet light of his eyes has been extinguished.[30] Here the complexity is the doubt about how the eyes functioned: did the light of the eye come from within to see the outside world, or did it gather its light from external sources? Whatever the source of the eye's light, everyone knew that when the light went out of a person's eye, it was a sign of grief or worse. Finally, Jacopo da Varagine's retelling of the legend of Barlaam and Josaphat brought to western readers a dim echo of the Buddha's life in the guise of the eastern prince Josaphat.[31] This admirable noble had most beautiful and healthy eyes, able to look safely at a magic stone. This case implies that the good character within made the eyes capable of taking in a sight that injured lesser people. This typical collection of stories conforming to the canons of physiognomy left its readers with a clear sense of good and bad faces, as well as some idea that the eyes were the most revealing feature.

Medieval physiognomists treated the works of their predecessors with respectful awe. Peter of Abano's treatise on physiognomy, dated to 1295, drew on a comprehensive range of classical, Jewish, and Muslim authors.[32] What is most striking is how he synthesized astrology and physiognomy to create an overarching system for understanding human types. Michael Scot, working earlier in the thirteenth century, also attempted to see the big picture by trying to unify physiognomy with a theory of human temperaments or complexions that derived its data from organs like the liver, lungs, and stomach.[33] Of course, at times this reasoning became circular; the liver was not so easy to observe, so its state might be deduced from liverish behaviors or moods. The Muslim world, conflicted about the moral value of the classical inheritance, nonetheless had a deeper and more continuous contact with ancient physiognomy, and scholars working in the Christian parts of the Mediterranean depended on the Muslim world for good texts. A great Muslim synthesis, the *Kitāb al-Firāsa* by Al-dīn al-Rāzī (d. 1210) naturally drew on a different vision of the world where the five great races or nations were the Arabs, Greeks, Persians, Indians, and Turks.[34] His gaze began in the eastern Mediterranean, where Greeks stood as proxy for all the peoples to the west. Al- Rāzī knew ancient works like Polemon well and brought to the science the fruit of centuries of Arab views on gender and how the eyes worked. Only this type of source reveals that the Arabs admired women with blinking eyes.[35] The more famous Zakariyyā al-Rāzī, whose vast work on early medieval medicine contained a section on physiognomy, stressed in a chapter on examination of slaves before purchase why it was important to learn their physical and moral health.[36]

The Eyes Have It

The point to introducing physiognomy into this study is to determine how the science shaped medieval perceptions of ethnic difference. Since the science was vast and this book's interest in it rather narrow, it seems best to focus attention on one feature, the eyes, which all the texts regarded as most important. After all, in Matthew 6:22–23, Jesus famously observed that the eye was the light (*lampada,* lamp) of the soul and that the good or evil in the eye revealed the status of the entire body and, by extension, the soul. The great sixteenth-century synthesis on physiognomy by Giovan Battista Della Porta observed that the color of the eyes followed the color of the body, so there was a natural connection between eye and skin color.[37] A fourth-century anonymous Latin text, a great summary of ancient physiognomy, provides the best and lengthiest analysis of the eyes shaping medieval attitudes on the subject. Knowing the eyes was the real test of a physiognomist's skills, and the main attributes were color, moistness, size, and movement.[38] Color was the most obvious feature, and the pupil was always black, surrounded by a colored circle and then the iris proper, with its own tint. Black eyes were a sign that the person was stupid, bad, and greedy. (It is fair to observe here that all the texts, after bowing to inclination rather than determinacy, discussed the traits as unambiguous signs.) Eyes labeled *glauci* seem to cover a wide group typified by being colored like the sea—a sort of blue-gray-green depending how they appeared in the light. Grey eyes were not easy to distinguish from *glauci,* but they were usually a good sign. Because there were so many types and varieties of these eyes they were hard to read, so other traits helped to define temperaments. For example, small pupils signified a servile, wily, and greedy person. Dry glauci eyes indicated somebody who was fierce, wild, and untamed. It is easy to see how these signs would be very useful to someone peering into the eyes of slaves, looking for the right type. Deep blue eyes that were moist were better than dry ones, but a whitish blue denoted timidity, always a bad sign. The best eyes were *glauci* (undoubtedly among the most common) when they were moist, tranquil, big, and quite shiny. By inference, the worst eyes were black, darting, shifty or spinning, and small. It is remarkable that this text, like the others, did not mention brown eyes.

Eyes moved in a variety of ways; they might be wall-eyed, crossed, looking up or down, left or right, trembling, or darting here and there. Straightforward eyes (and people) were best but shifty eyes disturbed observers. The anonymous text cites

Polemon as an authority on the emperor Hadrian's eyes, which were grey, moist, piercing, big, and very bright—altogether good.[39] Yet even brightness was not always a good sign; in black eyes it was a sign of trickery. Hence, the eyes revealed emotional states and sanity as well as temperament. There were laughing and cheerful eyes, as well as somber ones.[40] Frequently blinking eyes revealed fear and weakness, and when they were also dry the person was planning tricks and ambushes.[41] This science yielded nothing to some more modern and supposedly scientific means of detecting lies and the people who tell them. This text concluded its analysis of the eye with a brief word on the preferred condition for eyelashes: black, thick, and rigid.[42] On the head such hair would be a bad sign but for eyelashes it was good. Thin, soft, red eyelashes were yet another sign of a weak character.

Medieval commentators inherited these great and complex texts and repackaged the material for the special concerns of their audiences. The task here is not to write the neglected history of medieval physiognomy, or even the crucial part of it concerning the eyes, but rather to convey some sense of the refinements introduced by these subsequent writers. Since the connections between these texts have been barely established, noting something in one author is no guarantee that the observation was original to him. But the science of physiognomy was cumulative, and the texts convey the impression that these authors had a strong sense that they were participating in a profound tradition to which they might nevertheless add a few fresh insights. A tenth-century Byzantine book on interpreting dreams taught that "eyes symbolize faith, reputation, and spiritual illumination," hence the terrible fear of dreaming that one was blind, which meant that bad things were bound to happen.[43] In the early thirteenth century Al-dīn Al-Rāzī was convinced that the state of the eyes indicated what was going on in the mind, and the connection for him was the humors that loomed so large in his understanding of the human body.[44] Size of the tear ducts was a sign of the heat coming from the brain, and so dry eyes indicated a lack of this cranial fluid. Hence, tears without cause (he means here grief and the like) or their lack were signs of deeper things. A pupil bleared with fluid looking like a spider's web was a sign of approaching death. Again, what could be more valuable to a potential slave purchaser than seeing this harbinger?[45] Al-Rāzī's strong reliance on humors helped to explain to his satisfaction why black eyes were a sign of fearfulness—too much black bile—and why blue eyes, here called white, were a sign of too much lymph and hence proof of timidity.[46] The causes here were different and so were the expressions of fearfulness, one type more gloomy and depressed, the other more lethargic. It is perhaps not surprising to read in an Arabic text that blue eyes were signs of stupidity, laziness, and other bad things.[47] He concluded that grey eyes were the best and the only ones to praise, placed as they were in the (Aristotelian) middle of the other colors—black, blue, and green—which were to be blamed, presumably on account of the bad traits associated with them. He claimed to know that both the lion and the eagle had grey eyes.

Michael Scot was more interested in the shape and movement of the eyes than their color.[48] He observed that people with large eyes like cows were simple, slow-witted, had bad memories, and ate too much. He too favored an eye color he considered to be in the middle, in this case rather tending toward blackness; he uses no word close to grey. But he spells out in more detail the good qualities of such people. They were peaceful, mild, and smart, with good ideas and serviceable to others; they seem to be good advisers. (It is worth noting here an unusual feature of the way Scot appreciated colors. He believed that particular colors characterized dreams, so a black, dark, or smoky-colored dream signified death, sadness, corpses, illness, and the like.[49]) Peter of Abano knew and cited the pseudo-Aristotelian *Secret of Secrets*, but he was an abstract thinker who wrote about color in general terms, mixing in comments on hair, skin, and eyes. For example, he offered the specific view that a shade between pale yellow and black, which inclined toward a bright brown, was generally the best.[50] The obvious problem is that there was no agreement on what constituted the appropriate spectrum and the best color in the middle. Peter also clearly knew Al-Rāzī or some other Arabic source (or indeed a common Greek text) because he made similar points about the timidity of black and pale eyes, though he did not connect them to the humors.[51] He followed the same path to the best eyes, concluding that strongly black tending toward yellow—which he learnedly called *caropi*--matched the eyes of eagles and lions. It is clear that he, too, was reaching for the color gray, however defined as some implausible mix of black and yellow.

Eyes were the most complex but by no means the only signs the body displayed. Enough has been seen here to support a few generalizations about physiognomy and ethnography. The legacy of ancient physiognomy to the Middle Ages was a form of racism that still valued or devalued people on the basis of skin color, indeed even the color of the iris. When medieval descriptions of people appear similar or formulaic, the canons of physiognomy were at work, supplying human types that fit the heroic king or the sly slave. This was not a science requiring further elaboration; the ancient texts were so sophisticated that no subtlety of the human form escaped their scope. Only when medieval people came upon new groups not included in physiognomy texts would a need arise to incorporate the latest observations into the old, respected theory. Ethnography needed physiognomy in order to turn mere description into a useful and above all predictive set of facts. In the thirteenth century, first the Mongols and then other new peoples farther to the East brought before physiognomists fresh faces that needed explaining. These encounters happened in a European cultural context already well prepared to plug new observations into entrenched theory.

The human face and especially its eyes offered the soundest basis for generalizing about the whole person's temperament and behavior. Still, the path to this knowledge was blocked at every turn by puzzling inconsistencies and contradictions. Where exactly was the middle between too light and too dark? What was the best size for an eye or the best tone of skin color? Somatic norms and ethnic loyalties could carry analysis only so far. What was truly best, and how could one learn it? A clue had already surfaced in the faces of the saints, but here too impermanence and variety baffled synthesis. What better place to look than the depictions of angels to discover what might be best in humans?

The Appearance of Angels

Physiognomy may at first glance seem an inappropriate tool for studying spiritual beings whose bodies are at best a kind of temporary disguise for the benefit of humans. Obviously, historians cannot explain angels' choices about how to appear to people, but they can study how people perceived and illustrated angels. Ethnography also might seem a poor way to investigate angels, as their heavenly division of labor does not correspond to ethnic cleavages in humanity. If ethnic groups differ in how they portray angels, however, then patterns in these styles should reveal local hierarchies about what constituted a pleasing face or its best color. The task here is to distinguish the vast literature about the symbolism of angels, properly a discipline in itself called angelology, from the narrow and relevant interest in the literal facts about angels and most importantly how they appeared and were recreated by artists. An enduring lesson about angels is that people always wanted to have good relationships with them, and these ties, obviously mixed, create yet another model for how people chose to interact with different categories of the Other.

Physical people wanted relationships with these spiritual angels, but with what type of being, exactly, and on what level? As Ibn Khaldûn observed, angels lived in a world of pure intellect, were free from bodies and matter, and understood the world perfectly.[52] The Jewish philosopher Moses Maimonides (1135–1204) was also emphatic that angels "are not endowed with bodies" and have "no fixed corporeal shape."[53] Human understanding of angels was at best partial because they were so clearly not human; no matter how they might appear at times, they did not think or act like people. Here, the historian's task is to occupy the territory of the literal without straying into reductionism or absurdity. There is so much kitsch in contemporary popular culture about relationships with angels that must be put aside in order to look usefully at the historical issues surrounding the model of these ties. So these angels are not touching us or crashing through the ceiling, but instead posing literal questions about hierarchy and difference.

A very old and puzzling story from Genesis (6:1–4), really a prelude to the account of the flood, briefly explains how some angels mated with the attractive daughters of humans and produced a mixed breed of giants. The ensuing evils convinced God to destroy all of his creation, sparing only Noah and his kin. A longer version of this story exists in the first book of Enoch, an apocryphal work whose core dates from the Maccabean period and which is known in its most complete form only through an Ethiopian translation of a lost Aramaic original.[54] The authors of the book of Enoch drew upon old traditions that find echoes in other books of the Bible and indeed the Quran. Since the fullest story was unknown in the period covered here, Enoch had no direct effect outside Ethiopia on the ways people perceived angels. But the atmosphere of the story reflects a general sense of what happened when people and angels misbehaved together, and faint lessons about this problem appear everywhere as one of the first findings concerning the ethnography of angels.

Enoch knew this story from a vision transmitted to him by the good angels. Two hundred angels, known as the Watchers, formed a pact to mate with the beautiful daughters of human beings. These angels were spiritual, immortal beings whom God never intended to have children, so they were making a very big mistake. The angels taught these human women all about the many powers of plants, and most important had children with them, the mixed breed called giants. Misguided unions of spirit and flesh produced a new species of bloody, evil oppressors, known above all as great consumers who literally chewed up the resources of the earth. It is worth pausing to consider the lesson of the giants, who were so wicked that they needed to be destroyed and hence prompted the deluge. Inappropriate mixing across a barrier not meant to be breeched violated the order of nature and God's plan. The resulting giants were an abomination oppressive to all people, not just their mothers, and an eventual offense to the good angels as well. The lesson found in Ecclesiasticus 13:15—that every beast loves its like, and that all creatures flock together with their own kind—served as an ethnographic biblical reminder to stick to one's one kind when it came to having children. Angels and people were clearly different (but somehow close enough to mate); the problem arose when applying the lesson within the human family.

Azazel, the chief teacher among the Watchers, brought to people a knowledge of weapons and cosmetics, and other angels taught about alchemy and astrology. But these skills did not compensate for all the problems the giants caused. Good angels saw all this and took the case of humanity to God, who promptly ordered the flood. God directed Raphael to bind the chief bad angel Azazel and throw him into darkness, and sent Gabriel to act against the children of the Watchers, who hoped for eternal life and instead were placed on the path to self-destruction. The fate of the mixed breed is complex, but it seemed fitting to have them fight among themselves. Michael was dispatched to bind all the other rebellious angels in Hell, where they were to await their final judgment, and to destroy their women and their children, the giants. Righteous people would escape all this and restore a peaceful and just world. The drama of the ensuing sections of the book partly derives from Enoch's selfless desire to intercede for these wicked angels, and he will not succeed in averting God's wrath on them. It is interesting to note that among the many troubling ideas coming from the Egyptian Christian exegete Origen was the thought that maybe fallen angels and even the devil could be saved, and people and demons could change places.[55] The children of the Watchers seem by all accounts to be beyond the pale. Nothing about their appearance or the qualities of their parents, apart from the attractiveness of their mothers, comes up in any biblical source, but giant size is a clue that they were bad news for their Lilliputian cousins. As hyperconsumers, the giants were a warning against mixed relationships, which literally crushed communities.

Angelology early on established a vivid and detailed model of a celestial hierarchy. This learned discipline should be distinguished from angelolatry, a popular tendency in some times and places to worship angels in inappropriate ways.[56] It is good to begin with this image because, drawing on pieces from Hebrew and Christian scriptures, it becomes a thread through the entire common era, coming through Saint Augustine, Pseudo-Dionysius, Gregory the Great, and becoming even better known through works by Jacopo da Varagine and Dante. It is clear that the celestial hierarchy according to the shadowy Pseudo-Dionysius (early sixth century) was born in the eastern Mediterranean and reflected certain common assumptions about the world, most obviously hierarchy and subordination. Some details on this process of transmission are provided later, but for now what is important is the general model itself. The celestial hierarchy consisted of three sets of triads: the highest, those closest to God, were the seraphim, cherubim, and thrones; the next, dominations, virtues, and powers, mysterious beings seeing and praising God; and, lastly, the principalities, archangels, and angels—the last two connecting this hierarchy to people in this world.[57] By common (and right-thinking) agreement, God had created all of these levels of angels in an act of monogenesis, probably on the first day of creation, when light was separated from dark.

From the beginning, these angels were not equal, and therein rests the argument that they were not the same in proximity to God, or in powers, or, most importantly, in their roles in human affairs. The heavenly host consisted of unequal entities who gave and received commands, but all were superior to the subsequently created man and woman. This hierarchy of functions mimicked a division of labor among the angels in which groups specialized in various tasks. For example, Jacopo da Varagine explained the jobs of the third triad of angels.[58] Principality angels watched over the interests of empires, archangels protected big groups of people or cities, and angels guarded specific people. Angelology hence posited that work itself—in human terms, the hierarchy of trades—taught people important lessons about inequality and how to justify it. Distinguishing beings by function was not the only social lesson to be learned from angels. Pseudo-Dionysius stressed that these angels glowed by fire, and this was neither a human attribute or one easily understood by the human mind.[59] These angels also participated in a color symbolism, along with stones and other material objects, that associated white with light, red with fire, yellow with gold, and green with youth and the flower of the soul. Naturally, only the good colors appeared in this description of the celestial hierarchy. To think in literal terms about these angels was also to consider their own ethnography—their behaviors and powers, but most crucially, their physiognomy or appearance. For example, a common and inexplicable fact about the seraphim is that they were frequently portrayed with wings covered with human eyes, a startling image. Even more vivid than the peacock's markings, these eyes amaze the viewer with the idea of how great a soul must rest behind so many windows. Such eyes were almost never black or brown. All these angelic traits, so different from their human equivalents, provided a model for thinking first about their relations with people and then, inevitably, about the nature of human inequality itself. The inequalities among angels trained humans to expect the same ordering among people, but they were, of course, not the only way to understand hierarchy among humans. Color would help those so inclined to divide people into those who commanded and those who obeyed.

The western tradition about angels begins with the ancient Hebrews, who, like their fellow monotheists, would never accept that these angels had anything in common with pagan spirits or daemons, or that they represented some sort of fallen assembly of the gods who succumbed to the Lord of Hosts.[60] As James Kugel has rightly stressed, the nature of angels was not static but changed over time as these mysterious messengers existed in various historical contexts.[61] Also, he located the origins of these beings securely in the heart of the eastern Mediterranean: "Angels are a peculiarly Israelite phenomenon in the ancient Near East."[62] From the somewhat vague three visitors to Abraham to the being Jacob wrestled and the ones he saw on the ladder, through the more specific images of Isaiah and Ezekiel, to the numerous appearances in the New Testament of Gabriel and the Annunciation, to the same archangel Gabriel in the desert speaking to the Prophet Muhammad, these stories are among the most famous in the western tradition. Think about some other stories: the sacrifice of Isaac, Moses receiving the law, Daniel in his den, the angels announcing the birth of Jesus, and the ones at his baptism, crucifixion, resurrection, and ascension. And there is the parallel set of stories from Creation forward about the bad angels, whose chief, Satan, or Iblis in the Islamic tradition, had a long and unhappy role in the affairs of humanity. In all the monotheistic religions, the trend seems to be that the two levels of angels closest to people became more humanoid, sometimes had names, and often had more personal relationships with individual people.[63] This is nowhere more vivid perhaps than in Islam, with its clear sense that each person had a specific recording angel, one on the right and one on the left, who noted good and bad deeds that would be weighed in the final judgment.[64]

How people in the eastern Mediterranean conceived of angels was becoming more complex over time. To move toward some medieval understandings about angels, we need to establish a sort of benchmark or generic set of ideas about the literal qualities of angels. Again, the entire field of angelology is not relevant here; instead the focus is on the literal because it was the easiest part of this matter for most people to relate to, and the most literal of the literal—how angels might appear to the human eye—was, of course, most important to those who wanted to recognize the messengers as well as the message. People understood that these angels were not quite real, hence the value of thinking about them as humanlike beings who, after a time of appearing as smoke or pillars of fire, more commonly manifested themselves in a form people recognized as resembling their own. Inevitably, people found it impossible to have a relationship with a cloud of smoke, so from a human perspective anthropomorphizing these spiritual beings was a logical step in the process of relating to them. For example, the tenth-century Byzantine book on interpreting dreams analyzed what it meant when someone dreamed about angels. If the angel was one of the approved ones listed in holy books, then the dream signified good, happy news. If someone being persecuted had the dream, he would be saved. Even in dreams, it was possible and desirable to have a relationship with angels.[65]

With this context in mind, consider some of the grandest themes about angels.[66] (1) Angels were very numerous spiritual beings that could take on human form. They were rational creatures, even if their minds were incomprehensible to humans. (2) Judaism and Islam, with their special horror of graven images, provide no tradition of an iconography of angels in the visual arts but there are verbal descriptions. Christianity differs profoundly from the other monotheistic traditions on images and hence supplies virtually all the visual evidence. And here is the entire story in miniature: the Christian tradition is the only place to look for the medieval physiognomy and ethnography of angels and all they entail. (3) Angels connected this world to the divine and conveyed messages between them, though the great majority of communication descended from heaven to earth. They spent much of their time interceding for or protecting individual people or even nations, but they were not to be worshiped. (4) Michael the archangel became a saint with a popular cult throughout the eastern Mediterranean. In general, however, angels, even those coming down to earth, were not saints, and the saints were true humans who eventually joined the humanoid angels in heaven. (5) Angels were joyous, kindly, amazing, and beautiful—at least, the good ones. They therefore represented a model for what people might be and, by extension, how they might appear. (6) Angels were eternal, and when not disguised they had feathered wings and could fly. The feathers should be kept in mind, because along with footprints, they were something tangible an angel might leave behind in this world. (7) Angels appeared on earth, but their natural home was heaven, and wherever they might visit they would need to return home, to ascend, to rise. (8) Angels were gendered in oddly masculine, sexless ways. After a few early exceptions they were never bearded, and they were never, ever, old. (9) They loved light; they did not eat or drink but might seem to at times, and maybe there was something special for them called angel food. They were creatures of brightness who preferred white robes, or a sleeved *dalmatic* (shift) with a mantle (*pallium*) over it. Some angels, notably Michael, appeared as warriors in military dress with a cuirass. (10) When angels appeared, their primary function was to convey God's word, so angels spoke and hence had a sound accompanying their appearance. A Talmudic tradition holds that except for Gabriel the angels did not speak Aramaic.[67] Later peoples did not care about this tradition, but they needed to consider just what languages the angels spoke. (11) Fallen angels, the devil and his minions, existed. They conveyed a powerful set of literal images concerning the symbolic contrasts between good and evil as also being between light and dark. So all the negative associations of darkness surface again, this time clearly tied to malignant forces. Still, there were, alas, some people who wanted relationships with these demons, and their ties provide yet more models of disastrous mixed relationships.

The lowest two orders on the celestial hierarchy, the archangels and angels, being closest to humans and their guardians, were the ones with whom humans could hope to form bonds. An infernal hierarchy, less easily defined, also offered scope for making ties that doomed the people in them. A bit of angelology from Saint Augustine and the Quran is useful here because it illustrates the developing sense of the rules that governed the interactions between people and angels. Throughout his discussion of angels in the *City of God*, Augustine stressed the role of choice—the devil's pride and subsequent fall resulted from a free decision to be that way.[68] Hence, the angels of light were good by nature and choice, while the angels of darkness were good by nature (as their creator intended) but evil by choice.[69] Augustine here reinforced the strong connection between lightness and good, and darkness and evil, with inevitable consequences for people assigned to these categories. He also made clear that it was possible for people to be in fellowship, his term for relationship, with angels, and by this choice the good people were destined to join the angels in heaven.[70] Studying angels was worthwhile precisely because fellowship with them led to so many good consequences as people chose good and eschewed evil. Augustine had no trouble in associating these devils with pagan deities and demons, a word no longer conveying a classical, neutral sense of a spirit but now in a Christian context something deeply evil. Another distinguishing feature was that "the good angels hold cheap all the knowledge of material and temporal matters, which inflates the demons with pride."[71] Augustine was not interested here in how angels appeared, but as symbols of good and evil, both angels and demons evoked images of light and dark that became embedded in the discourse about them.

It is thus no surprise that the revelations vouchsafed to the prophet Mohammad contained nothing about how angels appeared, so strong was the injunction against images. Tradition held that usually when Mohammad saw Gabriel, he appeared in human form and took on the attractive aspect of his good friend Zahya.[72] Gabriel educated and guided Mohammad, and helped to establish his role as a true prophet in a monotheistic setting.[73] Gabriel was the angel of revelation, "the constant councillor and helper of the Prophet."[74] Also, prevailing Jewish and Christian ideas about angels found many points of contact in Islam: the primary job of angels was to praise God, but they were also sent with a purpose—to warn people or convey revelations, as Gabriel did for Mohammad. Those people who gave angels female names did not believe in the hereafter and were doomed, so it was clear that angels were male (Sura 53:27). All the angels bowed down before man except Iblis, or Satan, and that was why he was banished from heaven. Angels prayed for people in general and hence had the power to intercede (Sura 42:5). Most vividly, each person had a set of two angels, one on the left and one on the right, who recorded one's bad and good deeds (Sura 50:17-19). Hence every word and deed in this life were marked down in the accounts of the appropriate angel. Another tradition held that one angel was a moral and intellectual biographer while the other one recorded actual deeds. Bad thoughts not acted upon did not weigh against a person.[75] A tradition outside the Quran taught that two angels questioned a person at the grave, which for the unbeliever became Hell, and for the believer served as a place to prepare for Paradise.[76] Here, as with Augustine, there may appear to be some overlap with the functions of saints, but the difference is in fact stark: saints were human and hence had bodies just like other people; angels and demons were spiritual beings that occasionally appeared as humanoids.

Since holy texts conveyed so little information on how angels appeared, artists were left to bring the key episodes to life by using their imaginations within the rules or conventions governing religious themes. So, for example, the demonic face displayed a grimace or could be portrayed as laughing, while the angelic face was calm and limited to a pleasant smile not displaying the teeth, which were sometimes part of a menacing visage.[77] Simple physiognomy therefore taught that the angels were pleasant and attractive while the demons were threatening and ugly. Little else was known about the face except that some biblical passages referred to it as fiery or glowing.[78] One study has collected some examples of a famous episode from the New Testament when an angel tells the three women visiting Christ's tomb that he has risen.[79] Andreas Petzold concluded that this angel often had "a bright red, reddish brown or pink face," that was more than a "medieval conception of lightening" but also signified the fires of love and damnation.[80] Many other illustrations of angels from throughout the eastern Mediterranean place them at the birth of Jesus and especially as announcing this event to the shepherds. In such scenes, there is often a contrast between the pale angels and the much darker shepherds, who after all worked outdoors and would be in any naturalistic setting darker than most people, and certainly the angels.[81] Here too there is a simple symbolic lesson; in the contrast between light and darkness the angels were invariably on the white or brighter side of the line, while the demons were dark or black. This finding is to be expected, but it remains to be seen how it holds up in parts of the eastern Mediterranean where the people themselves were darker, closer to the shepherds, and therefore likely to portray the differences between angels and demons in different ways. As an example, some of the earliest sub-Saharan African angels that can be securely dated appear in an Ethiopian manuscript from the late thirteenth century.[82] These angels appear in tan colors, with dark hair and eyes, and no doubt conform to the expectations of Ethiopian viewers rather than, say, contemporary Italian standards for portraying angels.

Before analyzing the artistic evidence for one angel in more detail, it is useful to consider what Dante had to say about the appearance of angels, since they figure so prominently in his *Paradiso*, itself a work of great importance in shaping medieval opinions about angels. Dante's angels were pure spiritual beings who appeared as the heavenly hosts ringing God. He accepted the learned traditions of angelology concerning the nine orders of angels, whom Dante saw in all their intelligent purity. Angel eyes were always turned toward God (*Paradiso* 29), and the angelic host was like a golden swarm of bees (*Paradiso* 31). And then Dante makes his most specific comment on how angels appeared: all their faces had a living flamelike quality (there is scriptural support for this), and they had golden wings (like the bees) and had faces whiter than any snow.[83] Not surprisingly, Dante places the angelic face at the purest end of the color spectrum with the most common simile—white as snow. Anyone looking at the innumerable images of angels portrayed in Florentine or Sienese art in the fourteenth or fifteenth centuries will see thousands of such white angels, so often with a detail Dante omits—the blondest of hair. This type conforms to one of the contemporary standards of beauty for women, yet these ostensibly male angels follow the same prototype or archetype of human attractiveness.

Saint Michael the Archangel

Michael for a number of reasons seems the best choice of angels for detailed analysis. Michael was important everywhere but certainly a strong force in the eastern Mediterranean, and he was among the most frequently discussed and portrayed angels in pictures and statues. His name, which in Hebrew means "Who is like God?" prompts the inevitable answer: no one. Yet this angel was close indeed to the divinity and soon enough came to occupy the position of chief among the archangels. Michael also serves to return this study to its starting point and the themes of relationship. People wanted to have relationships with Michael, and this tie, inevitably profoundly mixed, reveals a great deal about the many things people expected from him. The bond was plainly asymmetrical because Michael, and the rest of the host he represents here, did not want anything from people. Most unusually, Michael became a saint with a common feast day, September 29 (Michaelmas), and hence, was an appropriate object for worship, which angels ordinarily were not. This exception is useful because it accounts for the many stories and pictures concerning Michael and his activities. Still, Michael may have wanted just a bit more from people than the rest of the angels did, and this too makes relationship a useful tool for exploring how people connected to the abstract, formless, spiritual, and illusory nature of angels.[84] Because the feast day eventually honored all angels, it serves as a reminder that Michael stood as a representative of his heavenly colleagues. Still, as Michel Rouche noted, it is odd that while the cult of the saints has received so much scholarly attention, the part angels played in this cult and other religious practices has been neglected.[85]

Written sources, as well as images, provide good evidence for elucidating the physiognomy and ethnography of Michael, as he stands for the rest of the angels, as well as in details unique to him, especially his being frequently depicted in military dress. Many trails lead back to Egypt, where Michael received early and detailed veneration.[86] Several times in this book Egypt has provided good reasons for looking more closely at issues of human skin color and how attitudes toward it shaped general views about hierarchy and subordination. But not only Egypt. The Ethiopic text of 1 Enoch contains an old core of Jewish tradition concerning Enoch's vision and the being that came down from heaven in the form of a snow-white person, with three companions also white (1 Enoch 87:1–3). This being has been plausibly identified with Michael as the leader, accompanied by three other archangels.[87] This part of Enoch's vision, also known as the *Animal Apocalypse*, describes a version of the future in which symbolic animals take leading parts, most notably white cows, who mysteriously become Noah and his sons (1 Enoch 89:1). Color symbolism once again privileged whiteness and from early on tied this good color of light to Michael. Students of angelology have naturally taken an interest in how Michael came to occupy so important a position in the earliest Christian thought; angels appear 175 times in the New Testament, archangels twice, and Michael twice.[88] Michael became a powerful force among early Christians, probably because of his prominent role in *Revelation* as the slayer of the Antichrist. Who Michael was naturally leads to the important question of how he functioned in human society.

One of the most pervasive images of the Mediterranean world is the evil eye, a disembodied organ that might cause or avert evil—another nice optical problem for the legacy of physiognomy. The evil eye was really a curse prompted by the ill wishes or envy of one person against another. Countermagic was needed to avert the evil eye, and what better instrument than a good one, in this case, the "much suffering eye," the talisman that could turn back envy and hate against their instigators.[89] A Byzantine story, contained in a magical work called the *Testament of Solomon*, told that the Archangel Michael gave King Solomon a signet ring giving him power over many demons, and this explained how the proverbially wise king learned that the much-suffering eye averted envy. That one eye countered another made sense, and that the powerful Michael was once again a friend to humans was no surprise—that was part of his job.

Jacopo da Varagine's life of Saint Michael became during the Middle Ages the best known account of this archangel's activities, and as an industrious compiler Jacopo helped to represent the tradition on angels going back to the early church.[90] Jacopo summarized at the beginning the most important things Michael did or would do, most notably, fighting successfully with the devil for the body of Moses (this an old story known from Jude 9), bringing the plagues on the Egyptians, and being the warrior for Christ who would eventually kill the Antichrist.[91] Michael was also singled out for his work as a psychopomp who conducted the souls of the saints to heaven. Other angels helped to accompany the souls of ordinary believers to the next world. This was yet another relationship that people wanted with the angels, for the alternative bond with demons conducting them elsewhere was terrifying.[92] Jacopo compared the angelic host to a princely court in the sense that duties were divided among various levels of angels for good reasons.[93] It was easy for people to understand his comparison of angels to the bureaucratic ranks of officials needed to run a kingdom or a city-state, from counselors at the top to bailiffs at the bottom. Michael's feast day served as a way to commemorate and honor all the angels, so Jacopo seems to have conceived this date as a close parallel to feasts honoring all souls or all saints. It helped to personify the myriad angels with a particular face—Michael's. Angels, with Michael standing for all, deserved to be praised and honored because they were our guardians, servants, brothers and fellow citizens, the conductors of our souls to heaven, the presenters of our prayers to God, and the most noble warriors of the Eternal King and consolers to the afflicted.[94] These tasks are familiar, but for the future Genoese archbishop Jacopo to use the word *concives* is important because it clearly established a fellowship between mortals and angels, who were fellow citizens in a community that encompassed this world and the next. Even though people and angels were distinct beings, they were brothers (never sisters) and shared with people a common membership if not equal status in God's creation. Jacopo would not have believed that all citizens were equal, but he would have understood and defended a threshold of minimum shared purpose and rights that defined the status of citizen.[95] Hence, on many levels, the truly mixed relationship between people and angels provided a fresh perspective and context for looking at all types of hierarchies in this world and the next.

Jacopo explained the angels' seven tasks or functions in detail, concluding on a strong note about how the angels comforted the afflicted.[96] Angels conveyed the basic message that people should be of good courage and not be consumed by fear. When they intervened in human affairs, as they did for Daniel, they brought courage to the despairing. As guardians, good angels were appointed to people in the womb and then after birth remained for life to protect their charges.[97] The relationship between a person and his or her guardian angel was as old as the one between mother and child. For all these reasons it is quite clear that people needed to have good relations with angels, with Michael standing as their best possible friend. Yet Jacopo did not write one word on what this friend might have looked like. This reticence was common even in references to the saints, about whose appearance there was often little said, and a physical description of Jesus himself seemed improper. Michael made himself known by his functions or works, and other sources have to supplement what can be learned about what types of physiognomy and ethnicity people placed upon him.

Jacopo's synthesis on angels takes the story to the late thirteenth century, and it is useful to have a few subsequent additions to these images before looking deeper into the Michael stories. Everywhere, pictures of the Last Judgment included Michael weighing souls. In the fourteenth century, a few angels appear as women, and it is important to be alert for signs of how images of the heavenly host began to include women.[98] At some point in the later Middle Ages, it became more common to equate angels with comets or stars, a natural connection to their heavenly abode and movements in the heavens.[99] Finally, in the fourteenth century visual sources showed angels playing musical instruments, which added an audio component to the heavenly experience.[100] These developments prove that angels remained a vibrant part of Mediterranean culture and became associated with deeper interests in music and astronomy. That female angels appear in the images must testify to a greater sense among artists and audience that a realistic equation of the celestial and earthly orders required an actual portrayal of gender. After all, the learned sources provided no support whatsoever for female angels, so the impetus for their creation must have come from some need to make the relationship even more like all the rest in human life, and, as half the people were women, perhaps they began to prefer female guardians and models.

With this context in mind, a closer look at the specific stories concerning Michael will fill in the gaps on the issues of faces, ethnicity, and relationship central to this study. An old hint from Saint Paul in Colossians 2.18 suggests a problem in southwest Asia Minor where some early Christians were making the mistake of worshiping angels. This prohibition, a legacy of ancient Judaism, would also become a tenet in Islam, and so in the first six or seven centuries of the Common Era in the eastern Mediterranean, the dominant discourse remained hostile to angelolatry. Glenn Peers has looked closely at a very early story about Michael, possibly fifth century in origin but reworked in the eighth century, which concerned a miracle that took place at Chonae, ancient Colossus.[101] Pagans were threatening the very early local hermit Archippus, so the context looks older than the surviving versions. In order to dislodge Archippus, the pagans try to flood his hermitage, but Michael appears and stops the water, and also strikes a rock that produces what becomes a famous healing stream. What is apparent at the outset is that Michael has powers over water, and this may be connected to his early prominence in Egypt and his role in fostering the reliable flooding of the Nile.

Peers has noted several important parts of this story relevant to this analysis. In order to make the waters disappear, Michael had to create a funnel that would drain them away, and there is indeed a river in the region that runs underground for part of its journey.[102] The funnel and the spring were the only relics of Michael's activities. In the earliest Chonae story Michael appeared in his biblical guise as a flash of light and a pillar of fire.[103] Archippus was rightly confused at first by this amazing apparition; his experience follows closely what Kugel and Peers have described as the biblical moment of confusion surrounding the appearance of an angel. Michael, had, however, a voice, and used it to announce who he was. Then Archippus was able to depend on

The Glory of Byzantium. Byzantine. Constantinople. Second half of twelfth century. *Icon with the Miracle at Chonai*. Tempera and gold on wood. 37.5 x 30.7 cm. (Cat. 66) *Source:* The Holy Monastery of Saint Catherine, Sinai, Egypt. Photograph © 1997 The Metropolitan Museum of Art. Photograph by Bruce White.

his friend who remained invisible to the pagans. Here the angel appears in his most formless ethereal state, but as Peers notes, there would be an inevitable anthropomorphism of angels concerning this type of experience as people needed to make these relationships more literal by illustrating them with understandable images.[104] An example of this, also used by Peers, is the twelfth-century icon of Saint Michael and the miracle at Chonae, from the monastery of Saint Catherine in Sinai. By this time established canons of the iconography of angels showed a humanoid Michael as a young black-and-red-winged male, clothed in white, with the power to divert waters. To be represented as a literal being, Michael acquired a face, skin color, hair, and all the other features that helped to locate him in a context people could comprehend. This Michael is not the blond angel common in Italy and elsewhere in the western Mediterranean. He is larger than the hermit, with brown hair and dark eyes and a tanned skin considerably darker than his robe. Michael seems to be conforming to eastern Mediterranean conceptions of young male handsomeness. But it is important to keep in mind that this particular image, like all the others of angels, is itself in relationship to angels and is in no angelic sense like them.[105]

Michael also needs to be situated in the distinctive Mediterranean context of microecologies defined by climate, hydrology, animals, plants, as well as the kinds of spiritual relationships people felt toward this generally harsh landscape and environment.[106] Horden and Purcell note that in 563 the emperor Justinian made his last journey to Germia near Ankara, where he sought help from a shrine to Michael where there was a miraculous healing fishpond. The same emperor also contributed to a shrine of Michael's at Pythia near Constantinople, which had once been a hot spring sacred to Apollo. Michael was not only connected to waters, however vital this resource was to the dry climates of the eastern Mediterranean; he was also found in high places, most notably Monte Gargano on the eastern spur into the Adriatic in central Italy. Jacopo da Varagine summarized and made even more famous the story of how the cavern shrine to Saint Michael at Monte Gargano was established. This story, from an early context in which pagans were still troubling early Christians, has the saintly archangel intervene and help destroy a hostile army.[107] An even more detailed story explains how a certain Gargano, out of frustration, shot an arrow at a straying bull that had wandered into a cave, but the arrow mysteriously turned on the archer and wounded him.[108] In this story Michael eventually reveals in visions that he averted the arrow because he wanted to dwell in this cavern. An important shrine and pilgrimage site developed in this place which would help spread the cult of Saint Michael even farther west, eventually to Mont Saint Michel and beyond. In order to confirm his legacy at this site, Michael left his footprints miraculously impressed into marble.[109] This truly original type of relic alludes to an entire genre of famous footprints stretching back to pagan antiquity and eventually including other notable divine, saintly, and angelic impressions.[110]

At this stage, with the image of Michael still so formless, impressions of his feet were all that people could have to remember him by. In a literal way, however, the relics confirmed that Michael had feet, which was another step on the path to anthropomorphizing his entire person. Michael's functions also came to include a role in fighting outbreaks of infectious diseases. He famously appeared in 590 in Rome when plague was raging through the city. Pope Gregory the Great set his statue on top of Hadrian's tomb, which became from that moment forward the Castel Sant' Angelo of Rome.[111] Here was another powerful reason to establish a relationship with the archangel. These late ancient and early medieval stories about Saint Michael help to explain how he became involved in the world and in struggles against paganism and illness, but another source provides a more nuanced explanation of how he and his images affected the world.

An encomium to Michael by Eustathius of Thrace survives in the northern Coptic dialect of Egypt. A thirteenth-century copy preserves an account most likely dating from the early seventh century.[112] The account describes an icon that does not survive, so here writing about an icon preserves the sense of how an image of Michael acted in the world. The story concerns the married couple Aristarchus and Euphemia, who were particularly devoted to Michael in their religious practices, honoring the twelfth day of every month as sacred to him. Euphemia worried about what might happen to her after her husband's death.[113] Sensing his own demise, Aristarchus had commended his wife to Michael's care because it was his job to pray for all people. Euphemia then requested that her husband commission an icon of Michael so that this object would protect her from Satan when he was gone, and Aristarchus had a skilled artist paint the picture of Michael on a wooden tablet also embellished with gold inlay and jewels. (It is necessary to note that this encomium contains not one word more on what Michael looked like.) Aristarchus soon died, and Euphemia kept the icon in her bed chamber and continued to pray to it three times a day.[114] This couple very much wanted a relationship with Michael; Aristarchus saw the angel as a friend who would watch over his wife, and Euphemia found a male protector who would safeguard her widowhood.

Inevitably, the devil found this challenge irresistible, and he soon began to appear to Euphemia to tempt her into evil ways. The devil appeared first as a nun, a trick that did not deceive Euphemia for long. Next, he tried another type of disguise: "the Devil appeared to her in the form of an Ethiopian of huge stature, and he was like a he-goat, and his eyes were very full of blood, and the hair on his head stood up straight like the bristles of a mountain boar."[115] This frightening person also carried a sword and had a foul smell. Every detail matters here. As an Ethiopian in this context the devil was surely black, and this, along with his inhuman hair, would certainly frighten Euphemia. Red eyes conveyed to students of physiognomy all the negative and dangerous qualities described earlier. Pigs and goats were not animals with positive associations, and the devil was also armed and smelly. This altogether nasty appearance was not intended to confuse Euphemia, and Satan railed at her, noting that the devils had left heaven because they did not want to see Michael's face, which terrified them.[116] As if Euphemia needed this hint, only then did she seize her icon and chase the devil away with it.

The greatest temptation, and the most important one for this analysis, occurred next. The devil cunningly appeared in the form of the archangel Michael.[117] He had great wings and also wore a golden girdle encrusted with jewels and a crown set in pearls. Showing himself as a mighty ruler, he carried in his right hand a scepter, but here Eustathius signals the key point of the story by noting that the scepter lacked its holy cross. Euphemia fell to the ground at this amazing sight and waited for the angel to convey to her God's commands. What followed was predictably bad advice: Euphemia should abstain from so much charity toward the poor and remarry to produce an heir to her great wealth. Euphemia naturally became suspicious about these scripture-contradicting messages and began to doubt that this messenger was in fact her archangel. The devil once again claimed to be Michael, and as a sidelight mentioned his role in praying to God for the waters of the Nile.[118] But Euphemia knew well that the devil could tempt people in many ways, so she asked, "Where is the figure of the Cross which should be upon your scepter, according to what I see painted in this picture in which the figure of Michael is depicted?"[119] There are a few more twists to this debate, but the crucial point has been reached; Euphemia appealed to her icon as a valid representation of Michael and rejected this devilish apparition. After she asked Michael for help, the real archangel appeared in all his royal splendor, filling the scene with amazing light, and carrying a scepter with a cross upon it. After punishing and dismissing the devil, Michael promised to continue to take Euphemia's prayers to God and then returned to heaven.

Some time later, at the time of the pious Euphemia's death, Michael attended her as a psychopomp who would take her worthy soul to heaven.[120] At this moment many witnesses saw Michael shining like the sun, with brass feet pouring out fiery flames, a harp in his right hand, and an emblem containing a cross in his left. Euphemia laid on her eyes her icon, which disappeared at the moment of her death but miraculously reappeared hanging in the air at her tomb. The author Eustathius claimed to have the icon before his own eyes as well as those of the congregation to which he was speaking these words, and the picture effected miraculous cures. The subsequent

Early Gondarine Illuminated Manuscript with the Archangels Michael and Gabriel. Ethiopian, early eighteenth century. *Source:* The Walters Art Museum, Baltimore.

history of this icon is not known, but for a time it acted like a battery storing up Michael's power in this world.

All its images of fire and light convey a positive, bright portrait, the opposite of the devil, the Ethiopian, and the negative symbolic as well as literal associations darkness conveyed. The angels were never human, and their physiognomy with its ethnic markers reveals what people admired about their images and expected from them. The best faces and colors remained the same, now enforced by a celestial hierarchy that privileged the same sorts of faces valued on earth. If people truly wanted to have relationships with these angels, then the bond, already so mixed in terms of spirit, at least offered a comforting similarity of how angels chose to appear, and how people decided to imagine and portray them. The color of the skin or eyes was indeed useless on one level when it came to portraying a being that after all did not have a real body.[121] But to the beholder (and creator), trained to peer into faces for signs and interpret them, such information was just as important as all the gold inlay, crosses, and halos intended to signify the truth. A late seventeenth-century Ethiopian text of *The Story of Euphemia* contains a two-page illustrated scene of the entire tale, from the request for the icon to the devil's defeat.[122] The human and angelic faces here, as in the rest of medieval and early modern Ethiopian art, are distinctly from that region, but the devil himself is quite black, with only the whites of his eyes betraying any positive humanoid trait.

In its long day physiognomy reigned as a respectable science or body of human knowledge because it yielded testable conclusions based on concrete evidence. The language of physiognomy became the best way to discuss human difference in terms that referred to meaningful signs like the eyes or the color of the skin. A practical gaze, informed by a close study of this art, benefited people as they learned which slaves to buy or what sort of person to trust in making a contract. This literal valuing of people crossed beyond simple color symbolism or even prejudice into a way of thinking that closely resembled modern forms of racism, in a vocabulary suited to the times. Faces and color proved to be the best clues indicating the deeper unalterable truths, and so it became important that angels had faces as well. Physiognomy had some valuable lessons on the consequences of human mixing and relationships, and these same issues concerned angels as well.

An icon dating from mid-twelfth-century Sinai helps to summarize and tie together the themes of physiognomy, ethnicity, and angels. Monks, presumably deceased, are being welcomed into heaven by Jesus, as their colleagues remaining on earth pray for their safe journey. A ladder reminds viewers of Jacob's dream and is an engaging image of a stairway to paradise, equating the good monks with angels. In the upper left appear some brightly clothed angels functioning as psychopomps helping the deserving monks on their way. Most startling are the smaller black demons, armed with snares and bows, harvesting their share of souls to be thrust down a kind of well leading no doubt straight to hell. Here the faces of the demons are not clear, but the memory of numerous other examples of frightening eyes and coarse features would remind the viewer of more than color symbolism. The demons, smaller than the monks, are in their way just as humanoid as the angels. Even the color of the wings is not a reliable marker; two of the angels have very dark, nearly black ones. Jesus and the angels have the largest eyes. In this eastern Greek Orthodox context, all the monks join with Jesus in having beards; only the angels remain without this marker of masculinity. Skin color reveals a community of tone among Jesus, the angels, and the monks saved and damned. The fallen angels have an unmistakable color that forever shaped attitudes toward people who shared anything like it. In a way the other features are irrelevant or subordinate to the main signifier of blackness. Michael is not in this icon, but it would be easy to imagine him leading the heavenly

The Glory of Byzantium. Byzantine. Sinai or Constantinople. Late twelfth century. *Icon with the Heavenly Ladder of John Klimax.* Tempera on wood. 41.1 x 29.5 cm. *Source:* The Holy Monastery of Saint Catherine, Sinai, Egypt. Photograph © 1997 The Metropolitan Museum of Art. Photograph by Bruce White.

host in the blank space on the right, as he appears in countless other images of the same memorable scene. Having a relationship with the angels on this and many other levels was a good thing, while to be ensnared by ties to the demons was an awful fate. Finally, the ladder is a metaphor for hierarchy, and the leaders of the monastic community are on the top rungs. So, too, do the angels, good and bad, teach that there is a universal order natural to this world and the next. Nothing from physiognomy or experiences with the angels taught strong lessons about human equality.

Conclusion

The long journey from attitudes about ethnicity and color prejudice through the commercial life, private and public contracts, renegades, physiognomy and even the angels of the eastern Mediterranean world has shown that ignoring the mirage of purity or any other value associated with it could be a costly endeavor. Each of these themes requires much more study, but the perspective of mixed relationship creates a fruitful way to explore the connections among them. Mixing was common in this region with its many boundaries. People inside relationships explored and explained these ties. The best the boundary breakers could hope for was to be allowed enough space to establish their relationships based on self-interest. The boundary makers were always busy sharpening the differences among humans, languages, creeds, and much else, because for them purity remained worth defending. Some ordinary people inside mixed relationships learned the wider context of their identities, more so than even the most sympathetic nonmixers ever understood. The passage of time had not lessened the purity of whiteness, made blackness a positive trait, or loosened the grip of any monotheistic religion on its claim to absolute truth. Still, in the fifteenth-century eastern Mediterranean, where the Ottoman Turks were employing a new style of holy warfare not favoring trade or other ties with enemies, their lands would still attract Jews expelled from Spain, Sicily, and eventually Portugal. Something about this region still offered a haven, an idea now made poignant by modern tragedies in places like Odessa, Beirut, and Sarajevo.

Big identities changed over time in the eastern Mediterranean. The Crusader kingdom vanished as did cosmopolitan Caffa, and the Byzantine and Mamluk states were incorporated into the Ottoman Empire. By the beginning of the early modern period, the Atlantic, Indian, and Pacific Oceans beckoned with even more varieties of mixed relationships and new boundaries to make and to break. Changes beginning in the fifteenth century dictate the end of this book because the Ottomans gradually imposed an order on the eastern Mediterranean which replaced these earlier opportunities and experiments in mixing. The story of what happened in between, especially from about 1000 to 1400, reveals a more complex history where no style of purity could quite overwhelm the others. Lessons from the eastern Mediterranean mattered to the rest of the world, even when some of its cultures disappeared without a trace. Enduring ideas about creed, color, and other boundaries survived and were transplanted everywhere Mediterranean peoples wandered in subsequent centuries.[1]

In the Mediterranean region with its climates of stark contrasts, Jews, Christians, and Muslims had all in their distinctive ways valued purity in every aspect of life—from diet and sexual behavior to worship, texts, and saints in this world and angels in the next. Everywhere the injunction to be perfect was heard, if not always followed. Even an admittedly pagan survival, physiognomy, shaped a way of thinking that matched unambiguous physical signs to clear temperaments. Yet these ideals about purity ran up against the necessity of exchange in an ecology where microregions and microclimates made trade an inevitable part of life for anyone who cared about food and water, let alone luxuries.[2] The pure ones often had to go far, deep into the desert or into a cave, to escape materialism and exchange, and sometimes even they could find no release from mixing with others.

I have not been able to explore every way in which this mixing occurred. Certainly, most people seem to have preferred to stick to their own kind, however defined, and they may have believed that mixing colors or creeds led to muddy outcomes. Economic self-interest still brought some people, groups, and states together into ties that violated somebody's standard of purity. Occasionally, they made relationships anyway, and when they did, some sort of material advantage, often accompanied by a claim to be pursuing some even higher ideal, justified mixing. Motives included love, honor, or other ideals that rivaled purity or profit. But a wider context shaped entrenched attitudes about human difference in this world from late antiquity to the first signs of modernity.

Facilitated by treaties, merchants, and pirates, trade in the Mediterranean easily moved people and commodities from Central Asia to Western Europe. But throughout these areas of the first world system, the lessons of color symbolism taught apparent truths about darker people. Ethnicity and color had become since late antiquity useful proxies for information about types of human beings. Ordinary circumstances of daily life out in the archipelago required that very different people make contracts, whether they wanted to get married or purchase a slave. Sometimes the boundaries between people were so formidable that interpreters were needed to facilitate communications between employer and employee, business partners, or even bride and groom. Mixed relationships, common in the activities of daily life as revealed in the notarial records surviving from places like Chios and Famagusta, show that economic and social concerns could foster profitable relationships across boundaries in the eastern Mediterranean where the paths of so many peoples crossed. Their children and successors, so hard to trace in the records, combined cultural and linguistic skills, making them more than the sum of their parts—truly new and adaptable people.

Contracts in business or between states in the form of treaties raised issues concerning personal and national identities. The act of treating with the Other on any level made it necessary to define, for example, who counted as a Venetian or a Genoese, who could be enslaved, and what were the rights of children of mixed parentage. No state policy consciously encouraged mixed relationships on anything approaching equal terms. Identities had to be clarified, and hybrids explained and deprecated. Here too, preconceptions about purity had to yield to the realities of daily life. Peoples like the Greeks, Armenians, and Jews, who eventually lacked states of their own which could negotiate for collective privileges, had to fall back on other ways to define their groups and sustain loyalties. Facing these issues required more careful thinking about the definition of a people in linguistic and national as well as racial terms. With all due caution about using the term *race*, it still emerges from this study that the classical inheritance as well as centuries of mixing taught the peoples studied here to distinguish ethnic groups that supposedly bred true and to assign them places in a hierarchy. Attitudes about skin color permeated views of the social order and in many cases justified subordinating others. Color symbolism gave birth to color prejudice, and it became more of a sustaining ideology as skin color tones or other unalterable physical traits down to the tiniest detail of the eyes became the vocabulary in which medieval people explained durable temperamental differences. *Racism* is a problematic modern word with a great deal of baggage, but something stronger than color prejudice or ethnocentrism is required to explain how long lasting and impervious to change these cultural attitudes about human inequality were. What matters most is the extent to which this study has succeeded in using a variety of perspectives to illuminate how the fates of mixed relationships demonstrate the underlying durability of the prescribed divisions among people.

Without renegades, the boundaries between states and creeds, and notions of Mediterranean honor, would not be as clear. Honor, like water, was a finite and precious resource in this world. Individuals and communities hoarded their honor, and defending it was considered a most admirable activity. When ideas about honor conflicted, as in the case of loyalty to a spouse or creed, sometimes people had to choose, and these choices reveal the important boundaries in the cultures. Hierarchical assumptions about how society worked reinforced general attitudes that there was more honor at the top of society than at the bottom, and certainly more in the brave, lighter-skinned people than in the timid, darker ones. Even the angels were ranked and colored from best to worst along the same spectrum. Brightness in the form of light became connected to whiteness; darkness imposed images of evil on anyone who could be perceived as black. These durable attitudes emerged from the ancient world and permeated the cultures of the eastern Mediterranean. The language used to justify hierarchy and inequality changed, but the message did not. If physiognomy had to yield to some other, more modern and scientific form of racism, the mental habits of those who were comfortable with human inequality easily made the switch.

Stepping outside entrenched assumptions about purity were some of the people who appeared on these pages as breaking the so-called rules. Their efforts carved out a space for creative private lives and may have had only a modest effect in softening public attitudes, especially in the East, about the boundaries or those who crossed them. Those inside mixed relationships perhaps became more tolerant of their partners, spouses, and co-workers. The master-slave tie was more likely to coarsen than civilize its parties, though manumitting a slave suggested that the bond had occasionally become something more than sheer exploitation. It was never easy to rebuke the claims of purity, although mixed relationships presumed that there were other choices. Those who crossed the boundaries had to make such choices. Essentialist thinking privileged stark contrasts of right and wrong, black and white, and seldom acknowledged the expedient gray. Even by the end of this study, there are few signs that this style of thinking is ever going to change. This book is not promoting looking at history as a model of progress toward modernity or pluralist, tolerant societies. Instead, it has asked the reader to focus more on the ties than the boundaries. Perhaps the patient realities of ordinary life in the eastern Mediterranean gave each mixed relationship a part in eroding the consensus on boundaries and purity, drop by drop, slowly dissolving rigid thinking. And yet it would be a long time before ideas about the color of water, or a better understanding of inner light, began to wear down the harsh attractions of purity.[3]

NOTES

Preface

1. See, of course, Said, *Orientalism;* this edition contains the important afterword.
2. See Kedar, *Crusade and Mission*, and Tolan, *Saracens*.
3. My translation of the Vulgate: "omne animal diligit similem sibi sic et omnis homo proximum sibi." The edition of the Vulgate used throughout this book is *Biblia Sacra iuxta Vulgatam Versionem*, ed. by Robert Weber (Stuttgart, 1969). Translations from all sources are my own unless otherwise noted.
4. This is a major and well-studied theme in American history; see, e.g., Sollers, *Interracialism*. Because in the medieval eastern Mediterranean mixed relationships were not so explicitly and legally defined, interracialism is not a useful tool for analysis for this book. Also, these mixed relationships do not exhaust the subject. Issues surrounding sex and gender roles, rich and poor, or urban and rural people, deserve separate analyses.
5. See McKee, *Uncommon Dominion*, 168–77, for an analysis that has helped shape this book.
6. Appiah, *The Ethics of Identity*, 64.

Introduction

1. For the major works of synthesis, see Abu-Lughod, *Before European Hegemony*, and Braudel, *The Mediterranean and the Mediterranean World in the Age of Philip II*. Chaudhuri, *Trade and Civilisation in the Indian Ocean* provides another excellent model.
2. Henri Pirenne, *Mohammed and Charlemagne*, trans. by Bernard Miall (New York, 1968); and Horden and Purcell, *The Corrupting Sea*.
3. Williams, *Truth and Truthfulness*, 11, 44, discusses a theme going back to the ancient historians.
4. Appiah, *The Ethics of Identity*, 112. Identity formation is a main subject of this book.
5. Connor, *The Book of Skin*, is the first general study of skin from a western cultural perspective but it neglects color. John Jeffries Martin, *Myths of Renaissance Individualism* (Houndmills, 2004), 14–15, 18, has some good insights on the skin as boundary between the interior and exterior self.
6. Isidore, Bishop of Seville, *Etymologiarum*, ed. W. M. Lindsay (Oxford, 1911), XI, I, 6.

Chapter One • The Perception of Difference

1. Ibn Khaldûn, *The Muqaddhima*, 2:305–7, 3:352.
2. Momigliano, *Alien Wisdom*, 86.
3. Hillenbrand, *The Crusades*, 331.
4. See Gilroy, *Against Race*, 7, 57, for more on this idea that permeates his book. For a succinct account of the rise of scientific raciology, see Proctor, *Racial Hygiene*, 10–20.
5. Jordan, "Why 'Race'?" See also his "The Medieval Background."
6. Fredrickson, *Racism*, 6, 24.
7. See, e.g., the founding study, Snowden, *Blacks in Antiquity*, 216–18, and Thompson, *Romans and Blacks*, esp. 157.
8. Goldenberg, *The Curse of Ham*, 2–4, 83–85, 167.
9. Benjamin Isaac, *The Invention of Racism in Classical Antiquity* (Princeton, 2004), p. 23, 35. Judith M. Lieu, *Christian Identity in the Jewish and Graeco-Roman World* (Oxford, 2004), 260–65, raises the prospect that there was a Christian race in late antiquity, but it was ambiguous and alterable.
10. Ibn Khaldûn, *The Muqaddhima*, 1:301, 171.
11. Fredrickson, *Racism*, 170.
12. Goldenberg, *The Curse of Ham*, 51. For what follows, see his introduction and conclusion, esp. pp. 2–3, 186, 195–200, and elsewhere, but he makes no reference to Gilroy.
13. Isaac, *The Invention*, 446.
14. I've been influenced here by the many astute points in Maalouf, *In the Name of Identity*.
15. Braude, "The Sons of Noah," 104.
16. Here I am citing the English translation by Edmund Howard, *The Aryan Myth: A History of Racist and Nationalist Ideas in Europe* (London, 1974). The original French is found in Poliakov, *Le mythe aryen*, 347–48, "La tradition judéo-chrétienne était 'antiraciste' comme elle était antinationaliste, et sans doute les stratifications et barrières sociales du Moyen Age, l'existence d'une hiérarchisation féodale et horizontale, favorisaient-elles l'action exercée par l'Église dans le sens de son idéal: tous les hommes étant égaux devant Dieu, les différenciations verticales et géographiques ne devaient donner lieu à aucun classement de valeur." It is interesting that Poliakov considered the one great exception to this rule to be the racist anti-Semitism of late medieval Spain, a subject taken up by Netanyahu, *The Origins of the Inquisition in Fifteenth Century Spain*.
17. Fredrickson, *Racism*, 141, points out that there is a sensible fear about modern essentializing of cultural difference.
18. Jacques Roger, *Buffon: A Life in Natural History*, trans. Sarah L. Bonnefoi (Ithaca, 1997), 116.
19. Balbi, *Catholicon*, is cited by alphabetic entry, as the pages are not numbered.
20. Buffon, *De l'homme*, 223. "La prèmiere et la plus remarquable de ces variétés est celle de la couleur, la seconde est celle de la forme et de la grandeur, et la troisième est celle du naturel des différents peuples . . ." See also pp. 266, 262, 316–17, and 320, for his grand conclusion. Oddly, he thought that after eight, ten, or twelve generations they would be much less black—such was the power of climate.

21. Origen, *Commentaire sur le Cantique des Cantiques*, 12, 18. The Middle Ages knew only the Latin translation by Rufinus.

22. Gregory of Nyssa, *Commentary on the Song of Songs*, 35.

23. For a study on the exegesis of this book of the Bible, see Matter, *The Voice of My Beloved*, which stresses the dominant trend of allegorical exegesis and does not explore issues of color or ethnicity.

24. Goldenberg, *The Curse of Ham*, 48.

25. Origen, *Commentaire*, 261–62. The words for dark or black, *fusca* or *nigra*, vary according to what text of the Bible the author or translator used. Jerome's Vulgate uses both terms, but in this line *nigra*. From early antiquity, Egyptians viewed themselves as red; see Donald B. Redford, *From Slave to Pharaoh: The Black Experience of Ancient Egypt* (Baltimore, 2004), 5.

26. Origen, *Commentaire*, 264; both are black because of the "ignobilitas generis."

27. Ibid., 298: "ex seminis carnalis successione nigredo."

28. See Origen, *Homélies sur le Cantique des Cantiques*, 71–72, for what follows. These homilies, better known than the commentary, were translated by Saint Jerome, who provided here yet another phrase: "nigra sum et speciosa."

29. Goldenberg makes the important point that the Hebrew Bible has nothing about an Ethiopian becoming white in the Song; this is based on an early mistranslation (*Curse of Ham*, 48–49, 84).

30. Here I use *Glossa Ordinaria Pars 22 In Canticum Canticorum*, 97–101, which, according to its editor Mary Dove, was composed in the early twelfth century in Laon. If it was not known to Abelard and Bernard, they certainly knew its main sources.

31. For the text of this part of the letter, see Muckle, "The Personal Letters Between Abelard and Héloïse," 84–85. Moses' wife is noted in Numbers 12:1; she is the first Aethiopissa. There is some question about whether this wife is Zipporah, the only one named in scripture; see Kugel, *The Bible as It Was*, 299–300.

32. Goldenberg, *Curse of Ham*, 26, concludes that the main problem for this wife was that, whatever her identity, she was not an Israelite—hence the problem of the mix.

33. For a profound survey of these issues, see Glacken, *Traces on the Rhodian Shore*, 80–115, 254–87.

34. Muckle, "The Personal Letters," 84.

35. Jeremiah 13:23: "si mutare potest Aethiops pellem suam aut pardus varietates suas et vos poteritis bene facere cum didiceretis malum . . ."

36. Bernard de Clairvaux, *Sermons sur le Cantique*, vol. 1 (sermons 1–15), pp. 102–4.

37. The best place is sermon 28 in de Clairvaux, *Sermons sur le Cantique*, 2:346–75.

38. Ibid., 2:352.

39. Ibid., 2:370.

40. Ibid., 2:372.

41. See *Secundum Salomonem*, 56. This edition also contains the Hebrew text by Rashi. See also *The Five Megilloth*, 1:9, which includes the Rashi text and other.

42. For more on Jewish exegesis on *Song of Songs* 1:5, see Goldenberg, *The Curse of Ham*, 79–83.

43. Rabbi Ezra ben Solomon of Gerona, *Commentary on the Song of Songs*, 43, 44.

44. Levi ben Gershom (Gersonides), *Commentary on Song of Songs*, 27–28.

45. Schorsch, *Jews and Blacks in the Early Modern World*, 296–98, where the author summarizes a vast survey of rabbinical exegesis, responsa, and other sources from the medieval and early modern worlds.

46. See Iacopo da Varazze, *Legenda Aurea*, xiii.

47. Ibid., 155. The image of the devil as black reaches deep into antiquity; for Athanasius, see *St. Athanasius: The Life of Saint Anthony*, trans. Robert T. Minor (London, 1950). Minor dates the text to 357 (p. 8); the reference to the devil as a black boy (p. 23) and a long note (p. 109) with references to other texts make a similar connection. See Goldenberg, *The Curse of Ham*, 50, for other references pushing the link back to Philo and Origen. This is a well-known example of ancient racism, brought into the Middle Ages by Jacopo, again with Egyptian roots.

48. Iacopo da Varazze, *Legenda Aurea*, 189, 215, 1004, 1231.

49. For details, see Simmons, *Arnobius*, 93–111.

50. Arnobius, *Adversus nationes*, ed. Augustus Reifferschied (Vienna, 1875), VII, ix, p. 274, a "spiritus unus"; VII, xix, p. 253; the cheerful white is *candor*, the gloomy dark *furvus*.

51. Lewis, *Race and Slavery*, 21, shares this view, though he sees racial and ethnic prejudices entering Islamic thought in the early conquests before 900. Hence he regards the idea that Islam remained free of prejudice and discrimination as a myth; see p. 99 and the book's central argument. A closer look at mixed relationships in the region should test this debatable finding.

52. For a recent survey of the vast literature on eastern travels, see Guéret-Laferté, *Sur les routes de l'Empire mongol*.

53. For the text of Brother Richard's memorial and Julian's observations about the Tartars, see Dörrie, "Drei Texte," 151–61.

54. Ibid., 165–82, 177, 178.

55. Ibid., 181, 182, and see Biller, *The Measure of Multitude*, 232–35.

56. Dörrie, "Drei Texte," 197–94, provides parallel texts from Matthew of Paris and the Annals of Burton, the best witnesses of this strange business. For a summary of what is known about Peter, see Ruotsala, *Europeans and the Mongols*, 153–55.

57. Dörrie, "Drei Texte," 188.

58. Anastasius van den Wyngaert, *Sinica Franciscana*, vol. 1 (Florence, 1929): 29.

59. Ibid., 30–31, 32–36.

60. Ibid., 36–45.

61. Ibid., 45–51.

62. Ibid., 51.

63. Mary Carruthers, *The Book of Memory* (Cambridge, 1990), 26.

64. For Brother Benedict's terse account of this mission, see *Sinica franciscana*, 135–43.

65. Ibid., 107–9, 127. Wyngaert and most authorities conclude that the "Saracenic" language referred to here was most likely Persian (Farsi) and definitely not Arabic. I think there is a faint chance the language was in fact Turkish.

66. Ibid., 116–17, and 123–24, on the letter.

67. For the Latin letter, see ibid., 142–43. Wyngaert also supplies a French translation of the Persian version for comparison!

68. Ibid., 143. The key sentence is "Sed quomodo scire potestis, cui Deus suam gratiam conferre dignetur?" This is the first inadvertent plea for religious pluralism in medieval Latin!

69. Saint-Quentin, *Histoire des Tartares*, 31–32.

70. See Jean de Joinville, *Vie de Saint Louis*, 232–42, for parallel old and modern French texts.

71. The best introduction to Rubruck and his work is now in the best English translation by Peter Jackson and David Morgan, *The Mission of Friar William of Rubruck* (London, 1990).

72. Only once does William of Rubruck mention the color of any people, and that is to compare them to the dark Spanish. Here I am using the standard Latin edition, which is *Sinica franciscana*, ed. Anastasius van den Wyngaert, 1:164–332, esp. 234, 220, 322, 205. See pp. 226–27 for a nice use of *terra* that includes *ideoma* (language) and *litteris* (script).

73. Ecclesiasticus 39:4.

74. *Sinica franciscana*, 164: "In terram alienarum gentium transiet, bona et mala in [omnibus] temptabit." Jerome's Latin is exactly "in terram alienarum gentium pertransiet bona enim et mala in hominibus temptavit." The small differences result from the vagaries of memory, but the larger change, his *omnibus* for *hominibus*, is even better; William sees the good and bad in everything, not simply the people.

75. Ibid., 220: "quos Deus suscitavit a remotioribus partibus populum nullum et gentem stultam."

76. Ibid., 220. William quotes Deut 32:21 with his gloss, "secundum quod dicit Dominus 'Provocabo eos' id est non custodientes legem suam 'in eo qui non est populus et in gente stulta irritabo eos.'" I paraphrase the translation supplied in the New English Bible.

77. For a brief note on the problems surrounding the identity of this interpreter, see Jackson and Morgan, *The Mission*, 279.

78. *Sinica franciscana*, 170.

79. Ibid., 191.

80. Ibid., 196: "Non faciatis me predicare, quia nescio talia verba dicere."

81. Ibid.: "Tunc videns periculum loquendi per ipsum, elegi magis tacere."

82. Ibid., 232: "interpres meus fatigatus, non valens verba exprimere, fecit me tacere."

83. Ibid., 249.

84. Kedar, "The Multilateral Disputation," 166, 167; the source here is a story the king of Armenia told about William.

85. *Sinica franciscana*, 300: "Si habuissem potestatem faciendi signa sicut Moyses, forte humiliasset se."

86. Ibid., 311.

87. Ibid., 183–84.

88. Ibid., 335, 341–43.

89. Ibid., 346–50.

90. Ibid., 352. Perhaps he used Phags.pa, the script recently created in 1269 at the order of Qubilai. This writing combined elements of Uighur and Tibetan scripts and like Mongol in the Uighur alphabet was written vertically; see *The Mongol Languages*, ed. Juha Janhumen (London, 2003), 58.

91. For more on Balbi, see Epstein, *Genoa*, 162–64.

92. For color, see Epstein, *Speaking of Slavery*, 20–22.

93. Balbi, *Catholicon*, cited by alphabetical entry, pages not numbered.

94. See H. Rushton Fairclough, trans., *Horace: Satires, Epistles, and Ars Poetica* (Cambridge, 1929), 55.

95. For background, see Kedar, *Crusade and Mission*, 180–83.

96. See *Wilhelm von Tripolis*, 71–74, where editor Peter Engels discusses the authorship of these two works traditionally attributed to William.

97. See ibid., 216–17, for William's version; it was slightly altered by the anonymous author (pp. 334–36).

98. I make a slight change in the Fairclough translation on p. 273.

99. Tolan, *Saracens*, 23, 139.

100. Kedar, *Crusade and Mission*, 85–91.

101. Jacques de Vitry, *Lettres*, 52, for this and what follows.

102. Said, *Orientalism*, considers the modern aspects of these themes. Daniel in his *The Arabs in Medieval Europe*, 209, refers to the *poulains* as "delatinized Latins de-Europeanized colonists" who were really "cultural defectors."

103. Margaret Jubb, *The Legend of Saladin in Western Literature and Historiography* (Lewiston, ME, 2000), 54–60.

104. For general background, see Evangelista, *Fidenzio da Padova*. For these details from the text, see Golubovich, *Biblioteca*, 2:1–9, and 9–60, for the text; for the discussion of the takeovers of the Holy Land, see pp. 9–12.

105. Ibn Jubayr, *The Travels*, 317; he also saw many Muslim captives there (p. 322).

106. Golubovich, *Biblioteca*, 13. Evangelista, *Fidenzio*, 41–42, notes this passage about diversity but makes nothing of it, instead concentrating on the images of Christian society in the text.

107. Golubovich, *Biblioteca*, 14–17.

108. For details on his early life and the text of the polemic, see Mérigoux, "L'ouvrage d'un frere precheur florentin," 1–144, text 62–144.

109. Daniel, *The Arabs*, 218, calls Riccoldo "the Crusader who knew most about the Arabs." For the text of the travelogue, see Riccold de Monte Croce, *Pérégrination*; see pp. 9–14 for biographical details.

110. Ibid., 118, clearly "lingua arabica," not Farsi.

111. Ibid., 156, 158–62; the population estimate for Baghdad is credible.

112. Ibid., 164–66, 168, 172.

113. Ibid., 172–78.

114. Ibid., 178–82.

115. This is Quran 19:28, not Sura 3 as Kappler suggests.

116. Riccold, *Pérégrination*, 182–84, for the rest of this part of the text.

117. See Michael Rocke, *Forbidden Friendships: Homosexuality and Male Culture in Renaissance Florence* (New York, 1996).

118. Riccold, *Pérégrination*, 194–98.

119. For a recent introduction to Polo, and one that credits his account, see Larner, *Marco Polo*. Wood, *Did Marco Polo Go to China?* argues that he did not.

120. Many manuscript versions of Polo's account survive and no standard edition exists. For a common French text, see Polo, *Le Livre*. An important Latin translation containing information not in some vernacular accounts appears in A. C. Moule and Paul Pelliot, *Marco Polo: The Description of the World*, vol. 2 (London, 1938); and for this reference, see Polo, *Milione*, 30. I prefer the Italian version because it is fuller in some respects than the others and uses a vocabulary that can be checked against other Italian sources from the

East, but I have checked these references against the French text and cite its words where appropriate.

121. Polo, *Milione*, 64–65.
122. Polo, *Milione*, 103; compare *Le Livre*, 205, women "moult belles et blanches."
123. Polo, *Milione*, 105; compare *Le Livre*, 214, but it is not noted there that these people were white!
124. Polo, *Milione*, 123–24; compare *Le Livre*, 258, "le vis blanc et vermeil, les yeux vairs."
125. Polo, *Milione*, 136; compare *Le Livre*, 288.
126. Polo, *Milione*, 197; compare *Le Livre*, 430, "belles genz, mais ne sont pas bien blanches, mais brunes gens."
127. Polo, *Milione*, 234, 251; *Le Livre*, 580.
128. Polo, *Milione*, 266; *Le Livre*, 627.
129. Polo, *Milione*, 289–90; *Le Livre*, 685.
130. My source here is the edited text in Latin with a French translation; see Adorno, *Itinéraire*, 425.
131. Ibid., 66–88, 104.
132. Ibid., 118, for sun's effects; 156, for his strange thoughts on Galata; 174, 210, for notices of the trucimani; 196–98; and 212, where the drug is called *tiriacum*—it must be *teriaque*.
133. Ibid., 342, 350, 316.
134. W. E. B. Du Bois, *Black Reconstruction*, quoted by David Levering Lewis, *W. E. B. Du Bois: The Fight for Equality and the American Century, 1919–1963* (New York, 2000), 370.

Chapter Two • Mixed Relationships in the Archipelago

1. McKee, *Uncommon Dominion*. No other island or colony has such an excellent study central to the themes of this chapter.
2. Ibid., 168–77. This paragraph is a gloss on the book, especially the conclusion.
3. A problem to which McKee is astutely sensitive—see her comments on the sources. Ibid., vi–xii.
4. *Benvenuto de Brixiano*.
5. Kate Fleet, *European and Islamic Trade*, 37–58, also considers some of these slave sales in the broader context of Ottoman-Genoese trade in slaves.
6. *Benvenuto de Brixiano*, 96–100, 104–8, 123–37, 148, for notices of his activities.
7. Ibid., 60, 28; for cows, 66, for a horse, 49. McKee, *Uncommon Dominion*, 34, defines the *villani* as "unfree peasants," and they were tied to the land and transferred with it.
8. See *Benvenuto de Brixiano*, 8, for some of Vergici's activities; see 60–61, 81, for examples of contracts.
9. McKee, "Inherited Status and Slavery," 31–53, esp. 37.
10. See Balard and Veinstein, "Continuité ou changement d'un paysage urbain?" for the general account.
11. Ibid., 83. See also Pistarino, *I problemi*, and Balard, *La Romanie génoise*, 1:114–18.
12. See Skržinskaya, "Storia della Tana," for background.
13. Balard, *Gênes et L'Outre Mer I*, no. 770, p. 307; no. 844, p. 246.
14. For Roman examples of child sales, see Keith Bradley, *Slavery and Society at Rome*

(Cambridge, 1994), 40–51. For ideas on how slaves affected their sales, see Walter Johnson, *Soul by Soul: Life Inside the Antebellum Slave Market* (Cambridge, Mass., 1999), 16–17, 163–64.

15. Balard, *Gênes et L'Outre Mer I*, no. 593, p. 215; no. 685, p. 263; no. 714, p. 278; no. 697, p. 269.

16. For details on the genesis of this unique surviving copy, see *Codex Comanicus*, ed. Vladimir Drimba, for the latest edition and a facsimile of the manuscript. See also the introduction by Louis Ligeti to the 1981 reprint of the less reliable 1880 edition by Geza Kuun.

17. See Airaldi, *Studi e documenti*, for an edition of the registry for 1381–82 by the notary Niccolo de Bellignano. References to the interpreters are numerous; see, e.g., 96, for Luchino; 92, for Filippo; 49, for Giovanni; and 83, for Raffo.

18. Ibid., no. 36, pp. 82–83. Coia is described as "valetudinarius et podragus."

19. See Epstein, *Speaking of Slavery*, for more details.

20. *Codex Comanicus*, ed. Drimba, 38v, facsimile text.

21. This notarial act appears in the appendix to the article by Musso, "I Genovesi," 167–69.

22. Domenico Gioffrè, *Il mercato degli schiavi a Genova nel secolo XV* (Genoa, 1971) contains an exhaustive appendix listing every notarial act he found concerning a slave in fifteenth-century Genoa. There is no sign of Angelo Squarciafico, nor any slaves of the right ethnicities arriving in the city in the 1470s, nor any notice of the six named relatives, two Giustiniani and four Lercari, to whom the slaves were consigned. The evidence is indirect, but all those who were hoping that the women escaped may be right.

23. Balard, *Gênes et L'Outre Mer I*, no. 385, p. 149; no. 728, p. 285; no. 406, p. 160; no. 781, p. 313; no. 873, p. 361.

24. Airaldi, *Studi e documenti*, no. 5, p. 48; Ibn Battuta, *The Travels*, 2:470–71.

25. See Balletto, *Genova, Mediterraneo*, 214–35, for an edition of the record of the auction; the Latin document found its way back to Genoa; see also pp. 252–54.

26. For an accessible edition of this document, see Enrico Basso, "Il 'Bellum de Sorcati,'" 25–26. This treaty is examined in detail in chapter 3, but it should surprise no reader that captured slaves were a big issue.

27. Lopez, *Storia*, 231.

28. Ibid.

29. Balbi and Raiteri, *Notai genovesi in Oltremare*, no. 12, p. 213.

30. Pistarino, *Notai genovesi in Oltremare*, no. 9, p. 16.

31. Ibid., no. 15, p. 22; no. 97, p. 175.

32. Ibid., no. 42, p. 70.

33. Balbi and Raiteri, *Notai genovesi in Oltremare*, no. 2, p. 198.

34. See Argenti, *The Occupation of Chios*, 477–78.

35. For more details on this remarkable person, see Lopez, *Benedetto Zaccaria*.

36. Argenti, *The Occupation of Chios*, and Epstein, *Genoa*, 209–11.

37. Argenti, *The Occupation of Chios*, 170, 483–88.

38. Ibid., 582. My generous estimate adds the Genoese and Jewish population.

39. For convenience, the documents from Chios are cited from these published editions: Argenti, *The Occupation of Chios*; Gioffrè, "Atti Rogati in Chio," 319–404; Balard, *Notai genovesi in Oltremare: Atti rogati a Chio*; and Roccatagliata, *Notai genovesi in Oltremare*.

40. Argenti, *The Occupation of Chios*, no. 416, p. 896.

41. Gioffrè, "Atti Rogati in Chio," 335.
42. Basso, *Notai genovesi in Oltremare*, no. 23, p. 70. This notary had an unusual precision and mentioned what languages were at issue when he noted the services of an interpreter. The languages are always Greek and Latin. What he means by "Latin" is revealed in no. 76, p. 143. A witness did not know "Latin" and needed an interpreter. Few ordinary people on Chios in the late fourteenth century, Greeks or Italians, actually knew spoken Latin, so the "locucio" at issue here is Italian.
43. Gioffrè, "Atti Rogati in Chio," 373. Fleet, *European and Islamic Trade*, 170, has a Chiot document from 1413 in which Greek was again the common language between Turks and Genoese.
44. Gioffrè, "Atti Rogati in Chio," 343.
45. Argenti, *The Occupation of Chios*, no. 86, p. 570.
46. Ibid., no. 321, p. 807. "Cum naturaliter omnes homines liberi naschantur et servitus per ius gentium contra ius naturale fuerit introducta ad cuius extinctionem per dictum ius gentium introductum est beneficium manumissionis."
47. Toniolo, *Notai genovesi in Oltremare*, no. 50, p. 102.
48. Roccatagliata, *Notai genovesi in Oltremare*, no. 120, p. 214.
49. Argenti, *The Occupation of Chios*, no. 321, p. 807.
50. Roccatagliata, *Notai genovesi in Oltremare*, no. 23, p. 31.
51. Balard, *Notai genovesi in Oltremare: Atti rogati a Chio*, no. 17, p. 58.
52. Ibid., no. 36, p. 108.
53. Roccatagliata, *Notai genovesi in Oltremare*, no. 36, p. 53.
54. Argenti, *The Occupation of Chios*, no. 274, p. 765.
55. Roccatagliata, *Notai genovesi in Oltremare*, no. 132, p. 232.
56. See Greif, "Reputation and Coalition in Medieval Trade."
57. This is a major theme in Burns, *Jews in the Notarial Culture*.
58. Gioffrè, "Atti Rogati in Chio," p. 348.
59. Ibid., 379.
60. Ibid. "In Dei nomine qui creavit cellum et terram cuius exemplo cotidie humanum genus, sua illustrante clementia manifesta documenta conspiciens, invenit doctrinam ut benemeritis premia et favores exhibeantur benigne..."
61. See Argenti, *The Religious Minorities of Chios*, 116–20, for more on this Jewish quarter, called a ghetto by the sixteenth century.
62. Gioffrè, "Atti Rogati in Chio," 393.
63. Balard, *Notai genovesi in Oltremare: Atti rogati a Chio*, no. 21, p. 70.
64. Argenti, *The Occupation of Chios*, no. 170, p. 629; no. 173, p. 630.
65. A clear example is the problem of usury among coreligionists and with strangers of another faith. Among the voluminous literature, see, for context, Odd Langholm, *Economics in the Medieval Schools* (Leiden, 1992).
66. Balard, *Notai genovesi in Oltremare: Atti rogati a Chio*, no. 30, p. 92: "iuravit super licteris ebraycis more iudeorum." In an act from the next century, a Jew swore on the "biblia" itself, presumably a torah scroll; see Argenti, *The Occupation of Chios*, no. 277, p. 769.
67. For the sale of the house, see Balard, *Notai genovesi in Oltremare: Atti rogati a Chio*, no. 39, p. 114; for transactions without interpreters, see, e.g., no. 48, p. 136.

68. Toniolo, *Notai genovesi in Oltremare*, no. 109, p. 157; no. 110, p. 158.
69. Epstein, *Wage Labor*, 116.
70. Argenti, *The Occupation of Chios*, no. 201, p. 647.
71. Ibid.: for Giustiniani, see no. 325, p. 810; for Theodora Greca, see no. 305, p. 797.
72. Basso, *Notai genovesi in Oltremare*, no. 69, p. 134.
73. Carlo Ginzburg, *Ecstasies: Deciphering the Witches' Sabbath* (New York, 1991), 33–86.
74. Epstein, *Genoa*, 212–13.
75. Dols, *The Black Death*, 109, 253.
76. Argenti, *The Occupation of Chios*, no. 323, p. 808.
77. See Edbury, *The Kingdom of Cyprus and the Crusades*, for the general background.
78. Ibid., 64–65.
79. Ibid., 204–8, and for the Genoese side of the story, see Epstein, *Genoa*, 236–37.
80. Polonio, *Notai genovesi in Oltremare*, no. 331, p. 396.
81. Pavoni, *Notai genovesi in Oltremare: Atti rogati a Cipro da Lamberto di Sambuceto (6 luglio–27 ottobre 1301)* no. 117, p. 148. (Hereafter this cite is referred to as *Atti 1301*.)
82. Pavoni, *Notai genovesi in Oltremare: Atti rogati a Cipro da Lamberto di Sambuceto (Gennaio–Agosto 1302)*, no. 248, p. 296. (Hereafter this cite is referred to as *Atti 1302*.)
83. Polonio, *Notai genovesi in Oltremare*, no. 269, p. 320; no. 256, p. 303; no. 399, p. 478.
84. Pavoni, *Atti 1302*, no. 122, p. 151.
85. Polonio, *Notai genovesi in Oltremare*, no. 63, p. 71; Pavoni, *Atti 1301*, no. 173, p. 211.
86. Polonio, *Notai genovesi in Oltremare*, no. 341, p. 405.
87. Pavoni, *Atti 1301*, no. 224, p. 267; no. 156, p. 194; no. 78, p. 105; no. 79, p. 106.
88. Ibid., no. 239, p. 284.
89. Balard, *Notai genovesi in Oltremare: Atti Rogati a Cipro: Lamberto di Sambuceto 1307, Giovanni de Rocha 1308–1310*, no. 63, p. 134.
90. Epstein, *Speaking of Slavery*, 96.
91. Pavoni, *Atti 1301*, no. 107, p. 139.
92. Pavoni, *Atti 1302*, no. 185, p. 219.
93. Balard, *Notai genovesi in Oltremare: Atti rogati a Cipro da Lamberto de Sambuceto (11 ottobre 1296–23 giugno 1299)*, no. 13, p. 17. (Hereafter this cite is called *Atti 1296–99*.)
94. Polonio, *Notai genovesi in Oltremare*, no. 165, p. 189;. no. 168, p. 196; no. 170, p. 198.
95. Pavoni, *Atti 1301*, no. 71, p. 95; no. 106, p. 137; no. 119, p. 150.
96. Pavoni, *Atti 1302*, no. 281, p. 336.
97. Balard, *Atti 1296–99*, no. 122, p. 145.
98. Polonio, *Notai genovesi in Oltremare*, no. 262, p. 310.
99. Balard, *Atti 1296–99*, no. 27, p. 37.
100. Pavoni, *Atti 1301*, no. 36, p. 45.
101. Pavoni, *Atti 1302*, no. 234, p. 279.
102. Polonio, *Notai genovesi in Oltremare*, nos. 13, 14, pp. 14–17; McKee, *Uncommon Dominion*, 6.
103. Polonio, *Notai genovesi in Oltremare*, no. 380, p. 456.
104. Pavoni, *Atti 1301*, no. 94, p. 123.
105. Polonio, *Notai genovesi in Oltremare*, no. 274, p. 328; no. 87, p. 100.
106. Lombardo, *Nicola de Boateriis*.

107. Ibid., no. 77, pp. 81–82.

108. Ibid. The phrases are "quia cum divina lex mandet ut unusquisque suum debeat diligere proximum ut se ipsum et iura communia per omnia faveant libertati melifluaque et suavi voce intonent hominem debere semper letari qui potitur beneficio libertatis . . ." and "restituens te iuri primevo, secundum quod omnes homines liberi nascebantur . . ."

109. Ibid., 121–24, for the three acts.

110. Ibid., 176–79.

111. Ibid., 178: " . . . quod firmiter scio quod non est gravida neque est in actu concipiendi, cum iam sit provecte etatis . . ."

112. The fundamental work is by Shelomo Dov Goitein, whose monumental *A Mediterranean Society* is in five volumes: vol. 1, *Economic Foundations*; vol. 2, *The Community*; vol. 3, *The Family*; vol. 4, *Daily Life*; and vol. 5, *The Individual*. A sixth volume containing a cumulative index appeared in 1993. Vol. 1:1–28 contains a useful introduction to the nature of these sources.

113. Ibid., 2:275–99; for useful comments on slavery in Cairo, 1:130–47; for quote, 2:276.

114. Fleet, *European and Ottoman Trade*, 141.

Chapter Three • Treaties and Diplomacy

1. 1. Al-Qalqashandī (d. 1418), a Muslim antiquarian and chancellery official, compiled a text that includes advice and examples of correspondence with foreign states but no treaties; see Lammens, "Correspondences diplomatiques." See Korobenikov, "Diplomatic Correspondence," for a way to use Mamluk formularies for clues to how Muslims perceived the Byzantine empire. Some Muslim treaties survive in narrative sources.

2. Zachariadou, *Trade and Crusade*, 183–84, for this and what follows.

3. Holt, *Early Mamluk Diplomacy*, 3–6, for some comments on Muslim treaties.

4. Isaac, *The Invention of Racism*, 239–42, for many references from Plato to Cicero.

5. Stephen J. Gould, *The Hedgehog, the Fox, and the Magister's Pox* (New York, 2003), 81–112, on what he called the old affliction of dichotomization.

6. Imperiale di Sant'Angelo, *Codice diplomatico*, 1:327–30. See also Jacoby, "Italian Privileges."

7. There is a detailed study on this topic; see Constable, *Housing the Stranger*, for more on the Muslim *fonduq*, Byzantine *embolo*, and western *fondaco*.

8. For more details on the treaty and its consequences for the complicated Mediterranean diplomacy of this period, see Epstein, *Genoa and the Genoese*, 72–78, and Day, *Genoa's Response to Byzantium*, 23–26.

9. Text here is from Manfroni, "Le relazioni fra Genova l'impero bizantino e it turchi," 791–809.

10. For more on Byzantine taxation in this period, see Oikonomides, "The Role of the Byzantine State in the Economy."

11. Constable, *Housing the Stranger*, 105, notes that in the Muslim *funduq* merchants mixed with travelers from other lands, but what the Genoese wanted was a place purely their own.

12. *Annales Ianuenses*, vol. 4, *Fonti per la storia d'Italia*, no. 14, ed. by Cesare Imperiale di Sant'Angelo (Rome, 1926): 41–44, for this and what follows.

13. Ibid., 101.

14. See *Pacta Veneta*, 27–47, for the text of this failed treaty, which survives in Greek and Latin copies. A failed treaty is ambiguous evidence on the state of relationships, the subject here, not diplomatic history. This edition contains fine introductions to the Venetian treaties.

15. Ibid., 57–65, for Latin text and what follows.

16. Ibid., 81–109, for parallel Greek and Latin texts. Greek resume dated 1285.

17. Ibid., 90. "Item Veneti guasmuli et heredes ipsorum, quos habebat et tenebat potestas Venetorum, quando tenebant Constantinopolim, sint liberi et franki, sicut Veneti." An anonymous author, in a tract dated 1332, was extremely hostile to guasmuls. He remarked that they were unstable, ignorant liars, regardless of which parent was Greek or Latin. See *Directorium ad passagium faciendum* in *Recueil des historiens des croisades, Documents arméniens*, vol. 2, ed. by Charles Kohler (Paris, 1906), 490–91. For more on the problems attributing this text to a known author, see Antony Leopold, *How to Reconquer the Holy Land: The Crusade Proposals of the Late Thirteenth and Early Fourteenth Centuries* (Aldershot, UK, 2000), 43–44.

18. *Pacta Veneta*, 115, 140, 158. The Greek equivalent is a direct transliteration, always beginning in *g* (e.g., *guasmul* for *vasmul*).

19. See McKee, "Inherited Status," 43, for signs that by the 1270s Latin paternity made the child of a slave woman free on Crete. By way of comparison, when King Peter of Cyprus confirmed Genoese privileges in 1365, he expansively counted as Genoese, besides the adults, their legitimate and illegitimate children, their slaves and freedmen still working for them, as well as servants receiving food, drink, and a salary. Even sailors receiving a wage were considered Genoese, whatever their origins. *Historiae Patriae Monumenta: Liber Iurium Republicae Genuensis*, ed. by Cornelio Desimoni and Luigi T. Belgrano, vol. 2 (Turin, 1857): 738, 741.

20. See Housley, *The Later Crusades*, 49–79, and for background on Ottoman ethnic complexity, Kafadar, *Between Two Worlds*, 14–28.

21. For background here, see Zachariadou, *Trade and Crusade*, 3–121. Zachariadou has also edited and published here the texts of eleven treaties, a few directly from *Diplomatarium Veneto-Levantinum* (*DVL*), most directly from manuscript collections. I use here these texts in Latin, in preference to the *DVL* versions.

22. Ibid., 218; at the end of the edited text of this treaty, it says that the copy was made by a Turkish notary who knew Turkish script.

23. Jean de Joinville, *Vie de Saint Louis*, 176–79, for this and what follows. The text supplies Old French and the modern French translation.

24. Ibid., 180, for the end of the story.

25. Zachariadou, *Trade and Crusade*, 205–6, for text of the oath.

26. See Kedar, *Crusade and Mission*, and Tolan, *Saracens*, for astute analyses of western knowledge of Islam.

27. Zachariadou, *Trade and Crusade*, 206; the Arabic creed is recorded in Latin letters.

28. Ibid., 187.

29. Ibid., 190. This pact lasted for one year, a rare concession to the Muslim dislike of permanent treaties with infidels.

30. Ibid., 197–98. "Item si fugerit aliquis scalvus ab una partium ad alteram et abstulerit aliquod habere, restitui debeat illud havere et sclavus ille sit liber . . ."

31. Ibid., 198: "et si aliquis patronus vel naucleri per audaciam levaverit sclavum illum cognoscens ipsum fore sclavum, quod dictus patronus vel nauclerus qui eum levaverit, solvere

debeat domino sclavi florenos duodecim." No gender-neutral language here, but there is no doubt that there were many female slaves to whom this provision would also have applied.

32. Ibid., 217–18.

33. Ibid., 220: "victualia, vel consilia, vel linguam a gente nostra."

34. M. Amari, "Nuovi ricordi arabici su la storia di Genova," *Atti della Società Ligure di Storia Patria* 5 (1867): 549–633; its publication in book form (Genoa, 1873), pp. 58–66, provides an Italian translation of the chronicle and also prints the Arabic text. Holt, *Early Mamluk Diplomacy*, 141–51, gives a good account of the Muslim context and an English translation of the same part of the chronicle. Amari's translation is stronger on Italian names and context; Holt is better on the Egyptian side.

35. The best edition of this text is Belgrano, "Trattato del sultano."

36. See Ashtor, *The Levant Trade*, 3–63, for details on Mamluk trade policies.

37. Constable, *Housing the Stranger*, 8, 328, also observes this imbalance—no *fondacos* for Muslim traders in the Christian west, especially Genoa.

38. Holt, *Early Mamluk Diplomacy*, 146.

39. Amari, "Nuovi ricordi," 63, is the most coherent source on these Genoese names.

40. For details, see the classic work by Spuler, *Die Goldene Horde*.

41. *DVL*, 2:188: "sicut eius maiestas plene nouit, conuersatio nostrorum mercatorum in partibus Tane et alijs partibus sui imperij est multum accomoda et utilis suo imperio et suis, et uersauice nobis et nostris, quia ex hoc non solum amor et perfecta amicitia generatur hincinde, sed propter imperium eius et sui fideles et subditi augentur . . ."

42. For details here, see Lane, *Venice*, 73–85, 174–81, and Epstein, *Genoa*, 146–47, 181–83, 219–21.

43. *DVL* (Venice, 1880), 1:243–44.

44. Ibid., 250.

45. Ibid., 251: "non possit . . . facere aliquem Venetum, etiam per modum predictum, nisi sit origine et lingua Latinus."

46. Ibid., 261–63, for what follows. The editor notes that one version of the treaty supplies the year 1344, for the Year of the Khan 759 (the Muslim year). The treaty itself is dated Year of the Horse, the eighth new moon.

47. Ibid., 262. The duty is clearly this high, and the 50 percent is repeated in subsequent treaties.

48. Ibid, 300–305; the operative paragraph is on 301.

49. Ibid., 301. The remarkable sentence is "Idcirco affectantes huic morbo dare medelam—iuxta verbum illud evangelicum, pasce oves meas, non monge, non tonde, ipse dominus imperavit." The editor G. M. Thomas noted the passage in John 21:17 but then wrote, "unde sequentia nescio, nec quo tendat monge." I'm assuming here a Latin borrowing of *mangiare*, and a play on the word *Monga* for Mongol.

50. Ibid., 311–13, for this and what follows.

51. *DVL*, 2:24–26, a rough and more formal version of the same pact, both in Venetian dialect.

52. Ibid., 49–51.

53. Ibid., 51–54. The Venetians eventually received the substantial sum of 10,998 white bezants, paid by leading Tartars, including the khan's wife.

54. See Epstein, *Genoa*, 238–42, for details on these years.

55. See Spuler, *Die Goldene Horde*, 109, 121–36, for details.

56. The treaties were published in Desimoni, "Trattato." Desimoni believed that these were two copies of the same agreement, but they are in fact separate agreements, currently in a poor state of conservation. Documents 23 and 24, Busta 2728, Negoziazioni e Trattati, Archivio Segreto, Archivio di Stato di Genova.

57. See the discussion of Caffa in chapter 2.

58. Desimoni, "Trattato," 162–65; this treaty is in the left column.

59. Ibid., 162: "e accresceran lo nome de lo Imperao segundo lo lor poey, si como I faxean per li Imperaoy passay."

60. Fugitives and runaway slaves had been concerns in treaties between Mamluk rulers and the crusader states; see Holt, "Qalāwūn's Treaty," 810–11.

61. Desimoni, "Trattato," 162–65, right column. The second treaty is written in a more regular Genoese, with much better spelling and grammar.

62. *DVL*, 2:188–90.

63. See Basso, "Il 'Bellum de Sorcati' "; the treaty is edited on pp. 25–26. The original is a formal copy of record, document 27, Busta 2729, Negoziazioni e Trattati, Archivio Segreto, Archivio di Stato di Genova.

64. Ibid., 25, and for what follows.

65. Kate Fleet, "The Treaty of 1387 between Murad I and the Genoese," *Bulletin of the School of Oriental and African Studies* 56 (1993): 13–33, here p. 15.

66. For details here, see Basso, "Il trattato."

67. Ibid., 454–60, for an edition of the long and complex Latin treaty.

68. Ibid., 457: "neque eciam ex uvis acerbis quas patres comedissent obstupescent dentes filiorum vel e contra, silicet quod neque eciam flius dabit penas pro scelere patris vel e contra ..." Surely, this is among the more remarkable images ever to appear in a treaty.

69. Ibid., 458: "et intelligantur esse Ianuenses et de familia ipsorum omnes et singuli qui declarati fuerint per consulem Ianuensium ipsos esse Ianuenses."

70. For citations to the massive literature, see Meyvaert, "An Unknown Letter," and Richard, "Un ambassade mongole."

71. The source is Al-Maqrīzī, and the letter and surrounding context are translated by Bernard Lewis, *Islam*, 1:84–88; see 84–85 for letter and what follows.

72. Meyvaert, "An Unknown Letter," 250; see 252–59 for the text of the letter, the source of what follows.

73. Ibid., 256–57; the khan's letter does not provide the actual dates.

74. For a brief account of Bohemund, the Mamluks, and the Mongols in this period, see Riley-Smith, *The Crusades*, 238–44.

75. For background, see Amitai-Preiss, *Mongols and Mamluks*, 26–48.

76. Golubovich, *Biblioteca*, 177–81, for introduction and text.

77. Ibid., 179, for the new details about Soldaia.

78. Ibid., 210–11, for text of the letter.

79. Diplomacy is a major theme in Olivia Remie Constable, *Trade and Traders in Muslim Spain* (Cambridge, 1994).

Chapter Four • Renegades and Opportunists

1. Northrup, *Africa's Discovery of Europe*, 27.
2. María Antonia Garcés, *Cervantes in Algiers: A Captive's Tale* (Nashville, 2002), 165.
3. I owe this approach to Assmann, *Moses the Egyptian*.
4. Ibid., 34–35, for a way to look at this story of Moses, and the plagues, from an Egyptian perspective.
5. The best look at the gray zone is in Primo Levi, *The Drowned and the Saved* (New York, 1989).
6. See Little, *Benedictine Maledictions*.
7. *Inferno* 31–34, Dante Alighieri, *La Divina Commedia*.
8. See *Digenis Akritis: The Grottaferrata and Escorial Versions*, xiii–lix, for an introduction to these complicated, vexing, and disputed two texts, not really versions of the same story. Renegades figure prominently in this Byzantine epic.
9. Ibid., 29. The Greek word for renegade here is *parabates*.
10. Horden and Purcell, *The Corrupting Sea*, 518.
11. *Digenis Akritis*, 63, line 323.
12. Ibid., 67, line 18.
13. Ibid., 79, line 198; 89, line 355.
14. Ibid., 125, line 970, on the Ethiopians; see p. 215, lines 205–9, about their descent from slaves.
15. *The Life of St. Andrew the Fool*, ed. and trans. by Rydén, 15–16, 21, 35. Rydén considers this life to be a fiction pretending to be older than it is.
16. Ibid., 85, blessed here for righteousness' sake as in Matthew 5:10.
17. Obadiah has benefited from extensive study and several international conferences; the collected surviving fragments in Hebrew are published by Norman Golb, "The Scroll of Obadyah the Proselyte." Professor Golb has prepared an English translation of these documents which he presented to a conference in Oppido in 2004, and I am most grateful to him for a copy of this paper, cited here as "The Autograph Memoirs of Obadiah the Proselyte of Oppido Lucano." All my citations are to this work. A good discussion especially for context remains Prawer, "The Autobiography." I am also grateful to Benjamin Z. Kedar for a copy of his paper "The Voyages of Giuàn-Obadyah in Syria and Iraq and the Enigma of his Conversion." Angelo Lancellotti figured out that John wrote his name in Hebrew in the local dialect for Giuàn, Giuwan, but it seems better to call him simply John before his conversion and Obadiah after; see Angelo Lancellotti, "Nella cronaca di Giovanni-Abdia," 256–57. This volume contains earlier work by Golb and others presented in 1970.
18. The source for this account are the documents edited and translated by Norman Golb, "The Autograph Memoirs."
19. Prawer, "The Autobiography," 117–18.
20. Ibid., 115.
21. Ibid., 119. Golb's translation does not identify the exact source of Obadiah's fear, but fear of the "uncircumcised" is a reasonable hypothesis.
22. Golb, "The Autograph Memoirs," 3.

23. Goitein, *A Mediterranean Society*, vol. 2, *The Community*, 308–9.

24. Alfred Büchler, "Obadyah the Proselyte and the Roman Liturgy," *Medieval Encounters* 7, no. 2 (2001): 165–73, stresses the liturgical significance of this passage. It figures in the mass on one of the five days in the year set aside for the ordination of priests and deacons, so John would have heard it rather often.

25. Prawer, "The Autobiography," 120.

26. Golb comments on eclipses in Europe in 1095 and 1096 on p. iv of "The Autograph Memoirs."

27. Golb, "The Autograph Memoirs," 4; the context also invokes sexual worries about the Christian women being left behind.

28. Ibid., 1, and 13–19, for the translation of the key evidence from a letter of recommendation Barukh ben Isaac of Aleppo wrote for Obadiah when he arrived in the East, perhaps shortly after 1102. The hint that the conversion took place in Apulia comes from Golb's use of the surviving vowel marks from a missing line of text. This letter is especially valuable because the information in it comes from another witness.

29. Benjamin Z. Kedar, "The Voyages of Giuàn-Obadyah," 13–17. I compress his detailed argument.

30. For the fragments on the Baghdad phase, see Golb, "The Autograph Memoirs," 6–9.

31. Ibid., 8–9.

32. Golb was himself the first to spot the connections between Hebrew poetry set to this music, and for the texts, see the music pages at the end of "The Autograph Memoirs."

33. Ibid., 12, but Obadiah sees this as the Land of Israel.

34. See ibid., 12–13, for the last fragments from Obadiah.

35. For an edition of this remarkable text in Arabic with translation, see Samau'al al-Maghribī, *Ifḥām al-Yahūd Silencing the Jew*, 75–88, for the author's own accounts of his dreams and conversion. These events occurred in Marāgha today near Tabriz in Iran. For context here, see Lazarus-Yafeh, *Intertwined Worlds*, 69, and elsewhere.

36. The classic account is Riley-Smith, *The First Crusade*, where he emphasizes how the trials of the march remade the spirituality of some participants.

37. See John France, *Victory in the East*, and his essay "The Fall of Antioch during the First Crusade."

38. For what follows, see *Gesta Francorum*, 44–47, for the Latin and an English translation. The author was at Antioch during these events.

39. I cite here the translation in the useful collection *The First Crusade*, ed. by Edward Peters, 75.

40. D'Aguilers, *Le 'Liber' de Raymond D'Aguilers*, 64–66.

41. Ibid., 64. One version of the text stated that the Greeks and Armenians *turcaverant*, became Turks, Muslims, so it is possible that the unnamed traitor here was one of the recent converts.

42. For this text, see Guibert de Nogent, *Dei Gesta per Francos*, 200–207, for what follows about Firuz and Antioch.

43. Ibid., 251.

44. Ibid., 331–32.

45. I use here *La Chanson d'Antioche*, ed. by Suzanne Duparc-Quioc, lines 5886–96.
46. For more on the theme of women in this work, see Susan B. Edgington, "Women in the *Chanson D'Antioche*," 154–62.
47. *La Chanson d'Antioche*, lines 6217–20.
48. Ibid., line 6514.
49. Gabrieli, *Arab Historians*, 6.
50. *The Damascus Chronicle of the Crusades*, 44; al-Qalānīsī may have been a source for Ibn al Athīr.
51. Usāmah Ibn Munqidh, *An Arab-Syrian Gentleman*, 156–58.
52. Ibid., 159–60, for these stories.
53. *Decretales ineditae saeculi XII*, ed. by Stanley Chodorow and Charles Duggan (Vatican City, 1982), no. 94, pp. 166–67.
54. Usāmah, *An Arab-Syrian Gentleman*, 169–70.
55. Hillenbrand, *The Crusades*, 282.
56. See Prawer, "The Battle of Hattin," in his *Crusader Institutions*, 484–500, and Kedar, "The Battle of Hattin Revisited," in *The Horns of Hattin*, 190–207. See also Hamilton, *The Leper King*, 8–13, for a recent survey of the sources, including the vexed issues surrounding the vernacular French chronicles of the period.
57. See the old but still valuable study by Baldwin, *Raymond III*, 11–13, for the significance of this captivity.
58. Friedman, *Encounter between Enemies*, 6, where the author compares Raymond to Patty Hearst!
59. Baldwin, *Raymond III*, 83–84, for a good analysis on the sources for this episode; Hamilton, *The Leper King*, 216–24, for a more detailed investigation that supports the view that Raymond was a traitor.
60. For this and what follows, see Richard, "An Account"; the Latin text used here appears on 175–77.
61. The new insights on this Jean also come from Jean Richard, "The Adventure of John Gale, Knight of Tyre," in *The Experience of Crusading*, vol. 2, ed. by Peter Edbury and Jonathan Phillips (Cambridge, 2003), 190.
62. Ibid., 189. This is the same Jean, if indeed he is the object of Saladin's enduring desire for revenge in 1188, as Richard believes.
63. Morgan, *La Continuation*, 53–54. See her *The Chronicle of Ernoul* for astute arguments on why this version is especially valuable.
64. *Recueil des historiens des croisades*, vol. 2 (Paris, 1869): 65. This chronicle is known as *Eracles*.
65. For this version, see the anonymous but well-informed source *De Expugnatione Terrae Sanctae per Saladinum, Libellus*, ed. J. Stevenson, Rolls Series, no. 66 (London, 1875), 225, which offers a direct quotation from Raymond on the field of battle: "Qui potest transire transeat, quoniam non est nobis praelium. Sed et fuga quidam jam periit a nobis."
66. Richard, "An Account," 176.
67. Baldwin, *Raymond III*, 84.
68. Hillenbrand, *The Crusades*, 342, citing Imad al-Din.
69. Ralph of Coggeshall, *Chronicon Anglicanum*, Rolls Series, no. 66, p. 22: "Comes Tripolitanus cum terram suam tradere proposuisset Salaadino, inventus est mortuus in lecto suo."

70. *Recueil des historiens des croisades*, vol. 1, pt. 1, pp. 71–72, for what follows.
71. Morgan, *La Continuation*, 53.
72. *Gesta Regis Henrici Secundi*, ed. W. Stubbs, Rolls Series, no. 49 (London, 1867), 2:11–12.
73. John of Ibelin, *Le Livre*, 167. Jews were also excluded, but according to Joshua Prawer, they had no business in this court, see his *The History of the Jews in the Latin Kingdom of Jerusalem* (Oxford, 1988), 100.
74. Friedman, *Encounter between Enemies*, 137–39, quotation p. 139.
75. Kedar, "Multidirectional Conversion in the Frankish Levant," 193–94.
76. For what follows, I rely on the standard Latin edition of William's account, *Sinica franciscana*, 164–332.
77. Ibid., 252–53, for this and what follows.
78. Ibid., 261. Olschki, *Guillaume Boucher,* closely scrutinizes these notices in William.
79. *Sinica franciscana*, 270.
80. Ibid., 275–76.
81. Ibid., 278.
82. Ibid., 281–82 for this and what follows.
83. Ibid., 287.
84. Ibid., 305.
85. Ibid., 311.
86. For his text, the best source on his thoughts, see Adae, *De Modo*, 521–55.
87. Ibid., 524–26 for this and what follows.
88. Ibid., 528.
89. Ibid., 549–50.
90. Holt, *Early Mamluk Diplomacy,* text on pp. 122–28; for what follows, see p. 123.
91. Adae, *De Modo*, 531, for example.
92. Ibid., 526–27. And for the Officium, established in 1301, see Ausilia Roccagliata, *L'Officium Robarie del Commune di Genova 1294–1397* (Genoa, 1990).
93. Benjamin Z. Kedar, "Segurano-Sakrān Salvaygo: Un mercante genovese al servizio dei sultani mamalucchi, c. 1303–1322," was originally published in 1976, but the version used here, containing one additional reference, appears in his *The Franks in the Levant*.
94. Ibid., 89–91.
95. In addition to references in chapter 2, see the expanded essay by Ayalon, "Mamlūk: Military Slavery in Egypt and Syria," in his *Islam*, 6–7.
96. Kedar, "Segurano," 90.
97. Ibid., 81.
98. Ibid. Kedar draws his price data from E. Ashtor and David Ayalon's work on slavery in Egypt. Ayalon notes that the price of eunuchs was no doubt very high; see his *Eunuchs*, 300–301.
99. Kedar, "Segurano," 84–85.
100. Ibid., 90, for Kedar's find of the Muslim source.
101. See *Ramusio Navigazioni*, 504–7.
102. Ibid., 590.
103. Ibid., 607.
104. Ibid., 573, for the following story.
105. Ibid. "Come? La fede di Macometto cresce in questo modo?"

106. Karpov, "New Documents," 36.

107. *Montaigne's Travel Journal*, trans. by Donald Frame (San Francisco, 1983), 123–24.

108. See Lucchini, *La merce umana*, for comments about reintegrating captives back into Genoese society.

109. See Howard, *Venice*, for a good visual sense of how Venice incorporated so many aspects of the eastern Mediterranean into its fabric.

110. For a good study of the complex fates of Muslim captives in Italy, see Bono, *Schiavi musulmani nell'Italia moderna*, a study that covers from about 1500 to 1830.

Chapter Five • Human and Angelic Faces

1. See Aristotle, *Minor Works*, 84–137, here 806a, 808b. This Hellenistic work, though not by Aristotle, by common agreement reflects the opinions of his school, and in the Middle Ages remained the classic, most authoritative, and oldest work on physiognomy. For background on medieval physiognomy, see the collected essays by Jole Agrimi, *Ingeniosa scientia nature: Studi sulla fisiognomica medievale* (Florence, 2002).

2. See *The Talmud of Babylonia*, vol. 31.B, *Tractate Bekhorot*, trans. Jacob Neusner (Atlanta, 1984), here *Bekhorot* 43A–46A, p. 101. David Goldenberg dates and discusses this passage in *The Curse of Ham*, 113, giving special care to the words that mean very light (*lavan*) and very dark (*shahor*).

3. Campanella, *La Città del Sole*, 84: "e con modi magici li fanno venire al coito, che possan ben generare inanzi a cavalli pinti . . ." A note here points to the antiquity of this belief.

4. Scot discussed this problem in other, better-known works, and it preoccupied many scholars. See Cadden, *Meanings*, 200–201, 130–31 for some comments on Scot, but this work does not consider ethnic differences or mixing. Cadden has some valuable comments on physiognomy and reasons for its neglect on pp. 186–88. For an older but comprehensive look at Scot, see Lynn Thorndike, *Michael Scot* (London, 1965), esp. 87–91 on physiognomy.

5. Scot, *Liber Physionomie*, is not paginated so it is cited by capitulum (cap. 1) for this comment and what follows on color. "Et est sciendum quod si de semine uiri plus fuerit quam feminae foetus erit illi similis in pelle et forte in sexu. Verbi gratia mulier quaedam erat alba: et cum coiret cum aethyope peperit filiam albam. Alia mulier nigra coiuit cum viro albo et peperit filium nigrum: ut patet hoc toto tempore."

6. Other factors, like ethnic loyalty, could stress the free parent's status in determining the child's fate; see Sally McKee, "Inherited Status," esp. 42–43.

7. See Aristotle, *Minor Works*, 805a, where he singles out Egyptians, Thracians, and Scythians as examples.

8. Goldenberg, *The Curse of Ham*, 187–93, makes clear that the overwhelming majority of the negative references came from pagan and not Jewish sources. The Christian and Muslim legacies remain more ambiguous. A tenth-century Byzantine dream book stated that if someone (a man) dreamed "that his skin turned from white to black, like an Ethiopian's, he would be untrustworthy and a ludicrous liar . . ." and for a woman it meant that she would acquire the reputation of a prostitute—more signs that physiognomy was gendered and hostile to darker people. See *The Oneirocriticon of Achmet*, 118.

9. Benjamin Isaac also stresses how gendered ancient physiognomy was—positive traits

were male and negative ones female. See his *The Invention of Racism*, 149–59, on ancient physiognomy, here p. 154.

10. Scot, *Liber Physionomie*, cap. 13. "Lac mulieris nigrae et brunae est melius semper illo mulieris albae et rubae": and he goes on to extol the value of mother's milk in general over milk from a pig or goat.

11. For this detail, see Bartolomeo of Messina's Latin translation of the Pseudo-Aristotle *Physiognomika* in *Scriptores Physiognomici*, 1:73. This point is not clear in the Greek original.

12. Aristotle, *Minor Works*, 805b, 806a

13. For details here, see *Anonyme latin*, 28–29.

14. This version appears in the widely known section on physiognomy in the *Secretum Secretorum* as edited by Roger Bacon, *Opera hactenus inedita Rogeri Baconi*, fasc 5, 219.

15. Ibid., 166, for Bacon's gloss containing these comments, where he also explains that the word *physiognomy* comes from the Greek for the law of nature, its proper subject.

16. Peter of Abano, *Liber conpilationis phisonomie*; by my pagination, see p. 10, on Paduans, p. 34, on the eyes of Ezzelino.

17. The standard edition is now Iacopo da Varazze, *Legenda Aurea*, ed. by Giovanni Paolo Maggioni; see p. 35 for a comment appearing in the life of Saint Andrew.

18. Ibid., 1081, in life of Saints Simon and Jude.

19. Ibid., 402.

20. Ibid., 831. In this case, a demon was describing the face, which was cheerful, and its owner knew all languages.

21. Ibid. This face was described by an angel.

22. Goitein, *A Mediterranean Society*, 5:309.

23. Ibid., 5:477.

24. See interesting comments on Muslim and Jewish traditions on this and other matters in Lazarus-Yafeh, *Intertwined Worlds*, 29–32.

25. Samau'al al-Maghribī, *Ifḥām al-Yahūd*, 84; a previous dream, 81, briefly noted something about the appearance of his namesake the prophet Samuel.

26. Iacopo da Varazze, *Legenda Aurea*, 735.

27. Ibid., 287.

28. Ibid., 1195. The saintly victim was Faustianus; the story appears in the life of Saint Clement.

29. Ibid., 106.

30. Ibid., 183: "Quis dulce lumen oculorum meorum extinxit?"

31. Ibid., 1242. The likely source is John of Damascus (eighth century).

32. Peter of Abano, *Liber compilationis phisonomie*.

33. Scot, *Liber phisionomie*, cap 33 (the heart) to cap. 37 (the testicles).

34. The text has been edited and translated by Youssef Mourad, *La physiognomonie arabe*. See p. 89; I have substituted Indians for Hindus for clarity.

35. Ibid., 119.

36. Ibid., 55, 141. Gerard of Cremona translated this text into Latin and it influenced numerous other Muslim works on the medical diagnosis of slaves.

37. Della Porta, *Della fisionomia dell'uomo*, 358.

38. *Anonyme latin*, 66, 71–72, on color.

39. Ibid., 79.
40. Ibid., 80.
41. Ibid., 84.
42. Ibid.
43. *The Oneirocriticon of Achmet*, 105–6. For more on the Arabic background of this Greek work, see Mavroudi, *A Byzantine Book on Dream Interpretation*.
44. Mourad, *La physiognomonie arabe*, 102, for this and what follows.
45. Ibid., 55. Mourad notes in his introduction the strong role physiognomy played in the important Arabic genre devoted to medical examinations of slaves.
46. Ibid., 117.
47. Ibid., 118.
48. Scot, *Liber phisionomie*, cap. 53. The key passage on color is "Cuius oculi sunt in forma mediocres tendentes ad nigredinem significant hominem conuenienter pacificum:mansuetum: legalem ingenii boni magni intellectus: et conuenienter alteri seruitialem."
49. Ibid., cap. 49.
50. Peter of Abano, *Liber compilationis phisonomie*, 10–11. "Color intra crocedinem non tinctam et nigredinem qui uergit in brunum clarum . . ."
51. Ibid., 11, for this and what follows.
52. Ibn Khaldûn, *The Muqaddhima*, 2:421.
53. Maimonides, *The Guide of the Perplexed*, 108–9, where Maimonides also observed that angels might even appear in the form of women and that figurative language describing them was necessary for limited human intellects to comprehend them.
54. See *The Old Testament Pseudoepigrapha*, 5–12, for a historical introduction to this complex work. What follows is a summary of 1 Enoch 6–11.
55. Clark, *The Origenist Controversy*, 11–12. The catalogue of errors is from Jerome, and here it does not matter if they were fair or not.
56. For some useful ideas on these themes, see Peers, *Subtle Bodies*, 10–11.
57. Pseudo-Dionysius, *La hiérarchie céleste*, 105–33, for an extensive treatment of the three triads of angels.
58. Iacopo da Varazze, *Legenda Aurea*, 990–91.
59. Pseudo-Dionysius, *La hiérarchie céleste*, 169, and 184–86, for what follows.
60. For more on these themes, see Alexander Rofé, *The Belief in Angels*, which stresses the "pagan origins of angelology," xiii.
61. This is a major theme in Kugel, *The God of Old*.
62. Ibid., 15.
63. Angelic names had power and were part of Jewish request formula and adjurations since at least late antiquity; see Janowitz, *Icons of Power*, 88–91. For Jews, asking angels for things was a way to request what could not be sought directly from God.
64. Quran Sura, 50:17–19.
65. *The Oneirocriticon*, 88–89.
66. This list draws on all the sources, scholarly and scriptural, mentioned in this section as well as the numerous notices in Kugel, *Traditions of the Bible*, Stapert, *L'ange roman*, and Heidt, *Angelology*.
67. Bussagli, *Storia degli angeli*, 33–34.

68. Augustine, *City of God*, 446.
69. Ibid., 472. All the references are from book 11, where angels are a major theme.
70. Ibid., 471–73.
71. Ibid., 367.
72. Boloyan, "Gli angeli," 70.
73. Brooke Olson Vukovic, *Heavenly Journeys, Earthly Concerns: The Legacy of the Mi'raj in the Formation of Islam* (New York, 2005), 32–39.
74. *Encyclopedia of Islam*, 2:362–64, for Djibrīl, Gabriel, the Man of God, always more important in Islam than Michael.
75. Boloyan, "Gli angeli," 73.
76. *Encyclopedia of Islam*, 6:216–19, for *malā'ika* (angels).
77. Stapert, *L'ange roman*, 70.
78. Ibid., 270. Stapert pays more attention to clothing, perhaps a useful ethnographic marker.
79. Petzold, "'His Face like Lightening.'"
80. Ibid., 149, 155.
81. There was a long tradition in literature of seeing peasants in Europe as dark; see Freedman, *Images*, 139–42.
82. See *African Art*, 144, for image, and 176, for description.
83. Dante Alighieri, *La Divina Commedia,* Paradiso, 31:13:"Le facce tutte avean di fiamma viva / e l'ali d'oro, e l'altro tanto bianco, / che nulla neve a quel termine arriva."
84. Peers, *Subtle Bodies*, 63–66, 120, and elsewhere is emphatic on these essential points.
85. Rouche, "Le combat," 534. Kathryn M. Ringrose, *The Perfect Servant,* argues for a connection between angels, Michael, and eunuchs as beardless courtly servants of God—see esp. pp. 143–50—but this emphasis neglects both Hebrew and early Christian traditions about angels.
86. See Del Francia, "Angeli," 53, for the role of Michael in the Coptic church. Michael also had a strong tie to water and the flooding of the Nile.
87. Hannah, *Michael*, 36.
88. Ibid., 122.
89. For what follows, see Maguire, *The Icons*, 106–7.
90. See also Oldoni, "L'angelo," 74–78.
91. Iacopo da Varazze, *Legenda Aurea*, 986–1001, here 986.
92. In the early medieval trip to Hell ascribed to Barontius, Raphael guides the traveler, but he is not called a psychopomp; see John J. Contreni, "'Building Mansions in Heaven': The *Visio Barontii*, Archangel Raphael, and a Carolingian King," *Speculum* 78 (2003): 673–706, here 690–91.
93. Iacopo da Varazze, *Legenda Aurea*, 989.
94. Ibid., 995: "Ipsi enim sunt custodes nostri, ministratores nostri, fratres et conciues nostri, animarum nostrarum in celum portitores, orationum nostrarum apud deum representatores, regis eterni nobilissimi milites et tribulatorum consolatores."
95. See ibid., 998, where he returns to the theme of fellow citizen and explains in more detail how hierarchy was natural in this world and the next, relying on the angelology of Gregory the Great.
96. Ibid., 1000–1001.

97. Ibid., 996: "boni angeli . . . in natiuitate in utero et statim post natiuitatem ex utero et semper est cum ipso iam adulto."

98. Bussagli, *Storia degli angeli*, 175.

99. Ibid., 200.

100. Ibid., 278.

101. Peers, *Subtle Bodies*, 143–44.

102. Ibid., 163–65. See *Acta Sanctorum, Septembris*, vol. 8 (Paris, 1865) for September 29 and a collection of sources about Michael, and p. 39 for the course of the Lycus river.

103. Peers, *Subtle Bodies*, 181–83.

104. Ibid., 93–95.

105. See ibid., 120, where Peers is excellent on this point.

106. These are the main themes of Horden and Purcell, *The Corrupting Sea*; see 408–9, 413, and 416 for notices to Michael.

107. Iacopo da Varazze, *Legenda Aurea*, 992.

108. See *Acta Sanctorum*, September 29, pp. 61–2, for the full Latin version of this story. Peers, *Subtle Bodies*, 166–67, summarizes this Greek version of the story.

109. *Acta Sanctorum*, September 29, p. 62: "vestigia marmori diximus impresa."

110. Arnold, "Arcadia Becomes Jerusalem," 586–87.

111. *Acta Sanctorum*, September 29, p. 72 and p. 65, for an inscription from 1656 at Siponto invoking Michael's aid against the plague.

112. See Hunt, "For the Salvation of a Woman's Soul," 205–7. For background on icons as objects of study and sources, see Cormack, *Painting the Soul*.

113. See *St. Michael the Archangel*, 74*–108*, for the translation; 76*–77* sets up the story.

114. Ibid., 80*.

115. Ibid., 87*–88*.

116. Ibid., 89*.

117. See ibid., 91*–99*, for the dramatic conclusion to the encomium.

118. Ibid., 96*.

119. Ibid., 97*; here as elsewhere, the phrasing is slightly modernized.

120. Ibid., 102*–4*, for this and what follows.

121. Peers, *Subtle Bodies*, 205, makes this point to conclude that skin color is useless for analyzing icons of angels.

122. Horowitz, *Ethiopian Art*, 65.

Conclusion

1. For an example of how important ideas survived, see Brundage, "Immortalizing the Crusades," 251–60, esp. 260. The wanderings and mixings of the western Mediterranean peoples, before and after 1400, merit separate studies.

2. I take this theme from Horden and Purcell, *The Corrupting Sea*.

3. A view influenced by ideas in James McBride, *The Color of Water: A Black Man's Tribute to His White Mother* (New York, 1996).

SELECTED BIBLIOGRAPHY

Manuscripts

Archivio di Stato di Genova
Archivio Segreto, Negoziazioni e Trattati

Published Primary Sources

Acta Sanctorum quotquot toto orbe coluntur. Paris, 1863.
Adorno, Anselme. *Itinéraire d'Anselme Adorno en Terre Sainte (1470–1471)*. Ed. and trans. by Jacques Heers and Georgette de Groer. Paris, 1978.
Al-Quran: A Contemporary Translation. Trans. by Ahmed Ali. Princeton, 1994.
Alighieri, Dante. *La Divina Commedia*. Ed. by C. H. Grandgent and C. S. Singleton. Cambridge, Mass., 1972.
Anonyme latin. *Anonyme latin: Traité de Physiognomie*. Ed. by Jacques André. Paris, 1981.
Aristotle. *Minor Works I Physiognomonica*. Ed. and trans. by W. S. Hett. London, 1936.
Arnobius. *Adversus nationes*. Ed. by Augustus Reifferscheid. Vienna, 1875.
Augustine of Hippo. *City of God*. Trans. by Henry Bettenson. Harmondsworth, 1977.
Bacon, Roger. *Opera hactenus inedita Rogeri Baconi: Secretum Secretorum*. Ed. by Robert Steele. Oxford, 1920.
Balard, Michel. *Gênes e L'Outre Mer I Les actes de Caffa du notaire Lamberto de Sambuceto 1289–90*. Paris, 1973.
———. *Notai genovesi in Oltremare: Atti rogati a Chio da Donato di Chiavari (17 febbraio–12 novembre 1394)*. Genoa, 1988.
———. *Notai genovesi in Oltremare: Atti rogati a Cipro da Lamberto di Sambuceto (11 ottobre 1296–23 giugno 1299)*. Genoa, 1983.
———. *Notai genovesi in Oltremare: Atti rogati a Cipro: Lamberto di Sambuceto 1307, Giovanni de Rocha 1308–1310*. Genoa, 1984.
Balbi, Giovanna, and Silvana Raiteri. *Notai genovesi in Oltremare: Atti rogati a Caffa e a Licostomo*. Genoa, 1973.
Balbi, Giovanni. *Catholicon*. Mainz, 1460.

Basso, Enrico. "Il trattato con il principe Ivanko e la diplomazia genovese nel Mar Nero alla fine del '300." *Atti della Academia ligure di scienze e lettere* 47 (1990): 443–61.

——. *Notai genovesi in Oltremare: Atti rogati a Chio a Giuliano de Canella.* Athens, 1993.

Belgrano, Luigi T. "Trattato del sultano d'Egitto col commune di Genova nel 1290." *ASLSP* 19 (1887): 163–75.

Benedict the Pole. *Relatio* in *Sinica Franciscana*, vol. 1. Ed. by A. Van den Wyngaert. Florence, 1929.

Benvenuto de Brixiano: Notaio in Candia 1301–1302. Ed. by Raimundo Morozzo Della Rocca. Venice, 1950.

Bernard of Clairvaux. *Sermons sur le Cantique.* Ed. and trans. by Paul Verdeyen and Raffaele Fassetta. 2 vols. Sources Chrétiennes, no. 414. Paris, 1996.

Boccaccio, Giovanni. *Decameron* in *Tutte le opere.* Ed. by Vittore Branca. Brescia, 1974.

Campanella, Tommaso. *La Città del Sole.* Berkeley, 1981.

La Chanson d'Antioche. Ed. by Suzanne Duparc-Quioc. Paris, 1977.

Codex Comanicus. Ed. by Vladimir Drimba. Bucharest, 2000.

Codex Cumanicus. Ed. by Geza Kuun. Budapest, 1981.

The Damascus Chronicle of the Crusades. Trans. by H. A. R. Gibb. London, 1932.

Della Porta, Giovanni Battista. *Della fisionomia dell'uomo.* Ed. by Mario Cicognani. Parma, 1988.

Desimoni, Cornelio. "Trattato dei Genovesi col Chan dei Tartari nel 1380–81: Scritto in lingua volgare." *Archivio storico italiano* 30 (1887): 161–65.

Digenis Akritis: The Grottaferrata and Escorial Versions. Ed. and trans. by Elizabeth Jeffreys. Cambridge, 1998.

Diplomatarium Veneto-Levantinum. Ed. by George Martin Thomas. Venice, 1899.

Dörrie, Heinrich. "Drie Texte zur Geschichte der Ungarn und Mongolen." *Nachrichten der Akademie der Wissenschaften in Göttingen, I.* Philologisch-Historische Klasse, no. 6. (Göttingen, 1956).

Ezra ben Solomon of Gerona. *Commentary on the Song of Songs.* Trans. by Seth Brody. Kalamazoo, 1999.

Firenzuola, Agnolo. *Prose scelte.* Florence, 1957.

The Five Megilloth. Trans. by A. J. Rosenberg. New York, 1992.

Gesta Francorum. Ed. by Rosalind Hill. London, 1962.

Gioffrè, Domenico. "Atti Rogati in Chio nella seconda metà del XIV secolo." *Bulletin de L'Institut Belge de Rome* 34 (1962): 319–404.

Glossa Ordinaria Pars 22 in Canticum Canticorum. Ed. by Mary Dove. Turnholt, 1997.

Golb, Norman. "The Scroll of Obadyah the Proselyte." In *Studies in Geniza and Sepharadi Heritage Presented to Shelomo Dov Goitein*, in Hebrew. Ed. by Shelomo Morag and Issachar Ben-Ami. Jerusalem, 1991.

Golubovich, Girolamo, ed. *Biblioteca Bio-bibliografica della Terra Santa dell'Oriente francescano.* Quaracchi, 1913.

Gregory of Nyssa, *Commentary on the Song of Songs.* Trans. by Casimir McCambly. Brookline, 1987.

Guibert de Nogent. *Dei Gesta per Francos.* Ed. by Robert B. C. Huygens. Turnholt, 1996.

Guillelmus Adae. *De Modo Sarracenos Extirpandi.* In *Recueil des historiens des croisades, Documents arméniens.* Vol. 2. Ed. by Charles Kohler. Paris, 1906.

Iacopo da Varazze (Jacopo da Varagine). *Legenda Aurea.* 2 vols. 2d ed. Ed. by Giovanni Paolo Maggioni. Florence, 1998.

Ibn Battuta. *The Travels of Ibn Battuta A.D. 1325–1354.* Ed. and trans. by H. A. R. Gibb. Cambridge, 1962.

Ibn Jubayr, *The Travels of Ibn Jubayr.* Trans. by R. J. C. Broadhurst. London, 1952.

Ibn Khaldûn, *The Muqaddhima.* 3 vols. Trans. by Franz Rosenthal. New York, 1958.

Imperiale di Sant'Angelo, Cesare. *Codice diplomatico della repubblica di Genova.* Vols. 1 and 3. Rome, 1936, 1942.

Jackson, Peter, and David Morgan. *The Mission of Friar William of Rubruck.* London, 1990.

Jacques de Vitry. *Lettres de la Cinquième Croisade.* Brepols, 1998.

Jean de Joinville. *Vie de Saint Louis.* Ed. by Jacques Monfrin. Paris, 1995.

John of Ibelin. *Le Livre des Assises.* Ed. by Peter W. Edbury. Leiden, 2003.

John of Monte Corvino. *Letters* in *Sinica Franciscana.* Vol. 1. Ed. A. van den Wyngaert. Florence, 1929.

John of Plano Carpini. *Ystoria mongolorum* in *Sinica Franciscana.* Vol. 1. Ed. A. van den Wyngaert. Florence, 1929.

Lammens, Henri. "Correspondences diplomatiques entre les sultans mamlouks d'Égypte et les puissances chrétiennes." *Revue de l'Orient chrétien* 9 (1904): 152–87, 359–92.

Latini, Brunetto. *Il Tesoretto.* Ed. and trans. by Julia Holloway. New York, 1981.

Levi ben Gershom (Gersonides). *Commentary on Song of Songs.* Trans. by Menachem Kellner. New Haven, 1995.

The Life of St Andrew the Fool. Ed. and trans. by Lennart Rydén. Uppsala, 1995.

Lombardo, Antonino. *Nicola de Boateriis: Notaio in Famagusta e Venezia (1355–1365).* Venice, 1973.

Maimonides, Moses. *The Guide of the Perplexed.* Trans. by Shlomo Pines. Chicago, 1963.

Manfroni, Camillo. "Le relazioni fra Genova l'impero bizantino e I turchi." *ASLSP* 28 (1898): 577–858.

Michael Scot, *Liber Physionomie.* Venice, 1490.

Mingana, A., ed. and trans. "The Apology of Timothy the Patriarch before the Caliph Mahdi." *Bulletin of the John Rylands Library* 12 (1928): 147–290.

Morgan, Margaret Ruth. *La Continuation de Guillaume de Tyr.* Paris, 1982.

Mourad, Youssef. *La physiognomonie arabe.* Paris, 1939.

Muckle, J. T. "The Personal Letters Between Abelard and Héloise." *Mediaeval Studies* 15 (1953): 47–94.

The Old Testament Pseudoepigrapha. 2 vols. Ed. by James H. Charlesworth. New York, 1983, 1985.

The Oneirocriticon of Achmet. Ed. and trans. by Steven M. Oberhelm. Lubbock, 1991.

Origen. *Commentaire sur le Cantique des Cantiques.* Ed. by L. Brésard and H. Crouzel with M. Borret. Paris, 1991.

———. *Commentaire sur L'Évangile selon Matthieu.* Trans. by Robert Girod. Paris, 1970.

———. *Homélies sur le Cantique des Cantiques.* Ed. by O. Rousseau. Paris, 1954.

Pacta Veneta: I trattati con Bisanzio 1265–1285. Ed. by Marco Pozza and Giorgio Ravegnani. Venice, 1996.

Pavoni, Romeo. *Notai genovesi in Oltremare: Atti rogati a Cipro da Lamberto di Sambuceto (Gennaio–Agosto 1302).* Genoa, 1987.

———. *Notai genovesi in Oltremare: Atti rogati a Cipro da Lamberto di Sambuceto (6 luglio–27 ottobre 1301).* Genoa, 1982.

Peter of Abano. *Liber conpilationis phisonomie.* Padua, 1474.

Pistarino, Geo. *Notai genovesi in Oltremare: Atti rogati a Chilia da Antonio di Ponzò (1360–61).* Genoa, 1971.

Polo, Marco. *Le Livre de Marco Polo.* Ed. by M. G. Pauthier. Paris, 1865; reprint, Geneva, 1978.

———. *Milione: versione toscana del trecento.* Ed. by Valeria Bertolucci Pizzorusso. Milan, 1994.

Polonio, Valeria. *Notai genovesi in Oltremare: Atti rogati a Cipro di Lamberto di Sambuceto (3 luglio 1300–3 agosto 1301).* Genoa, 1982.

Pseudo-Dionysius. *La hiérarchie celeste.* Ed. and trans. by G. Hall and M. de Gandillac. Paris, 1958.

Ramusio, Giovanni Battista, *Navigazioni e Viaggi.* Ed. by Marica Milanesi. Turin, 1978.

Raymond D'Aguilers. *Le 'Liber' de Raymond D'Aguilers.* Ed. by John H. and Laurita L. Hill. Paris, 1969.

Riccold de Monte Croce. *Pérégrination en Terre Sainte et au Proche Orient: Texte latin et traduction.* Ed. by René Kappler. Paris, 1997

Roccatagliata, Ausilia. *Notai genovesi in Oltremare: Atti rogati a Chio (1453–1454, 1470–1471).* Genoa, 1988.

Samau'al al-Maghribī. *Ifḥām al-Yahūd Silencing the Jew.* Ed. and trans. by Moshe Perlmann. New York, 1964.

Scriptores Physiognomici. 2 vols. Ed. by Richard Foerster. Leipzig, 1893.

Secundum Salomonem: A Thirteenth Century Latin Commentary on the Song of Solomon. Ed. by Sarah Kamin and Avrom Saltman. Ramat Gan, 1989.

Simon de Saint-Quentin, *Histoire des Tartares.* Ed. by Jean Richard. Paris, 1965.

Sinica Franciscana, Itinerarium Willelmi de Rubruc. Ed. by Anastasius van den Wyngaert. Vol. 1. Florence, 1929.

St Michael the Archangel: Three Encomiums. Ed. and trans. by E. A. Wallis Budge. London, 1894.

Toniolo, Paola Piana. *Notai genovesi in Oltremare: Atti rogati a Chio da Gregorio Panissaro (1403–1405).* Genoa, 1995.

Usāmah Ibn Munqidh. *An Arab-Syrian Gentleman and Warrior in the Period of the Crusades: Memoirs of Usāmah Ibn Munqidh.* Trans. by Philip K. Hitti. Princeton, 1987.

Wilhelm von Tripolis (William of Tripoli). *Notitia de Machometo De statu Sarracenorum.* Ed. by Peter Engels. Würzburg, 1992.

Yule, Henry, ed. *Book of Ser Marco Polo the Venetian.* London, 1905

Secondary Works

Abu-Lughod, Janet L. *Before European Hegemony: The World System A.D. 1250–1350.* New York, 1989.

African Art: The Sacred Art of Ethiopia. Ed. by Roderick Grierson. New Haven, 1993.

Airaldi, Gabriella. *Studi e documenti su Genova e L'Oltremare.* Genoa, 1974.

Amitai-Preiss, Reuven. *Mongols and Mamluks: The Mamluk-Īlkhānid War, 1260–81.* Cambridge, 1995.

Appiah, Kwame Anthony. *The Ethics of Identity.* Princeton, 2005.

Argenti, Philip P. *The Occupation of Chios by the Genoese and Their Administration of the Island, 1346–1566.* Cambridge, 1958.
———. *The Religious Minorities of Chios: Jews and Roman Catholics.* Cambridge, 1970.
Arnold, John Charles. "Arcadia Becomes Jerusalem: Angelic Caverns and Shrine Conversion at Monte Gargano." *Speculum* 75 (2000): 567–88.
Ashtor, Eliyahu. *The Levant Trade in the Later Middle Ages.* Princeton, 1983.
Assmann, Jan. *Moses the Egyptian: The Memory of Egypt in Western Monotheism.* Cambridge, Mass., 1998.
Ayalon, David. *Eunuchs, Caliphs, and Sultans.* Jerusalem, 1999.
———. *Islam and the Abode of War.* Aldershot, 1994.
Balard, Michel. *La Romanie génoise.* 2 vols. Rome, 1978.
Balard, Michel, and Gilles Veinstein. "Continuité ou changement d'un paysage urbain? Caffa génoise et ottoman." *Le paysage au Moyen Age* (Lyon, 1981).
Baldwin, Marshall. *Raymond III of Tripolis and the Fall of Jerusalem (1140–1187).* Princeton, 1936.
Balletto, Laura. *Genova, Mediterraneo, Mar Nero (secc. XIII–XV).* Genoa, 1976.
Basso, Enrico. "Il 'Bellum de Sorcati' ed I trattati del 1380–87 tra Genova e L'Orda D'Oro." *Studi Genuensi* 8 (1990): 11–26.
Biller, Peter. *The Measure of Multitude: Population in Medieval Thought.* Oxford, 2000.
Boloyan, Kegham Jamil. "Gli angeli nel Corano e nel pensiero islamico." In *Lo ali al Dio: Messageri e guerrieri alati tra oriente e occidente.* Ed. by Marco Bussagli and Mario D'Onofrio. Milan, 2000.
Bono, Salvatore. *Schiavi musulmani nell'Italia moderna.* Naples, 1999.
Boyarin, Daniel. *Border Lines: The Partition of Judaeo-Christianity.* Philadelphia, 2004.
Braude, Benjamin. "The Sons of Noah and the Construction of Ethnic and Geographical Identities in the Medieval and Early Modern Periods." *William and Mary Quarterly,* 3d ser., 54 (1997): 103–42.
Braudel, Fernand. *The Mediterranean and the Mediterranean World in the Age of Philip II.* Trans. by Siãn Reynolds. New York, 1976.
Brundage, James A. "Immortalizing the Crusades: Law and Institutions." In *Montjoie: Studies in Crusade History in Honour of Hans Eberhard Mayer.* Ed. by Benjamin Z. Kedar, Jonathan Riley-Smith, and Rudolf Hiestand. Aldershot, 1997.
Büchler, Alfred. "Obadyah the Proselyte and the Roman Liturgy." *Medieval Encounters* 7 (2001): 165–73.
Buffon, Georges. *De l'homme.* Paris, 1971.
Burns, Robert I. *Jews in the Notarial Culture: Latinate Wills in Mediterranean Spain, 1250–1350.* Berkeley, 1996.
Bussagli, Marco. *Storia degli angeli: Racconto di immagini e di idee.* Milan, 1991.
Cadden, Joan. *Meanings of Sex Differences in the Middle Ages.* Cambridge, 1995.
Chaudhuri, K. N. *Trade and Civilisation in the Indian Ocean: An Economic History from the Rise of Islam to 1750.* Cambridge, 1985.
Clark, Elizabeth. *The Origenist Controversy.* Princeton, 1992.
Connor, Steven. *The Book of Skin.* Ithaca, 2004.
Constable, Olivia Remie. *Housing the Stranger in the Mediterranean World: Lodging, Trade, and Travel in Late Antiquity and the Middle Ages.* Cambridge, 2003.

Cormack, Robin. *Painting the Soul: Icons, Death Masks, and Shrouds.* London, 1997.
Daniel, Norman. *The Arabs in Medieval Europe.* New York, 1979.
Day, Gerald. *Genoa's Response to Byzantium, 1155–1204.* Urbana, 1988.
Del Francia, Loretta. "Angeli in Egitto." In *Le ali al Dio.* Ed. by M. Bussagli and M. D'Onofrio. Milan, 2000.
Di Tucci, Raffaele. *Il genovese Antonio Malfante: La famiglia, la vita, l'esplorazione del Sahara nel 1447.* Bologna, 1935.
Dols, Michael. *The Black Death in the Middle East.* Princeton, 1977.
Edbury, Peter. *The Kingdom of Cyprus and the Crusades, 1191–1374.* Cambridge, 1991.
Edgington, Susan D. "Women in the Chanson D'Antioche." In *Gendering the Crusades.* Ed. by Susan D. Edgington and Sarah Lambert. New York, 2002.
Encyclopedia of Islam. 2d ed. Leiden, 1994.
Epstein, Steven A. *Genoa and the Genoese, 958–1528.* Chapel Hill, 1996.
———. *Speaking of Slavery: Color, Ethnicity, and Human Bondage in Italy.* Ithaca, 2001.
———. *Wage Labor and Guilds in Medieval Europe.* Chapel Hill, 1991.
Evangelista, Paolo. *Fidenzio da Padova e la letteratura crociata-missionaria minoritica.* Naples, 1998.
Evans, Helen C. *Byzantium: Faith and Power, 1261–1557.* New Haven, 2004.
Evans, Helen C., and William D. Wixom. *The Glory of Byzantium: Art and Culture of the Middle Byzantine Era, A.D. 843–1261.* New York, 1997.
The First Crusade. Ed. by Edward Peters. Philadelphia, 1998.
Fleet, Kate. *European and Islamic Trade in the Early Ottoman State: The Merchants of Genoa and Turkey.* Cambridge, 1999.
France, John. "The Fall of Antioch during the First Crusade." In *Dei gesta per Francos: Études sur les croisades dédiées à Jean Richard.* Ed. by Michel Balard, Benjamin Z. Kedar, and Jonathan Riley-Smith. Aldershot, 2001.
———. *Victory in the East: A Military History of the First Crusade.* Cambridge, 1994.
Fredrickson, George M. *Racism: A Short History.* Princeton, 2002.
Freedman, Paul. *Images of the Medieval Peasant.* Stanford, 1999.
Friedman, John B. *The Monstrous Races in Medieval Thought and Art.* Cambridge, Mass., 1981.
Friedman, Yvonne. *Encounter between Enemies: Captivity and Ransom in the Latin Kingdom of Jerusalem.* Leiden, 2002.
Gabrieli, Francesco. *Arab Historians of the Crusades.* Berkeley, 1969.
Gilroy, Paul. *Against Race: Imagining Political Culture Beyond the Color Line.* Cambridge, Mass., 2000.
Gioffrè, Domenico. *Il mercato degli schiavi a Genova nel secolo XV.* Genoa, 1971.
Glacken, Clarence. *Traces on the Rhodian Shore: Nature and Culture in Western Thought from Ancient Times to the End of the Eighteenth Century.* Berkeley, 1967.
Goitein, Shelomo Dov. *A Mediterranean Society: The Jewish Communities of the Arab World as Portrayed in the Documents of the Cairo Geniza.* 6 vols. Berkeley, 1967–93.
Goldenberg, David M. *The Curse of Ham: Race and Slavery in Early Judaism, Christianity, and Islam.* Princeton, 2003.
Greif, Avner. "Reputation and Coalition in Medieval Trade: Evidence on the Maghribi Traders." *Journal of Economic History* 48 (1989): 857–82.

Guéret-Laferté, Michèle. *Sur les routes de l'empire mongol: Ordre et rhétorique des relations de voyage aux XIIIe et XIV siècles.* Paris, 1994.

Hamilton, Bernard. *The Leper King and His Heirs: Baldwin IV and the Crusader Kingdom of Jerusalem.* Cambridge, 2000.

Hannah, Darrell D. *Michael and Christ: Michael Tradition and Angel Christology in Early Christianity.* Tübingen, 1999.

Heers, Jacques. *Les négriers en terres d'Islam: La première traite des Noirs VIIe–XVIe siècle.* Paris, 2003.

Heidt, William G. *Angelology of the Old Testament.* Washington, D.C., 1949.

Hillenbrand, Carole. *The Crusades: Islamic Perspectives.* New York, 2000.

Holt, P. M. *Early Mamluk Diplomacy (1260–1290).* Leiden, 1995.

———. "Qalāwūn's Treaty with Acre in 1283." *English Historical Review* 91 (1976): 802–12.

Horden, Peregrine, and Nicholas Purcell. *The Corrupting Sea: A Study of Mediterranean History.* Oxford, 2000.

Horowitz, Debora E., ed. *Ethiopian Art: The Walters Art Museum.* Lingfield, UK, 2001.

Housley, Norman. *The Later Crusades: From Lyons to Alcazar 1274–1580.* Oxford, 1992.

Howard, Deborah. *Venice and the East.* New Haven, 2000.

Hunt, Lucy-Anne. "For the Salvation of a Woman's Soul: An Icon of St. Michael Described within a Medieval Coptic Context." In *Icon and Word: The Power of Images in Byzantium.* Ed. by Antony Eastmond and Liz James. Aldershot, 2003.

Isaac, Benjamin. *The Invention of Racism in Classical Antiquity.* Princeton, 2004.

Jacoby, David. "Italian Privileges and Trade in Byzantium Before the Fourth Crusade: A Reconsideration." *Anuario de estudios medievales* 24 (1994): 349–69.

Janowitz, Naomi. *Icons of Power: Ritual Practices in Late Antiquity.* University Park, 2002.

Jordan, William C. "The Medieval Background." *Struggles in the Promised Land: Toward a History of Black-Jewish Relations in the United States.* Ed. by Jack Salzman and Cornel West. Oxford, 1997.

———. "Why 'Race'?" *Journal of Medieval and Early Modern Studies* 31 (2001): 165–73.

Kafadar, Cemal. *Between Two Worlds: The Construction of the Ottoman State.* Berkeley, 1995.

Karpov, S. P. "New Documents on the Relations between the Latins and the Local Populations in the Black Sea Area (1392–1462)." *Dumbarton Oaks Papers* 49 (1995): 33–41.

Kedar, Benjamin Z. "The Battle of Hattin Revisited." In *The Horns of Hattin.* Ed. by Benjamin Z. Kedar. Jerusalem, 1992.

———. *Crusade and Mission: European Approaches toward the Muslims.* Princeton, 1984.

———. *Franks in the Levant, 11th to the 14th Centuries.* Aldershot, 1993.

———. "Multidirectional Conversion in the Frankish Levant." In *Varieties of Religious Conversion in the Middle Ages,* pp. 190–99. Edited by James Muldoon. Gainesville, 1997.

———. "The Multilateral Disputation at the Court of the Grand Qan Möngke, 1254." In *The Majlis: Interreligious Encounters in Medieval Islam.* Ed. by Hava Lazarus-Yafeh, Mark R. Cohen, Sasson Somekh, Sidney H. Griffith. Wiesbaden, 1999.

Korobenikov, Dimitri A. "Diplomatic Correspondence between Byzantium and the Mamlūk Sultanate in the Fourteenth Century." *Al-Masāq* 16 (2004): 53–74.

Kugel, James T. *The Bible as It Was.* Cambridge, Mass., 1997.

———. *The God of Old.* New York, 2003.

———. *Traditions of the Bible: A Guide to the Bible as It Was at the Start of the Common Era.* Cambridge, Mass., 1998.

Lancellotti, Angelo. "Nella cronaca di Giovanni-Abdia il proselita normanno la prima pagina di storia di Oppido della Lucania." In *Antiche civiltà lucane.* Ed. by Pietro Borraro. Galatina, 1975.

Lane, Frederic C. *Venice: A Maritime Republic.* Baltimore, 1973.

Larner, John. *Marco Polo and the Discovery of the World.* New Haven, 1999.

Lazarus-Yafeh, Hava. *Intertwined Worlds: Medieval Islam and Biblical Criticism.* Princeton, 1992.

Lewis, Bernard. *Islam: From the Prophet Muhammad to the Capture of Constantinople.* Oxford, 1974.

———. *Race and Slavery in the Middle East.* New York, 1990.

Little, Lester. *Benedictine Maledictions: Liturgical Cursing in Romanesque France.* Ithaca, 1993.

Livi, Ridolfo. *La schiavitù domestica nei tempi di mezzo e nei moderni.* Padua, 1928.

Lopez, Roberto S. *Benedetto Zaccaria: ammiraglio e mercante nella Genova del Duecento.* Messina, 1933; reprint, Genoa, 1996.

———. *Storia delle colonie genovesi nel Mediterraneo.* Bologna, 1938; reprint, Genoa, 1996.

Lucchini, Enrica. *La merce umana: schiavitù e riscatto dei liguri nel seicento.* Rome, 1990.

Maalouf, Amin. *In the Name of Identity: Violence and the Need to Belong.* New York, 2000.

Maguire, Henry. *The Icons of Their Bodies: Saints and Their Images in Byzantium.* Princeton, 1996.

Matter, E. Ann. *The Voice of My Beloved: The Song of Songs in Medieval Christianity.* Philadelphia, 1990.

Mavroudi, Maria. *A Byzantine Book on Dream Interpretation: The Oneirocriticon of Achmet and Its Arabic Sources.* Leiden, 2002.

McKee, Sally. "Inherited Status and Slavery in Late Medieval Italy and Venetian Crete." *Past & Present* 182 (2004): 31–53.

———. *Uncommon Dominion: Venetian Crete and the Myth of Ethnic Purity.* Philadelphia, 2000.

Mérigoux, Jean Marie. "L'ouvrage d'un frere precheur florentin en Orient à la fin du XIIIe siècle." *Memorie Domenicane* 17 (1986): 1–144.

Meyvaert, Paul. "An Unknown Letter of Hulagu, Il-Khan of Persia, to King Louis IX of France." *Viator* 11 (1980): 246–59.

Momigliano, Arnaldo. *Alien Wisdom: The Limits of Hellenization.* Cambridge, 1975.

Morgan, Margaret Ruth. *The Chronicle of Ernoul and the Continuations of William of Tyre.* Oxford, 1973.

Musso, Gian Giacomo. "I Genovesi e il Levante tra Medioevo ed Età Moderna." In *Genova, La Liguria e L'Oltremare tra Medioevo ed Età Moderna.* Ed. by Raffaele Belvederi. Genoa, 1974–81.

Netanyahu, B. *The Origins of the Inquisition in Fifteenth Century Spain.* New York, 1995.

Northrup, David. *Africa's Discovery of Europe, 1450–1850.* Oxford, 2002.

Oikonomides, Nicolas. "The Role of the Byzantine State in the Economy." In *The Economic History of Byzantium.* Vol. 3. Ed. by Angeliki E. Laiou. Washington, D.C., 2002.

Oldoni, Massimo. "L'angelo e la 'Legenda Aurea.'" In *Le ali al Dio.* Ed. by M. Bussagli and M. D'Onofrio. Milan, 2000.

Olschki, Leonardo. *Guillaume Bouchier: A French Artist at the Court of the Khans.* Baltimore, 1946.

——. *Marco Polo's Asia.* Berkeley, 1960.

Peers, Glenn. *Subtle Bodies: Representing Angels in Byzantium.* Berkeley, 2001.

Petzold, Andreas. "'His Face Like Lightening': Colour as Signifier in the Representation of the Holy Women at the Tomb." *Arte Medievale* 6, no. 2 (1992): 149–55.

Pistarino, Geo, ed. *I problemi de Mar Nero nel passato e nel presente.* Genoa, 1993.

Poliakov, Léon. *Le mythe arien: Essai sur les sources du racisme et des nationalismes.* Paris, 1971.

Prawer, Joshua. "The Autobiography of Obadyah the Norman, a Convert to Judaism at the Time of the First Crusade." In *Studies in Medieval Jewish History and Literature.* Ed. by Isadore Twersky. Cambridge, Mass., 1979.

——. *Crusader Institutions.* Oxford, 1980.

Proctor, Robert N. *Racial Hygiene: Medicine under the Nazis.* Cambridge, Mass., 1988.

Richard, Jean. "An Account of the Battle of Hattin Referring to the Frankish Mercenaries in Oriental Moslem States." *Speculum* 27 (1952): 168–77.

——. "Un ambassade mongole à Paris en 1262." *Journal des savants* (1979): 295–303.

Riley-Smith, Jonathan. *The Crusades: A Short History.* New Haven, 1987.

——. *The First Crusade and the Idea of Crusading.* Philadelphia, 1986.

Ringrose, Kathryn. M. *The Perfect Servant: Eunuchs and the Social Construction of Gender in Byzantium.* Chicago, 2003.

Rofé, Alexander. *The Belief in Angels in the Bible and in Early Israel.* Jerusalem, 1979.

Romano, Dennis. *Housecraft and Statecraft: Domestic Service in Renaissance Venice, 1400–1600.* Baltimore, 1996.

Rouche, Michele. "Le combat des saints anges et des démons: la victoire de Saint Michel." In *Santi e demoni nell'alto medioevo occidentale, Settimane di Studio 36.* Vol. 1. Spoleto, 1989.

Ruotsala, Antti. *Europeans and the Mongols in the Middle of the Thirteenth Century.* Helsinki, 2001.

Said, Edward. *Orientalism.* New York, 1994.

Schorsch, Jonathan. *Jews and Blacks in the Early Modern World.* Cambridge, 2004.

Seed, Patricia. *American Pentimento: The Invention of Indians and the Pursuit of Riches.* Minneapolis, 2001.

Simmons, Michael Bland. *Arnobius of Sicca.* Oxford, 1995.

Skržinskaya, Elena C. "Storia della Tana." *Studi veneziani* 10 (1968): 3–45.

Snowden, Frank. *Blacks in Antiquity.* Cambridge, Mass., 1970.

Sollers, Werner. *Interracialism: Black White Intermarriage in American History, Literature, and Law.* Oxford, 2000.

Spuler, Bertold. *Die Goldene Horde: Die Mongolen in Russland, 1223–1502.* Wiesbaden, 1965.

Stapert, Aurelia. *L'ange roman dans la pensée et dans l'art.* Paris, 1975.

Thomas, Rosalind. *Herodotus in Context: Ethnography, Science, and the Art of Persuasion.* Cambridge, 2000.

Thompson, Lloyd A. *Romans and Blacks.* Norman, Okla., 1989.

Thorndyke, Lynn. *Michael Scot.* London, 1965.

Tolan, John V. *Saracens: Islam in the Medieval European Imagination.* New York, 2002.

Weitzmann, Kurt. *The Icon: Holy Images—Sixth to Fourteenth Century.* New York, 1978.
Williams, Bernard. *Truth and Truthfulness.* Princeton, 2002.
Williams, Steven J. *The Secret of Secrets: The Scholarly Career of a Pseudo-Aristotelian Text in the Latin Middle Ages.* Ann Arbor, 2003.
Wood, Frances. *Did Marco Polo Go to China?* Boulder, 1996.
Young, Robert C. *Colonial Desire: Hybridity in Theory, Culture, and Race.* London, 1995.
Zachariadou, Elizabeth A. *Trade and Crusade: Venetian Crete and the Emirates of Menteshe and Aydin (1300–1415).* Venice, 1983.

INDEX

Aaron, 44
Abdullah, interpreter, 33–34, 159, 161
Abgar of Edessa, 178
Abraham, 187
Abelard, Pierre, 18–19
Abiram, 140
Abkhazians, 61, 71
Abusa, Tartar prince, 134
Acre, 37, 39, 40, 49, 80, 106, 115
Adam, Guillaume, 162–165
Adam and Eve, 10, 14, 16, 20, 32
Adorno, Anselme, 48–49
Aegean Sea, 69, 108, 110–115, 139
Africa, Africans, 47–48, 138, 176
'Ain Jalut, battle, 132
Alamut, 132
alchemy, 185
Aleppo, 106, 147, 155
Alexander III, pope, 154
Alexandria, 93, 116, 163
Ali the Farsighted, 153–154
Allah, 79, 112–113
Alum, 165
Andreas, archbishop of Bari, 145
Andrew the Fool, Saint, 144
Anea, 102
Angelology, 186, 189
angels, 173, 179, 184–203; appearance, 189; color, 191–192; dreams of, 188; faces, 201; fallen, 189–190, 203; guardian, 194; Hebrew attitudes, 187; and Jesus, 188; and Jews, 229n63; and music, 195; qualities, 188–189; recording, 190; Watchers, 185–186; wings, 187
Animal Apocalypse, 193

animals, 23, 43, 177, 199
Anthony, Saint, 22
Antioch, 115, 133, 149–153, 155
antisemitism, 12, 13
Antoninus Polemon, 177, 180, 182
Apollo, 197
apostate, 138, 170, 172
Appiah, K. Anthony, xiii
Arabs, 37–38, 144, 180
Aragon, 106, 139
archangels, 186
Archippus, 195
Aristarchus, 198–199
Aristotle, 19, 174, 176, 177, 182
Armenia, Armenians, 31, 60, 89, 106, 115, 132, 150, 168
Arnobius of Sicca, 23
Assassins, 132
astrology, 185
auction, 64–65
Augustine, Saint, 189–190
autobiography, 23, 144, 153
Aydin, 111, 113–114
Azazel, 185
Azov, sea of, 118

Babylonian Talmud, 174
Bacon, Roger, 177
Baghdad, 42–44, 132, 147
Bahira, monk, 38, 45
baillis, Venetian, 109
Balbi, Giovanni, 36
Baldwin V, king of Jerusalem, 155
Banyas, 148

baptism, 10, 12, 62, 152
Barbaro, Iosafa, 166–168
Bari, 145
Barlaam and Josaphat, 180
Bartholomew, Saint, 178
Basil, Saint, 180
bath (bagno), 122
Batu, 25, 28
beards, 24, 176, 178–179, 203
beeswax, 65, 67, 128
Beijing, 34
belts, 161
Benedict the Pole, 25, 27
Bernard of Clairvaux, Saint, 19–21
Bible, 193, 217n66
Birdi Beg, 123, 124
black, blackness, 11, 17–21, 36, 38, 47, 62, 176, 201; eyes, 182. *See also* color
Black Sea, 55–56, 65, 105, 115
blasphemy, 43, 113
Bohemund I, prince of Antioch, 145, 149–153
Bohemund III, prince of Antioch, 157
Bohemund VI, prince of Antioch, 132
Bosphorus, 108
Bouchier, Guillaume, 159–162
boundaries, xii, 5, 204
brokers, 120
brownness, 46–47, 62, 84
Buddha, 180
Buffon, Georges, 15
Bulgars, 65, 69, 128–130
Byzantine Empire (Romania), 68, 80, 97–110, 139, 143

Caffa, 55–65, 124–127, 169
Cairo, 93–94
Campanella, Tommaso, 175
Candia, 53, 54, 113
Cappadocia, 143
captives, 55, 130, 154, 155, 159–162, 169–172
Cassiodorus, 22
Castel Sant'Angelo, 198
Castile, 106
Catalan Grand Company, 139
Catalans, 82, 166
Catherine, of Sinai, Saint, monastery, 197
Catholicon, Latin dictionary, 15, 36
Cembalo, 126

cemeteries, 104
Cervantes, Miguel, 138, 170
Chanson, d'Antioche, 151–152
charity, Christian, 199; Jewish, 147; Muslim, 42–43
cherubim, 186
chess, 48
children, in Caffa, 58; on Crete, 54–55; on Cyprus, 84, 87; at Dobrugia, 128; mixed, 109, 175; slave, 163; at Tana, 121
Chilia, 65–67
China, 34–35, 47, 160
Chingiz Khan, 24, 27, 29, 132
Chios, 67–80, 102, 164; population, 68
Chonae, 195
Christianity, Christians, 10, 22, 29–30, 31, 37–38, 72, 133, 168, 188–189; Coptic, 117; Nestorian, 29
Circassians, 61, 69, 71, 72, 127, 164, 167
circumcision, 82, 145, 147, 169
citizenship: and angels, 194; Genoese, 57, 101, 130, 220n19; Venetian, 109–110, 121
The City of the Sun, 175
climate, 15–16, 18, 48–49
Codex Cumanicus, 59–60, 62
coffee, 170
Coffin, Nicola, 92–93
colonialism, 55, 68, 80, 95
color, 15–16, 46, 49–51; of angels, 187, 191, 201; of bones and teeth, 18–19, 23; of clothing, 49; mixed, 174–176; prejudice, 10–11, 51, 206; of slaves, 62, 84; symbolism, 10, 16, 23, 47, 187, 191, 201, 205. *See also* skin: black, white
Colossus, 195
commerce, 46, 75–76, 98, 164–165, 169
Constantinople, 99, 100, 102–104, 107
consuls, Genoese, 56, 65–66, 116, 124, 126, 130, 158; Venetian, 121
Contarini, Ambrogio, 167
conversion, 9, 40–41, 72, 88, 133–134, 143, 145–148, 151, 154, 157–158, 167, 169
cosmetics, 185
Cotolboga, 125–128
Council of Lyon, 25
Crete, 52–55, 102, 113–115
Crimea, 55, 118–128, 163
crows, 37–38
crusades, to Egypt, 30–31; first, 145–146; fourth, 100
Cumans, 24

currency: in Caffa, 57; in Chilia, 65; in Crimea, 128
Cyprus, 80–93, 106, 124

Damascus, 106, 132, 147
Dan, 148
Dandolo, Andrea, 122
Daniel, prophet, 188
Dante Alighieri, 44, 139, 140, 191–192
Danube, 65
Dardanelles, 108
Dathan, 140
Datien's wife, 151–152, 172. *See also* Firuz
da Varagine, Jacopo, 22, 178, 187, 193–194
de Guasco, Pietro, 167
Della Porta, Giovan Battista, 181
Delphi, oracle, 37
demons, 22, 47, 161, 190, 203
de Montaigne, Michel, 169–171
de Murta, Giovanni, 122
de Sauli, Manfredo, 169
De statu sarracenorum, 37
Deuteronomy, 32
devil, 22, 189–190, 198–200, 212n47
de Villehardouin, Geoffrey, 106
dictionaries, 36
Digenis Akritis, 141–144
diplomatic correspondence, 130–134, 219n1
dishonor, 111, 144. *See also* honor
diversity of peoples, 40–41, 46
Dniester, 65
Dobrugia, 128–130
dogs, 177
dominations (angels), 186
Dominic, Saint, 179
Don, 56
dowry, 63, 73, 77, 88–89. *See also* marriage
dragoman, 33, 58–59; terguman, 33; turjumān, 33; truciman, 58
dreams, 77, 145, 148, 179, 183, 227n8; interpretation of, 182, 188
Du Bois, W. E. B., 51

Ecclesiasticus, xii, 31, 185
Egypt, 49, 139, 145, 148, 164, 192–193, 195
Ellias bey, 125–126
embryo, 175, 194
emotions, 172, 174, 182
endogamy, 15

England, 106, 179
Enoch, 185, 192, 193
equality, xii, 6, 10, 50, 134, 173, 186–187, 201, 206–207
Erguil, 46
Ethiopians, 17, 18–19, 22, 144, 175, 191, 198–199
ethnicity, 14–15, 94, 176, 181, 205; in Caffa, 61, 65; in Chilia, 67; on Crete, 53; on Cyprus, 80–82, 91
ethnikos, 141, 143
ethnography, 25–27, 31, 34, 48, 155; and angels, 184; and physiognomy, 183
eunuch, 144, 226n98
Euphemia, 198–200
Eustathius of Thrace, 198
evil eye, 193
excommunication, 107
exile, 139, 141
eyelashes, 182
eyes, 178–179, 180–184; blue, 182; blue-grey, 181, color, 181–183, dry, 181; movement, 181–183, much suffering, 193; of slaves, 181, Tartar, 30
Ezekiel, prophet, 187
Ezra ben Solomon, 21
Ezzelino da Romano, 178

faces, 173; angelic, 179, 191, 201; demonic, 179; Mongol, 26, 30; saintly, 173, 178–179
Famagusta, 80–81, 88–89
family life, 86–87
fascism, 10
Fidenzio of Padua, 39–42
Firuz (Pyrrus, Datien), 149–153, 172
flaws, human, 174
Fleet, Kate, 95
Florence, 44
Foglietta, Antonio, 71
fondaco, Genoese, 99, 102, 219n11; Venetian, 108, 120, 123
France, 106, 151–152
Franciscans, 66
Franks, 39–41, 109, 126, 149–150, 153–158
Fredrickson, George, 10, 11, 15
Fulcher of Chartres, 150

Gabriel, archangel, 37, 186, 187; and Muhammad, 190
Gale, Jean, 156
galleys, 105–106; and slaves, 169

Gambek Khan, 121–122
Gazaria, 56, 127. *See also* Crimea
gender, 175, 176; of angels, 189, 195
gener, 31
Genesis, 185
Geniza records, 93–94, 144
Genoa, Genoese, 48, 56, 64, 83, 100, 103–104, 162–165; in Black Sea, 118–130; in Chilia, 67; commune, 126
gentes, 31
genus, 15
Georgians, 46
Gesta Francorum, 149
gifts, 161; diplomatic, 99, 104–105, 127, 164
Gilroy, Paul, 10
Giuseppe, renegade, 169–171
Giustiniani family, 68
Goitein, S. D., 93–94, 146, 179
Golb, Norman, 146
Goldenberg, David, 10
Golden Horde of Tartars, 56–57, 66, 118–130, 164–165
The Golden Legend, 22–23, 178, 180
goldsmiths, 78, 159–162, 167
Greeks, 49, 91, 150, 180; in Caffa, 63, on Chios, 68–69, 72; on Crete, 53–54; on Cyprus, 82; Orthodoxy, 72
Gregory of Nyssa, 16–17
Gregory the Great, pope, 179, 198
guasmuls, 109, 135, 220n17
Guibert of Nogent, 150–151
Guy of Lusignan, 80, 156
Güyüg Khan, 28, 29–30, 130–131

Hadrian, 182
Hagar, 37, 144
Hagarenes, 38, 122
hagiography, 22, 144
Hattin, battle, 155–158
Hav, xi
hell, 140, 186
Héloise, 18
heresy, 38
hierarchy: of angels, 184, 186–187, 193–194, 203; of color, 176, 206–207
Hippocrates, 18, 177
Holt, Peter, 117
Holy Land, 39–41, 49; recovery of, 162

honey, 128
honor, 142, 144, 152–154, 172, 173, 206. *See also* dishonor
Horace, 36–38
Horden, Peregrine, 142
Hospitalers, 106, 107, 110
Hülegü Khan, 131–133
humanity, 14–15, 31–32, 48, 49; and animals, 23, 177; movements and gestures, 177
humors, theory, 20, 50, 176, 182
Hungary, 24–25, 30, 159, 160–161
hybrids, 173
hypocrisy, 44, 137, 168

Iblis, 188, 190
Ibn 'Abd al-Zahir, 116
Ibn al-Athīr, 152
Ibn al-Qalānīsī, 152
Ibn Battuta, 64
Ibn Jubayr, 40
Ibn Khaldûn, 9, 11, 184
iconography, of angels, 188, 191, 196, 198, 201–203
icons, 198–199
identity, xii–xiii, 4, 12–13, 48, 53, 67, 135, 138, 204
India, 34–35, 47, 62
Indian Ocean, 163
indigenes, 40, 95
inheritance of traits, 11, 15, 17, 174–176
Innocent IV, pope, 25
insurance, 73–74
interpreters, 28, 33–34, 49, 58–60, 66–67, 70, 73–74, 77, 79, 88, 111–112, 117, 124, 127
interracialism, 209n4
iris (of eye), 181
Isaac, 188
Isaac, Benjamin, 11
Isabella, princess of Armenia, 92–93
Isaiah, 187
Ishmael, 37, 144
Isidore of Seville, 5, 18
Islam (Muslims), 12, 23, 37–39, 42–45, 48, 133, 142, 163, 167–168, 188; hadith, 44. *See also* Muslims

Jacob, 176, 187, 201
Jacques de Vitry, 39
Jeremiah, 19, 41
Jerome, Saint, 22
Jerusalem, 17, 33, 146–147; kingdom, 106, 155, 158

Jesus, 20–21, 112, 141, 150, 178, 181, 188
Jews, 12, 15, 37, 144–148; attitudes toward Song of Songs, 21–22; in Caffa, 64–65; in Cairo, 93–94; on Chios, 68–69, 74–78; on Crete, 53; on Cyprus, 82, 89–90; Karaite, 94; Rabbanite, 94. *See also* Judaism
Joel, 146
John, evangelist, 122
John XXII, pope, 133, 134
John of Ibelin, 158
John of Monte Corvino, 34–35
John of Plano de Carpini, 25–29
John the Almoner, Saint, 22
Joinville, Jean de, 30–31, 111
Jordan, William C., 10
Judaism, 12, 147–148, 188. *See also* Jews
Judas, 140
Judges, book of, 41
Julian, Dominican missionary, 24–25
Julian, Saint, 22
justice, 103, 116, 120, 129, 134
Justinian, Roman emperor, 197

Karakorum, 26, 159
Karām al-Dīn, 106
Kashmir, 46
Kedar, Benjamin Z., 34, 147, 164
Kiev, 27
Kitbogha, 132
Korea, 160
Kugel, James, 187

Laban, 175
Lamberto de Sambuceto, 81–82, 89
Landrimiti, 102
languages, 9, 24, 45, 119, 160; Arabic, 40, 93–94, 97, 111, 117, 155; Aramaic, 185, 189; Armenian, 59; Chinese, 34; Coptic, 198; creole, 60; Cuman, 29, 59, 120, 160; Ethiopian, 185; Farsi (Persian) 28, 59, 119–120; French, 88, 160; Genoese, 70, 124–125; Greek, 33, 59, 97, 110, 150; Hebrew, 93, 147; Latin, 28, 59, 99, 117, 149, 160, 217n42, 221n49; Mongol, 25, 27, 34, 124, 213n90, 221n49; pidgin, 60; Ruthenian, 28; Slavic, 27–28, 61; Tartar, 127; Turkish, 60, 70, 171; Uighur, 25, 28, 97, 124–125, 127
Last Judgment, 194
law, Byzantine, 103; Genoese, 57, 103; Latin Kingdom, 158; Muslim, 97–98; natural, 71; Roman, 61, 72; Tartar, 120; Venetian, 20
leprosy, 79
Lesbos, 102
Levi, Primo, 139
Levi ben Gershon, 21–22
Licostomo, 65
Liguria, 83, 101
loans, 76, 90
Louis IX, king of France, 30–31, 11–112, 130–132, 161
love, 143, 172
loyalty, 152–154, 158, 164, 172
Lucca, 169–170

Maimonides, Abraham, 179
Maimonides, Moses, 184
Mamluks, Mamluk Egypt, 41–42, 49, 80, 106, 111, 115–118, 132–133, 162–164
Manuel Comnenus, 98–99, 104
manumission of slaves: on Chios, 43; 70–72; on Cyprus, 85, 91; by will, 85–88
Maona of Chios, 68, 75, 78
Mark, Saint, 178
marriage: Arab-Byzantine, 143; in Caffa, 63–64; in Cairo, 93–94; on Chios, 72–73; on Crete, 54; on Cyprus, 88–89, 92, Islamic, 44, 93; mixed, 18, 39, 145, 154, 174; Mongol, 26. *See also* dowry
Marta, innkeeper, 167
Mary of Egypt, Saint, 22
mass, 160
mastic, 68
Maurocastro, 65
McKee, Sally, xii, 53–54
Mecca, 111, 113, 167
medicine, 175, 181, 183
Menteshe, 111, 114
mercenaries, 139, 145
merchants. *See* trade
messiah, 146–148
Michael, archangel, 189, 192–201; appearance, 197; footprints, 197–198
Michaelmas, 192
Michael Palaeologus, 100–107, 163
Michael Scot, 175–177, 180, 183
Midianites, 25
milk, 79, 176, 228n10
miscegenation, 173
missionaries, 33, 35, 36, 42, 60, 165

Möngke Khan, 32, 33–34, 159
Mongols (Tartars), 23–36, 159
monogenesis, 16
Monte Gargano, 197
Montferrat, 106
Mont Saint Michel, 197
Moors, 22, 48
Moses, 17, 32, 34, 44, 112, 138–139, 140, 188
mourning, 19–20
Muhammad, prophet, 23, 37–38, 112, 142, 152, 179, 187, 190
mule, 109, 173
multitude of people, 25, 41
Murad I, 128
murder, 168
music, 35, 147, 171, 195, 224n24
Muslims, 82; in Caffa, 64, 141–144. *See also* Islam

names, 61–62
Negroponte, 91–92
Nestorian Christians, 35
new worlds, 13
Nicola de Boateriis, 90
Nicosia, 81, 88
Niger. *See* black
Nile, 195
Noah, 185
Normans, 144–146
notaries: in Caffa, 63; on Chios, 69, 71, 74–75; on Crete, 53–54; in Crimea, 125, 127; on Cyprus, 81; Mamluk, 117; Tartar, 28, 127
Notitia de Machometo, 37
Nymphaeum, treaty, 100–108

oaths, 76, 79, 97, 111–113, 116–117, 128, 130
Obadiah the Norman (John), 144–148, 172, 223n17
Officium Robarie, 164
Ögödei Khan, 28
Oppido, 144
opportunists, 139, 159
orientalism, xii
Origen, on angels, 186; on Song of Songs, 16–17
Ottoman Empire, Turks, 62, 69, 97, 106, 110–111, 167, 170, 204

paganism, 23, 195–198
Palatia, 113

pallia, 99, 104
papacy, 106, 107, 115, 131, 133, 166
Paquette, 159
Paradiso of Dante, 191
Paris, 159
Paul, Saint, 32, 195
Peers, Glenn, 195
penitence, 17
peoples, 32
Pera, 73, 124, 128–129
persecution, 21
Persia, Persians, 162–163, 166–168, 180
Peter, Saint, 179
Peter, archbishop, 25, 26
Peter of Abano, 178, 180, 183
Phags.pa, 213n90
Phocaea, 67–68
physiognomy, 5, 6, 47, 173–184, 227n4; ancient, 143–144, 173–174, 177, 181; of angels, 191, 201; and ethnic difference, 181; gendered, 227n9; Jewish, 179; medieval, 180, 227n11; Muslim, 180; as a science, 177–178
pilgrimage, 163
piracy, 98, 164
Pisa, 99, 103, 106
plague of 1347/48, 37, 79
Poland, 30
Poliakov, Léon, 13
Polo, Marco, 35, 45–47, 214n120
Portugal, 204
poulains, 39, 110, 135, 214n102
Prawer, Joshua, 145
preaching, 33–34, 39, 42
Prester John, 31
principalities (angels), 186
property sales, 76
prophesy, 146
protoracism, 11
Provence, 106
Pseudo-Aristotle, 183
Pseudo-Dionysius, 187
psychopomp, 193, 203
Purcell, Nicholas, 142
purity, xii–xiii, 5, 7, 40–41, 52, 173, 204–207; of language, 9

Qalāwūn, 163
Qubilai Khan, 34, 46–47

Quran, 23, 37–38, 43–44, 113; and angels, 190. *See also* Islam; Muhammad, prophet
Qutuz, 131, 132

race, 9–13, 143, 154, 206
raciology, 9, 14, 173, 210n4
racism, 11, 14, 50, 183, 201, 207
Ralph of Coggeshall, 157
Ramadan Khan, 123
Raphael, archangel, 185, 230n92
Rashi, 21
Raymond III, Count of Tripoli, 155–158, 172
Raymond D'Aguilers, 150
redness, 176, 211n25
relationships, xii–xiii, 4–5, 36, 50–52; human and angelic, 184–186, 188–190, 201, 203; mixed, xii, 5, 7, 13, 93–96, 135, 137, 174, 204–205
religion, 10, 45–46, 95, 204; Mongol, 26, 30, 24
renegades, 137–143, 146, 148–149, 155–156, 165, 168–169, 172, 206
Rhodes, 110
Riccoldo da Monte Croce, 42–45
Richard, Jean, 156
Richard I, king of England, 80
Richard the Pilgrim, 151
Rome, 198
Rustichello da Pisa, 45

sainthood, 30, 192
Saladin, 39, 156–157
Salonika, 102
Salvaygo, Segurano, 162–166, 172
Samau'al al-Maghrībībi, 148, 179, 224n35
Saracens, 37, 38–45, 82
Sarai, New Sarai, 118
Satan, 22, 138, 188. *See also* devil
science, 174, 181, 183, 201
Secret of Secrets, 183
Seraphim, 186, 187
shoemakers, 90
Sicily, 83, 106, 108, 145, 204
Simon Magus, 179
Simon of Saint Quentin, 30
sin, 21, 40, 163
Sitia, 114
skin: black, 17–21, 22; as boundary, 4, 209n4; color, 5, 14, 18–21, 35, 51, 176, 203; white, 17–21
slavery, 20, 35, 49, 83, 95, 144, 176, 207; ancient, 13, 215n14; in Caffa, 57–58, 61–63; in Cairo, 93–94; in Chilia, 66–67; on Chios, 69–72, 73, 79; on Crete, 54–55; on Cyprus, 81–88, 90–92, 220n19; prices, 54, 84; runaways, 62, 73–74, 114, 128, 167, 171; trade, 114, 123, 162–64
sleepwalking, 77
Smyrna, 102, 104, 110
societas, 78
sodomy, 44, 144
Soldaia, 133
Solgat, 126–128
Solomon, 17, 20, 193
Solomon the Karaite, 148
Song of Songs, 16–22
Spain, 135, 204, 210n16
Spinola, Alberto, 116
Sultaniyeh, 162
Sun, latitude theory, 15–16, 22
Syria, Syrians, 39, 40–41, 142

Tabriz, 35, 42, 167–68
Talmud, 189
Tamerlane, 110, 111, 128
tamoga, seal, 120, 124, 127
Tana, 56, 118, 120, 121, 123, 166
Tartars, 67–68, 69, 118–130; captives, 166–167; correspondence, 130–134; defined, 25; reputation, 126
taxes, 113–114, 120–123, 129–130
tears of eyes, 182
temperaments, 5, 46, 61, 174, 176–177
Templars, 80, 107
Tenduc, 46
Teologo (Ephesus), 70, 113
teriaque, 49
Thomas of Canterbury, Saint, 180
thrones (angels), 186
tobacco, 170
Toktamysh Khan, 124, 127
tolerance, 94, 207, 212n51
Toulouse, 106
Tower of Babel, 27
trade, 51, 98, 135–136; in Aegean, 68, 73–74; in Black Sea, 56, 65, 118–130, 169; on Cyprus, 80–81; Genoese-Bulgarian, 128–130; Genoese-Byzantine, 102, 105; Genoese-Mamluk, 117–118, 162; Genoese-Ottoman, 95; in grain, 105, 129;

trade (*continued*)
  in hides, 121; Muslim-Christian, 163–165; Venetian-Tartar, 119–123; Venetian-Turkish, 113–114
travel, 48
treason, 137–140, 151, 157, 172
treaties, 97–98, 134; Byzantine-Genoese, 98–108; Byzantine-Mamluk, 163; Genoese-Mamluk, 115–118; Genoese-Tartar, 122–128; Venetian-Tartar, 122–128; Venetian-Turkish, 112–115
Tripoli, 88, 115, 157
truces, Venetian-Byzantine, 109–109
tughra, 97
Tunis, 106
Turks, 69, 82–83, 140, 149, 169–171, 180; Kipchak, 59, 164
Tyre, 106, 148, 154, 155

Uighur script, 25, 28, 35, 59
Urban IV, pope, 107
Usamah Ibn-Munqidih, 153–155
usury, 76, 217n65
Uzbeg Khan, 120, 133

Venice, 45, 52, 80, 90–91, 100, 103–104, 107–109, 118, 166, 170

Venier, Andrea, 123
Vincent of Beauvais, 30
violence, 24, 27, 43–45, 62, 84
virtues (angels), 186
Vlachs (Wallachs), 65, 69
Volga, 118

warfare, Genoese-Venetian, 119, 123–124; naval, 103, 105–106, 117, 135
water, 126, 142, 195–197, 207
wetnurses, 71, 79, 177
white, whiteness, 18–21, 46, 176. *See also* color
William of Rubruck, 31–34, 159–161
William of Tripoli, 37
Williams, Bernard, 4
wills, 92–93
women, 18–20, 46; and angels, 194; concubines, 130; eyes, 180, Mongol, 26, 34, 37; Muslim, 142–143, 151–154; renegades, 140–141; slaves, 58, 62
work, 78–79, 90, 93; on Chios, 71–72

Zaccaria, Benedetto, 68
Zakariyyā al Rāzī, 181
Zanzibar, 47
Zeno, Andreas, 119
Zeno, Raineri, 108